DAVID EDWARDS
'19

Becoming
Beauvoir

Becoming Beauvoir

A Life

Kate Kirkpatrick

BLOOMSBURY ACADEMIC
LONDON · NEW YORK · OXFORD · NEW DELHI · SYDNEY

BLOOMSBURY ACADEMIC
Bloomsbury Publishing Plc
50 Bedford Square, London, WC1B 3DP, UK
1385 Broadway, New York, NY 10018, USA

BLOOMSBURY, BLOOMSBURY ACADEMIC and the Diana logo are
trademarks of Bloomsbury Publishing Plc

First published in Great Britain 2019
Reprinted 2019 (twice)

Cover design by Irene Martinez Costa
Author photo by John Cairns
Cover image: *Simone de Beauvoir*, Paris, 1957 © The Irving Penn Foundation

A catalogue record for this book is available from the British Library.

A catalog record for this book is available from the Library of Congress.

ISBN: HB: 978-1-3500-4717-4
        ePDF: 978-1-3500-4718-1
        eBook: 978-1-3500-4719-8

Typeset by RefineCatch Limited, Bungay, Suffolk
Printed and bound in Great Britain

To find out more about our authors and books visit www.bloomsbury.com
and sign up for our newsletters.

'All these relationships between women, I thought, rapidly recalling the splendid gallery of fictitious women, are too simple. So much has been left out, unattempted. [. . .] almost without exception they are shown in their relation to men.'

VIRGINIA WOOLF, *A ROOM OF ONE'S OWN*

'To emancipate woman is to refuse to enclose her in the relations that she sustains with man, but not to deny them to her.'

SIMONE DE BEAUVOIR, *THE SECOND SEX*

For Pamela
in memoriam amoris amicitiae

Contents

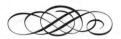

Illustrations

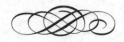

Abbreviations of Beauvoir's Works

A   *Adieux: A Farewell to Sartre*, trans. Patrick O'Brian, London: Penguin, 1984.

ADD   *America Day by Day*, trans. Carol Cosman, Berkeley: University of California Press, 1999.

AMM   *All Men Are Mortal*, trans. Euan Cameron and Leonard Friedman, London: Virago, 2003.

ASD   *All Said and Done*, trans. Patrick O'Brian, London: Penguin, 1977.

BB   *Brigitte Bardot and the Lolita Syndrome*, trans. Bernard Frechtman, London: Four Square, 1962. First published in *Esquire* in 1959.

BI   *Les Belles Images*, Paris: Gallimard, 1972.

BO   *The Blood of Others*, trans. Yvonne Moyse and Roger Senhouse, London: Penguin, 1964.

CC   *Correspondence croisée*, Paris: Gallimard, 2004.

CJ   *Cahiers de jeunesse*, Paris: Gallimard, 2008.

DPS   *Diary of a Philosophy Student: Volume I, 1926–27*, ed. Barbara Klaw, Sylvie le Bon de Beauvoir and Margaret Simons, Urbana: University of Illinois Press, 2006.

EA   *Ethics of Ambiguity*, trans. Bernard Frechtman, New York: Citadel Press, 1976.

FC   *Force of Circumstance*, trans. Richard Howard, London: Penguin, 1987.

FW   *Feminist Writings*, ed. Margaret A. Simons and Marybeth Timmerman, Urbana: University of Illinois Press, 2015.

LM   *The Long March*, trans. Austryn Wainhouse, London: Andre Deutsch and Weidenfeld & Nicholson, 1958.

LS   *Letters to Sartre*, trans. Quentin Hoare, New York: Arcade, 1991.

M   *The Mandarins*, trans. Leonard Friedman, London: Harper Perennial, 2005.

MDD   *Memoirs of a Dutiful Daughter*, trans. James Kirkup, London: Penguin, 2001.

MPI   *Mémoires*, tome I, ed. Jean-Louis Jeannelle and Eliane Lecarme-Tabone, Bibliothèque de la Pléiade, Paris: Gallimard, 2018.

MPII   *Mémoires*, tome II, ed. Jean-Louis Jeannelle and Eliane Lecarme-Tabone, Bibliothèque de la Pléiade, Paris: Gallimard, 2018.

OA   *Old Age*, trans. Patrick O'Brian, Harmondsworth: Penguin, 1977.

PL   *The Prime of Life*, trans. Peter Green, London: Penguin, 1965.

PW   *Philosophical Writings*, ed. Margaret Simons with Marybeth Timmerman and Mary Beth Mader, Chicago: University of Illinois Press, 2004.

PolW   *Political Writings*, ed. Margaret Simons and Marybeth Timmerman, Chicago: University of Illinois Press, 2012.

QM   *Quiet Moments in a War: The Letters of Jean-Paul*
         Sartre and Simone de Beauvoir 1940–1963, trans. Lee
         Fahnestock and Norman MacAfee, London: Hamish
         Hamilton, 1993.

SCTS   *She Came to Stay*, trans. Yvonne Moyse and Roger
         Senhouse, London: Harper Perennial, 2006.

SS   *The Second Sex*, trans. Constance Borde and Sheila
         Malovany-Chevallier, London: Vintage, 2009.

SSP   *The Second Sex*, trans. H. M. Parshley, New York: Random
         House, Vintage, 1970.

TALA   *A Transatlantic Love Affair: Letters to Nelson Algren*,
         New York: New Press, 1998.

TWD   *The Woman Destroyed*, trans. Patrick O'Brian, London:
         Harper Perennial, 2006.

UM   *'The Useless Mouths' and Other Literary Writings*, ed.
         Margaret A. Simons and Marybeth Timmerman, Urbana:
         University of Illinois Press, 2011.

VED   *A Very Easy Death*, trans. Patrick O'Brian, New York:
         Pantheon, 1965.

WD   *Wartime Diary*, ed. Margaret A. Simons and Sylvie le Bon
         de Beauvoir, Urbana: University of Illinois Press, 2009.

WML   *Witness to My Life: The Letters of Jean-Paul Sartre to*
         Simone de Beauvoir, 1926–1939, ed. Simone de Beauvoir,
         trans. Lee Fahnestock and Norman MacAfee, London:
         Hamish Hamilton, 1992.

WT   *When Things of the Spirit Come First: Five Early Tales*,
         trans. Patrick O'Brian, London: Flamingo, 1982.

Introduction:
Simone de Beauvoir –
Who's She?

One day in 1927 Simone de Beauvoir had a disagreement with her father about what it means to love. In an era when women were expected to aspire to marriage and motherhood, 19-year-old Simone was reading philosophy and dreamt of finding a philosophy she could live by. Her father claimed that 'to love' meant 'services rendered, affection, gratefulness'. She begged to differ, objecting with astonishment that love was more than gratitude – not something we owe someone because of what they've done for us. 'So many people,' Beauvoir wrote in her diary the next day, '[have] never known love!'[1]

This 19-year-old did not know that she would become one of the twentieth century's most famous intellectual women, that her life would become copiously written about and widely read. Her letters and autobiography alone would amount to over a million words,[2] and she would publish philosophical essays, prize-winning novels, short stories, a play, travelogues, political essays, journalism – not to mention her magnum opus, *The Second Sex*, which has been celebrated as 'the feminist Bible'. She would co-found political journals, successfully campaign for new legislation, object to the inhumane treatment of Algerians, give lectures around the world and lead government commissions.

Simone de Beauvoir was also to become one of the twentieth century's most infamous women. She was half of a controversial intellectual power couple with Jean-Paul Sartre. And, unfortunately, for much of the twentieth century popular perception was that he contributed the intellectual power and she contributed the couple. When she died in Paris in 1986, *Le Monde*'s obituary headline called her work 'more popularization than creation'.³ Reading the existing biographies, Toril Moi wrote in 1994 that 'one may be forgiven for concluding that the significance of Simone de Beauvoir derives largely from her relatively unorthodox relationship with Sartre and other lovers'.⁴

In the decades since these words were written a series of revelations about Beauvoir have come to light, surprising readers who thought they knew her. But they have also – ironically – obscured Beauvoir the thinker by perpetuating the illusion that her love life was the most interesting thing about her. After all, it was her philosophy that led her to live – and to continuously reflect on and re-evaluate – the life she lived. In her words: 'there is no divorce between philosophy and life. Every living step is a philosophical choice'.⁵

When the public figure Simone de Beauvoir picked up her pen she wrote not only for herself but for her readers. Her best-selling autobiographies have been described as embodying a philosophical ambition to show 'how one's self is always shaped by others and related to others'.⁶ But Beauvoir's point was more than that 'No man is an island', as John Donne said. For, in addition to being related to others, Beauvoir's autobiographies are upheld by a conviction that *being* a self does not mean being the same self from birth until death. Being a self involves perpetual change with others who are also changing, in a process of irreversible *becoming*.

Philosophers since Plato have discussed the importance of self-understanding to living a good life. Socrates claimed that to be wise one must 'Know Thyself!'; Nietzsche wrote that the task of each person is to 'Become who you are!' But Beauvoir's philosophical rejoinder was: what if, as a woman, 'who you are' is forbidden? What if becoming yourself simultaneously means being seen as a failure to be what you should be – a failure as a woman, or as a lover, or as a mother? What if becoming yourself makes you the target of ridicule, spite, or shame?

Beauvoir's century saw seismic shifts in the possibilities available to women. During her lifetime (1908–1986) women were admitted to universities on the same terms as men and gained the rights to vote, divorce and contraception. She lived through the bohemian blossoming of 1930s Paris and the sexual revolution of the 1960s. Between these cultural turning points, *The Second Sex* marked a revolutionary moment in the way women thought – and eventually, talked frankly – about themselves in public. Beauvoir's philosophical education was unprecedented in her generation, but, even so, when she was in her late thirties and began to apply her mind to the question 'what has it meant to me to be a woman?' she was shocked by her own discoveries.

In a century during which 'feminism' came to mean many different things, she wrote *The Second Sex* because she was irritated by the 'volumes of idiocies' that were churned out about women, tired of the ink that flowed in the 'quarrel about feminism'.[7] But when Beauvoir wrote her now-famous line – 'One is not born, but rather becomes, a woman' – she did not know how much this book would affect the rest of her life or the lives of those who came after her.

Much ink has been dedicated to the meaning of that sentence, to what it means to 'become' a woman. This book is dedicated to the question of how Beauvoir *became* herself. At the age of 18 Beauvoir wrote that she had reached the conclusion that it was impossible to truly 'put her life in order on paper' because it was a perpetual becoming; when she read what she'd written in her diary the day before, she said, it was like reading 'mummies' of 'dead "selves"'.[8] She was a philosopher, inclined to reflection and perpetually questioning the values of her society and the meaning of her life.

Because of the role Beauvoir assigned to the passage of time in the experience of being human, this biography follows the chronology of her life. As she grew older, she said, the world changed and so did her relationship with it. When Beauvoir wrote her life for the purpose of others reading it, she wanted 'to show the transformations, the ripenings, the irreversible deterioration of others and myself'. Because life unfolds in time she wanted to follow 'the thread the years have unwound'.[9] In this she resembled the young woman she had been, the teenage reader of Henri Bergson's philosophy. A self is not a thing, Bergson wrote – it is a 'progress', a 'living activity',[10] a *becoming* that continues to change until it meets its limit in death.

The woman Beauvoir became was partly the result of her own choices. However, Beauvoir was acutely aware of the tension between being a cause of herself and a product of others' making, of the conflict between her own desires and others' expectations. For centuries French philosophers had debated the question of whether it is better to live life seen or unseen by others. Descartes claimed (borrowing Ovid's words) that 'to live well you must live unseen'.[11] Sartre would write reams about the objectifying 'gaze' of other people – which he thought imprisoned us in relations of subordination. Beauvoir disagreed: to live well human beings must be seen by others – but they must be seen in the right way.

The problem is that being seen in the right way depends on who is seeing you, and when. Imagine that you are a woman in your early fifties and you have recently decided to write your life story. You start with your girlhood and youth, your coming-of-age as a woman, and publish two successful volumes in quick succession. In them, you describe two conversations you had at the age of 21 with a now famous man who was once your lover. You are also accomplished and internationally known. But it is the late 1950s, and women's life-writing has not yet reached the watershed moment in the twentieth century when women began to publicly admit that they had ambitions and felt anger, let alone that they had record-setting intellectual achievements or sexual appetites that could be disappointed even by a very famous man. Imagine that your stories become legendary – so legendary that they come to be a lens through which people read your entire life, even though they are just moments in it.

Beauvoir's public persona has been shaped – to the extent of being misshapen – by two such stories she told in her memoirs. The first takes us to Paris, in October of 1929, when two philosophy students were sitting outside the Louvre defining their relationship. They had just come first and second place (Sartre first, Beauvoir second) in a highly competitive and prestigious national exam and were about to embark on careers as philosophy teachers. Jean-Paul Sartre was 24, Beauvoir was 21. Sartre (as the story goes) did not want conventional fidelity, so they made a 'pact' according to which they were each other's 'essential love' but consented to the other having 'contingent loves' on the side.[12] It would be an open relationship, with first place in their hearts reserved for each other. They would tell one another everything, they said; and to start with it would be a 'two-year lease'. This couple would become, as Sartre's biographer Annie Cohen-Solal put it, 'a model to emulate, a dream of lasting complicity, an extraordinary success since, apparently, it seemed to reconcile the irreconcilable: the two partners remained free, equal, and honest with each other'.[13]

Their polyamorous 'pact' has provoked such curiosity that biographies have been written about their relationship as well as their individual lives; they are given an entire chapter in *How the French Invented Love*; they are called 'the first modern couple' in headlines.[14] Carlo Levi described Beauvoir's *The Prime of Life* as telling 'the great love story of the century'.[15] In her 2008 book about Beauvoir and Sartre's relationship, Hazel Rowley wrote that: 'Like Abélard and Héloïse, they are buried in a joint grave, their names linked for eternity. They're one of the world's legendary couples. We can't think of one without thinking of the other: Simone de Beauvoir and Jean-Paul Sartre.'[16]

In one sense, this book exists because it *is* difficult to think of one without the other. After working on Sartre's early philosophy for several years I grew increasingly suspicious about the asymmetries in the ways that the lives of Beauvoir and Sartre have been considered. Why, when Beauvoir died, did every obituary of her mention Sartre, while when Sartre died, some obituaries did not mention her at all?

For much of the twentieth century, and even the twenty-first, Beauvoir has not been remembered as a philosopher in her own right. In part this is due to a second significant story Beauvoir herself told. Earlier in 1929, also in Paris, by the Medici Fountain in the Luxembourg Gardens, Beauvoir decided to tell Sartre about her own ideas: about the 'pluralist ethics' she had been developing in her notebook – yet Sartre 'took it apart', and she suddenly became uncertain of her 'true capacity' intellectually.[17] There is little doubt that she was one of the star philosophy students of a famously stellar era; that summer – at the age of 21 – she would be the youngest person ever to pass the highly competitive *agrégation* exams. As well as Sartre, the budding philosopher Maurice Merleau-Ponty sought Beauvoir out for her conversation, and valued it enough to engage with her in person and in print for decades to come. But even later in her life Beauvoir would insist, 'I am not a philosopher ... [I am] a literary writer,' she claimed, and 'Sartre is the philosopher.'[18]

This conversation by the Medici Fountain has led later generations to ask: did Beauvoir – the very woman who wrote *The Second Sex* – underestimate or deceptively understate her own ability? Why would she do either of these things? Beauvoir was a formidable figure: many of her achievements were without precedent, blazing the trail for women to come. In feminist circles she has been celebrated as an exemplary ideal, 'a symbol of the possibility, despite everything, of living one's life the way one wants to, for oneself, free from conventions and prejudices, even as a woman'.[19] However, one of the central claims of *The Second Sex* is that no woman ever has lived her life 'free from conventions and prejudices'. Beauvoir certainly did not. And this biography tells the story of how, in many ways, she suffered from them – and how she fought back.

Close readers of Beauvoir have always suspected that she was editing her image in her autobiography, but it was not always clear how or why she did this. After all, the story of the pact showed a woman who was committed to telling the truth, and the author of *The Second Sex* wanted to shine light on the reality of women's situations. Did her commitment to scrutiny stop short at herself? If not, *why* would she hide significant parts of her life – intellectual and personal – from view? And why is it important to reconsider the way her life is remembered now?

The first answer to these questions – there are two – is that we have access to new material. Beauvoir's autobiographies were published in four volumes between 1958 and 1972. Over the course of her life she wrote many other works that included autobiographical material, including two chronicles of her travels to America (1948) and China (1957), and two memoirs of the deaths of her mother (1964) and Sartre (1981). She also published a selection of Sartre's letters to her (1983).[20]

During her lifetime some in the circle that grew around Sartre and Beauvoir – known patronymically as 'the Sartre family' (*la famille Sartre*) or more simply, 'the family' – thought they could see what Beauvoir was doing with the autobiographical project: putting herself in control of their public image. Many have assumed that she did this out of jealousy because she wanted to be remembered as first in Sartre's romantic life, as his 'essential love'.

But in the decades since Beauvoir's death in 1986 new diaries and letters have been made public that challenge this assumption. After Beauvoir published Sartre's letters to her in 1983, she lost some friends when the details of their relationships were brought out into the open. And when her war diary and letters to Sartre were published after her death in 1990, many were shocked to learn that not only had she had lesbian relationships, but that the women with whom she had them were former students. Her letters to Sartre also exposed the philosophical character of their friendship, and her influence on his work – but this drew less comment.[21]

Then came her letters to her American lover Nelson Algren, in 1997, and the public again saw a Beauvoir they had never expected: a tender, sensitive Simone who penned more passionate words for Algren than for Sartre. Less than a decade later, in 2004, her correspondence with Jacques-Laurent Bost was published in French, showing that within the first decade of her pact with Sartre, Beauvoir had another ardent affair with a man who remained close to her until her death. It was another shock, shifting Sartre from the romantic zenith he occupied in the public imagination. Sartre battled to establish Beauvoir's centrality to his intellectual life, publicly acknowledging her rigorous critical influence on his work. But evaluating Beauvoir's life seems to require the forcible displacement of Sartre from the centre.

Over the past decade more new publications and documents have been released that show Beauvoir in an even clearer light.

Beauvoir's student diaries – which show the development of Beauvoir's philosophy *before* she met Sartre and her early impressions of their relationship – reveal that the life she lived was very different from the life she recounted for the public. Although the diaries were published in 2008 in French, they are not yet available in full in English, so this period of her life is not well known outside scholarly circles. And in 2018 more new material became available to researchers, including letters Beauvoir wrote to the only lover she ever lived with or addressed by the familiar second person, *tu*: Claude Lanzmann.[22] In the same year, a prestigious two-volume *Pléiade* edition of Beauvoir's memoirs was released in France, complete with extracts from unpublished diaries and working notes for her manuscripts. In addition to these publications in French, in recent years the Beauvoir series, edited by Margaret Simons and Sylvie Le Bon de Beauvoir, have found, translated and published or republished many of Beauvoir's early writings, from her philosophical essays on ethics and politics to magazine articles she wrote for *Vogue* and *Harper's Bazaar*.

This new material shows that Beauvoir omitted a great deal from her memoirs – but it also shows some of the reasons behind her omissions. In the media-saturated internet age, it is difficult to imagine the extent to which Beauvoir's publication of autobiography defied contemporary conventions of privacy. Her four volumes (or six, counting the memoirs of her mother's and Sartre's deaths) cultivated a sense of intimate familiarity in her readers. But she did not promise to tell all: in fact, she told her readers that she had deliberately left some things obscure.[23]

The most recent new material – her diaries and unpublished letters to Claude Lanzmann – show that it was not just lovers she left in obscurity, but the early genesis of her philosophy *of* love and the influence of her philosophy on Sartre. Throughout her life she was plagued by people doubting her ability or originality – some even suggested that

Sartre wrote her books. Even the 'mammoth edifice' that is *The Second Sex* was accused of resting on 'two slender postulates' that Beauvoir took from Sartre's *Being and Nothingness*; she was accused of referring to Sartre's works 'as if to a sacred text'.[24] In some of her writings she explicitly condemns these belittlements as false. But they afflicted her in life and after death: in addition to the one that called her a popularizer, another obituary dismissively declared her 'incapable of invention'.[25]

It may come as a surprise to today's readers to hear this woman be accused of being unoriginal. But it was (and still is, sadly) an allegation frequently made against women writers – and often internalized by them. Beauvoir did have her own ideas, some of which were very like the ones Sartre became famous for; one year she published under his byline because he was busy and no one even noticed. Sartre acknowledged that it was her idea to make his first novel *Nausea* a novel rather than an abstract philosophical treatise, and that she was a rigorous critic whose insights improved his manuscripts before publication throughout his long career. In the 1940s and 1950s she wrote and published her own philosophy, criticizing Sartre and eventually changing his mind. In her later autobiography she defended herself against attacks on her own abilities, claiming outright that she had her own philosophy of being and nothingness before she met Sartre (who went on to write the book *Being and Nothingness*), and that she did not come to the same conclusions that he did. But these claims to her own independence and originality would be widely overlooked, as would her claims that some of the things people called 'Sartrean' weren't really original to Sartre.

This leads me to my second answer to the question of why we should reconsider Beauvoir's life now. Biography can reveal what a society cares about, what it values – and by encountering the values of another person in another time we can learn more about our own.

The Second Sex criticized many 'myths' of femininity for being the projections of men's fears and fantasies about women.[26] Many of these myths involve failing to take women as agents – as conscious human beings who make choices and develop projects for their lives, who want to love and be loved as such, and who suffer when they are reduced to objects in the eyes of others. Before she met Sartre, a year before she had an argument with her father about love, the 18-year-old Beauvoir wrote in her diary that: 'There are several things I hate about love.'[27] Her objections were ethical: men were not held up to the same ideals that women were. Beauvoir grew up in a tradition which taught that becoming an ethical self involves learning to 'love your neighbour as yourself'. But in Beauvoir's experience this injunction was rarely applied: people always seemed to love themselves too much or too little; no example of love from books or life satisfied her expectations.

It is far from clear whether Beauvoir's expectations were satisfied by the loves she went on to have. But it is clear that Beauvoir made and remade her decision to live a philosophical life, a reflective life guided by her own intellectual values, a life of freedom. She chose to do this by writing in several literary forms – and to do this in lifelong conversation with Sartre. It matters to reconsider Beauvoir's life now because Beauvoir and Sartre were united in the popular imagination by a very ambiguous word – 'love' – and 'love' was a concept that Beauvoir subjected to decades of philosophical scrutiny.

Reconsidering Beauvoir's life also matters because over time Beauvoir became dissatisfied with the way her life was depicted – with the way the persona 'Simone de Beauvoir' departed from the narrative of conventional marriage only to be subsumed by another erotic plot. Even after her death, widespread assumptions about 'what women want' and 'what women can do' affected the way Beauvoir's life is remembered. Whether romantically or intellectually, she has been cast as Sartre's prey.

Romantically, the idea that Beauvoir was Sartre's victim relies heavily on the assumption that where 'love' is concerned all women, if they're really honest with themselves, want lifelong monogamy with men. Over the five decades of the 'legendary couple' Sartre very publicly courted numerous 'contingent' women. Beauvoir, on the other hand, *appeared* (because they were omitted from her memoirs) to have few contingent relationships with men, all of which were over by her early fifties. On this basis some concluded that Sartre hoodwinked her into an exploitative relationship in which, despite being unmarried, they played the all-too-familiar parts of feckless womanizer and faithful woman. Sometimes her life is described as a casualty of patriarchal norms which suggest, among other things, that an ageing or intellectual woman was not as romantically desirable as an ageing or intellectual man. And sometimes she is the dupe of her own foolishness. As her former student, Bianca Lamblin, put it: Beauvoir 'planted the seeds of her own unhappiness' by refusing marriage and family.[28] Louis Menand wrote in the *New Yorker* that 'Beauvoir was formidable, but she was not made of ice. Though her affairs, for the most part, were love affairs, it is plain from almost every page she wrote that she would have given them all up if she could have had Sartre for herself alone.'

By contrast, Beauvoir's student diaries show that within weeks of meeting Jean-Paul Sartre she assigned him only one irreplaceable role: she was delighted to have found Sartre, writing that he 'is in my heart, in my body and above all (*for in my heart and my body many others could be*) the incomparable friend of my thought'.[29] It was friendship rather than love, she later explained in a letter to Nelson Algren, because Sartre 'does not care much for sexual life. He is a warm, lively man everywhere, but not in bed. I soon felt it, though I had no experience; and little by little, it seemed useless, and even indecent, to go on being lovers'.[30]

Was 'the great love story of the century' ultimately the story of a friendship?

Intellectually, Beauvoir has also been portrayed as a victim of Sartre, patriarchy, or personal failure. Did Beauvoir internalize misogyny? Did she lack confidence in her own philosophical ability? Throughout her public life Beauvoir was accused of 'popularizing' Sartre's ideas. She has been taken – to borrow Virginia Woolf's metaphor – as a magnifying mirror, with 'the magic and delicious power of reflecting the figure of man at twice its natural size'.[31] Even worse, she has been accused of being satisfied with playing this reflective role.

But it is difficult to know how much Beauvoir's purported 'secondary' status owes to Beauvoir and Sartre themselves and how much to attribute it to widespread cultural sexism. Even today, we know that women are: more often described in relational (personal or familial) terms than professional; more likely to be described with passive verbs than active ones; subject to negative gender distinctions (for example, 'despite being a woman, Simone thought like a man') and paraphrased rather than cited in their own voice.

Prominent commentary spanning Beauvoir's career provides illustration after illustration of her public definition as Sartre's derivative double, or worse:

The New Yorker, 22 February 1947
'Sartre's female intellectual counterpart'; 'the prettiest Existentialist you ever saw'

William Barrett (philosopher), 1958
'that woman, his friend, who wrote a book of feminine protest'[32]

La Petit Larousse, 1974
'Simone de Beauvoir: woman of letters, Sartre's disciple'

The Times of London, 1986
'In both her philosophical and political thinking, she follows his lead'[33]

La Petit Larousse, 1987
'Simone de Beauvoir: Sartre's disciple and companion, and an ardent feminist'

Deirdre Bair, Beauvoir's first biographer, 1990
Sartre's 'companion', who 'applies, disseminates, clarifies, supports, and administers' his 'philosophical, aesthetic, ethical and political principles'[34]

The Times Literary Supplement, 2001
'Sartre's sex slave?'[35]

Because many of Beauvoir's own words have not been available until relatively recently even some of her most insightful commentators have cast her as someone who passively succumbed to Sartre's spell. Intellectually, Beauvoir has been described as a 'closet philosopher', who renounced philosophy (becoming 'second to Sartre') because she saw intellectual success to be '*incompatible with seduction*'.[36] Romantically, Toril Moi wrote, Beauvoir's relationship to Sartre was 'the one sacrosanct area of her life to be protected even against her own critical attention'.[37] bell hooks writes that 'Beauvoir passively accepted Sartre's appropriation of her ideas without acknowledging the source'.[38] But personally Beauvoir was critical of Sartre from the early days of their relationship; and philosophically she did defend her own originality – although it is true that this would become more pronounced later in her life, after she saw just how inflated and one-sided claims of Sartre's influence on her became.

Alongside concerns that she was an exploited victim, Beauvoir has also been depicted as an exploitative vixen. The posthumous publication of Beauvoir's letters to Sartre and her diaries from the Second World War revealed that she had sexual relationships with three young women in the late 1930s and early 1940s, all of whom were her own former students. In some cases, Sartre would later have relationships with them too. It is bad enough, the objection goes, that she preyed upon women many years her junior and in dynamics of unequal power; but did Simone de Beauvoir 'groom' young women for Sartre? The couple of the pact clearly valued truth-telling – it was a central part of the public mythology of their relationship. So when details of their trios came to light they provoked shock, disgust and character assassination: 'It turned out that these two advocates of truth-telling constantly told lies to an array of emotionally unstable young girls.'³⁹

But the disdain they provoked was, again, suspiciously asymmetrical: whether because Beauvoir was a woman or because she was the woman who would go on to write *The Second Sex*, it seemed so much more surprising that *she* could be guilty of such behaviour. When Beauvoir's *Wartime Diary* was published in English in 2009 one disgusted reviewer entitled her review 'Lying and Nothingness', expressing shock that Beauvoir had written 'page after dishonest page' in her memoirs.⁴⁰ In the eyes of some readers this Beauvoir cared only for herself, and her novels were vanity writ large. When Beauvoir's letters to Sartre were published in English in 1991, Richard Heller called *her* 'vapid' and lamented the 'dispiriting, narcissistic quality of the material'.⁴¹

Readers may be tempted to give up on Beauvoir when they encounter the way she described these women. One of her lovers – with whom Beauvoir remained friends until her death – wrote a memoir after the posthumous publication of Beauvoir's letters to Sartre. Although it was decades after the events the letters depicted, she felt used and betrayed after reading them. Who should be believed – and when? What sense can be made of these accusations against the same woman who later wrote a rigorous ethics demanding that women should be treated with the respect befitting their dignity as free and conscious human beings? After all, it is because of Beauvoir that the word 'sexism' was added to the French dictionary.[42] She has been admired by feminists like Toril Moi and bell hooks as 'the emblematic intellectual woman of the twentieth century', 'the one female intellectual, thinker-writer who had lived fully the life of the mind as I longed to live it'.[43]

The answers to these questions matter because Beauvoir's authority has been invoked by many feminists to sanction their claims – whether or not she would have agreed with them. 'Simone de Beauvoir' has become an iconic feminist and post-feminist consumer product: 'a trademark of [her]self, a person turned into a brand'.[44] But brand perception is notoriously fickle. While some feminists celebrated her perceptive analysis of women's oppression, Beauvoir's criticisms of ideals of love, in particular, enraged some of her contemporaries, who retaliated by belittling and insulting her. When she published an excerpt from *The Second Sex* in May 1949, claiming that women did not want a battle of the sexes but rather (among other things) to feel 'both desire and respect' from men in sexual life, the prestigious author François Mauriac asked with derision: Is 'a serious philosophical and literary review really the place for the subject treated by Mme Simone de Beauvoir'?[45] When Pascal asked whether there was a conflict between love and justice, he was doing philosophy. When Kant and Mill discussed the place of love in ethics, they were doing philosophy.[46] But when Beauvoir extended discussions of love and justice to intimate relationships between men and women, she was called 'Madame' – to draw shameful attention to her unmarried status – and accused of lowering the tone.

In hindsight, it looks like Beauvoir was on the receiving end of an *ad feminam* offensive: If her critics could reduce her to a *failure* as a woman, highlighting her deviance from femininity; or a failure as a thinker, because she was unoriginal and owed everything to Sartre; or a failure as a human being, highlighting her deviance from their own moral ideals, then her ideas could be summarily dismissed rather than seriously debated.

As a matter of principle, clearly, both men and women can fall foul of the *ad hominem* fallacy, an argumentative strategy that diverts attention from the topic at hand by attacking a person's character or motives instead. But Beauvoir was not just accused of having poor character and unsound motives; she was accused of being against nature, of being a failure *as a woman*. Recent research in psychology suggests that women who achieve positions called *agentic* – that is, positions in which they show agency, including competence, confidence, and assertiveness – are often punished by 'social dominance penalties'. If women break out of gender hierarchies by competing for or achieving high-status, traditionally masculine positions, they are often perceived to be arrogant or aggressive, and penalized by being 'taken down' or brought down to size – sometimes entirely unconsciously – in order to maintain gender hierarchy.[47]

Beauvoir transgressed this hierarchy in practice and in theory: her ideas had the power to disrupt the lives of both men and women and she tried to live her own life according to them. In this sense, Beauvoir's story – on her own and with Sartre – raises questions not only about what is true about this woman and this man, but about what we can claim is true about men and women more generally. In today's intellectual landscape, increasingly little is held to be universally true of the broad categories 'man' and 'woman', and the categories themselves have come into question. In part, this has been possible because of Beauvoir's thoughts. But, as we shall see, Beauvoir was often penalized for having the audacity to think them.

Beauvoir's own philosophy – from her student diaries to her last theoretical work on *Old Age* – distinguished between two aspects of becoming a self: the view 'from within' and the view 'from without'. To get close to Beauvoir's view 'from within', for some parts of her life we are almost entirely reliant on her memoirs. There are reasons to doubt what she tells us in them, so where new material provides evidence of omissions or contradictions between accounts I have highlighted this as much as possible.

I have also drawn attention to the way that Beauvoir's understanding of her own becoming changed as she aged. We know that human beings' views of themselves change over time; psychological studies have shown repeatedly that self-concepts shift and our memories are selected to correspond to them.[48] We also know that humans present themselves in a variety of ways depending on their audience. For some parts of Beauvoir's life we have private letters and diaries – but letters are always written for a particular reader, and even diaries can be written with one eye on posterity. Voltaire wrote that all we owe to the dead is truth:[49] but between the stories we tell ourselves, the stories we tell others, and the stories they tell about us, where is the truth?

This question has no easy answer, and it is made even more difficult when the biographer's subject is a woman. As Carolyn Heilbrun notes, 'biographies of women, if they have been written at all, have been written under the constraints of acceptable discussion, of agreement about what can be left out'.[50] Beauvoir's life defied convention – quite apart from considerations for others' privacy and the legality of what she wrote, it would have been even more scandalous for her and alienating for her readers if she had been completely honest about her life. So she excluded much of her philosophy and her personal relationships; she left out much of the 'view from within'. There are many reasons why she might have done this, and we will explore them as they arise in the context of her life. But before we do, because Beauvoir was a philosopher, there is a final question to address about *why* biography matters in the case of her particular life and work.

Some philosophers think it is irrelevant to read the lives of great thinkers because their ideas can be found in the pages of their works. However interesting or boring the life in question, it belongs in a separate compartment to the philosophy. By contrast, others believe that a person's work cannot be understood without the life, and that learning about a philosopher's life is necessary to understand the true meaning of the work. The first, compartmentalizing, approach has the potential pitfall that its ahistoricity can lead to misunderstandings: for example, this way of reading philosophy has led to the misunderstanding that Sartre developed existentialist ethics (even though Beauvoir's work on this subject was written and published first, and Sartre never published his during his lifetime).

The second approach has the potential pitfall that it can result in *reducing* human beings to effects of external causes. 'Reductivist' biographies are frequently guided by a particular agenda that reads into a person's life rather than letting that life speak for itself. These approaches can be very illuminating, but they can also overshadow the agency of their subjects, portraying them as products of their childhood or class rather than selves they have decided to become.[51]

Beauvoir herself would have resisted a crude distinction between 'life' and 'work' – as if 'work' isn't living, and 'life' doesn't require work! One of her key philosophical insights is that every human being is *situated* in a particular context, in a particular body in a particular place and time and nexus of relationships. This situation shapes each individual's ability to imagine his or her place in the world, and shifts over the course of a lifetime. Moreover, in the case of women this situation has been shaped by centuries of sexism.

Writing about Beauvoir's life therefore presents the challenge of another kind of reductionism: for in addition to looking at her life on the basis of formative childhood experiences and other psychoanalytic lenses, or economic, class and other social considerations, there are structures of sexism to consider. We now know that her work has been cut, mistranslated or untranslated into English, and that in some cases the cuts and mistranslations altered her work's philosophical rigour and political message. But the very fact that this has happened to her work provokes the question: why? In the twenty-first century 'feminism' remains a contested concept with multiple meanings. One woman's 'free choice' is another's 'oppression'. One man's satire is another man's sexism. And this is precisely the kind of ambiguity that Beauvoir's mature philosophy explored.

Beauvoir's philosophical and autobiographical writings made the tension between freedom and constraint central to becoming an ethical self. Her literature also explored these themes, although its relation to Beauvoir's own life experience is contested. In Beauvoir's 1945 novel *The Blood of Others*, her character Hélène objects to having her thoughts or behaviour reduced to the fact that she is lower class: 'It's ridiculous, always explaining people's behaviour by exterior circumstances; it is as if what we think, what we are, doesn't depend on ourselves.'[52] And her philosophy explored this tension too: In her essay *The Ethics of Ambiguity* Beauvoir wrote that 'the very notion of action would lose all meaning if history were a mechanical unrolling in which man appears only as a passive conductor of outside forces.'[53]

This biography does not claim with finality to see the 'real' Beauvoir, because no biographer can attain a God's-eye point of view on a human life. Rather, this book is motivated by a desire to navigate the treacherous terrain between compartmentalizing Beauvoir's life and work and reducing the work to the life. It aims to give credit to the notion that what Beauvoir did depended on herself, and to acknowledge – with Beauvoir – that part of becoming a woman is not to be in control of all aspects of who you become. In *The Second Sex* she wrote that women are 'condemned to possess no more than precarious power: slave or idol, it was never she who chose her lot'.[54] Later in life, she realized that her public persona required her to be 'Simone de Beauvoir' – and that the persona had public power – but her philosophy committed her to the view that all she could ever do was keep becoming herself.

From the age of 15 Beauvoir felt a strong vocation to be a writer, but she did not always enjoy what she became. In an early philosophical essay entitled *Pyrrhus and Cinéas* Beauvoir wrote that no human being wills the same thing during an entire lifetime. 'There is no instant in a life where all instants are reconciled.'[55] Sometimes, Simone de Beauvoir felt that her life was a wellspring from which others would drink. Sometimes she felt overwhelmed by doubt or deeply regretted the way she treated herself and others. She changed her mind and she changed others' minds. She struggled with depression. She loved life; she was afraid of ageing, terrified of death.

When Beauvoir was near the end of her life she agreed to be interviewed by Deirdre Bair for a biography in part because Bair wanted to write about *all* of her life, not just her feminism.[56] Beauvoir did not like being reduced to a single dimension. Bair's book – the first posthumous biography (1990), to which many still refer to learn about her life – had the benefit of many interviews with her subject. But in several respects it retold the story Beauvoir had already made public.

This is the first biography to draw on the story she did not make public: showing the formation of the intellectual woman *before* she met Sartre, how she developed and defended her own philosophy of freedom, how she wrote novels because she wanted to appeal to the freedoms of her readers, how writing *The Second Sex* changed her life, and how she turned to life writing and feminist activism because she wanted to be an intellectual whose works left an impact not only on readers' imaginations, but on the concrete conditions of their lives.

Writing this book has been intensely intimidating – at times even terrifying. Beauvoir was a human person, whose memory I do not want to distort – whether at its most confusing, awe-inspiring, or unsettling. No matter how well documented a life is, the documentation of a life is not the life itself. I have been selective, knowing that I am guided by the interests of my own situation and reliant on information that has already been subject to the selection of Beauvoir. I have tried to show the full spectrum of her humanity: her confidence and her doubt, her energy and her despair, her intellectual appetites and her bodily passions. I have not included every lecture, every friend, or every lover. I have, however, included her philosophy, because I could not be truthful to her contradictions or her contributions without it.

Beauvoir lived an epic life: she was a globetrotter who crossed paths with Picasso and Giacometti, Josephine Baker, Louis Armstrong and Miles Davis, not to mention a monumental number of the twentieth century's literary, philosophical and feminist icons. Charlie Chaplin and Le Corbusier came to New York parties in her honour and she once claimed to have smoked six joints without getting high.[57] But without philosophy Simone de Beauvoir would not have become 'Simone de Beauvoir', and this is important for two very important reasons: because the myth that Beauvoir was Sartre's disciple has been perpetuated for long enough, and because their disagreements, their constant conversations, are a crucial part of the way she became herself.

But they are only one part. In 1963 Beauvoir wrote that

the public dimension of an author's life is precisely nothing more than one single dimension, and I think that everything having a relation to my literary career is but one aspect of my private life. And that is exactly why I was trying to figure out, for myself as well as for the readers, what having a certain public existence means from a private point of view.[58]

Beauvoir was critical of Sartre's philosophy and of his love – and yet he remained for her, as he quickly became in the weeks after she first met him – 'the incomparable friend of her thought'. Her thoughts were deeply challenging to her contemporaries, and they would be silenced, ridiculed and scorned. She chose a life that would allow her to think and write them because she valued her own mind and was convinced of its fertility. At the age of 19, Beauvoir wrote in her diary that 'the most profound part of my life is my thoughts'.[59] And despite everything else that she had become in life, 59 years later the 78-year-old Beauvoir still agreed: 'to me the most important thing was my mind'.[60]

Virginia Woolf wrote that there are 'some stories that have to be told by each generation'.[61] But in the case of Beauvoir much of her story has been too invisible to be told. The account we read in Beauvoir's diaries and letters – about her love of philosophy and her desire to love in unprecedented ways – changes the shape of the life that came after it.

Figure 1 *Simone de Beauvoir surrounded by her paternal family at Meyrignac, Summer 1908. From left to right: Georges, Ernest (Simone's grandfather), Françoise, Marguerite (Simone's aunt) and her husband Gaston (Georges' brother).*

1

Growing Like a Girl

At 4.30 a.m. on the morning of 9 January 1908 Simonne Lucie Ernestine Marie Bertrand de Beauvoir was born into the sixth arrondissement of Paris and stifling social conventions.[1] The first air she breathed came through second-storey windows overlooking the boulevard Raspail, and by the age of 4 she had mastered the art of extracting her engraved calling cards from the velvet bag she carried when making visits with her mother.[2] Beauvoir would live in the same chic zone of Paris for nearly all of her life, but at the time of her birth the family's fortunes were waning.

The Bertrand de Beauvoirs were high bourgeoisie, originally from Bourgogne. One of their ancestors was given an aristocratic title in 1786 only to lose his head, after the Revolution, in 1790. Despite occurring over a century before her birth, this incident has divided biographers of Beauvoir, who diverge in their estimation of her family's social standing: Bair makes a great deal of Beauvoir's pedigree, but Simone's sister Hélène assigned it much less importance. After the decapitation of their esteemed ancestor the family did not make much of their aristocratic pretensions.[3]

They did, however, still own land with a château in Limousin. But Simone's father, Georges de Beauvoir, was not firstborn so would not inherit it. He was intellectually gifted and charming, but his aspirations did not align with his parents' – he wanted to be an actor. His father encouraged him to pursue a more respectable profession and propriety prevailed: Georges studied law and worked in the office of a well-known Parisian lawyer. He was not ambitious: neither his father nor his brother needed to work to earn a living, and although his mother had attempted to instil the value of work in him it never took root. He did want to be married, however, so eventually he left his secretarial role to practise law in his own right, in the hope that it might improve his prospects.

Through the brokerage of his father a suitable contender was found: Françoise Brasseur, a young woman from a northern family with a sizeable dowry. Although their name did not have an aristocratic particle (like the 'de' in Bertrand de Beauvoir), the Brasseurs were much wealthier than the Bertrand de Beauvoirs. Gustave Brasseur, the father of the bride, was a very successful Verdun banker. Françoise was his first born but least loved child: her birth had disappointed his hopes for an heir. She was educated in a convent and her parents took little interest in her until they encountered financial challenges, which reminded them that she was well into marriageable age. This wasn't the only time that the Brasseurs would exhibit disappointment at a female birth: after encountering it as a daughter, Françoise faced it as a mother, and throughout her life she suffered from her parents' coldness.[4]

When the two families met for met for the first time in 1905 it was on the neutral terrain of a Houlgate resort, in Normandy. Françoise was unenthusiastic about the meeting, but she was also nervous on account of the artificial ritual that was expected of her: according to custom her suitor's first sight of her was carefully prearranged. In the hotel she was surrounded by her classmates from the convent in a scenario that displayed her beauty and social bearing, so that he could assess the aptitude of his potential companion as she presided over conversation and tea. Within a few weeks of meeting, Georges proposed. And although the marriage was arranged, by the time of their wedding on 26 December 1906 they were also united by love.[5]

In its early years Simone remembered her parents' relationship as a passionate one, emotionally and physically.[6] Just after their first anniversary, Simone was born. Although happy, her 21-year-old mother and 31-year-old father were still negotiating the combination of their lives and the competition of their expectations. Their address – 103 boulevard du Montparnasse – reflected Georges' status, but its furnishings did not. Georges wanted to recreate the splendour of his father's house; Françoise was young, provincial, and bewildered by the society in which she found herself.

Despite their differences (or perhaps because circumstances let them lay dormant), for a few blissful months the family fell into a harmonious rhythm: It was the role of their servant, Louise, to bathe and feed Simone as well as to cook and undertake other household chores. Georges went to work at the Courts of Appeal each morning, often returning in the evening with Françoise's favourite flowers. They played with their baby before Louise took her to bed, ate dinner together when Louise had returned to serve it, and passed the evening in reading aloud and needlepoint. Georges took it to be his responsibility to provide his wife with the culture befitting her class; Françoise took it to be her responsibility to ensure that her learning never exceeded the quantity or kind befitting her sex.

Two and a half years after Georges' and Françoise's marriage, in 1909 they had still not yet received Françoise's dowry when her father fled Verdun in disgrace. Gustave Brasseur's bank was ordered into liquidation in July 1909, and everything was seized for sale, including the personal possessions of the Brasseur family. To add insult to ignominious injury, he was sent to jail, where he spent thirteen months before he was tried and condemned to a further fifteen-month sentence. His former influence still exerted some of its power, however; he was released early. So he moved to Paris, with his wife and youngest daughter, to live near Françoise and start over.

This turn of events meant that Françoise's dowry would never be paid, but at first the family remained harmonious and hopeful even so. They were happy and their fortune seemed secure: Georges had a reasonable income from his work, and his own inheritance (although modest) had been invested in a way they thought wise. Georges' attention to Françoise was tender, and she blossomed into a laughing and lively woman.[7]

On 9 June 1910 a second daughter was born. She was christened Henriette-Hélène Marie but was called Hélène or, within the family, 'Poupette' (meaning 'little doll'). Although she was only two and a half years younger, Simone saw Hélène as a student in need of her expert tutelage; she was already a teacher in the making. The family had hoped for a boy, and Beauvoir detected their disappointment at her birth, writing in her memoirs (with characteristic understatement) that 'it is perhaps not altogether without significance that her cradle was the centre of regretful comment'.[8] In Hélène's own memoirs we read that after the birth announcement her grandparents had written a letter congratulating Georges and Françoise on the arrival of a son. They didn't bother to soil new paper when they were informed that it was a girl – they simply added a postscript: 'I understand that the birth was a little girl, according to the will of God.'[9]

Beauvoir described her earliest years with a feeling of 'unalterable security' broken only by the realization that eventually she, too, was 'condemned to be an outcast of childhood'. She loved to be outdoors exploring nature, relishing in running through lawns and examining leaves and flowers, seed pods and spiders' webs. Each summer the family spent two months in the country: one month at Georges' sister Hélène's house (a turreted nineteenth-century château called La

Grillère) and another at his father's estate, Meyrignac. The château at Meyrignac was set in a large property of more than 200 hectares, providing ample opportunity for Simone to lose herself in the beauty of nature. Her wonder at natural spaces would be a permanent feature of her life; she continued to associate the countryside with solitude, freedom and the highest heights of happiness.[10] But for all its grandeur, much to the surprise of some Parisian visitors, the château had neither electricity nor running water.[11]

Their Paris apartment, by contrast, was now plush, sparkling, and overwhelmingly red – red moquette upholstery, a red Renaissance dining room, curtains of red velvet and red silk. The drawing room walls were mirrored, reflecting the light of a crystal chandelier, and there were silver pose-couteaux for resting their table knives. In the city Françoise would say goodnight to her daughter in dresses of tulle and velvet before going back to play the grand piano for their guests. Here solitude and natural spaces were harder to come by: Simone had to settle for that 'common playground', the Luxembourg Gardens.[12]

Simone was a precocious reader and her family cultivated her curiosity with great care. Her father made an anthology of poetry for her, teaching her how to recite it 'with expression', while her mother enrolled her in one book subscription service or library after another.[13] The year of Simone's birth was the year in which French state schools were finally granted permission to prepare girls for the *baccalauréat* – the exam which allowed access to universities. But a girl of Beauvoir's milieu did not go to a state school. In October 1913 (when Beauvoir was 5½ years old) it was decided that she would attend a private Catholic school, the *Adeline Désir Institute* (which she nicknamed *Le Cours Désir*). Although Beauvoir later recalled jumping for joy at the prospect of going, it was a black mark for a girl of her status to be educated in a school at all – those who had the means had governesses at home. She only attended two days a week – Wednesdays and Saturdays – and the rest of the time her schoolwork was supervised by her mother at home, with her father taking interest in her progress and successes.[14]

Hélène missed her sister on school days and their relationship remained very close, partly because of a deep affection and partly because the girls were not allowed to socialize with anyone their mother had not vetted, and their mother did not think many of their

Figure 2 *Françoise de Beauvoir with her daughters, Hélène (left) and Simone (right).*

peers passed muster. Georges and Françoise doted on their eldest but did not consider Hélène an individual in her own right. Hélène knew that her parents were proud of Simone: When Simone came first in her class, she was praised profusely by their mother; when Hélène also came first Françoise credited her success to the fact that she had it easier with an older sister to help her. Hélène recognized that 'as the second-born girl, I was not really a welcome child. But Simone valorized me even though she could have crushed me by siding with our parents, and that's why I remained attached to her. She was always nice, always defending me against them.'[15] The family had few toys, but the sisters enjoyed playing imaginary games and confiding in each other.[16]

At the age of 7 Simone had her first private communion – beginning a practice that she would continue to observe three times a week, either with her mother or in the private chapel at the Cours Désir. The same year she wrote her first surviving story, *Les Malheurs de Marguerite* (*The Misfortunes of Marguerite*) – it was 100 pages long, written by hand in a little paperback notebook she received from her grandfather Brasseur.[17]

Until the age of 8 there was only one other child that Simone thought worthy of her respect: her cousin, Jacques. He was six months older than her, but had had a boy's education – and a good one, at that: she was dazzled by his confidence. One day he made her a stained-glass window, inscribed with her name. They decided that they were 'married in the sight of God' and she called him 'her fiancé'.[18] In hindsight Hélène wrote that if it weren't for their isolation, Simone would not have assigned this childish fiancé so much importance – but for at least a decade she thought she really would marry him.

The day Beauvoir entered the fourth-first form (at the age of 9) she met a second outsider, beyond her immediate family, who was worthy of her respect: someone whose life and death would have a profound effect on her. Elisabeth Lacoin – Zaza, as Beauvoir called her[19] – was a bright and vivacious student at the Cours Désir, and after meeting at school the two developed an amicable rivalry. She introduced Simone to a new and delicious dimension of life: friendship. With Hélène, Simone had learned what it meant to say 'we'; with Zaza she first tasted what it meant to miss someone.

Hélène de Beauvoir described Zaza as highly strung – 'like a sleek and elegant racehorse ready to bolt out of control'[20] – but in Simone's eyes she was a marvel. She played the piano beautifully, wrote elegantly, became womanly without losing her 'boyish daring', and had the nerve not only to admire Racine (as one should) but to hate Corneille (as one shouldn't). She had subversive ideas, stuck her tongue out at her mother during a piano recital, and despite such displays of 'personality' she was greeted by her mother with love and affection.

So along with the sweetness of friendship Beauvoir discovered a bitter aftertaste: comparison.

She later realized that it was not a fair contest to compare her own life, and her own mother, with Zaza's: 'I felt myself from within, and I saw her from without.'[21] By the age of 18 Beauvoir was using this distinction, which would go on to play a significant role in her work, between the 'duality so often observed between the being that I am within myself and the being seen from the outside.'[22]

With the benefit of hindsight, Beauvoir recognized that Zaza's mother, Madame Lacoin – as Simone's parents noted the day they started to encourage friendship with Zaza – was from a good Catholic family, made a good Catholic marriage, and was a good Catholic mother of nine. She was also wealthy, and secure enough in her status to tolerate Zaza's defiance because she could afford to laugh at convention. The same could not be said for Madame de Beauvoir.

If a childhood could be summarized in commandments, the two greatest commandments of Simone's de Beauvoir's were 'Thou shalt not *do* what is improper' and 'Thou shalt not *read* what is unsuitable'. Françoise de Beauvoir had an unshakably rigid upbringing, with 'provincial propriety and the morals of a convent-girl'.[23] Her unwavering faith in God was accompanied by an equally impregnable zeal for etiquette: she 'never dreamed of protesting in any way against an illogicality sanctioned by social conventions'.[24] If this meant that a male friend, living 'in sin' with a woman, could be received in their house but the woman could not: so be it. Françoise was, in her daughter's words, 'apt to confuse sexuality with vice': she mistook desire itself for sin. Since convention allowed men indiscretions so did she; women bore the brunt of her dissatisfaction. She was sickened by 'physical' questions, and never discussed them with her daughters – Beauvoir had to learn about the surprises of puberty from her cousin Madeleine.

Madeleine was older than Simone, and knew more about bodies and the 'improper' uses of them. One summer day in the country, she told Simone and Hélène about the changes their bodies would soon undergo: that there would be blood and bandages. She offered definitions for mysterious terms – 'lover', 'mistress' – arousing curiosity about the causal chain preceding childbirth. Emboldened by new knowledge, when the sisters returned to Paris and their mother, Hélène asked Madame de Beauvoir where babies came out. She said they came out of the anus, painlessly. In this and other instances, Françoise misled her daughters about their own bodies' possibilities in shocking ways: Beauvoir would grow to view her body as 'vulgar and offensive'.[25]

Minds, on the other hand, Françoise did not neglect – she even learned English and Latin in order to better help her children. Georges and Françoise both placed a high value on education – a well-bred girl was a well-read one – but they were less than unified about religion. Her mother was as devoutly Catholic as her father was dogmatically atheist. This polarity was to have a profound impact on Beauvoir. Her father provided her with book after book, carefully curated selections from the great works of literature. Her mother provided her with religious literature and a living model of self-sacrificial Catholic devotion. She attended her daughters' classes (which the Cours Désir allowed mothers to do until the girls were 10) and regularly took them to mass at Notre-Dame-des-Champs or Saint Sulpice. By her mid-teens, both the education and the Catholicism would prove to be sources of tension between Beauvoir and her parents. She later described her childhood as suspended between scepticism and faith, and credited this 'imbalance' with making her life 'a kind of endless disputation': it was, she thought, the main reason she became an intellectual.[26]

When the First World War was declared in August of 1914 Georges and Françoise feared occupation, and the family stayed at La Grillère until they could determine whether it was safe to return to Paris. There Simone remembered canning and knitting for the war effort as 'the only time in my life I did those sorts of feminine occupations with any pleasure'.[27] The previous year Georges had been discharged from the army with a weak heart. But he was called to active service even so, and was at the front by October. Within weeks he had a heart attack so was again discharged from active duty and sent to a military hospital to recover. When he left the hospital for Paris in early 1915, he reassumed duty in the Ministry of War. Paris was beset by inflation, his income was miniscule, and his investments were paying hastily diminishing returns. His expenditure, however, did not adapt accordingly.

During these years Simone's beautiful girlhood moved into awkward adolescence. While Hélène's healthy, doll-like features made her epithet 'Poupette' increasingly apt, Beauvoir ate little, looked sickly, and was diagnosed with scoliosis. The strictness of her mother's moral code, the tightening of the family finances, and the rules of Paris under blackout provided her increasingly compulsive tendencies with other avenues for gaining her parents' approval.

She was becoming a dutiful daughter – but then her universe began to totter.

2

The Dutiful Daughter

As a small child, Simone remembered her family with a rapturous sense of belonging.[1] But from the age of 11 onwards, she began to feel increasingly confused by what was expected of her, and shocked that what she wanted to become was not what her family wanted her to be. They had raised her to be precocious, to read, to question: so why did they tell her to stop thinking, stop reading, stop questioning? She began to feel miserable and unhappy, in part because of her unanswered questions and in part because she was witnessing an unwelcome transformation in someone she loved. As a girl Beauvoir thought her father a rarity among men.[2] No one she knew rivalled his wit, his brilliance, his wide reading, his ability to recite poetry or his passion in argument. He enjoyed acting and loved being the life of the party. But the family's misfortune eventually cost him even his good humour. The *boulevardier*, the man about town, was déclassé and dispirited.

After the First World War, Georges de Beauvoir's already precarious fortunes took a turn for the worse. His investments (in pre-revolutionary Russian stocks) were now worthless, and suddenly the family had only his earnings to live on. Simone overheard vexed conversations about money: Françoise could not understand why Georges would not return to Law; Georges offered a retaliatory reminder that things would be different if her dowry had been paid. Their passion for each other was now mixed with bickering and spite. One night, when Simone returned home with Louise, her mother had a swollen lip.[3] The truth was that Georges could not afford to return to legal practice: he didn't have the capital to pay for office rent or furniture or any of the things needed to start the business, let alone the means to support the family while waiting for his business to become profitable. He was 40 and had already had two heart attacks: he lacked the health, the means and the will to do what Françoise wanted.

Fortunately for Georges, the previously disgraced Gustave Brasseur (Françoise's father) had a habit of landing on his feet and came to his son-in-law's rescue. For the last two years of the war he had been the director of a shoe factory. He had secured military contracts for boots and shoes, making his business highly profitable, and so offered Georges the role of co-director.[4] This was not a seemly profession for a Bertrand de Beauvoir, but he had no alternative but to accept. He treated his title as honorary and worked irregularly, only when it could not be avoided. After the war the demand for military boots died out, and so did the factory's prosperity. Once again Georges was rescued by a family member, who offered him a role as a newspaper advertising salesman. Since he was neither a natural salesman nor a reliable worker, that work too was soon lost.

From then on, he drifted from one role to the next. His daily habits cost him several jobs; despite his family's straitened circumstances Georges rose at 10 a.m., went to the Stock Exchange around 11 a.m. to be seen, ate lunch, briefly visited his office, played bridge all afternoon, had an evening drink at the café and then went home for dinner.[5] According to Hélène, Simone always spoke too charitably of their father; in Hélène's view, 'all the men in the Beauvoir family were lazy and did not like to work; the women are the strong ones who did it all and saved face for the men'.[6] It seems unlikely that Beauvoir's generous depiction of her father was motivated by genuine affection in view of what later years had in store, but it is possible that some kind of family loyalty moved her to paint him in flattering tones. A more compelling possibility is that Beauvoir knew, by the time she was writing her memoirs in the mid-1950s, that if she portrayed herself as a 'bitter' woman who was unsympathetic towards her own father, hostile readers would use her bitterness in *ad feminam* rebuttals of everything she stood for.

For a year after the end of the First World War life continued much as usual in the boulevard du Montparnasse. But by the summer of 1919 the Beauvoir family could make no more economies. They moved to a flat in the rue de Rennes, number 71. On the fifth floor, it was dark and dirty, and had no lift, no running water, no bathroom and no central heating.[7] Although their father still had a study in addition to the parental bedroom and reception rooms, Simone had no space to call her own: the sisters shared a room so tiny that the gap between their beds only allowed them to stand one at a time. They still had Louise, at first – the sixth floor of their building had rooms for the servants of its occupants. But soon after Louise was married and moved to the rue Madame and Françoise had to run her dilapidated apartment alone.[8] At first she attributed this state of affairs to the difficulty of finding good help, but the truth was that the family couldn't afford to look.

This was a clear sign of the depths to which they had fallen: one of the ways of distinguishing between the *haute bourgeoisie* and the middle class was that the former always had at least one live-in servant; the latter never did. Françoise had always had a temper but in the rue de Rennes she lost it more and more frequently, while at the same time attempting to turn indignity into an opportunity for virtue. She began to show neglect and contempt for her body; the girls, too, wore worn and dirty dresses. But this was not a cause of shame in the mind of their mother, who had begun to calculate life in a different currency. They may have had little cash, but they had culture and piety – commodities of much greater value.

As a woman Simone de Beauvoir would be remembered for her distinctive style, and as a novelist and memoirist her prose is textured with textiles: whether the material of a woman's dress or the pattern of a Mexican blanket. But as girls, both Simone and Hélène remembered suffering from a 'lack of elegance' for much of their childhoods – in later life Simone referred to their situation as one of 'semi-poverty'.[9] There were other girls at the Cours Désir who were poorly dressed on account of their 'decent poverty' – after all, no respectable girl should dress in a way that could attract accusations of coquetry – but their classmates observed that 'Simone de Beauvoir was dressed even worse'.[10]

Even after she had escaped from its scarcity, Beauvoir's childhood left her with a lasting sense of economy. At school, her notebooks became so crammed with tiny handwriting that her teachers complained. She was frugal not only with money and material things, but with herself: 'I remained convinced that one must make use of everything, and of oneself, to the utmost'.[11] She applied herself to her studies and simultaneously learned the ways of a good Catholic girl: her efforts were so successful that the chaplain praised her mother for 'the radiant beauty of her soul'.[12] She joined a lay religious order for children called the 'Angels of the Passion'. In her own words: 'I had made a definite metamorphosis into a good little girl. Right from the start, I had composed the personality I wished to present to the world; it had brought me so much praise and so many great satisfactions that I had finished by identifying myself with the character I had built up: it was my one reality'.[13] But she irritated many of her classmates: she was a know-it-all with a healthy dose of holier-than-thou.

Although Beauvoir's relationship with religion would become increasingly ambivalent as she approached her twenties, in childhood it inspired her to question the role of girls in her society. In the sight of God, she wrote in *Memoirs of a Dutiful Daughter*, her soul was no less precious than those of little boys: so why should she envy them?[14] In a 1965 interview, Beauvoir reiterated that her strict religious upbringing 'helped her enormously' precisely because she thought of herself as 'a soul'. 'At the level of souls,' she said, there was no variable valuation of human beings: 'God would have loved me as much if I had been a man, there was no difference between male and female saints, it was a completely asexual domain.' Before encountering intellectual egalitarianism, Beauvoir wrote, she found in her religion 'a species of moral, spiritual equality' that counted for a lot in the shaping of her life's convictions.[15] But a dissonance dawned in her awareness – between equality preached and inequality practised. She remembered her father saying with pride, 'Simone has a man's brain; she thinks like a man; she *is* a man.' And yet, she objected, 'everyone treated me like a girl'.[16]

As she grew, Beauvoir noted that her father's interest in her education increased – and so did his interest in her appearance.[17] Beauvoir wrote in her memoirs that she 'began to take an interest in the sort of figure I thought I should cut in life', taking inspiration from Jo March in Louisa May Alcott's *Little Women*. Even at the age of 11 Beauvoir was captivated by her.[18] Jo was not the most virtuous or beautiful of her sisters, but her passion for learning and desire to write shone like a beacon in the imagination of the young Simone. Georges de Beauvoir saw things differently. As long as he approved of her, Beauvoir felt, she could be sure of herself. But gradually the years of flowing praise gave way to disappointment. He appreciated elegance and beauty in women; her sister demonstrated these qualities to a higher degree and so she, like Amy in *Little Women*, won affirmation and affection.

Simone, like Jo, threw herself into books: she read religious works – *The Imitation of Christ*, a *Handbook of Ascetic and Mystical Theology* – and parentally approved works of history and literature, French and English. She loved English literature, reading *Alice in Wonderland* and *Peter Pan* as a child, honing skills she would later use to read the Brontës and Virginia Woolf in their native tongue.[19] Over time, her parents' prohibitions and her cousin Madeleine's insinuations led her to realize that books could teach her things her parents wouldn't. Madeleine was allowed to read whatever she wanted to; what was she missing?[20] When left alone in the flat, she raided the bookshelves, reading her father's worn copies of Bourget, Alphonse Daudet, Marcel Prévost, Maupassant and the Goncourts: they supplemented her sexual education.[21]

Novels also helped her see the questions hanging unanswered in the world around her. Jo March did not want to do housework because it kept her from what she loved: so why did so many women do it when so few men did? Convention told her that marriage was her future, but Jo March resisted this unwanted fate: could she, too?[22] George Eliot's *The Mill on the Floss*, which Beauvoir read at the tender age of 11 or 12, raised other questions that would recur in her life and her philosophy. Eliot's character Maggie Tulliver hated wasting her time on the repetitive labour of patchwork, where the same stitches had to be sewn again and again. How, if this domestic drudgery was what was expected of her, could Beauvoir be faithful to both herself and the desires of others? If 'love' meant that women sacrificed much and men little, was it worth it? In Beauvoir's student diaries in 1926 she was still pondering the question of how much of herself to keep and how much to give away.[23] Maggie Tulliver had fallen in love with the unworthy Stephen; but Beauvoir could not understand her attraction: 'The only relationship I could imagine was a love-friendship one; in my view, the exchange and discussion of books between a boy and a girl linked them forever.'[24]

Books offered Beauvoir more than an education: they were a refuge from the physical and emotional deprivation she encountered when she lifted her eyes from the page. They charted paths of resistance to the life that had been mapped out for her, even if they didn't yet lead to places where women could make choices or give and receive bodily affection without shame. While the young Beauvoir was inspired by characters' intellectual lives, she was discomfited by the physical; she was, to use her own word, prudish. She knew her own parents' relationship was physically passionate – and later grieved the injustice of her mother's loss when, at the age of 35, her father spurned her for extramarital pleasure.[25] But the young Beauvoir found the sexual a matter of disgust: 'Love, in my view, had nothing to do with the body.'[26]

In the five years after the move to the rue de Rennes Beauvoir experienced the tumult of adolescence, the increasing tensions between her parents, and the end of two lives. After marrying, her beloved Louise had a baby, a little boy. But the boy developed bronchial pneumonia and died. It was an abrupt death, the first Simone had ever known, and she found it terrifying. Louise and her husband lived in a single room in a sixth-floor garret with their child – when they went to visit her afterwards she saw not only death for the first time, but also the sixth-floor hallway, where the landing had a dozen doors, each of which led to single rooms that housed entire families.[27] Not long afterwards, the concierge's son in the rue de Rennes became ill. He had tuberculosis and meningitis – and died a painful and protracted death. Simone and her family daily watched his decline; anyone who entered or exited the building had to pass the sick child on the way to the staircase. She worried, since children were dying, that she or Hélène would be next.

Beauvoir would later write narratives that closely resembled her life in her novels, which has often obscured the line between the facts and fictions of her own biography. In her 1946 novel *The Blood of*

Others she revisited these childhood memories of premature death. The novel's protagonist, a man by the name of Jean Blomart, discovers 'original evil' when he hears the words 'Louise's baby is dead':

> Once again I see the twisted staircase, the stone corridor with those many doors, all alike; mother told me that behind every door there was a room in which a whole family lived. We went in. Louise took me in her arms, her cheeks were flabby and wet; mother sat on the bed bedside her and began to talk to her in a low voice. In the cradle was a white-faced baby with closed eyes. I looked at the red tiles, at the bare walls, at the gas ring, and I began to cry. I was crying, mother was talking, and the baby remained dead.[28]

How, Blomart asks a few pages later, can he smile when he knows Louise is weeping? Throughout her life Beauvoir would find herself aghast at the scandal of human indifference to the suffering of others.

At home, however, Simone wished that her mother would show her daughters a little *more* indifference. Both sisters described their adolescence as painful, and their relationships with their mother as particularly tense. From the age of 12 or 13 Simone found her hostile and even 'unbearable'; Hélène described her concept of motherhood as 'totally tyrannical'[29] and thought that she wanted to live through her daughters, and for her daughters to live for her – a desire they were unwilling to fulfil.[30]

It is not difficult to understand their unwillingness: their mother played the dutiful wife while their father's behaviour became ever more objectionable. Bridge in the afternoon had already given way to bridge after dinner; he spent more and more of his hours and his earnings on drinking and games while Françoise scrimped to meet the needs of their household. By daylight, Simone and Hélène watched their mother struggle to provide and care for them and their father make scenes when she asked for housekeeping money; after nightfall they heard late homecomings, fights, and talk of brothels, mistresses, gambling.

In *A Very Easy Death*, Beauvoir recounted her mother's loss of patience with the situation – eventually Madame de Beauvoir would slap and needle her husband, making scenes in private and public alike. Later in life, Beauvoir reflected on the way her mother felt torn between contradictory desires:

> It is impossible for anyone to say 'I am sacrificing myself' without feeling bitterness. One of Maman's contradictions was that she thoroughly believed in the nobility of devotion, while at the same time she had tastes, aversions and desires that were too masterful for her not to loathe whatever went against them. She was continually rebelling against the restraints and the privations that she inflicted upon herself.[31]

How to resolve these conflicting desires – to live a life of devotion to others or to live life for oneself – was to become one of the central questions of Beauvoir's student diaries, existentialist ethics and feminism. Madame de Beauvoir was a devout Catholic woman, who raised her daughter on a spiritual diet of saints and martyrs. This provided Simone with a catalogue of exemplary lives in which self-sacrifice was always a key ingredient. In some cases, this self-sacrifice resulted in apotheosis – making oneself nothing was the way to become divine. Simone began to find solitude the most exalting state; she wanted to reign 'alone over [her] own life'.[32] Religious refrains would reverberate in her later works, as would her mother's loss of prestige. Although she does not claim it to be autobiographical, there is a passage in *The Second Sex* where Beauvoir discusses the rebellion of daughters as especially violent when daughters have watched their mothers sacrifice themselves on undeserving altars: they see that in 'reality this thankless role does not lead to any apotheosis; victim, she is scorned; shrew, she is detested. [. . .] Her daughter wants *not* to take after her'.[33]

The circumstances at home were increasingly stressful, but school still offered stability and one companionship that rivalled even the deliciousness of solitude. Zaza's friendship continued to bring Simone pleasure and confidence: they were competitive, studious and dubbed 'the inseparables' by their teachers and peers. Their fathers were of the same social class, and by some miracle Madame Lacoin endeared herself to Madame de Beauvoir, so the girls were allowed to go to the Lacoins' house for visits. The Lacoins did not know about the Beauvoirs' relative poverty, and the Beauvoirs did not know about the Lacoins' relative informality at home (their children were allowed to run and jump indoors, to overturn furniture!),[34] but apart from Hélène – who initially felt displaced by the presence of Zaza in Simone's affections – all parties were satisfied that this friendship was suitable.

Both girls were interested in ideas: Simone could talk with Zaza about the things that interested her and voice her questions aloud. Simone usually came in first place in academic subjects at school, but Zaza beat her in athletics and music. As they grew into young women together, Zaza became increasingly pretty and graceful; Simone's face grew blotchy and her body awkward. This changed when Simone was around 17; but at the time she was self-consciously aware that her friend's life had many physical, financial and familial charms that were conspicuously absent from her own.

They shared a great deal – but Simone's desire for closeness was not fully reciprocated, in part because Zaza wanted a kind of relationship with her mother that Simone either did not want or could not have. Zaza had a full life, with eight siblings and a successful father, but she only felt special when she was singled out in her mother's attention. Simone believed that Zaza was Madame Lacoin's only confidante –

once, in a rare moment of intimacy, Zaza told Simone that her mother had told her about the 'horror' of her wedding night. Madame Lacoin told her daughter that she was disgusted by sex and that the conceptions of her nine children had all been devoid of passion.[35] Madame Lacoin had only had an elementary education, and while it was fine for Zaza to get good grades it was more important that she assume her family responsibilities, for these would prepare her for her own future as a wife. She expected her to make the best marriage in the family.

Simone had always been perplexed by the dynamics of this family, but she was taken aback one summer when she went to visit Zaza at the Lacoin's estate in the Landes. When she arrived, Zaza was confined to a sofa with a large gash on her leg. Once they were alone, Zaza admitted that the wound was self-inflicted: she had hit her own leg with an axe. Why!? Beauvoir asked. Because she wanted to be free of the expectations of her able-bodied self: social visits, garden parties, watching her younger siblings. Although she didn't mention Zaza by name, Beauvoir would write this incident, too, into *The Second Sex*.[36]

As Simone and Hélène grew older, their shared loneliness gave way to shared resentment. The sisters were also beginning to rebel – albeit in less violent ways. They sneaked out of the apartment when their parents weren't home to have café-crèmes at La Rotonde – a place whose glamourous clientele had fascinated them for hours as they watched from the balcony of their flat.[37]

When their parents were home it was increasingly clear that their father took it to be a sign of personal failure that his daughters required formal qualifications: had they had dowries they could have aspired to good marriages rather than employment. After the First World War this situation was far from unique: the dowries of many bourgeois Frenchwomen had been destroyed by inflation, and education was the necessary path in ensuring that they would have the means to live. But this did not stop people of Simone's parents' class thinking it was beneath them for their daughters to receive higher education. For them, training for a profession was a sign of defeat.

0   Simone's father's early pleasure in her precocious intelligence was rooted in his expectation that it would help her shine in the glittering social spheres of his childhood: to succeed there a woman needed to be beautiful, of course, and to be well read in order to be a good conversationalist. He liked intelligence and wit, but he did not like intellectuals and women's rights. Even so, eventually the reality sunk in that, unlike her cousin Jeanne, who would go on to be the *châtelaine* of the family estate, Simone would inherit nothing. He used to say to his daughters that they would never marry, announcing with bitterness in his voice that they would have to work for their living.[38]

So Simone confronted confusingly contradictory expectations: to succeed as a woman she must be accomplished and educated; but not too accomplished, not too educated. Her mother's wishes provided her with a catch-22 of a different kind. Since their household had no servants, Françoise would have liked her daughters' help. But Simone needed to study to succeed, and refused to spend time learning the 'feminine' skills she had no desire whatsoever to employ. The anger and ambivalence Françoise felt at her own situation was often unleashed on Simone.

Everywhere Simone looked she felt the weight of the expectations of others: often these were oppressive; occasionally they would let in fresh air instead of shutting it out. Jacques Champigneulle, Simone de Beauvoir's childhood fiancé, admired both Beauvoir sisters as they were, and continued to pursue their conversation when their father no longer considered them worthy interlocutors. Jacques' father owned a stained glass manufacturing plant on the boulevard du Montparnasse, and he frequently visited the Beauvoirs: Georges listened to him, treating him like an adult; Françoise loved his manners.

When Georges no longer found Simone's ideas interesting or amusing – reminding him, as they did, of his own failure – Jacques filled the conversational gap. At first Simone was puzzled by the way they would sit in the drawing room: Jacques and Georges would discuss something interesting while the women, much like Maggie Tulliver, were expected to sit quietly and sew or sketch. Initially Jacques deferred to Georges, but then became more liberal and more vocal, challenging his uncle's conservatism. So Georges decided not to delay his nightly bridge game by staying in the apartment to chat; he dismissed Jacques to his daughters. This intended slight delighted the cousins: now they could be together, exchanging ideas and books more freely. Conversations with Jacques led Simone to realize that her body was not the only attractive thing about her; a man might be – in fact, this man *was* – attracted to her mind.

But Jacques' attentions were hot and cold: sometimes he visited regularly and sometimes he was absent for unexplained and prolonged periods of time. Although she later downplayed the relationship, claiming in *Memoirs of a Dutiful Daughter* that she looked on him 'as a sort of elder brother',[39] for a long time Simone dreamed of a future with him – and even at the time of meeting Sartre, he was one of the three men who, in different ways, vied for her affections.[40]

Although it lasted for years, Simone's desire for Jacques may have arisen as a response to parallel movements in the life of Zaza, whose mother had started introducing her daughter to one man after another. This repulsed Zaza, who didn't see the difference between marrying 'for convenience' and prostitution. She had been taught to respect her body and it seemed to her that – whatever financial or family reasons there may be – it was not respectful to give it to a man without love. And yet, in the Lacoin family there were two paths open to women: a marriage or a convent.[41] Zaza was beginning to dread both.

Nevertheless, her family – with dowries of more than 250,000 francs for each of their five daughters – were identifying potential suitors in a systematic fashion. The Beauvoirs were in no position to do the same, so in later years Simone thought Jacques was her way of coping: to keep in step with Zaza she imagined her love for him. But those around her at the time – and, indeed, her diaries from the late 1920s – attested to the strength of her feelings for him. They also expressed indignation at his treatment of her: Hélène thought Jacques played the coquette, and that he wasn't worthy of her sister.

These romantic courtships and confusions unfolded in the context of sweeping educational reforms in France and significant decisions about Beauvoir's future. Simone graduated from the Cours Désir in 1924. Ten years earlier a teacher in a girls' lycée wrote that education and employment were becoming necessities for women:

> The majority of girls [...] now have the intention of continuing their studies to prepare themselves for some profession. [...] As is natural, nearly all desire love in marriage and motherhood. But they know that in our unjust society, dominated by the cult of gold, not every girl will be able to realize the motherly life that ought to be the norm for every woman. [...] They understand that instruction will open careers for them, which will enable them if need be to support themselves without masculine aid.[42]

For Beauvoir the promise of masculine aid through marriage was much less certain than that of her own abilities – she knew herself to be reliable in a way that masculine 'aid' (at least as instantiated by her father) was not. She studied hard, accumulating qualifications rapidly. At 16, in July 1924, she received her *premier baccalauréat* (a school-leaving certificate that had only recently been conferred to women on the same terms as men) with distinction. When she went to pick up her certificate an examiner acidly mocked her: 'Have you come to pick up a few more diplomas?'[43]

The Cours Désir, although conservative in many respects, was one of the leading institutions encouraging women to complete the first and second baccalauréats. After the first baccalauréat, bright students like Simone were encouraged to stay on for a year to qualify in subjects like philosophy, literature or science, which enabled them to teach in similar schools. This course was intended to make a virtue of necessity: it was a lower-status option than marriage, but at least the women who followed it stayed within the bourgeois circles of their birth.

The second examination was much more rigorous. The headmistress had recently added philosophy to the curriculum, since it was popular in the lycées and she wanted to boost her enrolments. A priest taught the course, and although Simone loved the subject she found its delivery woefully inadequate. He merely read or dictated passages from philosophical texts, and Simone complained in the *Memoirs of a Dutiful Daughter* that everything ended with 'the truth according to St Thomas Aquinas'.[44] Even so, she was captivated by philosophy and wanted to study more: she had had her first taste of it and all the other disciplines she had excelled in now seemed 'poor relations'.[45]

Simone passed the second baccalauréat but this time without distinction. Georges took her to the theatre to celebrate. He was beginning to take a bit more of an interest in her, perhaps because her face had cleared up and she was growing slim (he placed undue significance on such things), and perhaps because the practical questions of her future were becoming unavoidable.[46] He did not approve of her studying philosophy, which he thought was 'gibberish'. Françoise objected for other reasons: she did not want her daughter to be morally corrupted or lose her faith.

But Simone had made up her mind. She had read about an elite training school at Sèvres, which was established to educate women as teachers for the state lycées and collèges. Françoise would hear none of it. She had heard rumours about the strict exercise, lax morals and irreligiosity of this place. Simone's parents had spent years paying for a private education and did not want her to waste their investment by becoming a functionary of the state school system. To top it all off, Sèvres students boarded, which meant they could not be closely supervised by their mothers.

Georges saw no intrinsic value in philosophy, but he conceded that it might provide a good grounding for a career in law, which had become open to a few women since the war. If Simone qualified for a legal position in the civil service, her income would be guaranteed for life. Not being one to make rushed judgements, Simone read the Napoleonic Code before giving her answer, which was crystal clear: No. Her mother suggested training as a librarian. Again, Simone's answer was resolute: No.

She was determined to study philosophy; they were determined that she would not. So Simone resorted to a campaign of silence. Whenever they tried to discuss her future, she said nothing. As time passed, the window for avoiding embarrassment grew smaller and the air grew thicker. Her parents finally capitulated, but not without shouting matches.

One day, in a magazine, Simone found an image of the future she wanted. There was an article about the first woman *docteur d'état* in France, Léontine Zanta. The picture accompanying it showed her in a thoughtful pose at her desk, and the article said that she lived with an adopted niece: this woman was both intellectual and responsive to what Beauvoir called 'the demands of female sensibility': someday she dreamed of having such things written about her.[47]

But if Simone had been just a few years older nothing might have been written about her at all. Five years earlier she would not even have been able to take the qualifying exam. She knew her chosen road was not well travelled by women: at this point only six women had passed the *agrégation* in philosophy. It was a highly competitive national exam and Beauvoir 'wanted to be one of those pioneers' who passed it.[48]

Very little of Beauvoir's writing survives from this early period of her education. But there is one essay, written at the end of 1924, analysing a classic text in the philosophy of science, Claude Bernard's *Introduction to the Study of Experimental Medicine*. In it, the 16-year-old Beauvoir wrote that 'the most interesting part' of his 'interesting work' was the way Bernard valued philosophical doubt. Bernard wrote that 'the great experimental principle' is 'doubt, that philosophical doubt which leaves to the mind its freedom and initiative'. He thought that some forms of scepticism were barren, but that there was a kind of 'fertile doubt' that recognized the limitations of the human mind: 'our mind is so limited that we can know neither the beginning nor the end of things; but we can grasp the middle, i.e., what surrounds us closely'.[49]

Beauvoir's philosophy textbook at school – *Manuel de Philosophie* by Father Charles Lahr – had also discussed doubt. But it warned against taking it too far, since doubt could corrupt or even extinguish religious faith. Already as a student Beauvoir was rejecting a certain way of doing philosophy for enslaving the mind in systems, taking away its freedom.[50] This early interest in the philosophy of freedom is very important for understanding Beauvoir's later personal decisions, her philosophy, and the way her life has been misunderstood. In the 1920s she also read Alfred Fouillée, a nineteenth-century philosopher who disagreed with his better-known compatriot Jean-Jacques Rousseau about freedom. Fouillée argued that 'Man isn't born, but rather becomes, free.'[51] He claimed that freedom is an '*idée-force*' – which is to say an *idea* that has the power to shape the evolution of an individual. Fouillée was interested in the age-old question of whether human actions are free or determined, whether we make our fates or are destined to them. Against those who think human beings are determined to act in certain ways, Fouillée argued that the human desire for freedom itself enables us to become free.

Others worried that desire and emotion compromise freedom. But Fouillée claimed that the desire for freedom was unlike all other human desires because the desire for freedom *opposed* the influence of other desires. The desire for freedom leads human beings to want not 'the Good' or even 'a good decision', but rather a decision that is uniquely *mine*.[52]

Beauvoir wanted her future to be *her* decision; she wanted to live a life of freedom – and she wanted to study philosophy. When her mother told the teachers at Cours Désir Simone's chosen subject, the nuns stoked the fire of her maternal anxiety, saying that one year at the Sorbonne would ruin Mademoiselle de Beauvoir's faith and character.[53] So the family made a compromise: she would start by studying literature.

In 1925 the most prestigious path to her chosen profession was closed to her: women were not accepted at the École Normale Supérieure, which trained the crème de la crème of the Parisian philosophical elite. She would have to do a *licence* at the Sorbonne, then a teaching diploma, then the *agrégation*. In 1925 she began studying mathematics at the Institut Catholique and literature and languages at the Institut Sainte-Marie. Both institutions prepared Catholic students for the Sorbonne's exams – and were intended to limit pupils' exposure to the dangers of its secular culture.

Madame de Beauvoir did not know how excellent her choice of institution would be for her daughter. She chose the Institut Sainte-Marie for its Catholic respectability, but here Simone was under the tutelage of Madeleine Daniélou, a woman who held more degrees than any other in France. She believed that education was the key to liberation; she was married to a member of the French parliament who shared her ideas (Charles Daniélou). Françoise, who had more free time now that her daughters were older and Georges was so rarely at home, dedicated her time to reading and learning, and she followed Simone's studies. Françoise was intelligent, and the more she read the more she admired Madame Daniélou's curriculum.

Simone found this attention bittersweet: she knew her mother wanted their relationship to be one of friendship, and to have the closeness that she had never had with her own mother. But she attempted to achieve this proximity by force rather than by invitation, provoking resentment and withdrawal. According to Hélène, Françoise opened and read all of Simone's letters, even when she was 18, and threw away those she found unsuitable.[54] Simone's already miniscule handwriting grew even tinier – as if she wanted the words in her notebooks to be invisible to her mother's prying eyes.

The sisters felt stifled, which made it all the more surprising, one day, when Jacques came back to the rue de Rennes and Madame de Beauvoir loosened her reins. He hadn't been to visit for almost a year, but he had just bought a sporty car and wanted to show it off. He was a man in need of an audience, and Simone listened eagerly to his opinions on writers she hadn't yet read and the gossip about the writers and artists who lived in Montparnasse. Hélène quickly realized that he wasn't there to see her, and she saw by her sister's blushes that Jacques' interest was reciprocated. When Jacques suggested taking Simone out in the car Hélène was shocked that Françoise gave her permission. Hélène resented being left behind, but it meant that she was home to witness her mother's 'ecstasy' after the cousins departed. Françoise hoped Jacques might marry Simone, dowry or no dowry.

What followed was, to all appearances, a courtship – the only traditional courtship in Simone de Beauvoir's life. With Jacques she drove around Paris, walked in the Bois de Boulogne, read banned books, visited galleries, discovered music. Then, all of a sudden, Françoise stopped them going out alone. She hoped the absence might make Jacques' heart grow fonder, but she was also beginning to be suspicious: Simone had begun to discover nightclubs and cafés, and her clothes smelled of tobacco and alcohol.

That year Simone passed her exams with good marks, and her philosophy instructor encouraged her to continue at the Institut Sainte-Marie and to follow as many courses as she could at the Sorbonne. She had passed exams for three Certificates of Higher Studies – in mathematics, French literature and Latin. To put this achievement in perspective, the average *licence* (comparable to a bachelor's degree) was composed of four certificates, and the average student would earn one certificate per year.

Meanwhile, Jacques had failed his law examinations so would have to repeat the year's work. He was lazy and starting to drink a lot, but Simone overlooked these defects in character: she didn't want to admit he was stringing her along. Their relationship was not physical: they never even kissed. He was often absent – and even when present, aloof – but Beauvoir attributed his distance to defects in herself rather than him. As a mature woman it is hard to imagine her reading her diaries from this period without disappointment. (She drew heavily on them in writing her *Memoirs of a Dutiful Daughter*, and in her mature philosophy.) Jacques did speak of marriage vaguely, saying things like, 'It seems I will have to marry soon.' But an actual proposal never came. Beauvoir later wondered why she wanted it so badly, reflecting that her reasons were probably instrumental: through marriage she might finally earn her family's love and respect.

Her heart was divided: in her diaries she contrasted her imaginary life as Madame Jacques Champignuelle with what she called 'a life of freedom'. She spent the summer of 1926 struggling to be happy, even in the country with her relatives. When she returned to Paris in September she wanted to see Jacques, but Françoise forbade it.

That summer, at the age of 18, she made her first attempts at writing a novel, *Éliane*, but she only wrote nine pages.[55] Although philosophy was becoming her passion she did not want to create a grand philosophical system, but rather to write 'the novel of the inner life':[56] she wanted to show what was happening *within* the rich worlds of her characters. This project was inspired in part by reading the philosopher Henri Bergson, who celebrated a 'bold novelist' in his *Time and Free Will*. He described (and Beauvoir quoted in her diary) the way literature can tear 'aside the cleverly woven web of our conventional self'. When she read him she had a 'great intellectual rapture' because she saw in his philosophy not the 'logical constructions' but 'palpable reality'.[57]

In her diary Beauvoir wrote that she wanted to 'think life', to transpose her questions into fiction, and over the next two years she continued to refine her efforts in several short stories. Her commitment to attentive descriptions of experience was typical of the kind of phenomenology she would become interested in as a philosopher. Phenomenology – the study of the structures of consciousness from a first-person point of view – would also shape the methodology of her feminism, and she would reshape it for feminist ends. But in 1927 she wanted to write 'essays on life', which 'would not be a novel, but philosophy, linking them together vaguely with a fiction'.[58]

In *The Prime of Life* (1960) Beauvoir wrote that she was not the philosopher – Sartre was.[59] But her diaries show that in the summer of 1926 she had an experience that shocked her, made her feel ashamed, and led her to reflect philosophically on something that would become a central theme of her mature work. She wouldn't meet Sartre until three years later, and over time this theme would come to play a significant role in his work, too.

She was making a pilgrimage to Lourdes with her aunt when she saw the physical suffering of the sick who sought healing. She was overwhelmed, feeling 'disgust at all the intellectual and sentimental elegance before the invalids', and that her own sorrows were nothing compared with their physical pain and distress. She felt ashamed in that moment, and thought that a life of complete self-giving – even 'self-abnegation' – was the only appropriate response.[60]

But then, after reflection, she concluded that she was wrong. In her diary she urges herself not to be ashamed of living: she has been given a life and it is her duty to live it in the best possible way. To give herself away completely, in fact, would be 'moral suicide'. But it would also be easier than deciding how much of herself to give and how much to keep. She called what was needed 'equilibrium': in which people gave themselves without 'annihilat[ing] the consciousness of themselves in order to serve others'.[61] She wanted to live a life of self-giving without self-loss.

Six days later she returned to this theme in her diaries, discussing two poles of possibility: devotion and egoism. Given her childhood experiences it is tempting to read these poles along parental or gendered lines. Her mother's abject devotion and her father's unrepentant egoism are not mentioned in the diaries, but given what she would later write about her parents it is clear that one thing she inherited from her childhood home was an intense sense of injustice. In the diaries, Beauvoir writes that she wants to be devoted to others because she has 'a liking for beings'. She wanted her emotions to agree with her ideas, so she asked herself: could a moral code be built on appreciation for others? Whether or not it was sufficient for others, she decided, it was sufficient for her.[62]

Certainly, I am very individualistic, but is this incompatible with the devotion and disinterested love of others? It seems to me that there is one part of me that is made to be given away, another that is made to be kept and cultivated. The second part is valid in itself and guarantees the value of the other.[63]

At 18 she was dissatisfied by philosophical discussions that 'remained in a vacuum', and was already reflecting on the distance between knowing something intellectually and feeling it in real life.[64] Literature, she thought, bridged the gap: 'the writer pleases me when he rediscovers life, the philosopher when he rediscovers the writer who will serve as an intermediary with life'.[65] Beauvoir wanted to serve as such an intermediary, and in particular to show how human beings are 'dualities' that can be seen 'from within' and 'from without', both intensely inner and yet engaged in the world with others. She tried writing another novel in September, and this time finished a 68-page manuscript called *Tentative d'existence* – 'An attempted existence'.[66]

During the autumn of 1926 Beauvoir continued to wrestle with her affection for Jacques. At this stage she sincerely believed 'a reciprocal love' was possible between them. What Beauvoir wanted, in her own words, was 'a love that accompanies me through life, not that absorbs all my life'. She thought that love should 'not make all else disappear but should simply tint it with new nuances'.[67]

Although she was soon to change her mind, she thought she might marry someday, and that under the right circumstances marriage might be a 'great and beautiful thing'. But her mother annoyed her: she didn't think things with Jacques were moving quickly enough and worried about 'a precise conclusion': a proposal.[68] Françoise schemed, sending Simone on errands so that her path would cross Jacques's. She thought this would make Simone happy, but in fact it made her squirm. In November she wrote in her diary: 'How little I myself choose, how much life imposes itself upon me, *my* life to which after all I have to resign myself.'[69]

As her mother pushed her along the path of propriety, Beauvoir wrote in her diaries that every position in life was acceptable – but to have value, it had to be *valued* by the person adopting it. It was painfully clear that she did not see love, life and happiness the way her parents did. She didn't want to walk through life unthinkingly doing what was proper, reading what was suitable: by 1926 she had come to the conclusion that she could only genuinely have esteem for: 'beings who think their lives, not for those who only think, or for those who only live'.[70]

According to Deirdre Bair, shortly after the New Year of 1927, Françoise decided that Simone's birthday should be commemorated with a photo portrait. Birthdays were often marked in this way, but Simone knew that her mother had another agenda: Jacques. Instead of the traditional birthday pose, Françoise arranged her daughter in the traditional posture of an engagement announcement, holding flowers in a hand that ought to bear her fiancé's ring. Jacques accepted a copy of the portrait graciously, and that was that. Françoise was fuming.

We don't know how Simone felt about this, possibly because she did not record it and possibly because it didn't happen. Sylvie Le Bon de Beauvoir denied the existence of such a photo, and Beauvoir's diaries are silent on the subject, with no entries from early December 1926 to April of 1927. But the story as Bair tells it does not end there. In the spring of 1927 Hélène graduated from the Cours Désir and the sisters – who had grown apart somewhat during the periods when Jacques distracted Simone's attention – were again unified against their mother's irascibility. Françoise's anxiety about Jacques was noxious; she felt frustrated and powerless because the cards were all in his hand. When her confused emotions were not channelled into sarcasm and scorn for her daughter, they erupted on a humiliating scale. One night, frustrated after a proposal-less dinner with the Champigneulles, Françoise returned home. She paced for several hours, then screamed that she would deliver her daughter from disgrace and left the apartment. Georges was home but didn't get out of bed; Hélène woke up, threw on clothes, and chased her mother down the boulevard du Montparnasse. Françoise stopped in front of the Champigneulle residence, shouting. The noise woke Simone, who rushed down to the street. The daughters silently escorted their shrieking mother back inside.[71] From the vantage point of the twenty-first century, this story – if true – raises questions about Françoise de Beauvoir's mental health. Later, the female characters in Beauvoir's works often felt trapped, sometimes hovering on the verge of madness.[72]

We know from both sisters' memoirs that in the period from 1926–1927 they were gradually allowed to venture out more without suitors or chaperones: Simone went to read in the ladies-only section at the Bibliothèque Saint-Geneviève (Lucretius, Juvenal, Diderot) and began teaching at a social-service institute called the 'Equipes Sociales', which was founded by a young philosophy professor to help the working classes in north-east Paris.[73] Her mother approved of such philanthropic pursuits, so Simone gave the impression of teaching more nights than she actually did in order to escape the house. She walked around Paris some evenings, and on others she went to watch Hélène paint and draw: her sister's world had expanded in fascinating directions. At the Equipes Sociales and Hélène's life-drawing classes she saw men and women discussing their ideas and dreams, confidently nude models and their nonplussed observers. The sisters had never been exposed to so many, and such diverse, people.

In addition to Gide and Proust, Jacques had introduced Simone to cocktails; now she made herself a habitué of bars. Simone and Hélène continued to visit La Rotonde, sometimes skipping art classes and teaching to spend evening hours in bars and cafés instead. Simone now had a little money at her disposal because she had taken a job as a teaching assistant at the Institut Sainte-Marie. It wasn't much, but she could cover her expenses and books and have a small amount left over.

Despite distress at home and distractions at night, she continued to shine in her studies. In March 1927 Simone passed her certificate in the history of philosophy. In April she reflected that this year had brought her 'a serious philosophical formation' that sharpened her '(alas!) too penetrating critical mind and [her] desire for rigor and logic'.[74] What, one wonders, made her write this 'alas!'? What is there to object to in having a penetrating mind that values rigour and logic? Did she lament this mind because, as we will see in the next chapter, God became anathema to it? Or because she thought it was anathema to femininity? Her happiness?

In June she received another certificate in 'general philosophy', coming second to Simone Weil. Weil would become a prominent thinker, whose politics and self-sacrifice inspired many around her, including Albert Camus and Georges Bataille (philosophically, Beauvoir thought she accepted the conclusions of her teacher Alain without enough questioning). The third runner up in this exam would also become a leading French philosopher: Maurice Merleau-Ponty. Beauvoir obtained a certificate in Greek as well: in just two years, she had already earned a *licence* and a half.

Writing in *Memoirs of a Dutiful Daughter* Beauvoir claimed that education and success brought more than esteem to her: it brought feelings of profound loneliness and a lack of direction. 'I [...] was breaking away from the class to which I belonged: where was I to go?'[75] We see this loneliness expressed in the diaries, where she wrote, in May 1927, 'I am intellectually very alone and very lost at the entrance to my life. [...] I feel that I have worth, that I have something to do and say.' Reflecting on the way that Jacques dismissed 'her 'intellectual passions' and 'philosophical seriousness' 'with a smile', she wrote determinedly (and highlighted in the margins): 'I have only *one* life and many things to say. He will not steal *my* life away from me.'[76]

That day she was thinking about freedom again, writing that 'it is only by free decision and thanks to the interplay of circumstances that the true self is discovered'. People around her talked about making choices (like deciding to marry) as if you did it once and for all. But she never felt like choices were *made* in that way – every choice was 'constantly in the making; it is repeated every time that I become conscious of it'. That day she concluded that marriage is 'fundamentally immoral' – how could the self of today make decisions for the self of tomorrow?

She could still imagine a life in which she loved Jacques, but she had had a conversation with another man – Charles Barbier – who talked with her about philosophy and literature with intelligent interest instead of dismissive smiles. The experience made her realize that her future held many possibilities (she called them her *possibles* in French), and that bit by bit, she would have to 'kill all but one of them', so that on the last day of her life there would be one reality; she would have lived 'one life'. The question was, which life?[77]

Instances like these show that from an early age Beauvoir felt a strong sense of vocation and the importance of her own voice. In *Memoirs of a Dutiful Daughter* she would even invoke the language of Hebrew prophets – messengers of God – to express her calling. In one of the relevant stories in the Bible, God needs an emissary, and asks the people of Israel, 'Whom shall I send?' The prophet Isaiah replies to him: 'Here I am. Send me.' In the *Memoirs*, Beauvoir describes a voice that whispered within her, over and over again, 'Here I am.'[78] God or no God, she knew that what she had to say was important, and she had already begun to realize that some people would try to convince her otherwise – whether through outright confrontation or diminutive dismissals.

Simone was determined, but she was not immune to self-doubt and others' expectations of her. Her parents were beginning to make explosive scenes about what she was reading; she began to feel that they did not accept her – 'at all'.[79] She had more and more arguments with her father, who talked about sending her away and told her she had 'no heart'; that she was 'all brain and no feeling'.[80]

The week before Jacques smilingly dismissed her intellectual passions, she had an argument with her father about what it means to love. He said it was 'services rendered, affection, gratefulness'. She had been reading more now-forgotten philosophers – Alain and Jules Lagneau – and claimed that she had found in Lagneau 'how I would have to live'. So many people, she thought, had never known true love, in which 'reciprocity is necessary'.[81] In July Beauvoir again resolved to 'clearly spell out my philosophical ideas'. She wanted to study in depth the questions that interested her, especially 'love' (which she put in quotation marks in her diary)[82] and 'the opposition of self and other'.[83] For Beauvoir, even at this age, the concept of love was not just a romantic ideal, but an ethical one.

In her diary she enjoined herself: 'Don't be "Mlle de Beauvoir." Be me. Don't have a goal imposed from outside, a social framework to fill. What works for me will work, and that is all.'[84]

With Zaza, too, she discussed love – their shared love of philosophy and a shared concern over their futures brought them closer together than ever. They had been discussing the nature of love in their philosophy class at school, and their discussions continued throughout the week, while visiting museums or playing tennis.[85] The friendship still met with Françoise's approval, but Madame Lacoin was starting to worry that Zaza's interest in education was going too far, and Simone was a bad influence in that respect. Zaza wanted to enrol at the Sorbonne instead of pocketing her 250,000-franc dowry: her parents found this incomprehensible.

Slowly Simone began to make other friendships that stretched and softened her world. When she was 20, and on a visit to Zaza's family's country estate in the Landes, Beauvoir met Stépha Awdykovicz, their family governess, who would become one of her closest friends. In the eyes of Beauvoir, this Polish-Ukranian emigré was exotic and daring: she was wealthy and well educated but chose to work as a governess because she was curious about bourgeois Parisian life. She was not afraid of her sexuality and spoke frankly with Beauvoir about it. When they returned to Paris they met almost daily: Stépha lived nearby and worked for the Ministry of Foreign Affairs translating – she earned a sizeable amount, which she was happy to spend on her friends. She laughed Beauvoir out of some of her prudery, simultaneously challenging her reserve and expressing sisterly concern for her naivety.

Hélène introduced Simone to Geraldine Pardo, whom she had met through her art classes. Gégé, as they called her, was a working-class girl who enjoyed her job so much that she planned to continue working whether she married a man or not. Simone was attracted by Gégé's enthusiasm and eloquence; Gégé helped her see more clearly that social class did not determine human behaviour by necessity.

But Stépha's concerns about her naivety proved to be well founded. Simone started to indulge in 'adventures', which she thought were innocent pranks but could have had disastrous consequences. At first Stépha played too, but what started as accepting drinks from men gave way to more risky behaviour: frequenting the seediest bars, going on drives and back to apartments with no intention of delivering to their drunk companions what their drunk companions expected. Although she always managed to disentangle herself, Stépha was furious that Simone put herself in these situations, and confused that she did so when Simone gave the impression that she was still 'almost betrothed' to Jacques.

The 18-year-old Simone was philosophically precocious, but her behaviour could be perilously reckless and rather prim. When Simone came to visit Stépha, who was soon to marry Fernando Gerassi, she was shocked to find him inside her room with the door shut: wasn't Stépha worried about her reputation? When Fernando later painted Stépha nude Beauvoir was horrified and refused to look at the picture. Her friends found her prudery pompous: she told both Stépha and Gégé that their opinions and conduct were the sad consequences of their inferior upbringing.[86] This Simone de Beauvoir was easily scandalized: she would have been shocked to see the scenes her later novels – and life – contained.

In her diaries Simone continued to reflect on the question of the 'equilibrium' between self and other. She started to split her existence into two parts: one 'for others' and one 'for myself'.[87] This distinction importantly predates a famous one Sartre would make in *Being and Nothingness* (1943) – between 'being for itself' and 'being for others'. Many have mistakenly seen Sartre's distinction at work in Beauvoir's novels and in *The Second Sex*, but Beauvoir arrived this way of seeing things early and independently.[88]

In the 1927–28 academic year Beauvoir planned to do three more certificates in order to gain a double *licence* in classics and philosophy. She didn't always enjoy the demands she made of herself, sometimes complaining that so much of her time was spent at home or in the library; she felt 'like a rat on a treadmill'. In March 1928 she gained the remaining two qualifications in philosophy – ethics and psychology – but she found philology (the remaining requirement for classics) too dry and dull to deserve persistence. She decided she didn't need the classics *licence*. Her father objected: if she was not going to be conventionally successful in marriage she might as well be as unconventionally successful as possible. But she stood her ground, and ditched classics.

Her brilliance was unquestionable, and it was beginning to attract attention: Maurice Merleau-Ponty wanted to meet the young bourgeoise who had beat him in general philosophy. Of course, two women had beat him in general philosophy, but Simone Weil was Jewish so not a contender for the kind of intellectual friendship two Catholics could share – or so he thought.[89] Neither Simone would become a 'Catholic woman' in any conventional sense, but Weil would be remembered as a woman of fervent faith, Beauvoir of avid atheism.

3

Lover of God or Lover of Men?

On the eve of her nineteenth birthday Beauvoir's diaries include reflections on a painful absence. As a child she believed that God governed her universe, and however questionable his governance looked in hindsight she was now left confronting different problems. If there was no one to *call* her to her vocation, could she have a vocation at all? If there was no God, what gave humans – or anything – their value? 'Maybe I have value,' she says; but then 'values must exist.'[1] She was not alone in asking these kinds of questions. Since the turn of the twentieth century, Paris's philosophical elite had been debating the merits of religious belief and experience in the aftermath of Nietzsche's famous declaration that 'God is dead!'[2]

In Simone's life, the disappearance of God coincided with the courtship and death of her devout and beloved friend, Zaza. Both of these losses would leave lasting legacies. For the better part of three decades, Beauvoir would feel that her own freedom had come at the cost of Zaza's life.

By 1928 Beauvoir had discovered some of the alternative lives that Paris had to offer: bohemianism and revolt, surrealism, cinema, Ballet Russe.[3] That year she began her studies at the Sorbonne in the company of an impressive cohort. The two Simones (Beauvoir and Weil) did <u>not</u> become friends – although this seems like a missed opportunity in hindsight. Beauvoir was intrigued by Weil's reputation, not so much because of her intelligence but because of her passionate concern for others' suffering. Beauvoir heard that Simone Weil wept when she heard about a famine breaking out in China, and was impressed that her heart was large enough to ache even for people on the other side of the world. She wanted to meet this woman, but their meeting took a disappointing turn when the conversation shifted to the question of which was more important: revolution (so said Weil) or finding the reason for our existence (so said Beauvoir). Weil ended their exchange with the words: 'It's easy to see you've never gone hungry.' As Beauvoir saw it, Weil had looked her up and down and judged her 'a high-minded little bourgeoise'.[4] At the time Beauvoir found this irritating – after all, Weil didn't know her circumstances and was making mistaken assumptions – but in later years she became sympathetic to this judgement of her young self.

Merleau-Ponty, on the other hand, was to become Beauvoir's dear 'Ponti'. He was a student at the École Normale Supérieure, from a similar background to Beauvoir, and struggling with questions of faith. He sought Beauvoir out after the results of the general philosophy exam were published, and the two of them grew to be close friends – first exchanging heartfelt conversation and later reading each other's work. Merleau-Ponty liked her so much he introduced her to his friend Maurice de Gandillac, who found her brilliant and fascinating – he was especially interested in the state of her faith. She liked Merleau-Ponty so much she introduced him to Zaza, and soon the foursome was playing tennis together every Sunday morning. Merleau-Ponty was the first intellectual Zaza had ever met, and before long she began to hope for something that hadn't seemed possible: that she could fulfil her familial duty in marriage without relinquishing love or the life of her mind.

At first Simone, too, was thrilled with her conversations with Merleau-Ponty. They did have a great deal in common: he was also raised in a devout home and, at least initially, considered himself a quiet unbeliever. At the École Normale Supérieure, Merleau-Ponty belonged to a group that had irreverently been christened the 'Holy Willies' on account of their piety and respect for priests. Beauvoir had few female friends at school, and in later life admitted that she often dismissed women whose intellects she found interesting on account of their religion or social background or both.[5] Instead she became friends with other 'Holy Willies', including Jean Miquel, who was, like her, preparing a thesis under the noted scholar Jean Baruzi.

In her memoirs Beauvoir wrote that she 'went to hear Jean Baruzi, the author of a thesis that was very well thought of on St John of the Cross'.[6] But in fact Beauvoir did more than go to hear Baruzi; she wrote a thesis of her own under his guidance. In her diaries Beauvoir wrote that she liked Baruzi because he took her seriously and would criticize her.[7] But in the memoirs Beauvoir is curiously silent about the philosophical content of her thesis, saying only that it treated 'the personality'[8] and that Baruzi returned it to her with 'copious praise', telling her that it was 'the basis of a serious work'.[9] The diaries show that her work for Baruzi included discussions of love and ethics.[10] The discrepancy between accounts raises the recurrent question: why does her story lack consistency? Beauvoir's thesis itself has not survived, so we can't turn to it for possible answers.[11] But on the basis of what Beauvoir was writing about it in her diaries at the same time, it seems likely that her discussions of love here prepared the ground for what she would go on to write in the 1940s about ethics, when her ideas were assumed to be indebted to Sartre's. So did she hide her early work from readers because she was concerned that it would somehow jeopardize Sartre's reputation? Or was it because she didn't think her 1950s readers would believe – let alone identify with – a female protagonist whose philosophy went on to shape Jean-Paul Sartre's?

In the 1920s, Beauvoir had found few women who shared her intellectual passions. She recognized that she was beginning to turn to the company of men more and more for connections of the mind; she enjoyed men's conversation and friendship. In *Memoirs of a Dutiful Daughter* she wrote that she found it dismaying when women took up a challenging attitude towards men: 'from the start men were my comrades, not my enemies. Far from envying them, I felt that my own position, from the very fact that it was an unusual one, was a privilege'.[12] In hindsight she recognized that she was a token woman, but it was only later that she began to see this tokenism as problematic. In her student days, the friendly relations between Beauvoir and her male contemporaries were eased by the fact that they did not see her as a rival because the French education system did not treat them as equals. Simone, and all other female students, were accepted as 'supernumeraries' and were not competing for the same jobs. (The women were expected to teach in girls' lycées; the French state was providing education for girls, but it was still a widely held view that men should not educate them.)

As Deirdre Bair tells the story, Beauvoir lost some of her initial enthusiasm for Merleau-Ponty when it became clear that he was not an atheist;[13] she was disappointed that he thought the truth was to be found within the religious boundaries of their upbringing. But once again, the details of Beauvoir's diaries tell a different, and much less dispassionate story about her loss of faith than the bold lines of her memoirs suggest. As soon as she 'saw the light' about God, she wrote in the memoirs, 'I made a clean break'.[14] After that, Beauvoir told her readers conclusively, her 'incredulity never once wavered'.[15] In language reminiscent of Saint Augustine and Blaise Pascal, she described the experience of losing God as accompanied by the abrupt discovery that everything had 'fallen silent'. For the first time she felt the 'terrible significance' of the word 'alone'.[16]

But the story in the student diaries is less sudden and once-and-for-all. As late as 1928, at the age of 20, she was 'tempted by Catholicism'.[17] Although she later dismissed her childhood faith as enculturated and ingenuous, when she started university she suddenly found herself in the company of intellectual believers whose commitments coexisted with doubts and a willingness to question. She was a budding philosopher, and when she encountered a new argument she did not dig in her heels and remain unaffected in the name of consistency: she considered its merits.

But let us retrace the account she gave in the memoirs before looking at the diaries themselves. In the version of events published in 1958 Beauvoir acknowledged that as a child she developed a passionate faith in God – the kind of faith a pious mother couldn't fake. Simone attended mass three times a week and regularly undertook retreats for days at a time. She meditated and kept a notebook for recording her thoughts and 'saintly resolutions'. She 'desired to grow closer to God, but [...] didn't know how to go about it'.[18] She decided that the best life this world could offer was a life spent contemplating God, and resolved to be a Carmelite nun.

In later life Beauvoir would be converted to politics, but as a young woman she found social questions remote – in part because she felt so powerless to change the world around her. Instead she focused on what she could control: the world within. She had heard that in addition to the morality-infused religion of duty there was a mystical kind: because she had read stories of saints whose passionate lives reached fulfilment in mysterious unions with God that brought them joy and peace, she 'invented mortifications' for herself, scrubbing her skin with a pumice stone until it bled and fustigating herself with a necklace chain. There is a long tradition of *odium corporis* in Christian history, and of bodily asceticism producing mystical experiences in many world religions. But Simone's efforts did not deliver the enlightened states she sought.

In *Memoirs of a Dutiful Daughter* Beauvoir described her desire to be a nun as 'a convenient alibi'. But she did not see it that way at the time. During her childhood summers in the countryside, she would wake early in order to watch nature awaken, enjoying the 'beauty of the earth and the glory of God'. Several times in her memoirs she describes this association of the presence of God and the beauty of nature: but in Paris, she wrote, 'He was hidden from me by people and their top-heavy preoccupations.'[19]

She began to be more troubled by the hiddenness of God, concluding that God 'was a total stranger to the restless world of men'. Her mother and teachers alike took the Pope to have been elected by the Holy Spirit; both parents agreed that it was not his place to interfere in worldly matters. When Pope Leo XIII devoted encyclicals to 'social questions', therefore, her mother took him to have betrayed his saintly mission and her father took him to have betrayed the nation. So Simone had to 'swallow the paradox that the man chosen by God to be his representative on earth had not to concern himself with earthly things'.[20]

She also had to face so-called 'Christians' who handled earthly inhabitants – herself included – in objectionable ways. At school she felt her confessor betrayed her confidence. And when she was 16, in a religious bookshop near Saint Sulpice, she asked the shop assistant for an article. He walked towards the back of the shop and beckoned for her to follow. When she reached his side he revealed not the item she sought, but his erect penis. She fled, but took with her the feeling that 'the oddest things could happen to [her] without any warning'.[21]

Hélène also described their childhood as weighed down by God, and noted that the weight of God was not felt equally by everyone.[22]

None of the men in her family – either in Paris or Limousin – went to mass. This gave Hélène reason to comment that 'men – a superior race – were exempt from God'.[23] It is not difficult to see why Beauvoir objected to the Catholicism of her childhood: its values were taken to affirm double standards of colossal proportions – profligate husbands expected saintly wives, while ideals of self-sacrifice consecrated women's suffering.

In the *Memoirs of a Dutiful Daughter* Beauvoir describes her unbeliever Papa and her devout Mama as representing two extremes within herself: her father represented the intellectual, and her mother the spiritual. And these two 'radically heterogeneous fields of experience' had nothing in common: she began to think that human things – 'culture, politics, business, manners, and customs – had nothing to do with religion. So I set God apart from life and the world, and this attitude was to have a profound influence on my future development'.[24]

In the end, faced with philosophical gaps and religious hypocrisy, she concluded that 'it was easier for me to think of a world without a creator than of a creator burdened with all the contradictions in the world'.[25] After she rejected God for the first time, she confided to Zaza that she wanted to be a writer. But Zaza shocked her by replying that having nine children, like her mama had, was just as good as writing books. Beauvoir could not see anything in common in these two modes of existence. 'To have children, who in turn would have more children, was simply to go on playing the same old tune *ad infinitum*.'[26]

As is often the case with Beauvoir's 'life' and 'work', her life provided questions that her work sought to answer; she would return to religious questions in several books, including *The Second Sex*. But during the period of her studies she had to wrestle with her own faith, first for academic reasons and then because one of the most significant losses of her life brought her face to face with death and injustice.

During the period from 1926–27, she recorded in her diaries that despite her intellectual reservations she wanted to believe in God. She *wanted* to believe in something that would 'justify her life', something absolute, and throughout her life she would be revisited by this yearning for meaning, if not salvation. In May 1927 she wrote, 'I would want God.'[27] And again in July: she wanted 'God or nothing'. But philosophically speaking, she couldn't find a satisfactory answer to the question: 'Why the Christian God?'[28] She had several conversations about faith with Maurice Merleau-Ponty, but she thought that he put too much confidence in both Catholic faith and reason. On 19 July 1927 she wrote in her diary that 'Ponti supports his [philosophy] with faith in reason, I on the powerlessness of reason. Who proves that Descartes prevails over Kant? I am maintaining what I wrote for the Sorbonne – use your reason, you will end up with remainders and irrational elements.'

More and more, Beauvoir's diaries show that she found a certain kind of philosophy alienating on account of its requirement to 'reason coldly': she said that 'young girls' such as herself 'have not only a reason to satisfy, but a heavy heart to subdue – and in this way I want to remain a woman, still more masculine by her brain, more feminine by her sensibility'.[29] She kept trying to find a philosophy she could live by, and became interested in Jules Lagneau, a philosopher who wrote about freedom and desire as well as reason.[30] Beauvoir agreed with Lagneau that her own desire was a powerful impulse to believe: 'Oh! My God, my God, is this being whom we would like to love and to whom we would give all, does this being truly not exist? I know nothing, and I am weary, weary. Why, if he is, does he make seeking him so difficult?'[31]

Her heart felt achingly empty; she wrote that '*the one who would fulfil everything* doesn't exist'.[32] If these words had occurred a few pages earlier in her diaries it would be clear that they were penned for

God, for a divine beloved. But in the margins a later annotation is found: later on Beauvoir underlined the words in this sentence in ink and wrote and underlined in the margin, 'Sartre – 1929'. Could a man occupy the place her heart had previously held for God? After Sartre died in 1980, Beauvoir entitled a volume of his letters to her *Witness to My Life*. The French word *temoin* ('witness') was used by centuries of French Christians to describe the gaze of a God who saw everything.

Beauvoir's path to atheism unwound in the midst of significant personal events as well as philosophical explorations. Personally, she found much to admire in the faiths of Zaza and Merleau-Ponty. While the bodily exploits of Stépha and Gégé met with her disgust, the chaste courtship of Zaza and Merleau-Ponty brought the teenage Simone much joy.[33] She hoped, for Zaza, that marriage would not end up making a prostitute of her body and a mausoleum of her mind. Things had been blossoming promisingly, but suddenly it all came to a halt. Madame Lacoin decided not to allow her to return to the Sorbonne for a second year because her elder daughter was now married: it was Zaza's turn. She was to be kept at the family estates in the Landes so she could prepare to be presented to eligible men. This year, Simone was not invited to stay for weeks as she had done in the past, but only for a few days in July. Merleau-Ponty's family was from Bordeaux, so he and Simone decided to meet there while she was en route to Zaza's. One of their favourite authors, François Mauriac, was from the region and they wanted to make a literary pilgrimage – happily, this would give Simone an opportunity to bring Zaza fresh news of her beloved.

When Simone arrived, she found her friend agonizing over what were clearly becoming torturously divided allegiances. Zaza felt sure that she loved Merleau-Ponty, but she also wanted to obey her mother – who had decided that the match was unsuitable without giving any indication why. No one could understand this about-face on her mother's part: he was from a good Catholic family and her mother never said a bad word about him. But if the conversation ever turned in his direction she moved it onto another subject. Beauvoir was perplexed by Madame Lacoin's behaviour at first, but her perplexity gave way to anxiety and anger. Why on earth would she object? Did she not see the importance of her own daughter's freedom, her own daughter's dreams?

The previous year had been intense but emotionally high, and now Simone felt herself on an equally intense downward trajectory. She tried to cope as she always had: writing, and reading, voraciously. In August she wrote out a daily regime in her journal:

9.00–11.00 letters and journal
11.00–1.00 philosophy (in her journal she added 'meditation' in parentheses)
3.00–5.00 philosophy, reading
5.00–8.00 writing

That summer she set herself the goal of reading Stendhal, and Plato, as well as recent and contemporary writers whose books treated religion and mysticism: Henri Frederic Amiel, Henri Delacroix, Jean Baruzi.[34] Her diary contains reflections on her reading and correspondence and long passages professing love for Jacques and confusion about his intentions.

In September, having read back her diary, Simone thought 1927 had been a year of 'oscillation between the discouragement brought to me by love, the only great human thing in which I felt the nothingness of the entirety of what's human, and the desire to seek'.[35] Later that month she made herself a new programme of study: she was working on two assignments for her supervisor, Jean Baruzi, and writing a book. She wanted to finish the first part of her book by January, so she would need to be disciplined:

8.00 wake up

9.00–noon personal work in her room

2.00–6.00 serious study

6.00–8.00 conversations, painting, reading 'without vain strolls to which I have no right'

9.00–11.00 preparation for classes, for the club

11.00–midnight journal

She read novels by Paul Claudel, François Mauriac and many others, as well as books on mystics, philosophers and the lives of novelists.[36] She wrote notes for a novel that would chart the discovery of a woman's realization that she was 'free to choose herself'.[37] Her notes are fragmentary, but they explore the relationship between who we are and what we do (what philosophers would call the relationship between being and action).

At 19, she was already experimenting with ideas that would become famous in the 1940s for being 'existentialist' (in other words, Sartre's): '*The act* is the affirmation ourselves,' Beauvoir wrote. But if that's the case, she asked, then 'did this "ourselves" then *not exist* before the act? Or were we just unsure that it existed?' The philosopher Maurice Blondel had written a book on *Action* not long before – which explored big questions like whether or not human lives were meaningful, and whether or not individuals have destinies. Blondel wrote that 'The substance of man is action; he is what he makes of himself.'[38] Beauvoir's notes for the novel seem to reply to Blondel as well as Nietzsche. She wanted to know whether our actions acquaint us with ourselves – whether we were there all along – or whether they create us. Blondel said that the latter was the case: we are what we make of ourselves. But Nietzsche's command was to become who you are. But how could you become who you are if you don't know yourself? Beauvoir's notes are full of questions: 'Become who you are? Do you know yourself? Do you see yourself?'[39]

Her days were so regimented now that when she wasn't working she began to worry about 'scattering herself' too much in 'charming friendships'.[40] But even so, it was a blow when Zaza came back to Paris in November and told Beauvoir that she was being sent to Berlin. Ostensibly it was to perfect her already excellent German; really it was to try to make her forget Merleau-Ponty. She was anguished by her parents' opposition to him: what could they possibly object to? Beauvoir's bewilderment was exacerbated by conversations with Merleau-Ponty, who said little except that he put his trust in prayer and believed in the kindness and justness of God. His professions of faith made Beauvoir increasingly bitter; how could he be satisfied with the mere possibility of justice in the hereafter? Whether God was just or not, in her experience Madame Lacoin was not.

Zaza returned to Paris in the winter of 1929, looking well and even more convinced of her love for Merleau-Ponty. Her mother presented more and more obstacles to her meeting with Simone, but she could hardly forbid her daughter to read at the Bibliothèque Nationale; here Zaza and Simone found small pockets of space and time to drink coffee together illicitly and discuss life.

In January 1929 Beauvoir became the first woman to teach philosophy in a boys' school, the Lycée Janson-de-Sailly. Her fellow teachers there included Merleau-Ponty and another soon-to-be household name of twentieth-century French intellectual life: Claude Lévi-Strauss, the founder of structural anthropology. The lycée was full of just the type of boy Beauvoir used to envy. They didn't care much about philosophy – they took education for granted. But she did not take it for granted that she was now a guardian of the French intellectual élite. She felt like she was on the 'road to final liberation'; she described feeling that 'there was nothing in the world she couldn't attain now'. Her decision to reject classics had been the right one: she was now writing a dissertation on the philosophy of Gottfried Leibniz under the supervision of Léon Brunschvicg, a leading light of Parisian philosophy.

The spring and summer of 1929 were eventful seasons in Beauvoir's life. But for Zaza they were disastrous. In July she went to their summer home as usual. But before she left she confided to Beauvoir that she and Merleau-Ponty had become secretly betrothed – he was going into military service and they would wait another year, or possibly two, before making the case to her parents. Beauvoir was astonished. 'Why wait?' she asked her friend, shocking Zaza with her frankness: their affection was clear.

Figure 3 *Zaza and Simone, September 1928.*

Zaza's letters from the Landes became cryptic and confusing. Her Mama, she wrote, had told her something she couldn't explain. The next post brought a letter with more: 'Can children bear the sin of their parents? Are they guilty of it? Can they ever be absolved? Do others near them suffer from it?'[41] The correspondence that followed revealed that Zaza was disappointed by the messages she was receiving from Merleau-Ponty, for despite their promise to each other his tone became increasingly distant and his letters increasingly sparse. She missed Simone and said she was suffering, but she tried to give meaning to her suffering by comparing it to Christ's.[42]

This situation continued for some time and Simone became seriously concerned, urging both Zaza and Merleau-Ponty to make their intentions public: perhaps Madame Lacoin's hesitation was due to their lack of official announcement. But she met with resistance in both quarters: Zaza wrote to her that 'he has reasons for not doing so which to me are as valid as they are to him'.[43] Simone was not so easily satisfied, so she wrote to Merleau-Ponty, thinking he could not possibly act this way if he knew the suffering his so-called 'reasons' cost Zaza. But he wrote back explaining that his sister had just become engaged and his brother was about to go abroad, and his mother could not bear to lose all of her children at once.

Zaza had grown thin; she was to be sent to Berlin again. At first she seemed resigned to Merleau-Ponty's decision to sacrifice her for his mother. But not much later Madame Lacoin summoned Simone – Zaza was ill, very ill. Zaza had gone to see Merleau-Ponty's mother, delirious, asking whether she hated her and why she objected to their marriage. Madame Merleau-Ponty attempted to calm her down before her son arrived: he called a taxi, worried by Zaza's burning hands and forehead. In the cab she reproached him for never having kissed her and demanded that he make amends: he complied.

Madame Lacoin called a doctor and had a long conversation with Merleau-Ponty, after which she relented. She would not oppose their marriage; she could no longer be the cause of her daughter's unhappiness. Madame Merleau-Ponty agreed, it would all be arranged. But Zaza's temperature was 104 degrees – she spent four days in a clinic and it did not fall.

The next time Simone saw Zaza her body was cold, laid out on a bier clutching a crucifix.

Zaza died on 25 November 1929. Beauvoir would have to wait nearly thirty years to discover the truth about what happened. As she sank into the hopelessness of grief, she felt confused, angry horror at her conversations with Zaza and correspondence with Merleau-Ponty – they both 'spiritualized' their suffering, trying to cultivate virtue in themselves instead of castigating the real culprit: the vicious injustice of 'propriety'. It was the world, not them, that was at fault: and God had done nothing.

4

The Love before the Legend

While Zaza's hopes of a fulfilling fidelity were raised and dashed, Simone began to entertain hopes of a different kind. The friendship of Merleau-Ponty and Gandillac showed her that she was worthy of the interest of two *normaliens* – students at the École Normale Supérieure who were the *crème de la crème* of the Parisian intellectual elite. It also gave her confidence and during the spring and summer of 1929 she pursued the acquaintance of another *normalien* who attracted her – this time quite physical – attention.

That *normalien* was not – as legend might have it – Jean-Paul Sartre. Beauvoir's notebooks from 1929 paint a rather different picture of the genesis of their relationship from the one she made public during her lifetime. Once one accepts the premises that not all women want lifelong monogamy, and that not all original ideas come from men, the story of Beauvoir and Sartre reads rather differently from the start, for it is not true that once she met Sartre, he immediately occupied first place in her heart.

In the spring of 1929, Beauvoir became a close friend of René Maheu (called 'Herbaud' in her memoirs, and by the affectionate nickname 'Lama' in her diaries). Maheu belonged to a clique of three young men – the other members being the future novelist, Paul Nizan, and the future philosopher, Jean-Paul Sartre. In her memoirs Beauvoir writes that although she had broken into the circles of some *normaliens*, Maheu's group was the only one that remained closed to her. Beauvoir first noticed Maheu when he gave a talk at one of Brunzschvicg's seminars in 1929. He was married. But she liked his face, his eyes, his hair, his voice: in fact, everything. She decided to approach him in the Bibliothèque Nationale during lunch one day, and before long Maheu was writing her poems and bringing her drawings.

Maheu also gave Beauvoir the nickname that would stick with her for her entire adult life: *Castor* – the French word for beaver. One day he wrote in her exercise book, in capital letters: 'BEAUVOIR = BEAVER'. He explained his logic: like her, beavers 'like company and have a constructive bent'.[1]

In her memoirs Beauvoir describes Maheu's influence on her as similar only to Stépha's. In 1929 she wrote that 'I was tired of saintliness and I was overjoyed that [Maheu] should treat me – as only Stépha had done – as a creature of the earth.'[2] Beauvoir described Maheu as a 'real man', with an 'abundantly sensual' face, who 'opened up paths that [she] longed to explore without as yet having the courage to do so'. It is far from clear whether (and if so, when) the two became lovers – Beauvoir described their relationship guardedly – but certainly by the time she met Sartre Maheu occupied the central place in her affections. When she reflected on their time together she described it as one of 'perfect joy and numerous pleasures' during which she learned 'the sweetness of being a woman'.[3]

Many writers have claimed that Maheu was her first lover.[4] But precisely what this claim means is unclear so it is difficult to evaluate the truth of it. When Bair asked Beauvoir to confirm this she vehemently denied it, claiming that despite her clandestine adventures with Gégé and Hélène she had never even kissed a man on the mouth before Sartre.[5] But when Bair wrote her biography she did not have access to the letters and diaries that we now have.

Although Beauvoir and Sartre had caught glimpses of each other – in lecture halls, seminars, the Luxembourg Gardens – their official meeting was a long time in the making. Maheu was possessive: he wanted to keep Beauvoir to himself and deliberately did not introduce her to the infamous womanizer, Sartre. But Sartre had wanted to meet Beauvoir since the spring and was not shy about his interest: he had heard that her thesis was on Leibniz, so he sent her a drawing he had made for her. It depicted a man surrounded by mermaids and bore the title 'Leibniz bathing with the monads' (Leibniz called the basic substances of the universe 'monads': the mermaids were artistic licence on Sartre's part).[6]

During the three weeks before the written part of the *agrégation* examination Beauvoir saw Maheu daily. The written exam, on 17 June 1929, was a gruelling seven hours long, and required writing a dissertation on the spot, on a subject close to Simone's heart: 'freedom and contingency'. On 18 June was a further four-hour dissertation on 'intuition and reasoning in the deductive method'. And finally, on 19 June, four more hours on 'morality in the Stoics and Kant'.[7]

After the written component of the *agrégation* was completed, Maheu left Paris with his wife for ten days, telling Beauvoir that when he returned he would resume his studies with Nizan and Sartre. They all wanted her to join their elite group, he said – and Sartre wanted to take her out. Maheu delivered the invitation to the Beaver but asked her not to go without him. She liked the way he looked at her when he said it; and she did not like the look of Sartre.[8] So they decided that Hélène would go in her stead, to meet Sartre at the appointed place and time and tell him a white lie – that Simone had had to leave suddenly for the country.

Simone was starting to find her life joyful again: she had more and more friends these days, but most importantly she had Maheu, Merleau-Ponty and Zaza – still five months from her death – to share her life with, and she was excited to be 'creating' herself in the company of people who wanted her to become the woman she wanted to be (even if it was, as Zaza teased her, 'the amoral lady').[9] The evening that Hélène was out with Sartre, Beauvoir was euphoric, and wrote in her diary that she felt: 'Curious certainty that this reserve of riches that I feel within me will make its mark, that I shall utter words that will be listened to, that this life of mine will be a well-spring from which others will drink: the certainty of a vocation.'[10] That part, she put in her memoirs. But in the diaries themselves she added that she no longer felt her call a painful one – a *via delarosa*. She had the sense that she had been given something rare, something she could not keep to herself.

When Hélène came home she told her sister she had done well to stay in: Sartre took her to the cinema and was kind but he was not the conversational genius she'd been led to expect. 'Everything [Maheu] said about Sartre is pure invention.'[11]

Despite his failed bids for attention, Sartre was not dissuaded. He was intrigued by Maheu's praises of Simone's intelligence and wit, but he didn't have to rely on hearsay for what he could see for himself: her attractiveness. In 1973, Maheu wrote of her, 'what a heart! She was so authentic, so courageously rebellious, so genuine [...] and so distinctively attractive, her own genre and her own style, no woman has ever been like her'. Henriette Nizan (Paul's widow) remembered Beauvoir as a young woman with 'ravishing eyes', extremely pretty, with a slightly broken voice that only added to her allure. She was an 'unselfconscious beauty'.[12]

Sartre, meanwhile, was a notorious figure at the École Normale Superieure, where he had a reputation for both his mastery of philosophy and his irreverent mischief. He performed nude in a satirical sketch and threw water balloons out of the university's classrooms, shouting 'Thus pissed Zarathustra!' He was a prankster who – so he claimed – had been too bold in his exams the previous year: he was expected to place first in the nation but had failed because he wrote about his own philosophical ideas instead of following the rubric.

Sartre was suspicious when Simone sent Hélène in her stead: when she walked up and introduced herself he asked her: 'How did you know I was Sartre?' Hélène's reply gave her away: 'because . . . you are wearing glasses'. Sartre pointed out that another man was also wearing glasses. It didn't take a genius to figure out the adjectives she omitted from her sister's description: very short and very ugly.[13] Sartre was five foot one, and he knew he was ugly: it was one of the reasons he took such pleasure in seducing women – where looks failed, words conquered.

When Beauvoir was elated to receive Maheu's invitation to their study group it was because it meant more time with her Lama and also because it was a huge sign of respect. Sartre was a snob: he had had access to the best education Paris could offer a man and saw those who didn't as inferior and unworthy. In a 1974 interview Beauvoir confronted him with his arrogance, reminding him that in his student days he, Nizan and Maheu 'had the reputation of being extremely contemptuous of the world in general and of the Sorbonne students in particular'. His reply: 'That was because the Sorbonne students represented beings who were not quite human.'[14]

She was flattered and yet fearful, for the group's disdain was reciprocated by spite from the Sorbonne students, who described these men as heartless and soulless – and Sartre had the worst reputation of them all.[15]

When June ended, Sartre had still not met the woman he was 'dead set' on knowing. The legendary meeting finally occurred on Monday

8 July 1929, when Beauvoir arrived at the study group – 'a bit scared'. Sartre welcomed her politely, and all day long she commented on Leibniz's metaphysical treatise.[16] It may not sound like an auspicious start to a romance: from her point of view, it wasn't. But over the next few weeks the dynamics shifted.

First, the trio became a quartet. They would meet daily for the next two weeks. But on that first day Beauvoir's diaries leave little room to doubt the object of her affection: she describes the way Maheu's body was half-stretched out on the bed in his shirtsleeves, and when they were walking home it is only after Sartre leaves that their walk became 'delicious': she didn't remember what they discussed by the time she got home to her diary, but she filled it with praises for 'her Lama'.[17]

The next day they did more Leibniz, and Sartre gave Beauvoir a present – a Japanese painting, which she described in her diaries as 'atrocious'. The day after brought more Leibniz and more unwanted presents from Sartre: this time some porcelains she deemed 'absurd'.[18]

By Thursday she had begun to be impressed by the way he thought. They had finished Leibniz and moved on to Rousseau, with Sartre now taking the lead of their revision. Beauvoir began to see Sartre in an unexpected light, as: 'Someone who was generous with everyone, I mean really generous, who spent endless hours elaborating on difficult points of philosophy to help make them clear to others, without ever receiving anything in return. [...] he was a totally different person from the one the Sorbonne students saw.'[19]

But the day after that Beauvoir and Maheu slipped off and 'rented a room in a small hotel in the rue Vanneau' where she was, according to her memoirs, 'ostensibly helping him to translate Aristotle'.[20] In her diary that night she described the room, how the summer heat filtered in just enough to 'feel deliciously protected', how their friendship was 'modified by tenderness', in a way she would 'always, always remember'.[21] Maheu was worried that he had failed the written exams. Whatever else they did, the diaries are clear that they only worked a little.

Over the days that followed the diary is full of references to 'my Lama', who tells her, among other things, that Sartre is enchanted with her.[22] On 15 July the Lama teasingly whispered that he would kiss Simone and she confessed to her diary how disturbed she was by her desire for him. The day after that they told each other 'I love you' – *je vous aime*.[23]

On 17 July the results of the written component of the exam were posted at the Sorbonne. Passing the *agrégation* guaranteed a teaching post for life in the French school system; the number of successful candidates was limited to the number of teaching places available in the nation. Beauvoir was going in the door as Sartre came out: he told her that she, he and Nizan were among the twenty-six who had qualified for the orals; Maheu had failed.

Maheu left Paris that evening. And the same evening, Sartre swooped in. It is unclear how much he knew about Maheu and Beauvoir's relationship at the time, but these altered circumstances certainly worked to Sartre's favour. For one thing, Maheu no longer needed to prepare for the oral component of the *agrégation*, so the quartet became a trio again. Intellectually Sartre had already made a good impression on Beauvoir, so he had a foundation on which to build and now knew that the reports he had had of her were not exaggerated by affection or hyperbole: she was brilliant.

In the memoirs Beauvoir reports that Sartre said, 'From now on I'm going to take you under my wing.'[24] In the diaries Beauvoir did not record this; instead writing that Sartre 'makes me everything he wants', but that she loved 'his way of being authoritarian, of adopting me, and of being so harshly indulgent'.[25] He delighted her by mocking the men who told her she was 'unpleasant when she talked philosophy'[26] – and by seeking out her company to talk about just this. They continued to study together, and people around them started to notice.

After Maheu's departure, Beauvoir and Sartre met every morning in the Jardin du Luxembourg or local cafés, starting a conversation that would continue for fifty-one years. The arrival of Castor displaced some of Sartre's other friends: Raymond Aron wrote that 'our relationship changed the day Sartre met Simone de Beauvoir. There was a time when he was pleased to use me as a sounding board for his ideas; then there was that meeting, with the result that suddenly I no longer interested him as an interlocutor'.[27] It was also noted by Zaza, who did not like the 'frightful, learned Sartre', but who admitted that Beauvoir had chosen her path well before Sartre crossed it: 'The influence of Sartre might have hurried things along a bit,' she said, but he did not alter her course.[28]

Nine days after meeting Sartre, Beauvoir was comparing the two men's efforts for her attention in her diary, writing that the Lama could attach himself to a woman simply by caressing her neck; Sartre's approach was to show her his heart.[29] By 22 July Beauvoir described Sartre's influence on her as 'extraordinary'. In the thirteen days that she had known him, she wrote in her diary, he had 'understood me, foreseen me, and possessed me', such that she had an 'intellectual need' of his presence.[30] They had discovered 'a great resemblance' in their attitudes and their ambitions: in addition to their joint passion for philosophy, they shared passions for literature and dreamt of literary futures. They could glide easily through philosophical views and literary allusions – with each other, there was no tedium of having to define concepts or explain plots. Both had longed to be writers from an early age but now faced the ambiguous prospect of life after studenthood, when such dreams are often waylaid by pragmatism and disenchantment.

Of course, in significant respects, their dreams already had different degrees of reality: Sartre could name numerous men who had succeeded in his – the Panthéon was full of monuments glorifying the great writers of the nation, celebrating their literary and philosophical progeny. Beauvoir could name few women who were celebrated for their literature, and even fewer who were considered philosophers. Her predecessors had often had to pay a high price for their rejection of traditional values, frequently sacrificing their happiness in order to gain freedom. Beauvoir wanted better: why should freedom come at the cost of love? Or love at the cost of freedom?

Their revision sessions turned into trips to riverside bookstalls and the cinema, cocktails and jazz. He sang her *Old Man River*, talked about his dreams, and asked her questions about herself. Beauvoir later wrote that he tried to understand her in her own terms, 'in the light of my own set of values and attitudes'. He encouraged her to 'try to preserve what was best in me: my love of personal freedom, my passion for life, my curiosity, my determination to be a writer'. Even so, when she saw 'her Lama' again on 27 July everything changed. She asked herself why, when Sartre and Lama were in the same room, the former lost his importance? Her answer was that the second absorbed her more passionately.[31] But on 28 July she read Sartre's early attempt at a novel, *Er L'Armenien*, and they spent the following day together. *Er L'Armenien* includes dialogues with Chronos, Apollo and Minerva (among others) on topics such as time, art, philosophy and love.[32] Beauvoir started to use the same endearing epithets in her diary that she had previously reserved for her Lama. She slept poorly, feeling troubled.[33]

There is an essay by William James entitled 'What Makes a Life Significant?', in which he asks what is it that makes every Jack see his own Jill as charmed and perfect – as a beautiful wonder of creation – when she leaves the rest of her observers stone cold. Who sees Jill more clearly – the enchanted eyes of Jack? Or the eyes that are blind to Jill's magic? Surely, James writes, it is Jack who sees the truth when he 'struggles toward a union with her inner life'. Where would any of us be if no one was willing to see us truly and seriously, 'to know us as we really are'?

Beauvoir had eyes like Jack: but the trouble was, they saw Maheu's perfections and Sartre's charms (and to be honest, they still saw beauty in Jacques too). What was she to do?

In Beauvoir's memoirs, this dilemma was dramatically downplayed, whether for her reputation's sake or her readers'. It was the late 1950s, after all: would they be ready for the idea that a Jill could love a Jack – and a Jean-Paul and a René, too? In the simplified story she told in *The Prime of Life*, after Beauvoir met Sartre she recedes from the foreground. In the diaries she wrote that with Sartre, Maheu and Nizan she could finally be herself; in the memoirs she described her time with Sartre as the first time in her life that she 'had felt intellectually inferior to anyone else'.[34] This mood of inferiority intensified after the famous conversation – near the Medici fountain in the Luxembourg gardens – in which Beauvoir confided that she had been thinking up her own theory of morality. Sartre demolished it, and eventually she declared herself beaten. She found this disappointing in hindsight, but she looked back on it with humility: she wrote that, 'My curiosity was greater than my pride; I preferred learning to showing off.'[35]

Beauvoir's 'humility' in this instance – while laudable insofar as it expresses a preference for learning over blinding forms of pride – has perplexed feminists for decades. At many points in her life Beauvoir defined Sartre as 'the philosopher', despite the fact that when they took the oral part of the *agrégation* exam, she not only took second place but, at the age of 21, she was the youngest person ever to pass it. When the three-man jury deliberated, one judge held out for Beauvoir as 'the true philosopher', and at first the others favoured her too. But in the end their decision was that since Sartre was a *normalien* (someone who had studied at the elite École Normale) he should receive first place. (It is unclear whether the fact that he had sat and failed it the year before entered into their deliberations.[36])

Beauvoir's memoirs imply that it wasn't just Sartre who 'forced' her to take 'a more modest view' of herself. Her other *normalien* friends – Nizan, Aron, Politzer – had had several years longer to prepare for their exams, and their preparation was built on a foundation laid by much better educational opportunities. The situation in which they became philosophers was radically different from her own, because only men could be *normaliens* at that time, only men could get the most elite teachers and the confidence that ensued from debating with people who believed themselves to be the best.

Beauvoir's diaries support this story – to an extent. Shortly after the *agrégation* exams, she was having a drink with Sartre and Aron; they spent two hours discussing good and evil. She got home feeling crushed. It was so interesting! She wrote – but it was also a revelation: 'I'm no longer sure what I think.' Their intellectual lives were so rich compared with the 'too-closed garden in which she had been imprisoned'. She envied their mental maturity, the strength of their thought – and she promised herself that she, too, would achieve it.[37]

Despite her lack of access to the most elite philosophical pedigree, Beauvoir was remembered by her contemporaries as an excellent philosopher who wanted to *live* philosophy. Maurice de Gandillac described her as: 'Rigorous, demanding, precise and technically stringent, [...] everybody agreed that she *was* philosophy.'[38] It is perplexing, therefore, that she ever denied the title 'philosopher' and positioned herself in this subordinate way. 'Why', Toril Moi asks, 'does she seize every possible opportunity to declare herself intellectually inferior to Sartre?'[39]

Moi's conclusion is that Beauvoir sacrificed success for seduction.[40] And as she recounts the story in her early memoirs, Beauvoir gives the appearance of having done so: in the public persona she leaves philosophy to the 'great man', Sartre. But in her diaries we see that Beauvoir's early philosophical success occurred at the same time as a rather different seduction – of René Maheu, a man who failed his exams. In that case seduction required no sacrifice on her part. So why should it be different with the then-unknown Sartre? Moreover, we shall see that Beauvoir did not seize *every* opportunity to declare herself inferior – in fact, she publicly owned and in places fought to defend her own originality. Could it be that she described herself as inferior with a certain reader in mind: the kind of reader who doubts herself, who wonders whether she should listen to the voices that tell her not to try? For that kind of reader, it was remarkably bold of Beauvoir to comment publicly on the 'clumsiness' of the young Sartre's essays: after all, he was a genius.[41]

But in 1929, he wasn't the giant 'Jean-Paul Sartre' yet. He was barely 25 (three years older than her), had over twice as long to prepare for the exam, and was taking it for the second time. That Beauvoir's memoirs do not dwell on the uniqueness of her achievement may reflect insecurity, modesty or political savvy on her part. It may be a concession to the power of this institution (the École Normale) in the cultural landscape of France. The way she described herself as inferior to Sartre drew attention not to their relative abilities, but rather to differences in their confidence and cultural capital. He, prior to being a *normalien*, had attended the Lycée Henri IV, then Louis le Grand. On paper you couldn't be better qualified. Sartre did not have to list his *certificats de licence* because, as Toril Moi writes, 'a consecrated genius does not need to justify himself in such petty ways'.[42]

A female genius, by contrast, had to be careful not to shine too blazingly. In 1929, the French education system had also been trying to tread carefully through the delicate matter of women outperforming men in the *agrégation* exams. The outcome was public knowledge because *agrégation* results were publicly announced, like sports rankings. The candidate with the highest number of points came first, and so on. So, although their jobs were not under threat, the male students still had to experience the embarrassment (as some saw it) of being ranked lower than women in an official and influential context. (To avoid this humiliation the ministry of education separated the lists into male and female from 1891; they saw the better of this move and reintroduced the joint ranking system in 1924.)

To put Beauvoir's experience in perspective, it is worth noting that when Sartre's father died, not much more than twenty years before, his mother quickly left Paris because she was concerned that Jean-Paul would be taken away from her. As a woman, her legal rights to her own child were weaker than those of her dead husband's family. When Beauvoir was studying, women in France still didn't have the right to vote or open their own bank accounts. The year Simone took the *agrégation* female university students made up 24 per cent of the student population – a massive increase since the previous generation (in 1890 there were 288 female students, 1.7 per cent). But if a woman didn't have the right to vote, to open a bank account – or even to her own child – what right did she have to first place?

It was not that long ago that Simone had been reading philosophy by herself in the ladies-only section of the Bibliothèque Saint-Geneviève, writing in her diary that she wanted to *vivre philosophiquement* – to live a thinking life, rather than to just live, to just think – and to write out the riches she felt welling up within her. Later on she would read Ralph Waldo Emerson (an unrequited love of her beloved Louisa May Alcott) but even before she read him she had already come to share his conclusion that 'our chief want in life is somebody who shall make us do what we can'.[43]

By 22 July 1929 she knew that being with Sartre would force her to be a 'real someone'. He could be annoying. She felt afraid. But, be that as it may, she wrote that day: 'I will abandon myself to this man with absolute confidence.'[44]

Eventually, even she would wonder if she sold herself short.

5

The Valkyrie and the Playboy

When Beauvoir arrived at Meyrignac in August 1929, she needed to take stock of her situation. Meyrignac was the only place she had ever had a room to herself, so she took advantage of the privacy to do what she called 'an appraisal' of her life. She believed in Sartre, and believed that her growing tenderness towards him was not an infidelity to the Lama or to Jacques.[1] In the weeks since Maheu had left Paris, Beauvoir and Sartre became closer in mind and body: they had not yet consummated their relationship but in his room in the Cité Universitaire it was a case of, Beauvoir later told Bair, 'everything but sex itself'.[2]

Over the next week, as Beauvoir carried out her appraisal, she catalogued memories and feelings – which, being human, changed from day to day: 'doubts, devastation, elation'.[3] She didn't take this variation as a reason to upbraid herself but rather as deserving reflection. While she '*needed*' Sartre, she '*loved*' Maheu. In her own words: She loved what Sartre brought her; and she loved what Maheu was.[4] At this point, Sartre was not yet essential.

The weather in the Corrèze was beautiful and the family was drawn close by the recent death of Grandfather Bertrand de Beauvoir:

this was the first summer without him. Gandillac, Merleau-Ponty's Catholic friend, came to visit and proposed that the sisters should visit him, too – he was only an hour's train ride away. Françoise forbade it even though he was a respectable Catholic man, and she liked him: it wasn't proper. What about a day trip to Tulle? Gandillac asked. It was about half as far away. Their mother permitted this on one embarrassing condition – she was coming too, to chaperone.[5]

On 9 August Simone visited Uzerche with Gandillac and thought of nothing but Sartre; the day after, they walked on the banks of the Vézère and she thought of the Lama.[6] The workings of her mind were invisible to Françoise's escorting eyes, but it soon became evident that there were other means of escaping her vigilance. On 19 August the Bertrand de Beauvoirs moved from Meyrignac to La Grillère, Georges' sister's estate. At breakfast the next morning her cousin Madeleine rushed into the kitchen and told Simone that there was a man waiting for her in a nearby field.

It was Sartre.

She knew he would come: the prospect of his visit made her passionately happy.[7] At this point Beauvoir's diaries, in which she so regularly confided, stop. They are resumed after Sartre's stay, when she recounts their 'perfect days' of 'ideas and caresses'.[8] It seems reasonable to speculate that she found her usually regimented time too valuable to waste in writing when it could be spent with Sartre.

On the first day of his visit she suggested that they should go for a walk but Sartre declined, telling her that he was 'allergic to chlorophyll'. They sat in a meadow and talked instead; there was not enough time in the world to dry up the wells of their conversation. Sartre stayed in the Hôtel de la Boule d'Or in Saint-Germain-les-Belles. Simone woke up each morning feeling elated, running through the meadows thinking about what she would tell him that day. They lay in the grass and she talked to him about her parents, Hélène, Zaza, her school,

Jacques. On hearing about the latter Sartre said that he thought marriage was a trap, although he knew it was hard for women of her background to avoid. He admired her 'Valkyrie spirit' and told her he would be sad to see her lose it.

In parched August fields they began to plan a different future, together: they would travel, have adventures, work hard, write famous works and live lives of passionate freedom. He would give her much, he said, but he could not give her all of himself: he needed to be free. He had been engaged once already but now was terrified of marriage, children and possessions: she found 'sensitive Sartre' surprising when he told her. His goal was to be the great writer he was destined to be, and it was during this trip that Sartre gave her the spiel about how he needed to preserve his freedom in order to realize his destiny as a great man. He was a 'Baladin', a wanderer who needed to travel the world untethered in order to gain material for his great works. In characteristic Sartrean style this proposal was made with literary and philosophical sophistication: the 'Baladin' he fashioned himself on was the 'Playboy' of the Irish playwright J. M. Synge's *The Playboy of the Western World*.

The memoir version of this conversation has often been invoked to claim that Sartre set the expectations of their relationship, inflicting his infidelity on Simone. But the diaries show that her heart had many objects of affection, each of whom she found loveable for his own reasons. In Meyrignac that August, Sartre shared his notebooks with her and described his thinking on psychology and the imagination, as well as his theory of contingency. He had been reading many of the same things she had, so their conversations were buttressed by interests that stretched back into both of their pasts. Alongside the philosophy they had both read for the *agrégation*, their mutual love of literature gave them an uncommonly deep shared world. She found his ideas interesting, inspiring – hopeful, even – and began to realize that she was becoming more and more attracted to his 'beautiful serious head'.[9]

Simone had told her parents that she and Sartre were collaborating on a critical study of Marxism, hoping that their hatred of communism might overpower their concern for propriety. Would it work? Not for long. Four days after Sartre arrived they were together in a meadow when Georges and Françoise approached. The sprawling philosophers jumped to their feet and her father looked embarrassed. He addressed his words to Sartre: people were starting to talk; could he please leave the district? Simone was indignant, and asked her father why he spoke to her friend in this tone; her mother began to shout at her. Sartre assured them that he would leave soon, but said that they were working on a philosophical inquiry they needed to finish first. Whether or not her parents believed them, they returned to the house, and Sartre departed several days later on 1 September.

After Sartre left, Beauvoir wrote in her diary that she demanded 'nothing more from Sartre than the moments he wants to give her'. She had begun to imagine a future that enabled her to reconcile her hopes of independence *and* love, and it made her feel elated. In her diary she wrote: 'The Valkyrie hidden in the depths of this tender little girl, poured joy into her in great waves, and she knew herself to be strong, as strong as him.'[10]

After Sartre departed, she expressed delight at 'being alone, uniquely her own, free and strong'. In her solitude she had space to reflect on incertitude: for her heart was certain that she loved Sartre, she loved the Lama, and she could love Jacques, 'each in a different manner'. But she did not know how to reconcile all of her loves.[11]

So after Sartre left, on the 2–4 September, the Valkyrie continued her project of taking stock. She was happy, overflowing with possibility and feeling as though the life she had longed for had finally begun. Sartre was very much an ingredient in her happiness, but contrary to what has been widely written and assumed, he was not the *only* ingredient. Sartre's role was to be 'in my heart, in my body and above all (for in my heart and my body many others could be) the incomparable friend of my thought'.[12]

Beauvoir settled on a resolution: 'I will love each one as if he were the only one, I will take from each one all that he has for me; and I will give him everything I can give him. Who can reproach me?' There were days when she wasn't sure what her feelings for Sartre were, precisely, but felt certain that they were not yet love.[13]

Before their legendary pact, therefore, Beauvoir came to the conclusion that she would love multiple men in the ways she thought them loveable. As early as 1926 she wrote in her diary that she did not think she had the right to give a lover 'an image he likes in place of me, or to be really unfaithful to what I am': one should 'give only what one can give'.[14]

Two days later the Lama arrived and they stayed together in a hotel. They had hired separate rooms but she enjoyed the two mornings they spent together, tenderly remembering his blue pyjamas and the voice in which he said 'Bonjour Castor'.[15] Beauvoir's diary descriptions of Maheu are often imbued with physical attraction, drawing attention to his body, his face, his voice, his posture, what he wore and how it fitted him. But she began to see his attractiveness as 'partial' in comparison with Sartre's. She did not hold him in high esteem morally, and intellectually he didn't satisfy her.[16]

So was Maheu Beauvoir's first lover? The diary leaves this obscure. We have seen already that at the time of her interviews with Deirdre Bair, Beauvoir denied that her relationship with Maheu had been sexual. But Sartre and Maheu both said the opposite: Sartre confirmed to John Gerassi (Stépha's son) that 'Maheu was in love with her [...] And she was in love with Maheu; in fact he was her first lover'.[17] On this basis some have concluded that their 'translating Aristotle' was not what Beauvoir claimed. In *The Prime of Life*, Beauvoir wrote that she surrendered her virginity 'with glad abandon' – but she does not specify to whom.[18] However, a passage in the diaries may support Beauvoir's denials: she wrote that 'it was beautiful that with this sensual man [Maheu] nothing physical intervened between us, while with Sartre, who isn't sensual, the harmony of our bodies has a meaning that makes our love more beautiful'.[19]

This relationship presents us with a strange conundrum: Beauvoir denied that it was sexual; the men claimed it was. When I asked Beauvoir's friend and adopted daughter Sylvie Le Bon de Beauvoir she confirmed that Simone was attracted to Maheu and their relationship was intimate but not consummated in the period before Beauvoir met Sartre: at this stage, Beauvoir was a respectable Catholic woman, and there were things a respectable Catholic woman didn't do. In an interview given later in life Beauvoir was asked if there was anything she wished, in hindsight, that she had included in her memoirs. Her answer was 'a frank and balanced account of her own sexuality. A truly sincere one, from a feminist point of view'.[20] Even in her own diaries Beauvoir did not give an altogether frank account of her experiences. Did she fear that her mother might read them? She had yet to discover the way her personal life would be distorted by fame, used to distract attention from her philosophy and her politics.

6

Rooms of Her Own

When the 21-year-old Beauvoir returned to Paris in September of 1929 she moved out of her parents' apartment, renting a fifth-floor room in her maternal grandmother's property at 91 rue Denfert-Rochereau. Her grandmother had several lodgers and Simone had the same independence, and rent, as the rest. She decorated the walls with orange wallpaper; Hélène helped her redecorate some second-hand furniture. Her mother had tears in her eyes when she moved out; Simone was grateful to her for not making a scene.[1] Apart from during brief summer visits to Meyrignac she had always shared a bedroom with Hélène, so she was delighted to have – for the first time in her life – a room that was hers alone.

Simone did not yet have a job of her own: but she and Sartre had discussed their future as *their* future. While he was doing military service they would see as much of each other as possible. Beauvoir would stay in Paris rather than taking up a full-time teaching post, since that would give her time to start on a novel. She did some part-time tutoring and taught Latin and Greek at the Lycée Victor-Duruy a few hours a week, which gave her enough to live on.[2]

After the exacting schedule that led up to her examinations, Beauvoir found that working life was not as onerous as her parents had implied: without the constant threat of obstacles and failure life felt like she was permanently on vacation. She could now do – and *dress* – as she wanted to. Her mother had always dressed her in drab and durable cotton and wool: she now bought silks, crêpe de Chine, velours. One of Beauvoir's literary characters from the 1930s, Chantal, was a philosophy teacher who took pleasure in dressing stylishly; she describes the 'wonder-struck gaze of the pupils, who probably do not think I am quite real'.[3]

In *The Prime of Life* Beauvoir wrote that by the time she met Sartre again in October she had 'jettisoned' all other attachments and thrown herself into the relationship with Sartre wholeheartedly.[4] But once more the diaries tell a different story: from September to November Jacques and the Lama both still featured in her deliberations, with tenderness and love expressed for both. Again, Beauvoir's contradictory accounts raise the question: why? Why did she gloss over the other men in her life when she wrote her memoirs, assigning Sartre a more dominant place in narrative than he occupied in life?

In 1929 Beauvoir was still weighing up his merits. On 27 September she wrote that Sartre did not understand love because despite being an experienced player of the game he had never truly experienced love itself.[5] Her doubts persisted: on 8 October she wrote that she 'must learn not to regret this love any more than when I am near him.'[6] She had seen Jacques again when she got back to Paris in September, which renewed her interest and briefly demoted the Lama from her considerations. She thought her future required a choice between 'happiness with Jacques' and 'unhappiness with the help of Sartre'.[7] 'It is not funny,' she wrote, 'to love two men, and each one so passionately.'[8]

According to Beauvoir's memoirs, in the autumn of 1929 Sartre told Beauvoir that she had a double personality. Given the various disjointed accounts she gives, and her obvious feelings of being torn between possible lives, it doesn't take a great stretch of the imagination to see how he might have felt this way. (She even had a name for her possible lives – she called them *mes possibles*, my possibles.) Normally, he said, she was the Beaver. But sometimes the Beaver disappeared, and the less enjoyable (from his point of view) Mademoiselle de Beauvoir took her place. Mademoiselle de Beauvoir felt sadness and regret; the Beaver did not.[9] Episodes like this could be taken to support suspicions that Sartre gaslit Beauvoir, making her doubt herself in order not to challenge his dubious behaviour. But Sartre did not invent this distinction: we have already seen Beauvoir's diaries use a similar one as early as 1927, when she enjoined herself: 'Don't be "Mlle Bertand de Beauvoir." Be me. Don't have a goal imposed from outside, a social framework to fill. What works for me will work, and that is all.'[10]

On Monday 14 October Sartre and Beauvoir met in the Luxembourg gardens and went for a walk. That afternoon's conversation would inspire thousands of people to try to emulate them, because it contained the defining discussion of their open relationship: the pact. They would have a two-year lease, forsaking no others. And they would tell each other everything. To distinguish his relationship with Beauvoir from his relationships with lesser lovers, Sartre said to her: 'What *we* have is an *essential* love; but it is a good idea for us also to experience *contingent* love affairs.'[11] They called their relationship a 'morganatic marriage' – a marriage of people of unequal social rank, like Louis XIV and Madame de Maintenon. (They did not clarify for posterity which of them was considered royalty, and which the commoner.)

In the second volume of her memoirs Beauvoir wrote that at first she found their commitment to telling each other everything embarrassing. But then she came to see it as liberating: in Sartre she thought she had found an observer who saw her with much greater impartiality than she could ever have about herself: he would be her life's witness. They would be open books to each other, comfortable in the knowledge that their reader meant no harm.[12]

She trusted him so completely that he provided the 'absolute unfailing security' that she had once had from her parents or God.[13] Given her early insistence on the importance of 'the view from within' in her diaries, and the benefits of hindsight, it is difficult to know what to make of her confidence in Sartre's 'view from without'. Was her trust warranted? Truly mutual?

The Sartre and Beauvoir described in *The Prime of Life* were careful with the truths they told each other, since truths can be sharp weapons. Beauvoir made no claim, in later life, to having a timeless formula of successful communication – she thought that nothing she could say would grant couples perfect understandings of each other. She was often asked how they made their relationship work and her response was that people need to work together to decide the nature of their own agreements. In her youth she made the mistake of thinking that what worked for her was right for everyone; but it irritated her, by 1960, to be praised or criticized for the way they conducted their relationship.[14] (It's not hard to see why, given how little they really knew about it.)

As events unfolded in 1929, Beauvoir did reach giddy heights of love for Sartre. But she had also wavered since meeting him in July, and in the week after they made their pact she continued to have doubts. On 15 October they were together again and 'Mademoiselle de Beauvoir' threatened to appear: she felt dejected and regretted her choice, but managed to conceal her sadness from Sartre before he left and she broke down in tears.[15] On 21 October 1929 she decided, and underlined in her diary, 'I cannot live this year without Sartre.'[16]

It was just as well, for two days later Jacques embarrassedly informed her that he was engaged to someone else.[17] The next day the Lama and Stépha both came to console her. The Lama told her that men like Jacques were attractive at 18 but soon lost their lustre because they lived on their fortune instead of making it – Jacques had inherited his father's business; he accepted his place in the pre-established order of things in a way that Simone never would. Stépha took her for a hot chocolate at *Les Deux Magots*. She was grateful for their comfort: despite her growing attachments to other men, she still had tears to cry – whether for Jacques, the imagined future in which she fulfilled her family's expectations, or some combination of both.[18]

In *The Prime of Life* Beauvoir wrote that she and Sartre, in the early days of their relationship, succumbed to 'spiritual pride': they thought they were 'radically free' but in fact fell prey to several illusions. They didn't acknowledge any emotional obligations to others. They took themselves to be pure reason and will, failing to recognize how dependent they were on others and how sheltered they had been from the world's adversities. They didn't have much money, but they met luxury with disdain: what was the point of grasping for things that weren't within reach?[19] Instead they cultivated the riches of a shared imagination, stocking it with stories, ideas, images: when it wasn't literature it was Nietzsche, Marx, Freud or Descartes, regularly punctuated by excursions to galleries or the cinema.

In November Sartre went to Saint-Cyr to serve in the meteorological corps. After the two years were up, Sartre envisaged spending some time apart from Beauvoir: he had applied for a job in Kyoto, Japan, which – if he got it – would begin in October 1931. But then, he told her, they would meet each other in distant locations around the world (perhaps Istanbul?) to be together before parting ways again for new adventures alone.

Beauvoir did not share exactly the same dreams of solitary expeditions, but she did not feel able to tell Sartre what she wanted.

Even so, Sartre was still only part of her life. In the same 3 November entry of her diary she wrote about how she wanted Sartre's 'mouth against her mouth', followed by a paragraph about a letter from

Jacques, happiness to have seen Stépha, and another paragraph in which she describes wanting the Lama's hands in her hair, his body to brush her body.[20] It is unclear, at this stage, why Beauvoir took such pains to protect Sartre from her thoughts. But it is clear that she saw no contradiction in loving several people at the same time, whatever their respective faults.

Sartre's military service involved training at Saint-Cyr, which was close enough to Paris that three or four days per week Beauvoir could travel to meet Sartre for dinner – sometimes with their mutual friends Pierre Guille and Raymond Aron. On Sundays, Sartre came to Paris to see her. After the training was finished Sartre was sent to Saint-Symphorien meteorological station, not far from Tours. They wrote to each other most days, and Sartre had a week off each month plus Sundays, so between his trips to Paris and Beauvoir's weekly visits to Tours they saw each other regularly (even if it wasn't as often as she would've liked). He called her 'my dear little wife'; she called him 'my little husband'. But the euphoric highs of the previous summer quickly dissipated.

The next month, on 25 November 1929, was when Zaza died. Beauvoir recorded only the date in her diary; a teardrop blurred the ink.

Beauvoir's diaries go silent after Zaza's death, only resuming the next month after Sartre upset her. When she joined the study group at the Cité Universitaire she thought she had met people who accepted her as she was: a philosopher who wanted to seek the truth, and live it. But now Sartre seemed to have grating expectations: was he too telling her what to be and not to be, what she did and didn't understand? Among other things, she wrote, 'I understand the contingent life better than he wants to say.'[21]

The disagreement broke out the day before Zaza's funeral because Sartre had told her that she was too 'encrusted' in her own happiness.

So again tears flowed: 'Tears not bitter, tears where already a force is born, tears from which I feel that the Valkyrie will rise, awaken from this long sleep of happiness.'[22] At this stage in their relationship a pattern was starting to form: as the years went on Beauvoir would often turn to people other than Sartre when she needed emotional support. After Zaza died, Simone turned to Hélène, but even so at the funeral on 13 December she was overcome by the mournful vision before her – these were the same faces in the same spaces where she had imagined Zaza's wedding.[23]

Sartre clearly thought she had the capacity to write great things, but it is just at clear that at important moments he lacked compassion for her suffering. And over the first year of their pact Beauvoir had many doubts – about Sartre, herself and the impact of the pact on others. In December of 1929, when Maheu (*her* Lama) was visiting Paris, he discovered a letter from Sartre on her desk. She had not been open with Maheu about the changing nature of her relationship with Sartre; now the Lama said he could never trust her again, and wrote her a letter insisting that she see him while he was in Paris. Beauvoir copied out Maheu's words in a letter of her own to show them to Sartre: 'I have had my fill of the pretty situation that now exists, as a result of that September of yours and the two months of lying which followed it, and I deserve something better than the crumbs [...] that you both offer me with such elegance.'[24]

So Maheu did not want 'crumbs' – but what did he expect? He was married himself, so it was hardly consistent to expect her to be faithful to him when he clearly didn't practise fidelity himself. To Sartre she expressed little sympathy, condemning Maheu's jealousy as 'disagreeable'. But she was beginning to understand that 'contingent life' meant different things for Sartre and for her: she didn't want to hurt the people she loved, she wanted to be *with* them, and, frankly, this life 'didn't throw her into anything' now that Jacques was married,

Maheu was far away, and Sartre was leaving.[25] But it is unclear at this stage whether she was starting to doubt the value of 'the contingent life' itself, or just this particular chapter of it.

During Beauvoir's first year on her own, she continued to see her parents for lunch regularly but told them little about her life. Although she missed Sartre when he was away she enjoyed her curiosity-quenching pursuits of the previously forbidden: she went on 'dates with almost anyone' and visited a brothel. Her father didn't understand why she hadn't taken a teaching post, and dismissively told his friends that she was having her 'Paris honeymoon'. But she knew that her first teaching post was likely to be in the provinces, and she did not want to leave the Paris she was only just discovering. She briefly entertained the idea of becoming a journalist since that might allow her to stay in the capital, but the pull of teaching philosophy prevailed.[26]

In June 1930 she wrote in her diary that she had always had a desire to be strong, to work, to create her own works; and she could only agree with Sartre that she should give this first place in her life. But she had already begun to dread the end of their 'two-year lease', comparing it to a looming death. She was certain she wanted to write. But she underwent doubts about her abilities to realize her dreams of writing, thinking: 'I have no talent, I can't!' She berated herself for her laziness and lack of will power, on the one hand; on the other hand she could not tell whether Sartre was 'helping' as much as she anticipated. 'He speaks to me like one speaks to a little girl; he only wants to see me happy; but if I am satisfied with myself he isn't happy. [. . .] I have lied to him every time I was sad.'[27] Initially, she found his friendship incomparable: when they talked philosophy he seemed to be dedicated to the same thing she was: uncovering the truth. So why would he stop short of the truth when it concerned her feelings? And why was she, having rejected the role of dutiful daughter, accepting the part of a woman who pretends to be happy even when she is spoken to like a girl?

She felt like she had lost her joy, her inspiration to write, even her ability to believe his words when they said 'I love you'.[28] There is no record of exactly what Sartre said that she found so discouraging. But her father and her culture instilled in her the message that women were not creative: history was a testament to their lack of originality. Hélène de Beauvoir wrote that although the sisters clearly enjoyed literature and art in their childhood, neither she nor Simone had a eureka moment in which it was decided that they would be a painter or a writer. It took Hélène years to exorcize these words as she developed her painting. Simone, too, would later reflect on her youth as a time when she felt despair at her own lack of originality despite her strong sense of vocation. Letting her imagination speak, creating something herself, seemed impossible.[29]

Georges de Beauvoir's damning view of women's capabilities was shared, to some degree, by many of the philosophers Simone read: in her student diaries she quotes several lines from Arthur Schopenhauer, who, in an essay 'On Women', wrote that women are 'the second sex, inferior in every respect to the first', which exists solely for the continuation of the human species. He thought that it was possible for women to have talent, but never genius.[30]

When Simone was considering a career in journalism, one of her wealthy cousins (the same one who had helped her father in the past) had arranged a meeting for her with Madame Poirier, one of the joint editors of *L'Europe nouvelle*. She told Beauvoir that to succeed in journalism she needed to have ideas to contribute, and asked her: Do you have any ideas? 'No, I said, I didn't'.[31] Meanwhile Monsieur Poirier, the husband of this editor, suggested another kind of career progression, making unwanted sexual advances and telling Beauvoir that he would introduce her to powerful people if she was willing to get ahead that way. Beauvoir declined the advances and his offer, but when the couple invited her to a cocktail party she decided going along was worth a shot. When she arrived she felt very out of place; her wool dress was conspicuously modest in a room full of satin.

In the autumn of 1930 Simone began to think that her love of Sartre had taken too much of herself: that she had lived through him and 'neglected her own life'. 'I lost my pride,' she wrote, 'and that is how I lost everything.'[32] Looking back on her giddily high reunion with him the previous October she felt strongly that Sartre loved her less than she loved him: it seemed now that she was just one of Baladin's adventures, she had given him her soul in an awestruck moment, losing herself without realizing it.[33] She still loved him, but she described her love as 'more habitual, weaker, less purely tender'. He had lost the lustre of perfection: now she saw his desire to please, his amour-propre, the reddening of his face when he spoke loudly, and how easily he could be influenced.[34]

Her love had lessened but there was also a physical problem: her body's 'tyrannical desires' had been awakened and demanded satisfaction. This problem was made worse because Sartre did not suffer from it: he preferred seduction to sex. The circumstances in which Beauvoir agreed to the pact – namely, seeing both Maheu and Jacques as part of a present and future in which her heart and body would find love – may explain the readiness with which she accepted it. In their absence she was forced to admit the power of her physical appetites: but despite their promise to tell each other everything she did not, at first, raise this with Sartre.[35] Beauvoir's upbringing did not encourage her to express her desires or consider her emotions to be significant. But it is also possible that her censorious approach to emotion at this point in her life may have been exacerbated by Sartre's behaviour – and the philosophy that underpinned it.

Sartre, in his 1943 philosophical work *Being and Nothingness*, described sexual desire as 'trouble' because it clouded and compromised freedom. He was similarly intolerant of emotion, which he thought a free person could – and therefore *should* – choose not to feel. Once an ex-lover, Simone Jollivet, told the 21-year-old Sartre that she felt sad. The letter he sent by reply made no effort to conceal his disgust:

> Do you expect me to soften before this interesting pose you decided to adopt, first for your own benefit and then for mine? There was a time when I was inclined toward that kind of play-acting [...]. Nowadays I hate and scorn those who, like you, indulge their brief hours of sadness. [...] Sadness goes hand in hand with laziness [...] You revel in it to the point of writing to me 500 km away, who will very likely not be in the same mood: 'I'm sad.' You might as well tell it to the League of Nations.[36]

Beauvoir saw tears glisten in Sartre's eyes in the cinema once – but that was art, and there was no place for crying in life. So Beauvoir's mixed emotions and unwelcome sexual desire were committed to the pages of her journals, which didn't offer such rebukes.

In later life Beauvoir recalled having admired Sartre's detachment – sometimes. He claimed that great writers had to cultivate dispassion if they wanted to capture emotion rather than be taken captive by it. But at other times she felt like words had to 'murder reality before they can hold it', and she didn't want reality to die: she wanted to relish in it, to taste the richness of its flavours for herself rather than embalming it for posterity.[37] Although they agreed that literature was important they disagreed about what it was, and what it was for: Sartre knew words were powerful, but he thought all literature consisted of deception and disguise. Beauvoir thought it could do more and read Virginia Woolf with awe: here was a woman who wanted to close the gap between literature and life. Beauvoir wanted to know the world and to disclose it, truly.[38]

In her second volume of autobiography Beauvoir wrote that philosophically she frequently found Sartre to be careless and inaccurate; but she thought his bravado made his ideas more fruitful than her own precise and scrupulous thoughts.[39] In this and in many other instances Beauvoir portrayed herself as responding with reverence rather than recognition that Sartre had had advantages, which developed confidence, that she lacked. In the *Memoirs of a Dutiful Daughter* Beauvoir described Sartre as the perfect companion, the man she had been dreaming of since she was 15: 'I wanted husband and wife to have everything in common; each was to fulfil for the other the role of exact observer which I had formerly attributed to God. That ruled out the possibility of loving anyone *different*; I should not marry unless I met someone more accomplished than myself, yet my equal, my double.'[40]

But his observations weren't quite as exact as she later made them out to be: he refused to see her emotions as meaningful and dismissed her sexual desires.[41] Twenty years later, in *The Second Sex*, Beauvoir wrote about 'the woman in love' – a woman who makes her man so central to her life that she loses sight of herself.

The woman in love abandons even her own judgement, trying to see everything through the eyes of her beloved, to follow his preferences in books, art and music. She loses interest in the world if he is not there to see it with her; she is only interested in his ideas, his friends, his opinions. She thinks her value is conditional: that she has value because she is loved by a man. When she hears him say 'we', Beauvoir wrote, it is her supreme happiness, because she has been 'recognized by the beloved man as part of him; when he says "we" she is associated and identified with him, she shares his prestige and reigns with him over the rest of the world'.[42]

Writers such as Hazel Rowley have taken such passages to be autobiographical descriptions of the young Beauvoir; after all, in her autobiography Beauvoir described her young self as an 'ancillary being' and an 'intellectual parasite'.[43] As we have seen, some pages of the diaries can be taken to suggest that instead of asking herself what she wanted or expressing what she wanted to him, she asked how she could be what he wanted. But although Beauvoir elided Sartre's flaws in her memoirs, she chronicled them in her diaries. Before she met Sartre she was already reading the books he was reading: Gide, Claudel, Péguy, Alain, Pascal, Leibniz, Lagneau, Nietzsche – and a separate diet of English books that Sartre lacked the skill to read himself. She did use the word 'we', but not only with Sartre. And even if Beauvoir did portray herself as 'the woman in love' with Sartre in her memoirs, it is unclear whether she was that woman in real life. She may have depicted herself in this ancillary way not out of factual fidelity or narrative necessity, but feminist commitment – because she thought that telling the story in a certain way would give it greater power.

Despite the confidence of her 18-year-old self that she had something to say, that her intelligence was keen and penetrating – the young Beauvoir does not always seem to have realized that her intellect, too, was fecund enough to attract parasites. As the memoirs recount them, Beauvoir and Sartre's conversations about ideas continued on the railway platforms of Tours and Paris: Sartre would greet her excitedly and tell her about his latest theory, then she would point out the flaws in his argument. She helped him refine the ideas for which he became famous. He, in turn, told her she was not original: 'when you think in terms of *problems*, you aren't thinking at all'.[44]

This criticism can be read as a dismissal, but it can also be read as harsh but fertile encouragement. In *The Prime of Life* Beauvoir wrote that Sartre began to be irritated by her dependence on him, not because she was dependent but because he thought she was less full of ideas than she had been when they met, that she was in danger of being the kind of woman who relinquished her independence and contented herself with being a man's helpmate. When Sartre told her this she was furious with herself. But the reason she gave for her fury was that she had disappointed him.[45]

There are different vantage points from which to view this dissonant blend of dependence and independence in Beauvoir: at some points she was unsure that Sartre was best for her, or brought out the best in her. But it seems clear that despite her early sense of vocation as a writer, she lacked confidence and would resist praise for decades, downplaying the positive aspects of reviews of her work and focusing on the negative. To an extent, the image of their relationship that has been passed down to posterity reflects Sartre's self-confidence and her self-doubt – but that is not all it reflects.

By October 1930 her doubts about Sartre were strong enough that she imagined finishing it: at times she wanted to leave Sartre. She ached for Zaza and her previous self; although she had attained what she thought she wanted, she felt unfulfilled: 'caresses, work, pleasures: is this all there is?'[46] In the final entry of her diaries, we see Beauvoir grieve for lost futures, lost selves she should have become in the company of other friends:

> I have sinned, I have sinned, I have sinned! Oh! I do not want my life to be like this! Oh! This is not what I dreamed of. Tomorrow I will see the dear little man [Sartre] and all will be finished. But today I don't know where these regrets are coming from. Oh! Jacques, my purity, my dream, my love. But you weren't these things.
>
> Zaza. I cannot stand that you are dead. [. . .] But I am alone without you and I don't even know what I want. I want to go. I want to leave Sartre and go with you for a walk, just with you, to speak, and to love you, and to walk, far from here, far.[47]

At this point we become much more reliant on her memoirs and letters for the details of her life and so temporarily lose access to the view from within. Despite Beauvoir's doubts and fluctuations, she still chose Sartre. But she did not choose to restrict herself to his caresses, his pleasures, his work. Several writers and reviewers have speculated that Beauvoir would have been happier if she had married Sartre. But this claim overlooks two things: first, that she had already reached the conclusion that marriage was immoral before she met Sartre. And, second, Sartre's primary role in her life was clearly defined from the beginning: he was 'the incomparable friend of her thought'. It was in that respect that he was necessary to her. Sexually and emotionally, he was far from it.

During her first year in Paris after the *agrégation* she had lost touch with many of her previous friends: Zaza was dead, Jacques was married, others had moved away. She no longer saw Merleau-Ponty or the 'holy willies'. The only people she introduced to Sartre were Hélène, Gégé, Stépha and Fernando. But soon the Gerassis, too, left Paris for Madrid.

Even so, Sartre's friends provided ample diversion. Beauvoir later described this period of her life as 'a delectable but chaotic stew' of people and events.[48] She described herself as lazy at first, decompressing after the intensity of the previous year's studies, but eventually the scholar in her reasserted itself and she got back to reading and writing. She joined the Anglo-American library: 'Over and above the books I read with Sartre,' her memoirs say, Beauvoir read Whitman, Blake, Yeats, Synge, Sean O'Casey, 'all of Virginia Woolf', Henry James, George Moore, Swinburne, Frank Swinnerton, Rebecca West, Sinclair Lewis, Theodore Dreiser, Sherwood Anderson. She attributed to Sartre 'an interest in the psychology of mysticism' (in fact an interest of her own in the diaries of the 1920s), so they read Catherine Emmerich and Saint Angela of Foligno alongside Marx and Engels.[49] In most aspects of life she 'liked overdoing things'.[50] Even when she went on vacation it generally meant that she travelled and worked somewhere else.[51]

In these early days, their pact met with disapproval from their families. Sartre's stepfather, Joseph Mancy, flat-out refused to meet Beauvoir since they were not married or engaged.[52] But Sartre offered no protest; he continued to make weekly visits to his parents' house without her. His mother would sneak out to meet them on her own sometimes – but only rarely and always briefly.

Further problems arose when Sartre, true to his word, did not conceal his admiration for his first serious 'contingent' lover, Simone Jollivet. In fact he used Jollivet as an example to 'goad [Beauvoir] out of her inactivity'.[53] Beauvoir felt upset and jealous, but she also thought Jollivet was a fraud. She was a high-end prostitute who recited Nietzsche to the lawyers and town clerks she 'laid flat'; Beauvoir had never slept with a man she didn't love and did not understand Jollivet's ability to use her body so casually.[54] Sartre, in turn, found Beauvoir's feelings contemptible. He thought she should control her passions – since letting them rule her compromised her freedom. From his point of view, emotions were lame excuses: all she needed to do was use her freedom to choose otherwise.

Beauvoir attempted to purge her jealousy, but at points during their life together it was a real struggle. In addition to facing jealousy in herself she was also sensitive to, and suffered from, the pain others felt as a result of their jealousy over her. Beauvoir had started her relationship with Sartre with multiple men in her heart. And she continued to find things to appreciate about other men. But they did not always appreciate her divided attention: once, she was about to take a ten-day road trip with Pierre Guille (a mutual friend of Sartre's and Beauvoir's) when Maheu arrived in Paris. He was staying for two weeks, without his wife, and expected to spend time with Simone. They had made up after his discovery of Sartre's letter the previous December, but now she told him that she was about to leave Paris for ten days with someone else. Maheu told her that he would never see her again if she went; she objected that it was hardly fair to let Guille down: she thought it was an offence against friendship to back out of a 'joint project' unless it was unavoidable to do so. They had reached an impasse – Maheu was unconvinced and did not retract his ultimatum – so they went to the cinema together, still at odds. Beauvoir wept all the way through the film.[55]

Figure 4 *Drawing by René Maheu, 'The universe of Mlle Simone de Beauvoir', May–June 1929. Under the elliptical shape Maheu has written: 'Where the devil do you want me to go? Everything is packed.'*

Nevertheless she enjoyed her February vacation with Guille. Being in a car was still a novelty for her – she had enjoyed drives in Paris with the Nizans, but this would be many days of travel, seeing places that she'd only read about in books. They visited Avallon, Lyon, Uzerche, Beaulieu, Rocamadour and – her favourite – Provence. They spent leisurely days soaking in the heat of the Provençal sun. She loved seeing the Camargue, Aigues-Mortes, Les Baux and Avignon.

Alongside the beauty of new places this trip brought inequality before her eyes in ways she had never seen before. Contrary to Simone Weil's barb, Simone de Beauvoir had often been hungry. But she did not realize the extent of her privilege, even so. On their way south she visited a cousin who showed them around a factory: the workshops were dark and filled with metallic dust. During the preceding year Beauvoir had read Marx, and was beginning to see an important connection between labour and values – but what is read on paper in Paris can be rather removed from what is felt on the factory floor. She asked how long the labourers worked and her eyes teared at the answer: eight-hour shifts of hot monotony.[56]

When they got back to Paris Sartre had had a letter informing him that he had not got the job he wanted in Kyoto and Beauvoir had a letter from Maheu saying things were over between them. Sartre was now waiting for his future to be decided by the French Ministry of Education. That spring he was offered a post in Le Havre, not far from Paris: he accepted.[57] Beauvoir, too, was offered a post – in Marseille, 800 km away.

As this distance loomed large before her she became very anxious, realizing that although she sometimes longed for solitude she was also afraid of it. The previous year had taught her things about herself that made this exile fill her with dread. Sartre, seeing her turmoil, suggested marriage: as husband and wife the state would be obliged to post them near each other. There was no point suffering on principle, he said:

they were opposed to marriage, but what good did it do to be martyrs about it?

Despite his protest that marriage was merely a legality, Beauvoir was surprised by his suggestion. She saw reasons against it from both of their points of view. Marriage 'double's one's domestic responsibilities' and 'social chores'; she wanted neither. And she also did not want to be a source of resentment, and feared being Sartre's wife would make her precisely that. Sartre was already experiencing a crisis with respect to disappointed expectations: he had dreamed of a bold posting in Japan, fitting glory for a Baladin, and instead was going to be teaching in the provinces. Joining the order of married men was not what he needed. The memoirs put Beauvoir's reasons first (although she didn't spell out her philosophical objections). But nevertheless they have often been overlooked, with the result that it has been assumed that she accepted this arrangement for Sartre's sake.

In the memoirs Beauvoir said that the only thing that might have changed her mind about joining this bourgeois institution was children. And while in her teens she expected to be a mother she no longer foresaw this as a possible future: she had come to see childbearing as 'a purposeless and unjustifiable increase of the world's population'.[58] Whether for rhetorical or genuine reasons, Beauvoir frames her decision not to have children in terms of her vocation: a Carmelite nun 'having undertaken to pray for all mankind, also renounces the engendering of individual human beings'. She knew she needed time and freedom in order to write. So, as she saw it, 'By remaining childless I was fulfilling my proper function'.

So, instead of marrying, Beauvoir and Sartre revised the terms of their pact: their relationship had become closer and more demanding than it had been when they first made it. Now they decided that although brief separations were permissible, long solitary sabbaticals were not. Their new promise was not life-long; they decided they would reconsider the question of separation when they entered their thirties. So although Marseille would separate them, Beauvoir left Paris on a firmer footing – with a clearer future – with Sartre.

During the summer of 1931 Beauvoir crossed the French border for the first time in her life. She was 23 years old and had always wanted to travel; Zaza used to come back from Italy overflowing with mesmerizing descriptions of different people, different places. Beauvoir and Sartre were planning to visit Brittany that summer when Fernando Gerassi (Stépha's husband) invited them to Madrid. Sartre still had a little money left over from a legacy he'd inherited from his grandmother; he paid their fares and turned his final francs into *pesetas*. They visited Figueres on their first evening, and kept finding themselves repeating 'We're in Spain!' They travelled from there to Barcelona and Madrid, Segovia, Ávila, Toledo and Pamplona. At the end of September, they parted ways for Le Havre and Marseilles.

When Beauvoir later reflected on her arrival in Marseilles it stood out as a 'completely new turn' in her career'.[59] She arrived alone, with nothing she couldn't carry on her own back, knowing no one at all. The previous year had left her feeling as though she didn't know herself all that well, and her time in Marseille provided her with the space and time to resurrect parts of herself that had atrophied. She found the people provincial and uninteresting. But she had always loved to be outdoors; Sartre did not. So on her days off work she left early in the morning to walk – she started off with walks of five or six hours a day and gradually worked her way up, covering vast distances in an old dress and espadrilles. She hitchhiked despite friends' and colleagues' concern: it was dangerous for a woman to walk alone, and she had some narrow escapes. But she enjoyed the solitude of walking and thought this pastime saved her from boredom, depression and regret. She became compulsive about finishing the routes she planned – sometimes to endangering extremes.

Her new teaching post had eased some family relations: Françoise even persuaded Georges to take a week's holiday in Marseille. Françoise had begun to be impressed by Simone: she saw her as a professional woman with a good income. But she was disappointed that Sartre still figured in Simone's life: spinsterhood would have been preferable to his incomprehensible presence. Beauvoir was relieved when her parents returned to Paris: she wanted to get back to walking.[60] Hélène also came to visit twice – the sisters had never been separated for so long before that year, and they missed each other. Simone took Hélène walking with her, but one day Hélène became feverish. Simone was so determined not to be derailed from her plans that she left her shivering sister in a hospice to wait for a bus while she continued on her way. This would not be the only time in her life that her resolution to stick to a plan seemed to overtake her compassion.

At work she did not shy away from teaching what she thought, and she scandalized her pupils and their parents with her teachings on labour, capital and justice.[61] Her mind had grown liberal in many respects, but sexually she still sided with convention: she was scandalized when another teacher made sexual advances because the person wooing her was a *Madame* Tourmelin.[62]

Marseille offered fewer human distractions than Paris so on her teaching days Simone began to write again. She did not publish anything from this period but every plot she penned returned to the same thing: 'the mirage of the Other' and the relationship between honesty, freedom and love. She did not want 'this peculiar fascination to be confounded with a mere commonplace love affair', so she made her protagonists both women to save their relationship from sexual undertones.[63]

She visited Paris when she could: if her visit was brief she only saw Sartre and her sister – but if she stayed longer she enjoyed seeing other friends.[64] When she and Sartre were apart they wrote letters, and when they were together she read Sartre's work in progress and he read hers. He was writing a dissertation on contingency.

By June of 1932 Simone had heard that the following year's teaching post was in Rouen: only an hour from Le Havre, and an hour and a half from Paris. In *The Prime of Life* Beauvoir described herself emerging from this year triumphant: she had felt lonely living at such a distance from the significant others in her life but she now knew that she could rely on herself. In the 1980s she told Bair that her time in Marseille was 'the unhappiest year of my life': she loved Sartre and wanted to be with him, and couldn't tell whether to attribute her heartsickness to missing him or regret.[65]

That summer brought more travels – southern Spain, the Balearics, Spanish Morocco. When Beauvoir moved to Rouen at the beginning of the school year she took a room in the Hôtel La Rochefoucauld, near the train station. She found the trains' whistling reassuring: escape was within easy reach. She made a new friend in Rouen – Collette Audry. Nizan knew Audry from communist circles, and she was a colleague of Simone's at the lycée. Simone introduced herself, and at first Collette found her brusque and bourgeois.[66] Audry was a committed Trotskyite, and Beauvoir thought she was intimidating: she was well dressed, self-assured and always talking politics. Before long they were lunching regularly at the Brasserie Paul.

Audry admired Beauvoir's determination and enjoyed her laughter. She saw Simone's affections as ferocious. Beauvoir's forthrightness could be crushing when she wanted it to be; her reputation for not suffering fools stayed with her throughout her life. When Sartre came to visit Rouen they went out as a trio. Beauvoir had explained the nature of her relationship with Sartre to Audry, saying that it was based on truth rather than passion. Audry described the intense and ebullient conversations they had as a new kind of relationship, the likes of which she had never seen: 'I can't describe what it was like to be present when those two were together. It was so intense that sometimes it made others who saw it sad not to have it.'[67]

Rouen made the continuation of their pact much easier: Beauvoir and Sartre now spent their time between Rouen, Le Havre and Paris, where they took an increasing interest in theatre. Simone Jollivet's lover was a theatre director, Charles Dullin, and they took a keen interest in learning his art. Whatever the city, they populated their conversation with people. In the 1930s they developed the idea of bad faith (*mauvaise foi*): a concept of dishonesty that they thought did greater justice to human experience than Freud's concept of the unconscious.[68]

In *The Prime of Life* Beauvoir credits this concept to herself *and* Sartre. Beauvoir starts by saying that Sartre 'worked out the notion of dishonesty (*bad faith*)'. But she continues using *we*. 'We' set out to expose bad faith. There was a particular teacher, a colleague of Beauvoir's, whose behaviour led Beauvoir to a moment of clarity – 'I've got it,' Beauvoir told Sartre,

'Ginette Lumière is unreal, a sort of *mirage*'. Thenceforth we applied this term to anyone who feigned convictions or feelings that they did not in fact possess: we had discovered, under another name, the idea of 'playing a part'.[69]

The concept of bad faith would become one of the most famous in twentieth-century philosophy. The idea of 'playing a part' was famously illustrated by Sartre's 'waiter' in *Being and Nothingness*. So why does Beauvoir say that *we* discovered it? In the 1930s it is very difficult to determine the extent to which Beauvoir and Sartre were indebted to each other with any certainty. As Hélène's husband, Lionel Roulet, described it, their relationship then was one of 'constant talking': 'through their constant talking, the way they shared everything, they reflected each other so closely that one just could not separate them'.[70]

At this stage Beauvoir and Sartre became increasingly aware of politics, although the more mature Beauvoir would look back on herself and Sartre as 'spiritually proud' and 'politically blind'.[71] Through Audry and others their paths crossed with Troskyites and Communists – but they did not see the proletarian struggle as their struggle.[72] Their struggles were philosophical. They discussed problem of how to understand their rational and physical selves: they wanted to understand freedom, and Sartre saw the body – its physical appetites and habits – as posing a threat to it. Although in 1929 Beauvoir did not challenge Sartre's intolerance of passion and emotion, in the early 1930s she began to object to his position. He still thought his body was a bundle of muscles, detached from his emotions; it was weakness to succumb to tears or to be seasick. But Beauvoir disagreed: she thought eyes and stomachs were subject to their own laws.[73]

They wrote and researched, reading voluminously. One evening, near the turn of 1932–33, Sartre and beauvoir were sitting with Raymond Aron at the Bec de Gaz, on the boulevard du Montparnasse. Aron had been spending a year in Berlin, at the French Institute. He was studying the philosophy of Edmund Husserl, whose work – and the philosophical method for which he is famous, phenomenology – was still relatively unknown in France. As Beauvoir tells the story in *The Prime of Life*, Aron pointed to his cocktail glass and told Sartre they could make philosophy of it. Sartre went pale with excitement when he heard this. It was precisely what he wanted to do: to return philosophy to the everyday, and root it in descriptions of experience.

Sartre and Beauvoir would both employ phenomenological methods, although each with their own twists. In its founder Husserl's hands, phenomenology describes the 'things themselves' – phenomena – by trying to pare back the distractions, habits and presuppositions of everyday life and received opinion. It is a philosophy that recognizes that there is a distance between things as they appear to us and things as they are (or as we think they should be). For Sartre, this was a revelation. But the phenomenological method was not entirely new to Beauvoir: when she was at the Sorbonne she studied with Jean Baruzi, who had encountered phenomenology and whose work paid attention to the *lived experience* of Christian mystics. And Bergson's 'concrete metaphysics', too, used a similar approach.[74] We have already seen that before Beauvoir met Sartre she was thrilled when she read Bergson's praise of the novelist who could untangle the web of the conventional self; she wanted her work to express 'palpable reality'.[75] But neither Bergson nor Baruzi was as fashionable in 1930s Paris as Husserl. At the height of Bergson's fame people would crowd around the doors and windows of his lecture rooms, craning to hear what he said. But so many of them were women that men began to suspect that what Bergson was doing was not, in fact, philosophy. As one 1914 review put it: 'Bergson was nearly suffocated by scent when women attended his lectures; but had Bergson really been a philosopher, no woman would have listened to him.'[76]

In April of 1933 Beauvoir and Sartre spent their Easter vacation in London: they were amused by the English conventions they saw – bowler hats and umbrellas, Hyde Park speakers, taxis, teashops and peculiar fashions. Their differences frequently asserted themselves with greater force when they were travelling – perhaps because they did not have the separate living quarters and lives they had when at home – and in London this was as true as ever. Beauvoir, more fluent in English literature and culture, wanted to trace the steps of Shakespeare and Dickens, visit Kew Gardens and Hampton Court. Sartre wanted to linger in lower-class streets, guessing at the thoughts of their inhabitants.

In letters to Beauvoir Sartre sometimes wrote lovingly that they were 'but one'. But in London their twoness kept reasserting itself: in Oxford Sartre liked the city's streets and parks but he did not appreciate the 'snobbishness of the English undergraduate' and refused to go into the colleges. Beauvoir chided him for his churlishness, and went into the colleges by herself. In London, too, their wishes diverged: how could he not want to go to the British Museum?[77]

Beauvoir continued to find much to admire in Sartre's thoughts; but she did not like all of them. They were sitting in Euston Station when he explained how London fitted into his overall outline of understanding the world. Beauvoir was irritated by his habit of generalizing, and thought his hypothesis was spurious. This was old terrain – they had argued it before – but Beauvoir insisted once again that words could not do justice to reality, and that reality should be faced, warts and all: with all its ambiguity and uncertainty.

Sartre replied that observing and reacting to the world wasn't good enough: that they should try to pin it down in words. Beauvoir thought this was nonsense: London couldn't be understood after a twelve-day visit. He wanted to write their experiences instead of living them, which grated against her own prime allegiance: 'to life, to the here-and-now reality'.[78]

In January 1933 they saw Hitler become Chancellor; by 2 May the German Embassy in Paris was flying a swastika. In here-and-now reality, Beauvoir (and Sartre) watched as Jewish scholars went into voluntary exile and books were burned in Berlin. In her autobiographies Beauvoir would claim that she and Sartre had not yet been converted to political engagement, that their only concern during this period was 'themselves, their relation, their lives, and their books to come'. They had 'little interest in public and political events', instead preferring to retreat into their imaginations ('to keep the world at arm's length', she said).[79] 'At every level,' Beauvoir wrote in *The Prime of Life*, 'we failed to face the weight of reality, priding ourselves on what we called our "radical freedom".[80]

But she was not totally withdrawn from the world: that August Beauvoir was passionately interested in a story that was everywhere in Paris, about the crime and trial of a young working-class woman called Violette Nozière. Nozière had killed her father, after he raped her – although the press rarely put it that way, prompting many women to wonder: why did they call it 'incest'? The debate her trial provoked was so intense that it was compared to the Dreyfus affair.[81]

In Rouen Beauvoir continued to work on her philosophical and literary projects; she began a new novel in 1933 and had private German lessons two or three times per week with a refugee she met through Colette Audry.[82] She modelled her novel on Stendahl, and wanted to tell a story that paralleled her own, showing the stagnation of bourgeois society and the need for individual revolt. Although she was not one of its protagonists, Zaza was written into this story under the name Anne: a paragon of piety and loyalty. It was not the last time Beauvoir would re-write Zaza's life; she was just beginning to discover the cathartic and clarifying effects of writing literature. But she thought the characters in her first novel lacked depth, that they were not true enough to life, so she gave up on it not long after. But she returned to the same themes – and, indeed, characters – in subsequent work.

Although they didn't have much money during this period, Beauvoir and Sartre continued to travel whenever they could: in 1934 they visited Germany, Austria, Czechoslovakia, Alsace, Corsica. They went to Hanover to see Leibniz's house.[83] That year Beauvoir did not try to write anything, making a conscious decision to focus on reading and learning instead. She studied the French Revolution and read Husserl in German.[84] Sartre was working hard on a philosophical treatise on Husserl (*The Transcendence of the Ego*) and still editing the manuscript on contingency but without much success.

During Sartre's year in Berlin, Beauvoir took two weeks off to visit him. Sartre had met a 'contingent' woman there whose company he enjoyed a great deal: Marie Girard.[85] Beauvoir met and liked her; in her memoirs she wrote that although this was the first time that Sartre had taken a serious interest in another woman, she was as comfortable with their arrangement in fact as she was in principle (although she was capable of jealousy and did not underrate it).[86] She continued to feel secure in Sartre's estimation; they were discovering Faulkner and Kafka together, exploring the question of how to write life well. At this stage they both thought that salvation could be achieved through art.[87] Sartre's biographer, by contrast, calls this the 'first crisis' in their relationship.[88]

Personally, Beauvoir felt that her most serious problem was still the one she wrote about in her student diaries: how much of herself to keep and how much to give away. She still didn't know how to reconcile 'her longing for independence' with the feelings that drove her 'so impetuously towards another person'.[89] She made controversial claims in her classes – for example, that 'women were not exclusively intended for bringing children into the world'[90] – and lent her students books their parents found objectionable. Some parents raised formal complaints, accusing her of attacking the sanctity of the family; fortunately the schools inspector took her side.

During this period, while Beauvoir and Sartre were both unknown teachers, Sartre underwent a period of depression. He was disappointed and bored, and later called this time of his life 'the gloomy years'.[91] Sartre felt like a failure: he had not expected to end up a provincial schoolteacher, finding life so monotonous and his genius so unacknowledged. Comparison didn't help much, either. Paul Nizan had already published two books: *Aden, Arabie* in 1931 and *Antoine Bloyé* in 1933. The first was well received and the second, even more so. Even Maheu – who had failed the *agrégation* – was well on his way to a reputable career (he would go on to be Director-General of UNESCO). But Sartre had published nothing; he wasn't famous and was starting to get worried that, 'Whoever is not famous at twenty-eight must renounce glory forever.'[92] He knew it was absurd to think this, but he felt no less agonized by his lack of achievement.

One day in November they were sitting in a seaside café in Le Havre; both of them felt listless, worried that life had sedimented into relentless repetition and that nothing new would ever happen to them. Beauvoir was so upset that evening there were floods of tears and her 'old hankering' for the Absolute – that is, God – made a new appearance.[93] In these moods she felt like human endeavours were vain and reproached Sartre for making an idol out of 'life'. The next day she was still upset by her revelation and got into an argument with him: Sartre thought there was no truth to be found in wine and tears, and explained her mood by the depressing effects of alcohol rather than metaphysics. She thought that alcohol lifted a veil, revealing the ugly face of truth.

Both of them had to confront the disappointing dissonance between their expectations of adult life and its reality. Sartre was starting to lose his hair, and he didn't know what to do with his manuscript on contingency – it was still too dry. Beauvoir had an idea: why not make it a novel? It needed fictional depth and suspense. Sartre loved detective stories, so could he write his philosophical question as a fictional quest? In his third draft, he would set the novel in Le Havre and base the main character, Antoine Roquentin, on himself. Her criticism was detailed and exacting, but that was why he took her advice – 'invariably'.[94]

In the meantime he set it aside to work on his philosophical essay on the *Imagination*. It had been commissioned by Henri Delacroix for an academic publisher, Alcan, and researching the subject had made Sartre wonder about dreams and hallucination. A friend from the

École Normale, Daniel Lagache, had specialized in psychiatry and told Sartre that he would arrange for him to try mescaline if he wanted to have hallucinations for himself.

So in February of 1935 Sartre went into Sainte-Anne's hospital in Paris for a supervised mescaline injection. He was observed for several hours, and unfortunately did not experience the kind of trip he had hoped for: instead of happy hallucinations he was chased by the deformed shapes of the objects in his room, seeing crabs and other crustaceans, which haunted him for weeks to come. When he saw Beauvoir that evening he was not at all his usual self.[95]

Eventually he admitted that he was fighting depression and worried – he was a little prone to catastrophize – that he was on the edge of chronic hallucinatory psychosis. Beauvoir wryly reminded him that according to his own philosophy the mind controlled the body, that his only madness was believing that he was mad.[96]

In March 1935, Hitler enacted a conscription law reintroducing mandatory military service, increasing the army from 100,000 to 555,000 soldiers. France began to panic, Left and Right. They signed a pact with the USSR in which Stalin approved the French national defence policy. With Russia on one side and France on the other, peace seemed secure: Germany had no chance of winning a war, so surely they wouldn't be foolish enough to wage one. In retrospect Beauvoir would write that her 'way of reading the paper remained decidedly frivolous'; at this stage she took avoidance to be the best approach to the problems Hitler posed.[97] Only one of Beauvoir's letters from 1935 was published in *Letters to Sartre*, dated 28 July. She makes no mention of politics, save to say that the only newspaper she can get in the Ardèche is *Le Petit Marseillais*.[98]

That Easter they visited the Italian lakes, and Sartre seemed in good spirits. But when they returned he couldn't find it in himself to pretend that he was normal. He was listless and felt low – low enough that a doctor advised him to avoid being alone. So Beauvoir made every effort to be with him when she could, and to arrange others to be with him when she couldn't.

Writing in 1960 Beauvoir said that she couldn't really understand Sartre's crisis; she began to realize that although their situations looked very similar, they were not as alike as they seemed at first sight:

> To pass the agrégation and have a profession was something he took for granted. But when I stood at the top of that flight of steps in Marseille [in 1931, when she began teaching] I had turned dizzy with sheer delight: it seemed to me that, far from enduring my destiny, I had deliberately chosen it. The career in which Sartre saw his freedom foundering still meant liberation to me.[99]

Beauvoir continued to take deep satisfaction in reading philosophy, which she described as being a 'living reality' for her, and she continued to write. She worked on a collection of short stories, *When Things of the Spirit Come First*. One of them told the story of how Zaza was 'driven to madness and death by the puritan moral code of her environment'.[100] Another is now thought to have inspired Sartre's short story, 'The Childhood of a Leader'.[101] In the period between 1926 and 1934 Beauvoir made seven attempts at writing novels.[102] But she would have to wait over forty years to see any of this material published. And in the meantime, Sartre would at last meet with philosophical and literary success and their relationship would become (or at any rate, *appear* to become) a trio.

7

The Trio that Was a Quartet

In 1934, Beauvoir met the pupil whose role in her life and Sartre's became the subject of much conjecture and condemnation: Olga Kosakiewicz. Her part in their story was memorialized in *The Prime of Life* and fictionalized by both writers in their novels, as Xavière in *She Came to Stay* (by Beauvoir) and as Ivitch *The Road to Freedom* (Sartre). According to Hélène de Beauvoir, Olga resented their fictionalized depictions of her, but Olga and Castor remained friends until late in both their lives.[1]

From the mid-1930s to the early 1940s, Beauvoir had three intimate relationships with much younger women who were formerly her students, and in each case Sartre pursued these women, sometimes at the same time, and sometimes successfully. The French feminist Julia Kristeva called Beauvoir and Sartre 'libertarian terrorists' on the basis of the way they treated their contingent lovers, and it is this period especially that has given Beauvoir a reputation as a sexual libertine, and which features in many *ad feminam* rejections of her work.[2] Given the philosophy she would later go on to write, and the lasting legacies of these liaisons for her personal life and public reputation, it is very difficult not to wonder: what was she thinking?

Collette Audry first told Beauvoir about Olga, who was known at the lycée in Rouen as 'the little Russian'. She was the daughter of a noble Russian father and a French mother. She was strikingly pale and blonde, and wrote less positively striking essays: they were so short that Beauvoir struggled to mark them. So she was surprised when she handed back marks for the end of term exams: Olga had the highest results.

Soon afterwards there was another exam, a preparatory one for the *baccalauréat*. At the end Olga (having written nothing) burst into tears. Simone asked her whether she would like to meet about whatever was troubling her, so they met on a Sunday afternoon and walked by the river, talking about God and Baudelaire. They found each other fascinating: Simone thought the 19-year-old Olga was brilliant and wanted to build up her confidence; Olga found the 27-year-old Simone intriguing: unlike the other teachers at the school, Mlle de Beauvoir was elegant, sophisticated and unconventional.

Olga Kosakiewicz's parents had met in Russia: her mother had travelled there to be a governess for an aristocratic family in Kiev. She ended up marrying one of the sons, who was an engineer and became an officer of the Csar. Olga was born in Kiev on 6 November 1915,[3] and her sister Wanda was born there in 1917. But soon after the Russian Revolution the family joined the hegira of the high-born. They moved around a little, in Greece and elsewhere, before settling in France. So the Kosakiewicz sisters were raised on a parental cocktail of exiled nostalgia and noble superiority.

Olga did very well on her *baccalauréat*, especially in philosophy, and while she was home for the summer she and Beauvoir corresponded briefly before Olga's parents sent her back to Rouen to study medicine. She had no desire to be a doctor, and detested the right-wing nationalism of many of her classmates as much as others' communism. In the autumn and winter of 1934–5 the political situation shifted: the economy was getting worse, with large companies like Salmson laying people off and Citroën going bankrupt. Unemployment was rising, and so was xenophobia.

So Olga became friendly with other immigrants, many of whom were Jewish, and remained friends with Simone, with whom she discussed her day-to-day life and the questions arising from her new friendships. One day she asked what it meant to be a Jew. Simone replied: 'Nothing at all: There are no such things as "Jews"; only human beings.' Beauvoir later realized how deplorably abstract she was about questions like this – claiming that she knew that social categories were powerfully real but she utterly rejected her father's hierarchical ideology, in which Frenchmen and Jews, Men and Women occupied fixed orders.[4]

In the autumn of 1934, Olga and Beauvoir spent more and more time together: each found in the other relief from Rouen's penitentiary provinciality. They met about once a week for lunch, and occasionally for an evening at the opera or a political gathering: as far as Simone was concerned Olga was 'still a child', although she enjoyed her way of seeing the world.[5] She wrote to Sartre that it was 'a world rethought in an absolutely unexpected way by an original little consciousness.'[6]

By the time Olga met Sartre his legend had preceded him, and it had a layer of eccentric allure: the lobsters induced by his mescaline trip gave him a tragic air. 'Sartre had something of the medieval knight about him,' as Olga saw him: 'He was very romantic.'[7] During this period Sartre and Beauvoir usually met in Le Havre – which they preferred to Rouen – but by early 1935 Sartre had begun to visit Rouen, and spend time with Olga, more frequently. At first everyone seemed to benefit from their mutual friendship: Olga enjoyed their attention, Sartre was cheerfully fascinated by her, and Beauvoir was relieved to see Sartre emerge from his anhedonia. But then – from the spring of 1935 to the spring of 1937 – the black mood was supplanted by madness of a different colour: Sartre was obsessed with Olga.

The period that followed was intensely difficult for Beauvoir: she was very fond of Olga, and wanted her to see, and realize, the potential within herself. But through a series of events the relationship became complicated in ways that she had not anticipated. Beauvoir had moved into another hotel, recommended by Olga: Le Petit Mouton. Beauvoir tried to encourage Olga in her studies, and Olga also tried diligently – for a term. But then freedom went to her head and she spent her days and her nights drinking and dancing, reading and talking – but not working. She would go on to fail her medical exams twice in 1935, first in July and again in October.

With the situation with Olga increasingly complex, in the summer of 1935 Simone again set out on her own to walk her way through France, again with nothing better than canvas espadrilles on her feet. She walked on her own while Sartre was on a Norwegian cruise with his parents; then he joined her at Sainte-Cécile-d'Andorge. He could be a good walker too, when he felt like it, but he worried that Beauvoir pushed herself to unhealthy excesses.[8] He may have been overstating the case when he told her that he was allergic to chlorophyll in 1929, but he still preferred old stone to trees. So Beauvoir designed their route to take in towns, villages, abbeys and châteaux. After his mescaline trip Sartre was still suffering unwelcome visits from crustaceans. One day, they were sitting on a bus when he declared that he'd had enough of the lobsters: they had been following him throughout their trip, and he was going to will them away, once and for all. Walking had always been a good way for Beauvoir to exorcise her demons; now Sartre, too, was trying to rid his mind of its unwanted inhabitants.[9]

While Sartre struggled to will away his crustaceans, Beauvoir was thinking about why she hadn't had much success in writing lately. She was determined to get back to it. The only question was: what should 'it' be? It hadn't escaped her notice that Sartre was having more success with philosophical writing than novels at this point. So why didn't she try that? Sartre told her that she grasped philosophy more quickly and precisely than he did, and she acknowledged that his way of reading others tended to involve interpreting them in line with his own hypotheses.[10] In 1946 she would write that Sartre wanted to be dependent on no one for his creativity, that 'no idea ever comes to him from the outside' (apart from through her, of course): 'He reads little, and if by chance he feels like reading, any book can delight him – he asks only that the printed pages act as a support for his imagination and his thoughts, a bit like fortunetellers who look in coffee grounds for a support for their visions.'[11]

As she saw it, Sartre either couldn't get outside his own point of view or didn't see the value in doing so. But in Beauvoir's case the opposite was true: she felt little resistance when she attempted to understand other ways of thinking. She could see weaknesses in different opinions, and spot their potential for development. But when she met a convincing theory it did not leave her unaffected: it 'altered [her] relationship with the world, and coloured all [her] experience.'[12]

Although she hadn't been writing much, she hadn't been idle; she was working on her German – Sartre's, despite his year in Berlin, was terrible – and continued to read philosophy avidly. But she did not yet want to write it. In hindsight she did not remember feeling particularly anxious about not having published anything yet – Stendahl, the French novelist after whom she modelled *When Things of the Spirit Come First*, didn't even start writing until he was 40.[13]

Back in Rouen, it was clear that Olga was not going to make a success of medicine. Her parents wanted to send her to a boarding school in Caen: but all three of the 'trio' wanted to avoid that. The question was: what could she do well? She had done well in philosophy, so Sartre made a suggestion to Beauvoir which she found absolutely brilliant. They had enough money, between their two salaries, to pay for a room for Olga, and Sartre was running an honours course to prepare students for teaching diplomas. Beauvoir wrote to Olga's parents and arranged a meeting. They agreed to her proposal: Olga would study under her supervision. So Sartre and Beauvoir made a timetable of lessons, set her reading lists and essays, and rented her a room in the Petit Mouton, near Beauvoir's.

They also made a timetable of who would see whom when: they each wanted some time tête-à-tête, but they also wanted what they called 'plenary sessions' when the three of them were all together. In hindsight Beauvoir wrote that she never felt at ease in the trio with Olga. She frequently found herself in the middle of a relationship that was built on unstable foundations. Their efforts to teach her came to little fruition, academically: Olga did read when she felt so inclined, but she did not work unless she wanted to, and she rarely wanted to. Initially Sartre and Beauvoir thought they were consulting, and acting in, her interest, but Beauvoir later acknowledged that their relationship was not built on mutual equality: Sartre and Beauvoir 'annexed her' to themselves.[14] Both of them were starting to feel old and uninteresting: they lived vicariously through her youth and carelessness.

But Beauvoir did care about Olga very deeply: 'There are at the present time only two people in the world who count in my life,' she wrote to her, 'and you are one of them.'[15] Soon Olga's feelings towards Beauvoir 'reached a burning intensity'.[16] Olga's physical relationship with Beauvoir provoked several kinds of frustration for Sartre: throughout the two years of his obsession Olga wouldn't sleep with him.

Olga was the first of their 'contingent' loves that she and Sartre 'shared', but they did not share her sexually. Even so – and despite his disdain for, and freedom to overcome, emotion – Sartre grew very jealous.[17] His behaviour became increasingly erratic and strange.

More unsettling, from Beauvoir's point of view, was the undeniable fact that he experienced feelings for Olga that he had never had with her. Towards the end of Sartre's two-year obsession, Beauvoir was in an agony that went 'beyond jealousy', in her words, making her question whether her happiness was built on 'a gigantic lie'.[18]

But Olga was only part of the story. In Le Havre, one of Sartre's favourite students was a charming man called Jacques-Laurent Bost. He was the youngest of ten children, exactly six months younger than Olga. He came from a Protestant family and had an elder brother who worked as a reader for the prestigious Paris publisher, Gallimard. He was tall, with full lips and jet-black hair that fell into green eyes: and although she did write that she 'felt drawn towards him' Beauvoir said little about their relationship in her memoirs.[19] In fact, he was one of her most significant omissions – hidden for her whole life. It was only when their correspondence was published in French in 2004 (it is still unpublished in English) that their passionate, ten-year-long affair became public. When Olga betrayed Sartre (so it seemed to him) by sleeping with Bost, Sartre salved his wounded ego by seducing her sister, Wanda. Beauvoir thought Olga's decision to end the trio was the epitome of sanity, but Sartre was floored. To make matters worse, Gallimard rejected his novel.

For Beauvoir, the trio wreaked havoc with her daily life, but it also writ large the questions she had been pondering since the late 1920s. The 19-year-old Simone had written in her diary that she wanted to spell out *her* philosophical ideas on 'the opposition of self and other'. Ten years on, her relationships with Olga and Sartre made her face this problem in life in a new way. Although Olga enjoyed the attentions of both Sartre and Beauvoir, and stayed friendly with them until the 1970s, she knew she was playing a precarious part. She was moody and taciturn during this period, prompting Beauvoir to reflect that, 'When she stood apart from me she looked at me with alien eyes, and

I was transformed into an *object* that might be either an idol or an enemy.'[20]

Beauvoir's feelings about the relationship oscillated. In the public account of the trio in Beauvoir's autobiography, she wrote that the trio made her realize – yet again – that a harmonious relationship between two people should never be taken as given; it requires continuous work.[21] As early as 1927 she had reached the conclusion that love was not something that was established once and for all, but rather had to be 'unceasingly created in a perpetually renewed youth'.[22] But though she was honing her views about freedom, action and love, she had not fully realized the harm the 'essential' pair could inflict on their 'contingent' others.

Olga rarely gave interviews, but retrospectively she likened her young self – and Bost and Wanda – to mesmerized snakes: 'we did what they wanted because no matter what, we were so thrilled by their attention, so privileged to have it'.[23] Even before fame amplified their allure, Beauvoir and Sartre were a charismatic and captivating duo. But we do not have any evidence from this period that Beauvoir considered the unequal power relations between them a source of concern. Young or old, rich or penniless, their contingent lovers were free to choose their actions for themselves – weren't they?

That summer Sartre and Beauvoir travelled in Italy and Greece; Beauvoir was relieved to be just the two of them. There was also good news to celebrate: after the holidays she was finally moving back to Paris! She had won a post at the Lycée Molière. But when they returned in September they found politics harder to ignore: they were consumed by the Spanish Civil War. Their friendship with Fernando Gerassi had warmed their hearts to Spain, and after their travels they were whole-hearted hispanophiles. The Popular Front prime minister Leon Blum had decided that France would not intervene in the war, which Beauvoir found disgusting: Hitler and Mussolini were providing the rebels with men and material, but France declined to provide the Spanish Republic with arms, failing to honour its trade agreement.[24] Eventually Fernando couldn't bear to spectate from Paris so travelled to Spain to fight. Sartre and Beauvoir, with Stépha and other friends, saw him off at the station.

Once back in Paris Beauvoir rented a hotel room in the Royal Bretagne on the rue de la Gaîté. Although Sartre wouldn't be posted in Paris for another year, Bost was reading for his teacher's diploma at the Sorbonne and Hélène was still in the capital so she was happy to be near them again. Olga moved to Paris, too, to pursue acting with the help of Sartre's and Beauvoir's connections.

During the late 1930s Sartre went on a campaign of serial seduction, which has been fuel to the mythological fire of their pact. As the story goes, Beauvoir helped Sartre revise his novel, *Melancholia* (it would be published as *Nausea* in 1938), working for hours at the Dôme or La Rotonde annotating Sartre's manuscripts. She refined his literature while he gratified his *libido*. Sartre told everyone that *Nausea* was only publishable because of Beauvoir's extensive work on it. But the texts with her comments were lost: Sartre liked to neatly recopy the versions of his manuscripts that were to be preserved for posterity, and Beauvoir claimed to have thrown the annotated copies away.[25]

In the spring of 1937 Beauvoir had been working hard and resting little; she ran herself down and never felt she had an opportunity to replace her reserves. One evening in Montparnasse she was chatting with Bost in Le Sélect when she started to shiver.[26] She generally disregarded her body when it was being inconvenient, but this was too overpowering to ignore: she went home immediately, slept a feverish night, and stayed in bed the whole of the following day. By the end of the day, however, she felt that spending an entire day in bed was excessively lazy. So when Sartre arrived from Laon that night, they concluded that she was well enough to go out. She soldiered through getting dressed and out the door, but arrived at the party desperate to find somewhere to lay down again. Her friends were worried – was it serious? She protested at their concern but eventually Sartre took her home and called a doctor. Shortly afterwards she was hospitalized with serious pulmonary edema. She couldn't believe that this was happening to *her*; it was uncomfortable to realize that she, too, could be a statistic. She lay on the bed listening to the doctors talking about her body like an object, a thing; the realization that they were discussing *her* left her feeling alienated and insecure.

When she recovered she had more than health to be grateful for. Sartre was moving back to Paris – they would finally live in the same place again! – and he had booked them both rooms in the Hôtel Mistral, hers on the floor below his, so they could have 'all the advantages of a shared life without any of its inconveniences'.[27] The new hotel was in Montparnasse near all of their favourite cafés – La Rotonde, Le Dôme, La Coupole and Le Sélect. In May 1937 Sartre's literary fortunes, too, started looking up: his novel about contingency had finally been accepted.

That summer Beauvoir and Sartre travelled to Greece with Bost. They slept on rooftops and set off on long walks, tortured by their underestimation of the blazing sun. Sometimes Bost and Beauvoir went off alone, swimming together, while Sartre sat in a café working or writing to Wanda.

When the new school year started Beauvoir still wanted to write but didn't know what to write next. Sartre encouraged her to put *herself* in her books; it was only after he styled Roquentin after himself that *Nausea* had been accepted. *When Things of the Spirit Come First* was good, he said, but she was much more interesting than the Renées and Lisas she wrote about: why not write from her own life?

Her first reaction was that it made her feel too vulnerable to write from her own experience. Although she regularly chronicled her life for the consumption of Sartre and other correspondents in letters, it was quite another matter to publish it for all to see. But she kept returning to one of the philosophical problems she had been perplexed by since her teens: the consciousness of other people. She read a story in the news about a man who murdered his taxi driver because he was embarrassed that he didn't have enough money to pay his fare. She wondered: How could humans be so monstrously motivated by shame? Why did they sometimes live for others – attempting to appear a certain way in another's mind rather than living for the sake of one's own?

She thought about writing a fictional Simone Weil character as an anti-Beauvoirian protagonist: but then Sartre suggested that Olga would make a better juxtaposition.[28] Beauvoir needed no convincing: Olga was perfect. In September 1937 Beauvoir wrote to Sartre from Alsace, where she was on holiday with Olga – words which, quoted out of context, could lead to the wrong conclusions: 'K. is charming, perfectly idyllic with me, entranced by everything, and best of all much lustier than might have been thought, quite Gallic even.' But her celebrated lust was not sexual: Beauvoir goes on to say that Olga wasn't put off by rain or wind, and would walk for five, six, or even seven hours a day.[29]

In 1938 Sartre's *Nausea* was finally published – it was dedicated 'To the Beaver'. Soon afterwards praise rained in for Sartre, who was hailed as a rising star; *Les Nouvelles Littéraires* called it 'one of the distinctive works of our time'. When his collection of short stories *The Wall* came out soon after, André Gide wrote, 'Who is this new Jean-Paul? It seems to me we can expect a lot from him.'[30] But Beauvoir's *When Things of the Spirit Come First* was rejected twice – first by Gallimard, then by Grasset.[31] When Henry Müller wrote her rejection he commented that her portrayal of stifled bourgeois women was good, but that other people were writing about the same problems and she didn't resolve them: 'You are content to describe a disintegrating world, and then to abandon your readers on the very threshold of the new order, without giving any precise indication of what its benefits will be.'[32]

Beauvoir wasn't giving up – a decade later she would write a manifesto for the 'new order', *The Second Sex*. But while Sartre won the admiration of the Paris literati, Beauvoir won more and more spite from her father. Georges de Beauvoir mocked her unpublished writing and told her that she would never amount to being more than 'a worm's whore'.[33]

At work Beauvoir was very differently received. Her pupils at the Lycée Molière, a girls' school in the 16th arrondissement, remembered her making quite an impression. She dressed stylishly, in silk blouses and make-up, and had such good command of her subject that she always lectured without notes.[34] She taught her students Descartes, Husserl and Bergson. She discussed Freud only to reject him, preferring the epicureans, stoics and Kant.[35]

One of her students in the 1937–38 baccalaureate year, Bianca Bienenfeld, was awestruck by her – she wrote Beauvoir a letter saying that she enjoyed her philosophy classes and wanted to study the subject further at university. Would she be willing to meet her to discuss it?

The time and date were fixed: they met in Montparnasse. Bienenfeld was 17 at the time, a Jewish girl whose parents had moved to France in the disappointed hope that they would suffer less anti-Semitism there than they had experienced in Poland. Her father had been a doctor; the family valued culture and Beauvoir appreciated Bianca's intelligence and charm. She respected her a great deal, she told Bost; sometimes she forgot that she was talking to a young girl.[36]

Before long they were spending Sundays together, and Bienenfeld was running to the Metro station at Passy each week, excited to see her. Beauvoir explained her relationship with Sartre to Bianca: that they loved each other but wanted to preserve their freedom so didn't marry and had other lovers. Bianca was fascinated by her stories of the Kosakiewicz sisters, and felt slightly indignant that Beauvoir indulged them: from her point of view they were all laziness and caprice, and didn't deserve her support or so much of the time that Beauvoir could have spent with Bianca.[37] By the end of that June, Bianca would later write, she wanted to *be* Beauvoir.[38]

After the school year finished they were no longer student and pupil. They went on a backpacking trip in the Morvan, hiking long distances in mountainous terrain. At the end of the day they shared a room – and a bed – in a pension. It was during this trip, Bianca wrote, that their relationship consensually became physical.[39] Beauvoir later denied that she had ever had sex with women:[40] but her letters are explicit that she was sexually intimate with them. For a start, in a letter to Sartre dated 22 July Beauvoir wrote that she'd had letters from Bianca, 'full of passion'.

Bianca Bienenfeld was born in Poland in April of 1921, making her 17 years old that summer.[41] Her age is shocking by today's standards, but it was above the age of consent at the time – and there is no evidence that Beauvoir had concerns, in 1938, about the age gap between them or the fact that her role as Bianca's former teacher involved dynamics of trust and power that could be compromised in damaging ways by their relationship becoming sexual. After Beauvoir's death, Bianca painted Beauvoir as a predator who selected 'ripe young flesh from among her female students' to 'have a taste for herself before palming them off' on Sartre.[42] Bianca claimed that this 'pattern' explained what happened to her, and to Olga – although she seems not to have known that Olga refused Sartre's sexual advances.

It's impossible to piece together a complete picture of what happened – because some letters and diaries haven't survived for posterity, because of the upheavals of wartime, and because Bianca's

account of what happened was written over fifty years after the event
in the wake of a 'liberating anger' that followed the release of her name
to the public. Throughout her life, Beauvoir kept her vow not to
publish Bianca's identity. But when Deirdre Bair released her biography
of Beauvoir in English in 1990, she broke Beauvoir's confidence,
publishing both Bianca's maiden and married names. The French 'Law
of Private Life' prohibited the inclusion of potentially defamatory
information about people's private lives but American law did not.
So eventually news of Bianca's unwanted fame reached her from
across the Atlantic, prompting her to publish her own book in 1993.[43]
She was frank about her mixed motives for writing, and she was
also frank that it was only when Sartre entered the picture that 'the
drama' began.[44]

Nevertheless Bianca also described Beauvoir as a 'woman I had
loved all my life', and said explicitly that wounds she suffered were
not caused entirely by Beauvoir's behaviour but, as we shall see, by
a series of other betrayals. For a start, 'Before I met Sartre,' Bianca
wrote, 'Simone de Beauvoir and I shared only a passionate friendship.
As soon as he entered the emotional picture, everything became
much more difficult and much more complicated.'[45] Whatever
Bianca's reasons for waiting to publish her own account, it is clear that
her relationship with Beauvoir was complex and left her with very
strong – and very mixed – feelings.

The same July that Beauvoir and Bianca became intimate, Beauvoir
went for another hiking trip, this time in the mountains of Haute-
Savoie with Bost. Sartre took her to the station to say goodbye – he
was staying in Paris to work on his short stories and see Wanda. Sartre
had been pursuing Wanda for over a year by this point but she was
still not interested. Wanda found Sartre physically repulsive, and told
him he needed to improve his diet. Sartre was used to being rebuffed,
and took her disgust as a challenge to overcome. He found her

unintelligent – he likened her mind to a dragonfly's – but even so he was determined to succeed.

The day after Beauvoir left, Sartre wrote that he didn't like saying goodbye to her. He was imagining her on grey mountaintops: 'you'd still be with me right now, full of good little smiles, if you didn't have that strange mania for gobbling up kilometres'.[46] (In writing his tone can seem condescending but 'little' was also one of her favourite epistolary adjectives for him too.) When Beauvoir reached Annecy, Bost was waiting for her at the station, 'tanned and looking very nice in his yellow pullover'.[47] Bost was a keen walker himself – although even he struggled to cover the vast distances Beauvoir expected. They hiked all day and enjoyed hearty meals and local wine by night. They slept in tents or inns, depending on the weather. One night, five days in to their holiday, it was raining so they slept in a barn in Tignes. Beauvoir wrote to Sartre a few days later, describing the evening in detail:

> It was I who propositioned him, of course. Both of us had been wanting it: [...] In the end I laughed foolishly and looked at him, so he said: 'Why are you laughing?' and I said: 'I'm trying to picture your face if I suggested that you sleep with me' and he said: 'I was thinking that you were thinking that I wanted to kiss you but didn't dare.' After that we floundered on for another quarter of an hour before he made up his mind to kiss me. He was tremendously astonished when I told him I'd always felt incredible tenderness towards him, and he ended up telling me yesterday evening that he had loved me for a long time.[48]

Beauvoir and Sartre met in Marseille the following weekend to travel to Tangiers. Sartre asked her whether she had considered how complicated her life would be if she continued this affair; they both knew that Olga would object to her sleeping with Bost. Beauvoir and Olga were close friends – wasn't she being 'ignoble'?

Beauvoir wasn't so sure. Olga wasn't really the faithful type. And Beauvoir wanted Bost and Bost wanted her back: for now, she tried to decide not to let herself regret it. After she left to meet Sartre in July 1938 Bost completed more hikes in the Alps, but they had lost their appeal without her: he wrote that at least three times a day he had a strong desire to see her and his head incessantly replayed their final five days together.[49] His letters are equally full of tenderness and anticipation:[50] 'I love you *wonderfully* [formidablement], I would like you to know this and to feel it strongly, and for this to give you pleasure. I so love writing to you. I can imagine your face while I'm writing, and I imagine that I must have an idiot smile covering mine.'[51]

Bost's prose is not the prose of a Sartre or an Algren. But Beauvoir's letters to him reveal a passionate side of her that was never reciprocated by Sartre. Beauvoir felt no need to hide the bodily aspect of her passion for Bost: her letters to him express her desire to kiss his cheeks, his eyelashes, his chapped lips.[52] While Beauvoir toured Morocco with Sartre – taking in Tangiers, Casablanca, Marrakech, Fez, Ksar el Souk, Meknès – she heard love songs on the radio and had to fight back tears for Bost. On 22 August she wrote from Ksar el Souk just before going to bed. 'I have a terrible need to see you,' she wrote, 'my love, my love, how I wish to have you against me.'[53]

Figure 5 *Drawing by Jacques Laurent-Bost, representing Simone de Beauvoir walking him to his ruin, 1938.*

Bost went into their relationship with his eyes open: he was still courting Olga, whom he eventually married, and in addition to Sartre (whom Bost admired, and to whom he sent jocular postscripts in his letters to Beauvoir) he knew about Beauvoir's relationship with Bianca Bienenfeld. Sometimes, when Beauvoir was travelling and letters were more sure to reach Sartre, she asked Bost to write to Sartre to arrange his next meeting with her.[54]

In her memoirs Beauvoir deliberately redacted Bost, hiding her love for him and downplaying her appreciation of and respect for his friendship. According to Sylvie Le Bon de Beauvoir, this erasure represents the most significant thing Beauvoir left unsaid (although later there would be other contenders for this honour). Bost was a close and faithful friend from 1936 until her death in 1986, and for a long time he was much more.[55] But they decided not to tell Olga, and the secret was concealed until she died in 1983.

As early as 1939 Beauvoir's diaries show that her conscience was uneasy about this, and she recorded its weight more heavily there than in her letters to Sartre: a year into the affair with Bost, after a conversation with Olga, she wrote to Sartre: 'I don't feel any remorse as far as she's concerned, I do have a sense of superficiality and guile.'[56] At the end of August 1938 she and Bost arranged the next rendez vous: she wanted to be with him day and night. But should they meet in Le Havre, where his family was, or would Rouen be better? Paris was lovely, Simone said, but she was afraid they would run into Olga.

Even in 1938 Beauvoir felt ill at ease: she had arranged to spend ten days with Olga in September. She found it extremely unsettling to see Bost described from Olga's point of view, and suffered when she imagined them together.

I know that you don't forget me, but I feel separated from you, my love, and there are moments where I don't cope with it well. [...]

Write me, quickly, quickly, write long letters – tell me that we will pass long days together alone, that we will be happy like we were at Annecy. Tell me that your love for me is strong, my love – because I love you passionately.[57]

Bost's letters reassured her in no uncertain terms. He too sometimes felt weighed down when he thought of Olga, but he told Beauvoir that his feelings didn't last because 'I love you too much.' Before they were lovers they were friends, and he felt their love was built on such a solid foundation that they could not easily be separated.[58] It was all well and good that Bost loved her, but Beauvoir found her time with Olga difficult: Olga wrote to Bost daily and spoke of him frequently; Beauvoir tried not to write at first but then couldn't resist putting pen to paper, writing in quiet moments when Olga was not with her. She couldn't sleep for thinking about him, and sometimes tears filled her eyes when she imagined their reunion.[59]

They met on 26 September 1938. Events were such that they stayed in Paris: by the 28th war looked inevitable but the Treaty of Munich on the 30th seemed to assure peace. For a month Beauvoir and Bost enjoyed normal life in Paris, seeing each other daily. But on 3 November Bost had to rejoin his station at Amiens. Military service lasted two years; for Bost, ten months later, it would be active duty.

Beauvoir's concealed relationships with Bost, Olga and Bianca reveal not only her sexual dissatisfaction with Sartre but also a disturbing willingness to deceive others – in particular, other women. In the case of Bost, her relationship with him revealed her complicity in the life-long deception of a woman she called her friend. In a 1948 letter Beauvoir justified her behaviour by saying that Olga was 'the kind of girl who asks too much from everybody, lying to everybody, so everybody had to lie to her.'[60]

Whatever Olga's character, there is no doubt that Beauvoir's behaviour was deceptive and – for many readers, on many grounds – deeply problematic. While Beauvoir was in love with Bost and deceiving Olga she also continued a relationship with Bianca Bienenfeld. During the summer of 1938 – while Beauvoir was in Morocco and Bost was in France – she told Bost in a letter that Bianca's mother had read one of Simone's more passionate letters to her daughter, which had led to drama – she still wasn't sure how it was going to play out.[61] Madame Bienenfeld accused Beauvoir of being 'an old maid with unusual morals'.[62] But that did not put an end to the women's affair: in November 1938 Bianca told Simone she would never love anyone as much as she loved her.[63] Bianca was 18 now, studying philosophy at the Sorbonne, and they saw each other several times a week. But Beauvoir told her little about herself – and nothing at all about her relationship with Bost.[64]

That Christmas, Beauvoir introduced Bianca to Sartre. They went skiing in Mégève, and Bianca was staying nearby at Mont d'Arbois, so the three of them took to the slopes and talked philosophy. When they returned to Paris in January 1939 Sartre turned his attentions to Bianca. She found this flattering: many of her closest friends at the Sorbonne had been Sartre's pupils, and between their esteem, Simone's, and the recent reviews of *The Wall* that praised him as brilliant and innovative, she was starstruck.

Bianca wrote in her memoirs that, 'Just as a waiter plays the role of a waiter, Sartre played to perfection the role of a man in love.'[65] He was ugly, but his words were so beautiful they blinded her to her own repulsion. He asked her if she might be able to love him; Bienenfeld said that it was possible – but what about Beauvoir? She cared about her deeply and didn't want to hurt her. Sartre replied that the Beaver wouldn't mind. Sartre and Bienenfeld discussed consummating their relationship, and chose a day. It would be her first time with a man; she was full of anticipation. But as they walked to the Hôtel Mistral she shuddered inside: Sartre told her that housekeeping would be in for a surprise since he had slept with another virgin just the day before.

Sartre's actions were deeply unsettling, too – and not only where Bianca was concerned. He began another trio of his own, courting Wanda and sleeping with Bianca, and Beauvoir began to find their relationships with Bianca troubling. She wrote to Bost that the threesome's café conversations had become awkward, and that Bienenfeld did not know how to conduct herself with multiple lovers in the same place. 'She does not realize that effusions of tenderness work with two but not with three; she took our hands, squeezed them, let them go, took them again, taking care to share herself equally.'[66] Eventually Bianca told Beauvoir that she felt love for Sartre, but not passion; she wondered if Beauvoir could explain this to him?

Meanwhile, Bost had to perform the delicate balancing act of sharing himself between Olga and Beauvoir. Beauvoir's letters are full of impatience to see him, to hold him again – when he was on leave it was agony not to meet him at the station and share his first moments in Paris. Consequently Bost did not always tell her his plans in full.

Beauvoir still enjoyed spending time with Olga, but she was increasingly uncomfortable about the place of the Kosakiewicz sisters in their lives. Her discomfort has often been interpreted as jealousy or resentment of their place in Sartre's life – and she certainly was protective of her time with him – but she was also frustrated with Sartre for making matters so convoluted. He had begun to support Wanda financially, moving her to Paris and arranging for her to take painting lessons and share Hélène's studio space. Wanda was suspicious of Beauvoir, and challenged Sartre directly on the nature of their relationship. They were just friends, Sartre said.

By May 1939 Beauvoir found the situation 'grimy'. She was deceiving Olga. Wanda hated her. She wrote to Bost saying it was beginning to make her tremble with rage: it wasn't entirely anyone's fault, she thought, but it would have been easier if Sartre wasn't lying to Wanda. And she didn't like the feeling of being dissected by the consciousnesses of the two Kosakiewiczs. But even so, she said, it raised an interesting philosophical problem: is someone else's experience as real as your own?[67] She had been thinking about it for a long time, she wrote to him, because it was the subject of her novel. Every time she heard Olga speak about Bost it bothered her to think that in Olga's consciousness of Bost he had no link to Beauvoir.

Bost's reply rebuked her: he found it outrageous that she 'protested against the judgements and conversations that may be made about you and Sartre, and also about me, Wanda, and [Olga]. I think you must strike them as shady and dubious to the highest degree, and that is just right because they are so deceived in all senses.' He didn't want to discuss the matter further by letter, but he warned her that if she was withering – which she was, often enough to have a reputation for it – he wasn't backing down. She was lovely when he agreed with her, he wrote candidly, but this time he did not.[68]

Beauvoir didn't want a fight: she wrote back that she thought his judgement was impartial and true, and he had been honest with her. But a week later he reprimanded her treatment of others again. This time the other in question was Bianca, whom she was still sleeping with despite the fact that Sartre's waxing affections made hers wane. Beauvoir and Bianca had spent an afternoon together: a champagne lunch at La Coupole, coffee at the Flore, and then back to the Mistral to Simone's room for privacy. Beauvoir wrote: 'I think in the end that I'm not a homosexual since sensually I feel almost nothing, but it was charming and I love being in bed in the afternoon on a sunny day.'[69]

Bost jumped in the air when he read this sentence. He found the word 'charming' 'appallingly obscene'. It made him feel strange, he said. Not because she spoke so lightly of Bianca or treated her as an object – which he noted – but that word, *charming*, drew a blush.[70] He had been feeling sick with guilt about Olga, and in the same 'charming' letter Simone had confessed to feeling some remorse – though not regret. Olga was sincere with him, he said: but he was not sincere with her.

When Beauvoir read this, she felt numb for hours. She held herself together for a night out with Olga but when she got home she wept and wept. When she replied to Bost she told him his letter produced a 'pathological' anxiety, and she woke up to a morbid despair. She went to lunch with her mother, and again had to fight back welling tears.

So she decided to explain her side of the story to Bost in no uncertain terms: 'I have only *one* sensual life, and that is with you.' She didn't want him to be an episode of her life: she wanted him to be in all of it. That was not the case for Bianca nor, sexually speaking, for Sartre. 'With Sartre, too, I have physical relations,' she explained, 'but very little, and it mostly out of tenderness and – I'm not sure how to say this – I don't feel that engaged because he is not that engaged in it himself.'[71] By this point in their relationship she had explained this to Sartre several times. Now she was explaining it to Bost because she wanted him to know how seriously she took their relationship: he *was* the lover of her life.

Bost's reply didn't survive – but the relationship did.

Over that summer Beauvoir went walking in Jura, visited Geneva, and covered vast distances on foot in Provence. In July the French government passed the 'Code de la famille', a piece of pro-natalist legislation that offered incentives to mothers who stayed home with their children and banned the sale of contraceptives. The Napoleonic Code, established in 1804, had given authority to men – as husbands and fathers – over women. This Civil Code was in effect until the 1960s, when Beauvoir would be one of the women who dismantled it.

In August, Bost had a long leave, so he, Beauvoir and Sartre met in Marseilles where they stayed in the villa of a friend at Juan-les-Pins, near Antibes. Bost thought war was inevitable now, but Sartre was one of the last people to think it was not.

Bost's relationship with Olga was going well now; she had become more confident since, at Beauvoir's suggestion, taking acting workshops with Charles Dullin, and she had also become more committed to Bost. Things were getting more serious, Bost wrote, so it would be terrible if she found out: would Beauvoir burn his letters to her? He was thinking of doing the same. (Neither of them did.) After Bost left Juan-les-Pins, Beauvoir was tearful once again: with war coming she might lose both Bost and Sartre. War or no war, she wasn't at peace about Bianca and the Kosakiewicz sisters. Beauvoir found the end of the 1930s one of the lowest times of her life – war was coming, and her relationships with Sartre, Olga, Bianca and Bost left her feeling trapped.[72]

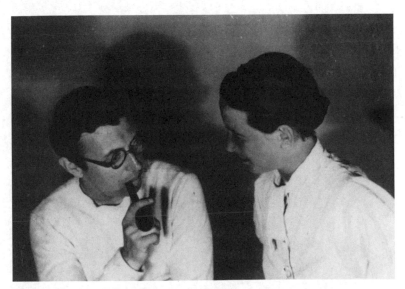

Figure 6 *Beauvoir and Sartre at Juan-les-Pins, August 1939.*

8

War Within, War Without

Bost was called to active service on 31 August 1939. On 1 September Germany invaded Poland. Paris was papered in posters mobilizing all fit men between the ages of 18 and 40, so Sartre went to the Mistral to pack. He wrote farewell letters to Bianca and Wanda but spent his final evening with Beauvoir: they had dinner and tried to sleep before the alarm went off at 3 a.m. She walked him to the Dôme for coffee before setting out for the Gare de l'Est. Sartre told Beauvoir he wouldn't be in danger at Nancy. He was in the meteorological corps so it would be just like it was before Paris, they would write to each other – please could she send him books? They embraced and parted; his retreating figure was blurred by her tears.

On 2 September Beauvoir had a 'breakdown' – the first of several: fear of Bost dying was her constant companion. Jacques-Laurent Bost went into service with ideas typical of the interwar Left. The generation whose thought shaped his had fought in the trenches and advocated unconditional pacifism: Alain, Giono, Romain Rolland, Gide. He could have been fast-tracked into leadership but he wasn't keen on this kind of entitled self-assertion; he felt it would compromise his commitments not to join the herd of cannon fodder. Beauvoir took to

writing a diary again, partly to record reality and partly to escape it –
'when one is writing, one doesn't think'.[1]

On 3 September 1939 Britain and France declared war on Germany.
In 1936 Beauvoir's sister Hélène had met one of Sartre's students from
Le Havre, Lionel de Roulet. He had heard rumours about 'the woman
philosopher with the ferocious intellect',[2] but it was Hélène who
captured his heart – by 1938 they were in love, the most constant of all
the couples in 'the family', as Sartre and Beauvoir had started to call
their circle. On the day war was declared, Simone offered Hélène the
funds to travel to Portugal to be with Lionel; she gratefully accepted
them and left.

The advent of war and so many significant departures severely
disrupted Simone's equilibrium; even before the war she had been
suffering from confusion and depression, but now she sank further
into both. By 4 September she detected a new diurnal rhythm: mornings
were liveable, but evenings brought breakdowns. By the 5th she was
having 'wild panic attacks'. Her sleep was fragmented by air raid sirens;
once, after being jolted awake by explosions and sirens she struggled to
find her clothes in the dark before evacuating the building; when she
went back to bed she decided it was easier just to sleep in them.[3]

Over the days that followed Paris was transformed: the men had
been deployed and many civilians fled. Her students brought gas
masks to their classrooms. But for the first eight months – the 'Phony
War' – it was neither war nor peace. Day after day, Beauvoir's diaries
show desperation at the thought that Bost or Sartre might die. Each
passing hour seemed to drain her of hope, and her reading material
hardly helped – she wanted to understand what it meant to be at war,
so she read Alain and Gide. She had to skip pages in Gide's 1914
journals – reading scenes from the trenches was 'needless torture'.[4]

Gradually, Beauvoir started to receive letters and to see new light in
herself: on days when she had news from Bost or Sartre she could feel

happiness, even joy. But then she felt guilty. (After all, Gide said, 'when one is safe oneself and with all one's family safe, it is a bit too easy to laugh and almost unseemly'.[5]) In retrospect, both Sartre and Beauvoir claimed that the war made them recognize the force of history; after the war, they said, their previous disinterest in politics – and their bystander mentalities – were no longer sustainable. But it did not, immediately, lead them to reform their personal lives. On 14 September Olga told Beauvoir that if Bost died it would be tragic, yes – but that 'deep down' it would not affect her. That, Beauvoir said, 'confirmed my resolution never to give up Bost because of her'. Olga didn't bother to arrange to have her mail forwarded when she moved, which meant going weeks without news from Bost – Beauvoir could not comprehend her indifference.[6]

Bianca, by contrast, wasn't quite indifferent enough for Beauvoir's liking. The Bienenfeld family had fled Paris, and on 16 September Beauvoir received a letter from Bianca reproaching her for not going to visit. Tension was emerging in their relationship: with Sartre gone Bianca wanted to occupy an even more central place in Beauvoir's life, but Beauvoir found Bianca increasingly entitled and controlling. In Paris she was just beginning to rediscover the happiness of her own solitude, and it bothered her that Bianca didn't respect her freedom.[7]

Even so, on 20 September she went to visit Bianca in Quimper. When Beauvoir arrived Bianca was waiting on the platform with tears in her eyes. They went for a coffee, and Bianca told Beauvoir that her mother was upset that Beauvoir had come – she had stolen one of Bianca's letters and threatened to send it to the minister of education. ('I didn't believe any of it and didn't get worked up about it,' Beauvoir wrote in her diary.[8]) They went for a long walk together, that day and the next. And then they had 'Embraces'. But Beauvoir didn't enjoy them: she felt a kind of 'blockage'.[9]

In addition to the dawning realization that they were part of history, absence made Sartre recognize just how much Beauvoir meant to him. He wrote that one thing would not change, no matter what. No matter what he became, he told Beauvoir, 'I will become it with you.' He thanked the war for showing him that they were *one*:

> my love, you are not 'one thing in my life' – not even the most important – because my life no longer belongs to me, because I don't even regret it, and because you are always *me*. You are so much more, it is you who permit me to foresee any future and realize any life at all. We cannot be any more at one than we are now.[10]

In hindsight, we know that Sartre could praise the unique irreplaceability of several women at once, which makes it hard to take his epistolary avowals very seriously. But even in his diaries Beauvoir took on a singular significance. In the days preceding 14 October, the ten-year anniversary of their 'morganatic marriage', Sartre reflected about how much he owed her: without her the world would be 'a desert'. He hadn't had letters from her for three days, and the lack of them made him realize the extent to which his courage to face this situation came 'from the certitude of being understood, supported, and approved by the Beaver'. Without that, he said, 'everything would fall apart'.[11]

They didn't know when they would next see each other; he wasn't even allowed to tell her where he was. As a lycée teacher he still drew his salary while in service so he had the means to keep Olga and Wanda in Paris: they would not have to leave or get jobs. With the men away Beauvoir spent more time with 'the Kosaks' as Sartre called the sisters: they moved together into a new hotel, the Hotel du Danemark, on the rue Vavin. But Beauvoir struggled with resentment: she was working hard, earning her own way through life. The sisters, whom she and Sartre supported (Beauvoir paid for the artist studio that Hélène shared with Wanda), were making little progress in their so-called pursuits.

Olga and Wanda openly wrote to Bost and Sartre as *their* men; Beauvoir clandestinely wrote to both as hers. Once when she was with Olga she caught sight of the thickness of her latest letter from Bost: it was bigger than the ones she received, could its words be tenderer? Beauvoir was struck by jealousy and guilt with increasing frequency. One night she had a dream that Olga asked her to show her a letter she was writing to Bost: she woke up in a cold sweat.[12] Two weeks later, Olga walked into her room just after Beauvoir had read a letter from Bost. Olga didn't know what she was reading, but Beauvoir felt an 'unpleasant feeling' – she tried to 'defend herself' against it but she knew that Bost loved Olga; she was just making excuses. 'It may be possible again for him to love her and for me to love him though I feel too depressed to make this effort.' She felt deeply unhappy, and wished Sartre was there to put things in perspective.[13] For weeks she had been descending into low moods and confusion: 'War is again in me and around me, and an anguish that doesn't know where to alight.'[14]

When she tried to distract herself from this void with relationships she just seemed to fall further into it. Another former student – Nathalie Sorokine – wanted a sexual relationship with her but she wasn't sure that was a good idea: 'I don't know what to do and it makes me feel really ill at ease.'[15] Things with Bianca, too, were taking a turn for the worse: she was sending letters telling Beauvoir to 'send all these people packing', which Beauvoir found stiflingly possessive and annoyingly self-important.[16] Her relationships with Sartre, Bost and Olga stretched back for years: she wasn't just going to walk away from them. The only thing that seemed to be going well was her novel – she had to fight to protect her writing time, but it was really starting to take shape.

At the end of October Sartre sent a letter to Beauvoir with details of his whereabouts, in code.[17] Beauvoir went to extraordinary lengths to see him, feigning illness to get a medical certificate so she could procure travelling papers. On 31 October she arrived late at night; the next morning she went to the tavern where he had breakfast so he'd know she'd arrived. They couldn't be seen out together since he was in uniform, so she took him to her hotel room. Her permit only lasted 24 hours – would she be allowed to extend it?

In the end she stayed until 5 November. They talked about philosophy, the complicated mess of their love lives, and their novels. She read his work in progress on *The Age of Freedom* and he read her work in progress on *She Came to Stay*. She told him that he needed to redo his book's female character, Marcelle. She had almost forgotten how good it felt 'to talk to someone, to find my intellectual life again'.[18] She had been teaching and reading, of course, but reading – even Husserl, Heidegger, Gide, Pearl S. Buck, Shakespeare, Gogol, Somerset Maugham, Jack London, Defoe, Agatha Christie, Arthur Conan Doyle and Dostoevsky – did not make up for deep conversation.

Beauvoir was beginning to be upset about sharing Sartre's and Bost's military leaves: she did not want Kosakiewicz leftovers, and now Bianca, too, wanted to take her share of Sartre's time. Sartre reassured her: Yes, he felt tenderly towards Wanda, but she was 22, childish and fickle; he really didn't expect the relationship to outlast the war. And yes, he was still writing to Bianca – often copying passages from his letters to Wanda verbatim – but he was losing enthusiasm. Of the four nights she was there they spent two – unusually passionate – together. The sexual relationship between Sartre and Beauvoir, despite this brief reignition during their separation in 1939, had now gone utterly flat.[19]

Beauvoir told Sartre that she was still upset that Bost loved Olga and now especially she didn't want to share Bost's leaves with her.

Sartre reminded her that she had *chosen* to love a man who loved Olga, and that in fact without Olga the relationship would be unstable. It was hardly fair to expect exclusivity from Bost when she had no intention of observing it herself.

Slowly, she was beginning to realize that she hadn't become the woman she wanted to be. 'In the past,' she wrote, 'I tried to believe I was what I wanted to be.' That year, however – because of Bost, she said – she realized that 'the presence of the contingent, the passionate'. It was interesting, she wrote in her diary, to find this out about herself: 'It's a step toward knowing myself, which is beginning to interest me. I think that I'm becoming something well defined. [...] I feel I'm a mature woman, though I would like to know what kind.'[20] She had become a successful teacher – that October she received a commendation from her school, and many students sent her cards or took her for coffees to express their thanks.[21] But was that enough?

A few days after Beauvoir returned from visiting Sartre, Bianca arrived in Paris to see her. Beauvoir wasn't thrilled – she had found Bianca's recent letters 'frenzied', which was worrying given the way her own feelings had cooled. She 'felt the lie' of Sartre's relationship with Bianca and 'cringed at the thought' of intimacy with her, but she went to bed with her anyway. Afterwards Beauvoir wrote in her diary that her physical pleasure with Bianca was 'perverse': she knew that she 'took advantage' of Bianca's body and that her own sensuality was 'deprived of any tenderness'. It was 'boorish', and she had never felt that way before. It was 'sickening', she wrote – 'like *foie gras* and not of the best quality'.[22]

When Beauvoir's letters and war diaries were published in French after her death, it was passages like this that led the Parisian press to call her '*machiste et mesquine*' – macho and petty.[23] It wasn't the first time Simone de Beauvoir was accused of acting or thinking 'like a man'. But it was shocking to the French press to hear her speak like such a carelessly unfeeling macho one. And it was disturbing to see that even after feeling 'boorish' and 'sickened' by her own behaviour, she didn't stop.

The next day, Bianca reproached Beauvoir for sending her sister Hélène financial support – Bianca's reasoning was that if she stopped doing that then she could pay for Bianca to come to Paris more often. And if Beauvoir stopped teaching she would have more time to see her, too. This was more than annoying; she told Bianca that she felt smothered. Then Bianca told Beauvoir that she had been fantasizing about offering herself to some friends who were about to leave for the war, so they wouldn't leave as virgins.[24]

By the visit's third day Bianca's presence had become a heavy burden: quite apart from her fantasies, it was increasingly clear to Beauvoir that Bianca did not see love in the same way that she did. Bianca viewed love as 'symbiosis'; she did not understand that people could actually find genuine pleasure in being alone or wanting to work. At one point, Bianca broke down crying, upset because Beauvoir loved Sartre more than her. Beauvoir was aghast: 'I never told her the contrary. I hate how easily she creates illusions for herself.'[25]

She tried to encourage Bianca to 'imagine herself in the center of her own life', instead of placing Beauvoir and Sartre there. 'She must become a person who is in touch with her own self,' Beauvoir wrote in her diary – but she could plainly see that Bianca found this difficult. As soon as Bianca left Beauvoir felt 'ill at ease' because of her own 'remorse and affection'. Beauvoir judged her own behaviour 'disgraceful'.[26]

As November unfolded she was still struggling with the dishonesty in her relationship with Olga. But then Olga told Beauvoir that she had stopped writing to Bost and feared she couldn't make herself start again. 'I'm not thinking all the time about Bost,' Olga said. Besides, how meaningful could a relationship be when you only saw each other for a few days every few months? Just a few months into the war, Olga was saying outright that it would be better to break things off. Beauvoir tried to defend Bost's interests – he didn't want his relationship with Olga to end, he just wanted her to write.

Beauvoir found Olga utterly unintelligible. If she loved Bost, why didn't she want to share her life with him? How could she see the effort it took to write a letter as a cost, not a benefit, when Bost was at war and a few warm words could bring him so much happiness? For Beauvoir, letters were a lifeline. She wanted to share in Bost's life, and Sartre's – though in the latter case she realized that 'the very fact of an intellectual life essential for both of us makes things so much easier'.[27]

In the final months of 1939 Beauvoir discovered that she could have an intellectual life in Paris even when Sartre wasn't there. Her friend Collette Audry invited her to dinner with the philosopher Jean Wahl, and at first she wasn't sure whether to go – alterations to her weekly timetable tended to provoke angry reactions from Olga et al. But she decided to do it; she needed 'to see people and have some serious conversation'. On the day of the dinner she had a premonition that her novel (*She Came to Stay*) would definitely be printed – 'I had the impression of being taken seriously'. And at the dinner itself she was amazed by her own ability to hold conversation. It was just like it had been at the Sorbonne twelve years ago, she wrote in her diary. Why, she wondered, did she always think that other people were more 'serious' than she was?[28]

More and more, she felt like she needed to study herself. A friend, Marie Ville, told her that Sartre oppressed her, ('Hardly amusing,' she said.) But it was true that she was starting to find things to disagree with in his philosophy – she agreed with his ideas about the will. 'But I don't know how he is going to give a content to his ethics.'[29]

Stépha, too, had been asking probing questions – after Bianca's visit to Paris in November she asked: was Simone a lesbian? Beauvoir never expressed any doubts about whether she was heterosexual, but she frequently attracted women – especially young women from her school – and the truth, she wrote to Sartre, was that she had 'developed a certain taste for such relations'.[30] She enjoyed sex with women but she seems to imply that, for her, it was second order. Her physical relationship with Bianca was still going on at Christmas 1939 – Bianca moved back to Paris in the middle of December – but now there was another young woman who was demanding her attention. Nathalie Sorokine was in her baccalaureate class; she had become infatuated with Beauvoir.

Nathalie Sorokine's parents were Russian by birth; they had left during the upheavals of the revolution and were now stateless. Nathalie was tall, tempestuous and bright, and she had done well in philosophy in her baccalaureate – Beauvoir enjoyed talking to her about Kant and Descartes. Nathalie wanted to study more philosophy but her mother was divorced and didn't have the means to pay for tuition at the Sorbonne. When she encouraged Nathalie to get a job rather than continue with her education Beauvoir offered to help pay her fees, so in 1939 Sorokine enrolled.

Sorokine – who was born in 1921, the same year as Bianca – had been pushing for a sexual relationship with Beauvoir since October. She was jealous of the presence of Sartre, Bost, Olga and Bianca in Beauvoir's life: she felt like she was in '5th place'. She was a troubled young woman, who stole bicycles and shoplifted pen sets from department stores. She resold the pens at the lycée to raise money for what she needed; she told Beauvoir that her parents called her a 'parasite' and had no qualms about taking money from her when they found it. In December Beauvoir told Nathalie that it wouldn't work for them to have a physical relationship. But then, on 14 December 1939, Sorokine tried to caress the clothed Beauvoir instead of working on Kant. That night she wrote to Sartre, 'There is nothing to be done, she wants to sleep with me.'[31] She didn't want to, she wrote in her diary, 'but that's what she really wanted – and the situation is disgusting and impossible'.[32]

A week later she wrote to Sartre that Sorokine had told her she loved her and tried to kiss her as if it was a legal romance. 'If I were free', Beauvoir wrote, she would throw herself into this story with momentum. But as it stood it made her feel strange to be passionately loved in this 'feminine and organic manner' by two women: Bianca and Sorokine.[33] It is unclear why she suddenly took herself to be 'unfree': she clearly didn't believe in monogamy with men, so why would she hold herself to a different standard with women? It is unlikely that she felt 'unfree' in a political sense: In 1942 the age of consent for homosexual relationships would be increased to 21 (while the age of consent for heterosexual relationships remained fixed at 13). But in 1939 Beauvoir's relationships were both consensual and legal.

Could her discomfort have arisen because that month Sartre had written to her to say he planned to end things with Bianca? Beauvoir didn't think ending things would be as easy as he thought: she could no longer avoid the recognition of (in her words) 'how used' Bianca was.[34]

Alone in Mégève that Christmas Beauvoir worked on her writing and amazed herself at how much she accomplished. She felt inspired and focused – and she was starting to feel sufficiently close to the end of her novel to imagine future projects. She wanted to write 'a novel about an entire life'.[35] She read and commented on Sartre's works, alongside her own. He had been working on the concept of freedom and sent Beauvoir some of his work in progress. She sent him a letter praising it, comparing it to the philosophies of Bergson and Kant – but, she told him, she couldn't really criticize it without the rest of the argument. If she had to raise an objection now, she wrote, her question would be: Once one recognizes one's freedom, what is one supposed to do?[36]

Beauvoir had been interested in philosophies of freedom since she read Bergson, Fouillée, Lagneau and others as a teenager. Since it was a central topic on their *agrégation* exam she and Sartre had spent a lot of time discussing it. It was all well and good to think about freedom as an abstract concept, and to claim, as Sartre did, that all freedoms are equal. But Beauvoir wanted a philosophy that could be *lived*. And when she looked at the lives people lived, she came to the conclusion that their freedoms were not equal, because (as she later put it) 'situations are different, and therefore so are freedoms'.[37]

On 12 January 1940 Beauvoir wrote to Sartre that she'd written the first 160 pages of her novel, *She Came to Stay* – she was looking forward to showing it to him when he came to visit. And she told him that she and Bienenfeld had had 'Embraces': 'If I'm to tell you everything, in addition to the usual rufous odour of her body she had a pungent fecal odour which made things pretty unpleasant. So far as friendship with her goes, no problem – but our physical relations couldn't be more distasteful to me.'[38]

Such a dramatic expression of disgust is startling and unsettling given that Beauvoir clearly did enjoy other lesbian relationships and that Bianca would remain her friend for life (on both women's accounts). Was Beauvoir really so disgusted by another woman's body? Could this be a psychosomatic expression of disgust with her own behaviour? When Beauvoir eventually broke up with Bianca she said that she preferred sex with men.[39] But despite her disgust and growing unease about their relationship – even an 'icy chill' when she first saw Bianca that January – she still agreed to see her two nights a week.[40]

At the same time Sartre wrote to Beauvoir that apart from her he didn't 'mean anything to the rest of the world (aside from my mother)'. He would 'slough off his old skin' at the end of the war, because 'not one of those good ladies will have acquired the rights of fidelity'.[41] But in a letter dated two days later Beauvoir describes being in bed with Nathalie Sorokine. As she described the event to Sartre, they were naked, thinking about reading some passages on the philosophy of the will together: 'The embraces started up again, this time with reciprocity. It's certainly not what it was with Kos. But I've a keen taste for her body.'[42]

Sartre's reply from 16 January reads: 'I've half forgotten what it's like to have anyone at my side at all, let alone you, who's interested in what I think and feel and who can understand it.'[43] The day after he exclaimed: 'What's going on? Such a lot of affairs and loves you're enjoying, little one!'[44]

Sartre was working away on the philosophy that would eventually be published as *Being and Nothingness*; when he told Beauvoir about it she replied: 'How seductive it sounds, that theory of Nothingness which solves every problem!'[45] The next month Sartre wrote to Beauvoir excitedly because he thought that at last he had found 'an intellectual niche' for himself. 'I'm beginning to see glimmers of a theory of time. This evening I began to write it. It's thanks to you, do you realize that? Thanks to Françoise's obsession: that when Pierre is in Xavière's room, there's an object living all by itself without a consciousness to see it.'[46] (Françoise, Pierre, and Xavière are characters in *She Came to Stay*.)

He didn't receive a letter the next day, so he wrote to her again. He was still working on his theory of time but he felt empty . . . why didn't she write? 'I wish you were here; then, everything would be fine.'[47]

The very day that Sartre was writing to thank her for inspiring his theory of time, Beauvoir received an unexpected note in her classroom. After six months of not seeing Bost at all, he was there. She trembled as she ran to meet him and they spent the day talking feverishly. They had three days and three nights together, after which he was going to see Olga. The previous year she had told Bost that she loved him 'with all her soul'.[48] Now she wrote to Sartre that she and Bost would 'never get to the end of what we have to say to one another'; that looking forward, 'Bost forms part of my future in an absolutely certain – even essential – way.'[49]

Perhaps it was because of this letter, perhaps it was because of Wanda's discovery of one of Sartre's jilted lovers from the previous year, or perhaps it was because he hadn't had another letter from Beauvoir for days: whatever the reason, Sartre began to be fearful:

> I'm in an odd state, I've never been this uneasy with myself since I went crazy. [...] My sweet, how I need you [...]. I love you. I'm afraid I must seem slightly underhanded to you with all of the lies I'm entangled in. [...] I'm afraid you might suddenly ask yourself [...] isn't he perhaps lying to me, isn't he perhaps telling me half-truths? My little one, my darling Beaver, I swear to you that with you I'm totally pure.[50]

The next day he wrote again, declaring that he no longer wanted to play the game of seduction. Intent on simplifying matters, he wrote a letter to Bianca to break up. Beauvoir saw her soon after: Bianca was hurt, angry and suspicious. It was a complete about-face on Sartre's part – his letters only a few weeks before had been talking about the future 'the three of them' would have after the war. She was right to be indignant, Beauvoir said to Sartre: the way they had treated people was 'unacceptable'.[51]

At last she was admitting her wrongdoing – and confronting Sartre's. But there was nothing they could do to undo it. In 1940 Bianca Bienenfeld had a breakdown; she felt 'crushed by abandonment and heartbreak'.[52]

What we know for certain is that Sartre broke up with Bianca by letter in February of 1940.[53] He wrote to Beauvoir to tell her about how harshly Bienenfeld had rebuked him; on 27 February Beauvoir briefly expressed sympathy for Sartre before adding her voice to the chorus of reproach: he 'really did go too far' with her – 'honestly, I don't know what got into your head'. Bienenfeld had come to see Beauvoir, showing her Sartre's letter. The letter's contents haven't survived – so it's unclear whether Beauvoir's reaction was hypocritical, given what we know about her own behaviour – but Beauvoir described Bianca as humiliated and disgusted: 'I found her estimable in her attitude that evening, and scathing, and right. [...] your letter was indefensible.'[54]

He replied remorsefully, agreeing that the letter was 'abysmal', that he had 'never' done anything 'so rotten as represented by the mailing of that letter'.[55] Over the following days and weeks the correspondence between Sartre and Beauvoir included a lot of discussion of Bienenfeld: Beauvoir thought she found the break hard at first but bounced back; Beauvoir continued to go for meals with her, discussing philosophy with her, and Bienenfeld gave Beauvoir feedback on her novel. She said that there was 'too much thought' in *She Came to Stay*, comparing it with American novels (like Hemingway's), which were pleasing because of their 'absence of thought'.[56] She wouldn't be the only contingent lover to tell Beauvoir that her novels had 'too much philosophy'. But few, if any, relationships in Beauvoir's life rival Bianca's for its absence of thoughtfulness. In the early months of 1940 Beauvoir admitted that they were responsible for causing her suffering – too much suffering. She wrote to Sartre on 3 March, 'I blamed us – myself as much as you, actually – in the past, in the future, in the absolute: the way we treat people. I felt it was unacceptable that we'd managed to make her suffer so much.'[57]

From 23 March to 11 July there is a gap in Beauvoir's correspondence.[58] On 7 May 1940 her novel was accepted for publication by Gallimard.[59] Three days later, on 10 May 1940, the Germans had invaded Holland, Belgium and Luxembourg, and Bost was transported to the Belgian border. On 12 May the Germans came around the Maginot line, surrounding the French divisions and attacking by air and on land. On 21 May Bost was hit in the abdomen by shrapnel. He was bleeding badly so he was taken to a Red Cross station on a stretcher, and from there to a military hospital for operation. He was lucky to have survived the hit, but even luckier to be off the line. Sartre wrote reassuringly to Beauvoir that 'it's the best possible news' that he had been evacuated from the front.[60] Bost's regiment dwindled; on 23 May Paul Nizan was killed by enemy fire.

On the evening of 9 June, 1940, Beauvoir received a note from Bianca. She had been looking for her all day, it said: no matter the hour please would she come to the Flore? Beauvoir arrived to a room full of distressed faces. Bienenfeld's father had connections and intelligence: the Germans were close to entering Paris. She was leaving with her father the next day. She knew it was less urgent for Beauvoir, not being Jewish, but she wondered if she would like to join them, even so.

Beauvoir wept, overcome by the bitter truth that France was on its knees, one of her lovers had been shot and another was about to become a prisoner of war. The next day Beauvoir joined the Bienenfelds and nearly 3 million others leaving Paris. On 14 June, Paris fell. In the days that followed surrender came quickly, and on 22 June Marshal Pétain signed an armistice with the Nazis. They would control the northern section of France, including Paris; Pétain would control the 'Free Zone' from the southern capital of Vichy.

Simone spent a month in the country at La Pouèze, a friend's country house near Laval. But she was impatient to return to Paris, and to news from Sartre and Bost. For all she knew, they might even be *in* Paris. So she set off to return, taking a lift in a German military truck. When she returned, the Nazi flag hung over the Senate in the Luxembourg Gardens. She saw her parents and Sorokine, and moved in at her grandmother's.[61] At the Hôtel Danemark there was only one letter waiting – it was from Sartre, from the day before she left Paris.

She phoned Bost's parents in Taverny to ask after him; he had been moved to a military hospital near Avignon.[62] She phoned Olga, who was with her family in L'Aigle; she was safe. Hélène was still in Portugal with Lionel, safe but not close.

Back in the capital, Beauvoir signed the Vichy oath, a declaration stating that she was not a Jew.[63] She later expressed embarrassment at having signed it, but at the time she saw no other option:

I signed it because I had to. My only income came from my teaching; my ration cards depended on it, my identity papers – everything. There simply was no other choice available to me. I hated it, but I did it for purely practical reasons. Who was I? A nobody, that's who. What good would it have done if some unknown teacher refused to sign a statement that had no meaning, no value, and certainly no influence or impact on anything? Refusing to sign such a statement would have had only one significance: that I no longer had a profession or an income. Who, in wartime, in my circumstances, would have been so foolish as to risk such a thing?[64]

According to Marshal Pétain, France had suffered from decadence in the interwar years, and the re-establishment of order was required. French people must return to their forgotten values: 'Work, Family, Fatherland' was the regime's slogan.[65] In Occupied Paris, Beauvoir said, 'the very fact of breathing implied a compromise'.[66] The clocks were on German time, and when Beauvoir watched the world from her balcony after the curfew it was uncannily light.[67]

Nathalie Sorokine was still in Paris, and Olga returned in mid-July. When Beauvoir met her there was so much to catch up on they talked for hours. For one thing, Olga was pregnant. The baby wasn't Bost's (he had been away on the front) but paternity aside she didn't want a child – she wanted an abortion. During the Occupation, it was difficult to find any way to have an abortion, let alone a safe one. But Beauvoir found her an address and nursed her for two weeks when she developed an infection afterwards.

In August Sartre was transferred to a prisoner-of-war camp near Trier, called Stalag XII D. The conditions there were good; he was allowed to write two postcards per week. He was reading Heidegger's *Being and Time*, writing his first play, and working on *Being and Nothingness*. In Paris Beauvoir passed swastikas on her way to work on her novel at the Dôme or read Hegel and Jean Wahl in the Bibliothèque Nationale.[68] In July she found an epigraph from Hegel's *The Phenomenology of Spirit* for *She Came to Stay*.

Beauvoir had first encountered Hegel in her philosophy textbook in the mid-1920s, and he was the kind of philosopher she would later distance herself from: he treated history as the logical development of a system, thought ideas could explain all events, and devalued individual experience. He was the target of famous criticisms by Kierkegaard and Marx, for giving us nothing but a 'palace of ideas' (in Kierkegaard's words) and being the kind of philosopher who was content to 'interpret the world' rather than change it (in Marx's). But during the Second World War Beauvoir found reading Hegel 'the most soothing activity I could find'. It reminded her of her *agrégation* year: 'there's the reality of books, of the ideas in the books and about human history of which this is only a moment – I felt more assured in the world than I had for a long time'.[69]

After work, she kept a carefully ordered timetable: two evenings a week with Olga, two evenings with Nathalie Sorokine. Sorokine was intensely jealous and resented Beauvoir's inflexible itinerary, calling her a 'clock in a refrigerator' for the inflexible way she insisted on having time to work. Sometimes she resorted to waiting for Beauvoir to come out of her hotel in the morning or to leave school in the afternoon to see her. Sometimes they went to the theatre or the opera: wartime tickets came cheap.

In September Bost returned to Paris and took a teaching job. This meant that Beauvoir was able to eat lunch with him most weekdays; Thursdays she ate lunch with her parents. As for nights, Bost's Saturday was hers. She kept writing, as signs went up barring Jews entry and denying them employment. Bost wanted to become a journalist, so she helped him with his writing. She was carefully reading Kierkegaard and Kant that winter. But now that Bost was back in Paris she wished that Sartre could be too.

After's Bost's return Beauvoir came clean with Bianca about her relationship with him, and said that she thought she and Bianca should see each other less often. It was a huge blow to Bianca to know that Beauvoir had lied to her; she felt like she was 'suffocating, sinking'. Sartre's about-face in February was bad, but this time she was 'desperate beyond words' because she was so much more strongly attached to Beauvoir.[70] Beauvoir still didn't fully realize how deeply they had hurt her; she wrote to Sartre that she had 'more or less broken with Bianca', but since Bianca was having a relationship with Bernard Lamblin (one of Bianca's classmates, a former student of Sartre's) she thought it would work out.

Bianca's father, however, wanted her to marry an American who would take her out of France: with a name like 'David Bienenfeld' he knew his family was not safe. Bianca didn't want to marry some unknown man, but her father insisted. He found a willing American in Montparnasse, paid him, and Bianca gave in. But on the appointed day, the American didn't show up for the wedding. So Bianca and Bernard married on 12 February 1941 – despite the danger of a mixed marriage between a Jew and a non-Jew. Her parents were relieved that she, at least, would have a more French-sounding name.[71]

By November 1940 Beauvoir was having 'days of dark depression', thinking that if she knew she would never see Sartre again she would kill herself.[72] By January reading philosophy and keeping history at

arm's length were no longer cutting it. In her diary she recognized that
she had been a solipsist – thinking that her consciousness and
freedom, her 'view from within', was real, but that the others around
her were like ants going about their business. (Sartre had written a
short story in the 1930s called 'Erostratus', in which the proud
protagonist looked down from a seventh-floor balcony and saw all of
the humans below as 'ants'.) She and Sartre had been 'antihumanists',
Beauvoir, wrote in her *War Diaries*, but she now judged that they were
wrong to have been so.[73]

When she read *She Came to Stay* now she looked at it with the
estrangement of something that belonged to her past. It wouldn't be
published until 1943, but in January of 1941 she had come to the
conclusion that 'it rests on a philosophical attitude that is already no
longer mine'.[74] She had become a different woman. She read Heidegger,
Kierkegaard, Kafka and Jaspers, and thought about old questions –
her desire for salvation. She wanted her next novel to be about
what she called the *individual situation*, and the moral tensions
that arise from being both individual and social – by the middle of
1941 she started writing the book that would become *The Blood
of Others*.

Beauvoir's diaries once again show a different side to her from the
version she presented in her memoirs. There, she described Sartre's
conversion to politics at the expense of her own thoughts and actions.
She wrote that she hadn't seen Sartre for eleven months when she
received a note at the end of March 1941: he was in Paris. He had lied
his way out of the camp, claiming to be a civilian and using his near-
blind right eye as a ploy. Beauvoir was elated to see him but within
days she wondered: was this the same man? He was moralizing and
impatient, shocked that she had signed a declaration that she was not
a Jew. It was all well and good to be free, he said: but now they must
act. He was speaking about resistance; about expelling the Germans

from France. She was, she claimed, still convinced that they, as individuals, were utterly powerless.

On 8 July 1941 Beauvoir's father died, leaving nothing. His last words to her were: 'You began to earn your living very young, Simone: your sister cost me a great deal of money.'[75] She shed no tears for him,[76] but afterwards she was struck by the courage with which her mother began a new chapter; for her, being widowed was a kind of deliverance. Françoise de Beauvoir had grown to loathe the family flat in the rue de Rennes, which Georges had 'filled with the noise of his ill-temper'.[77] So in 1942 she moved to a studio apartment in the rue Blomet. Françoise studied for exams and qualified to work as an assistant librarian in the Red Cross. She volunteered, learned languages, attended lectures, made new friends and travelled. But she did not give up what Beauvoir called her 'prudent attitude': she still considered her daughter to be living in sin.[78]

Less than six months later Françoise lost her mother, too.[79] On the day of Madame Brasseur's funeral Françoise had a nervous breakdown – she stayed in bed and Simone spent the night with her, watching over her 55-year-old mother as she slept. In the immediate aftermath of Georges' death Françoise was financially dependent on her eldest daughter. Beauvoir was already supporting Hélène to an extent by paying for her studio, as well as helping support other members of 'the family'. So she had to make economies: they would have to cut back on eating out.

The first meeting of their resistance group, 'Socialism and Liberty', met in Beauvoir's room at the Mistral – she and Sartre had moved back in, again in separate rooms. They made leaflets and met with other groups in Paris, and snuck across the border to Vichy France to try to establish links between their group and other members of the resistance. But their attempts were unsuccessful; the communist group was larger and seemed more effective so in May 1942 some of their members transferred ranks and soon afterwards the group dispersed.

Meanwhile Sartre refused to sign the declaration that he was not a Jew or a Freemason. He managed to keep his job at the Lycée Pasteur even so: the inspector general of education was part of the resistance so overlooked his insubordination. And in October he transferred Sartre to a more prestigious post: the Lycée Condorcet.

So life fell into a familiar pattern: they taught and they wrote. Winter times during the occupation were cold, so they took refuge in the Flore, on the boulevard Saint-Germain. Sartre continued to see Wanda, and to enjoy her possessive, proprietary affection. Some members of 'the family' were less than pleased that Sartre had returned to Paris: Nathalie Sorokine saw him as another person vying for Simone's attention. Before she met him Sorokine thought he was a 'phony genius'. But when they met in 1941 she seduced him. Like Sartre, she made a sport of seduction, and she also played it successfully with Bost.

In December of 1941 Sorokine's mother filed a complaint with the Vichy ministry of education. In it, she accused Beauvoir of corrupting her daughter: the official charge was 'inciting debauchery in a minor'.[80] The age of consent at the time was 13 years old; Nathalie Sorokine was 20 when the complaint was filed. And Mme Sorokine gave a lengthy report: Mlle de Beauvoir had seduced her daughter, and then introduced her to two men who also seduced her. Mme Sorokine drew attention to the irregular living arrangements of Mlle de Beauvoir, who was single, lived in a hotel, worked in cafés, making no secret that she was Jean-Paul Sartre's 'concubine'. She also taught her pupils the morally corrupting works of two homosexual writers, Proust and Gide. In short, any patriot would see why France did not need a woman such as her in their secondary schools. Under Pétain, France was attempting to regain lost dignity by a strategy that promoted French family values. Such a woman as Mlle de Beauvoir should not be shaping the futures of its youth.

The Ministry was inclined to agree, and began an investigation that would only conclude a year and a half later.

The story Beauvoir told Bair was that Mme Sorokine had come to her in March, asking Beauvoir to intervene in Nathalie's life. Nathalie was seeing a young man called Bourla, who was Jewish and poor – Mme Sorokine did not approve. Beauvoir said she would tell Nathalie about their meeting, but that she didn't think she held the influence her mother hoped. She thought that was the end of it. But then the complaint was filed.

During the 1941–42 academic year the philosopher Jean Wahl was dismissed from his post at the Sorbonne because he was Jewish. In 1942 he was interned at Drancy. That June Jews in Occupied France were required by law to wear the Star of David. Their freedoms were restricted even further: they could no longer own property or open bank accounts. It was illegal for anyone to cross the border to the Free Zone without permission. But that summer Beauvoir and Sartre sneaked across it with Bost. They went cycling in the Pyrenees.

The debauchery charges against Beauvoir were never confirmed. Sorokine denied that her relationship with Beauvoir was sexual, and the two men denied any such relations with her. So the Ministry of Education had no proof confirming these allegations. But they could confirm Mlle de Beauvoir's suspicious living arrangements and questionable inclusion of Proust and Gide on her syllabus. On 17 July 1940 a law had been created by Pétain's government to make it easier to eliminate government functionaries who did not contribute to its 'national renovation'. And this law was cited in the Ministry's decision of 17 June 1943, to sanction Simone de Beauvoir and to revoke her permission to teach.[81] Her dismissal went down like a badge of honour among some parts of the resistance. Her permission was reinstated in

1945, and other students from the period remembered her as an inspiring philosopher who introduced them to Husserl and Heidegger even before they were popular in French universities.[82] But Beauvoir didn't return to teaching: from now on, writing was to be her life.

In the memoirs Beauvoir skimmed over the debauchery charges, presenting them as Mme Sorokine's retaliation for Beauvoir's failure to get Nathalie to leave Bourla. But in the immediate aftermath of her dismissal the future looked uncertain. She knew she wanted to write – but she needed money to live on. Françoise had been saving a large fraction of the monthly stipend her daughter gave her and she volunteered to give it back to Beauvoir. Beauvoir asked her to keep it, in case it was needed.

Later that summer, Beauvoir got her first writing job, working as a features producer for Radiodiffusion Nationale (known as Radio-Vichy).[83] At the time, there were two national stations, Radio-Vichy and another, Radio-Paris, the latter of which shared the Nazi ideology. It was possible to work for Radio-Vichy without being seen as a collaborator – depending on the kind of work one did. Beauvoir worked on a programme about music in the Middle Ages, which was arguably neutral – although, unsurprisingly, her participation in this work raised questions about where to draw the lines between complicity and collaboration.

Research by Ingrid Galster has shown that the content of Beauvoir's broadcasts was not collaborationist. But even so Beauvoir's critics have charged that she was apolitical or, worse, that she actively participated in creating radio that encouraged listeners' evasion of their moral responsibilities to resist the Nazis. Beauvoir's defenders, by contrast, noted that in the episodes she worked on there was a certain spirit of refusal – she chose people and texts from French culture that defied the reigning values of their day. It was difficult, in Occupied Paris, to draw clean lines between resistance and collaboration.[84]

The existentialists would become famous for the slogan 'man is the sum of his actions'. And although Beauvoir was soon to become a woman whose actions inspired many, she was not proud of all of them. Beauvoir clearly resisted the values of Pétain's government in her classrooms and in her personal life. But she also failed to practise the ethics she would later preach: her relationships with women during this period were far from reciprocal. In the 'grimy' period between 1939 and 1942 she hit several low points before reaching the conclusion that she needed to think harder about the woman she'd become. And along the way she had written not one but two of the novels that would bring her fame and form her persona – *She Came to Stay* and *The Blood of Others* – although the second one would not be published until after the end of wartime censorship.[85]

9

Forgotten Philosophy

The year that Beauvoir lost her post in the French education system both she and Sartre published works that would secure their places in French intellectual life for good. Beauvoir's *She Came to Stay* was published in August, and Sartre's *Being and Nothingness* – dedicated to the Beaver – was published in June. Sartre was also beginning to produce plays to public acclaim, resurrecting innocent-looking plots from ancient Greek drama to convey messages of freedom and resistance.

The early 1940s mark a significant shift in Beauvoir's thought. Before the war she had been, by her own admission, solipsistic. As early as 1941 she realized that she had moved on from the 'philosophical attitude' of *She Came to Say*,[1] and her plays and novels from 1943–46 show a moral and political engagement that many people do not credit to her until the publication of *The Second Sex*. Already in 1943 she was asking: who is useful or useless to society? Who has the power to decide?

In July 1943 Beauvoir and Sartre moved to L'hôtel La Louisiane, 60 rue de Seine, where they lived (in separate rooms) until the end of 1946. They had left Montparnasse for Saint-Germain-des-Prés. And in the same month Beauvoir started an essay discussing Sartre's view of freedom and contrasting it with her own, putting to paper the objections that she had 'upheld against him in various conversations'.[2] From this point onwards we have more than 'constant conversation', diaries and letters to inform our picture of their intellectual exchange, because Beauvoir's voice became a public voice, available in print. And it was not just used to advertise Sartre's ideas, but to criticize them.

Well before the war Beauvoir and Sartre had discussed the ethics of their relationships with Olga and Wanda. Was it immoral to lie to someone whose happiness was false? Should she feel remorse for what she wasn't telling Olga? Or for what Olga wasn't telling Bost? In *She Came to Stay*, Beauvoir explored the philosophical problem that had preoccupied her since the 1920s: 'the opposition of self and other'. Ostensibly it was a book about the 'trio', in which a couple, Pierre and Françoise, invite a younger 'guest' into their relationship: Xavière. She provokes jealousy in Françoise, who becomes so frustrated that the only escape she can imagine is to murder her rival. Dedicated 'To Olga Kosakiewicz', the book's epigraph from Hegel reads: 'Each consciousness seeks the death of the other'.

But there is a fourth character: a tall, green-eyed man with dark hair – Xavière's boyfriend, Gerbert. 'I'm always fond of what belongs to me', Xavière tells Françoise: 'It's restful to have someone entirely to yourself.'[3] But in the novel Xavière does not have Gerbert to herself; he is also sleeping with Françoise. It's hard to imagine that Olga wouldn't have had suspicions when she read the book: in *She Came to Stay* Françoise and Gerbert go on a hiking trip together, and end up becoming lovers one night in a barn. When they return to Paris he tells Françoise he has never loved another woman like he loves her. And the reason for Xavière's murder is not the jealousy and frustration provoked by the trio with Pierre – but rather because Xavière discovers Gerbert's letters to Françoise. Françoise, like the man who killed his cab driver because he was too embarrassed not to have the fare, would rather kill Xavière than face her accusing gaze.

But Bost and Beauvoir insisted that this part of the novel – unlike the vivid conversations that echoed the real-life voices of Sartre, Beauvoir, and Olga – was fiction. In *The Prime of Life* Beauvoir felt no need to hide that she wrote the ending as catharsis: she thought that by killing Olga on paper she would purge herself of unwanted emotion and cleanse their friendship of its murkier memories.[4] For a long time this explanation would lead readers to assume that jealousy was the demon she wanted to exorcize. But in light of the publication of her correspondence with Bost in 2004, there is a new possibility: guilt. For the duration of Olga's life, she never knew that Beauvoir and Bost were having an affair.

Just as Simone had recoiled from her reflection in the Kosakiewicz sisters' eyes, Françoise struggles with the question of the relationship between herself and others:

'It's almost impossible to believe that other people are conscious beings, aware of their own inward feelings, as we ourselves are aware of our own,' said Françoise. 'To me, it's terrifying when we grasp that. We get the impression of no longer being anything but a figment of someone else's mind.'[5]

The novel brought mixed responses: some thought it was scandalous; others read it as a courageous rejection of the Vichy dogma of 'work, family, country'. But philosophically Beauvoir's novel presents two possible modes of relating to other people: the first involves acknowledging that others, like oneself, are conscious beings with rich and vulnerable inner lives. The second way refuses to see this, and refuses the possibility of reciprocity, taking it for granted that others just *are* either things for my use or obstacles in my way.

This is important because this second approach closely resembles something Sartre wrote in *Being and Nothingness*, and the next period in Beauvoir's life has long been reported as one of postwar fame, jazz and partying rather than intense philosophical productivity borne, in part, out of disagreement with Sartre. To understand why she has been so misunderstood, why she was later frustrated to be reduced to 'Notre Dame de Sartre', and why she had to walk a tightrope attempting to avoid (as best she could) *ad feminam* dismissals of her feminist work, we have to look more closely at precisely what it was about Sartre's philosophy that Beauvoir thought was wrong.

The British writer Angela Carter once wrote that 'every thinking woman in the Western World' must have asked herself, at one time or another: 'why is a nice girl like Simone wasting her time sucking up to a boring old fart like J-P?' Only love, Carter continued, 'could make you proud to be an also-ran'.[6] But in 1943 Sartre was worse than a boring old fart: he was an extremely pessimistic philosopher, with very low expectations of humanity even by the standards of extremely pessimistic philosophers. He thought that all human beings want to dominate each other, and that all relationships are conflictual – so conflictual that love is impossible (or, in his own words, an 'unrealisable ideal'). And Beauvoir was not an 'also-ran'. She was a philosopher who disagreed with him. She was also, as it happens, a woman whose own life would be wielded as a weapon against her – but that hadn't started yet.

In *Being and Nothingness* Sartre wrote that in all interpersonal relationships, one person plays the dominator and the other person plays the dominated. One person is a 'subject', seeing the world from his own point of view, and the other is the 'object', who internalizes the view of the person who has 'mastered' them. Sometimes we like to rule others, Sartre thought, and sometimes we like to be ruled by them. But we never engage with them on level ground.

Sartre wasn't the only Western philosopher to think these kinds of thoughts; Hegel wrote a famous passage on the 'master/slave dialectic' that said something similar, and long before him Saint Augustine thought all human beings had a *libido dominandi* – a drive to dominate

– and that this was the source of much human suffering. Because Beauvoir clearly studied Hegel during the war (taking solace in solitude and thinking) and made Hegelian themes central to her novel *She Came to Stay*, some scholars have gone so far as to claim that Sartre *stole* many of the central ideas of *Being and Nothingness* from her, and that if this was a story about two male philosophers, instead of a man and a woman, Beauvoir's ideas would have received the recognition Sartre's gained.[7] For although *Being and Nothingness* was published in June and *She Came to Stay* was published in August; Sartre had read *She Came to Stay* while he was on military leave – so he encountered her ideas in fictional form before writing his in philosophy. And one of the philosophical distinctions Sartre introduces in *Being and Nothingness* is a divide between 'being-for-itself' and 'being-for-others', which (once you get beneath the jargon) looks strikingly like the distinction Beauvoir made in her student diaries in 1927 between the view from within and the view from without, the 'for myself' and 'for others'.

But claiming that Sartre 'stole' Beauvoir's ideas is problematic, both historically and philosophically. Historically, it is problematic because their relationship was one of 'constant conversation' and mutual (if not exactly reciprocal) intellectual encouragement. And philosophically, it is problematic because both Beauvoir and Sartre were steeped in French philosophical sources that neither of them bothered to cite in their works, let alone claimed to *own*. An additional difficulty arises because initially Beauvoir was the kind of philosopher who thought that what mattered about a philosophy was not who had the idea; what mattered was whether it was true or not. In the 1940s, she would be very critical of the concept of 'possession'.

But she was also very critical of Sartre. Later in life she would realize that the idea of possession plays an important role in the perpetuation of power, and who is remembered by posterity. *Being and Nothingness* contained a concept that Beauvoir and Sartre had discussed together throughout the 1930s. It was present in *When Things of the Spirit Come First* and went on to inform Beauvoir's later work in powerful ways. But it was Sartre who would become famous for it: *bad faith*.

In her memoirs Beauvoir said that 'we' discussed bad faith when describing the emergence of this concept in their thinking in the 1930s. As Sartre described it in *Being and Nothingness*, bad faith was a way of fleeing from freedom, which consists in over-identifying with either 'facticity' or 'transcendence'. Facticity stands for all of the contingent and unchosen things about you such as the time or place in which you were born, the colour of your skin, your sex, your family, your education, your body. And 'transcendence' refers to the freedom to go beyond these features to *values*: this concerns what you *choose to make* of the facts, how you shape yourself through your actions.

For Sartre, bad faith arises when facticity and transcendence are out of joint in a way that makes an individual think they are *determined* to be a certain way. He gave the famous example of a waiter: he is in bad faith if he thinks his facticity – i.e., the fact that he is a waiter – determines who he is. The waiter is always free to choose another path in life; to deny this is to deny his transcendence. On the other hand, if the waiter thinks it doesn't matter that he is a waiter when he applies to be a CEO, then he is in bad faith for the opposite reason: he has failed to recognize the limits of his facticity.

This might sound trivial – but what if you replace the word 'waiter' with the word 'Jew' or 'woman' or 'black'? Human history is full of examples of people reducing other people to a single dimension of their facticity and, in doing so, failing to recognize their full humanity. In 1943, it was crystal clear that that habit did not only belong to humanity's past. But Sartre didn't make this ethical move in *Being and Nothingness*. Nor did he give a satisfactory answer to the ethical problem of objectifying others there. Rather, he said that we must not take ourselves to be determined by our facticity – because whatever the conditions of our existence, we are free to make the most of them.

Already in the 1930s Beauvoir was convinced that this was wrong. Sartre thought human beings were free because whatever their situation they were free to 'transcend' facticity by choosing between different ways of responding to it. Her challenge was this: 'What sort of transcendence could a woman shut up in a harem achieve?'[8] There is a difference between having freedom (in the sense of being theoretically able to make a choice) and having the *power* to choose in the actual situation where your choice has to be made. She would go on to articulate her philosophical criticisms in two philosophical essays in the 1940s, *Pyrrhus and Cinéas* and *The Ethics of Ambiguity*, but in the meantime she had to deal with the fallout from *She Came to Stay* in her personal life.

Before the publication of Beauvoir's first novel her mother knew little enough about her daughter's life to think her 'a good girl'. But, although after the publication of *She Came to Stay* 'public rumour destroyed her illusions', it also made her daughter a well-known writer, so Françoise was simultaneously shocked by Beauvoir's books and flattered by their success. And since Simone was the family's breadwinner, her success also brought some benefits to everyone.[9]

She Came to Stay has been read in three ways since its publication: before Sartre and Beauvoir became famous in 1945 it was read as a study of bohemian Parisian life; later, it was taken to be a *roman à clef* of their 'trio' relationship; and more recently it has been read by feminists as a portrait of three non-traditional women in an tyrannical traditional world. It is easy to find passages in the book where its protagonist, Françoise, seems to speak for Simone: Françoise does not like to waste 'precious working hours' on feeling upset about Pierre's other women.[10] She paints herself as 'the faithful sort',[11] who is uninterested in romantic affairs that have 'no continuity'.[12] Françoise 'loathed the thought' of being 'a woman who takes';[13] she wants her seduction of Gerbert to be reciprocal because of 'a deep-seated philosophical commitment to her own freedom'.[14] But – where Pierre is concerned – she also asks herself whether she is in bad faith. The novel is punctuated by passages in which Françoise reflects on her relationship with Pierre – passages which have led to speculation about Beauvoir's feelings about the Olga chapter of the Sartre–Beauvoir pact:

> She had loved him too blindly, and for too long, for what she received from him; but she had promised herself to love him for himself, and even in that condition of freedom of which he was now availing himself to escape from her, she would not stumble over the first obstacle.[15]

Her readers wondered: was this Beauvoir's voice speaking through Françoise's? Or the pure fruit of her imagination? In the novel, Françoise declares to Xavière: 'You think that you're something ready-made once and for all, but I don't think so. I think you make yourself what you are of your own free will.'[16] In making her fiction resemble the facts of her life – closely enough to provoke curiosity, at any rate – Beauvoir left herself open to being 'made' into many things by her readers.

Beauvoir herself encouraged the readings of some passages in this novel as autobiographical. Beauvoir's seduction of Bost, she told Francis and Gontier 'happened exactly as I tell it in *L'invitée* [*She Came to Stay*]' (although she didn't give his name, of course).[17] Beauvoir recounted her seduction of Bost in her letters to Sartre, so after his death (and Olga's) and the letters' publication it was possible to compare Beauvoir's letters with the novel's scenes. The letters to Sartre breezily present an unexpected sexual encounter: 'I slept with Little Bost three days ago. It was I who suggested it, of course. [...]

Both of us had been wanting it.'[18] In the novel, by contrast, Françoise describes 'a vague yearning' that accumulated over days until it became 'choking desire'; because Gerbert felt 'beyond reach', she was held back from taking any initiative.[19]

Before publication the novel's working title was *Légitime défense* – self-defence.[20] Looking back on it from a distance, Beauvoir thought that she had adopted a position of resolute blindness to others in the 1930s, that 'protected by the gaze of Sartre, she wanted to forget that there were other eyes that saw her'. When she was forced to admit this, it was intensely uncomfortable – and it was this feeling of discomfort that she 'pushed to paroxysm' in *She Came to Stay*.[21] She was no longer willing to be wilfully blind; as a philosophy to live by, this was a dead end.

After the successes of 1943, Beauvoir and Sartre's social scene began to expand rapidly. They were friendly with Albert Camus, and through him with other writers in the resistance including Raymond Queneau and Michel Leiris. Monsieur and Madame Leiris lived in an apartment on the Quai des Grands-Augustins; Beauvoir met Picasso there. La Louisiane was a much better hotel than any of their previous homes, so she began to invite people for hospitality at hers, too. She had parties with Leiris and Queneau, Camus, Sorokine and her boyfriend, Bourla, as well as Bost, Olga and Wanda. In the spring of 1944 they launched a series of all-night parties they called 'fiestas'. The writer Georges Bataille hosted the first of these; they all saved coupons so they could amass enough food for a wartime feast, with dancing, singing and drinking. Bost hosted one at his mother's house at Taverny; Simone Jollivet and Dullin hosted another in their apartment in Paris.

Although Beauvoir was starting to mix with the crème de la crème of 1940s Paris arts, she was also feeling the scarcity that was the abnormal normality of life under the Occupation. Fuel for heat had become scarce, as had food. Between 1938 and 1942, milk consumption halved and bread prices nearly doubled. The allied forces continued to target strategic ports, factories and stations.

On 20 and 21 April the northern parts of Paris were bombed by the allies. It was a controversial aspect of Operation Overlord, intended to disrupt all rail traffic leading into northern France. On 21 April the La Chapelle marshalling yards were hit, killing 641 people and wounding nearly 400 more. Sartre and Beauvoir were in La Pouèze, but Bost wrote to them describing the terrifying noise and the deafening thought of ending up a corpse in a pile of rubble. The previous month Bourla – Nathalie Sorokine's Jewish boyfriend – was arrested with his father. They didn't know it but he had already been transferred to Auschwitz.[22] But although the Nazi flag was still flying over the Senate people were talking about liberation, and from 19 August they could almost taste it. The Germans were retreating eastwards, and the French Resistance had placed posters all over the city calling citizens to arms. Sartre was stretched thin so Beauvoir wrote some articles for *Combat* under his byline.[23]

On 25 August 1944 Beauvoir was at Bost and Olga's room in the Hôtel Chaplain along with Wanda and Sorokine. They had cooked some potatoes for dinner, and as they ate them they heard the announcement on the radio: General de Gaulle was in Paris. People started to cheer and shout in the street – in front of the Dôme people were thronging near the rue Vavin. But then there were tanks; the crowds fled from gunshots and SS cars.

The next day the French flag was raised on the Eiffel Tower. De Gaulle marched through Paris, down the Champs-Elysées with French and American troops. Beauvoir and Olga cheered from the Arc de Triomphe.

The war was not over, but Paris was free.

The second volume of Beauvoir's autobiography covered the period from 1930–1944. It was only late in that period that her own writing began to be published, and *The Prime of Life* brushes very quickly over her philosophical preoccupations and achievements, giving what looks to many like disproportionate credit to Sartre. But the memoirs do not conceal that she read voluminously, including works on philosophy, psychology, religion and (although such material was much scarcer) women's sexuality. During this time she read Alfred Adler, Alain, American literature, Aron, Bergson, Georges Bernanos, Dostoevsky, Drieu La Rochelle, English literature, what she called 'entertaining trash',[24] Faulkner, Freud, Gide, Julien Green, Hegel's *Phenomenology of Spirit*, Heidegger, Hemingway, Holderlin, Husserl, Jaspers, Joyce, Kafka, Kierkegaard, La Rochefoucauld, Leibniz, Michel Leiris, Emmanuel Levinas, Jacques Maritain, François Mauriac, Maurice Merleau-Ponty, Nietzsche, Proust, Raymond Queneau, Saint-Exupery, Scheler, Sketkel's *Frigidity in Women*, Stendahl, Stoics, Valéry, Jean Wahl, Oscar Wilde and more Virginia Woolf.

So what was it that she omitted? Although written in 1943, Beauvoir's first philosophical essay *Pyrrhus and Cinéas* was published in September 1944, after the liberation. However, it was only published in an English translation in 2004; readers without French were not able to follow the full story of the philosophical dialogue between Sartre and Beauvoir, or to see the development of Beauvoir's thinking in her own right. *Pyrrhus and Cinéas* raised serious moral questions and inaugurated what Beauvoir called 'the moral period' of her literary career. Whether it was the war, her relationship with Bost, her narrow escape from the Sorokine affair, her realization that she and Sartre had harmed Bianca Bienenfeld, concern not to be associated with *all* Sartre's views – or, more likely, a combination of many of these factors – she wanted to know now: (how) could actions – and relationships – be ethical? And before answering these moral questions she had to answer a more basic existential one: why do anything rather than nothing?

When Sartre's magnum opus *Being and Nothingness* was published in 1943 it was criticized by many of his contemporaries for painting a very bleak picture of humanity. After hundreds of dense and depressing pages analysing the human condition, Sartre dedicated a mere two and a half pages to ethics. He wrote that bad faith leads many to the nihilistic conclusion that 'it amounts to the same thing whether one gets drunk alone or is a leader of nations'.[25] Sartre didn't clearly say here why *it doesn't* amount to the same thing, nor did he elaborate on how the nihilist is wrong – for example, by saying why life does have meaning, or how it can be lived authentically. Instead, he offered his reader a list of unanswered questions: Could freedom itself be the source of all value, the reason human lives matter? Or did freedom have to be, as many religious philosophers thought, defined in relation to a 'transcendent value' (that is, God)?[26]

Like Beauvoir, Sartre had been fascinated by the concept of freedom and the human desire for meaning since his student days. Both of them wondered whether 'a transcendent' such as God was needed to give human freedom value and life meaning. But, unlike Beauvoir, he had not yet seen a way to incorporate ethics into his philosophy of freedom, and solve the problem of the transcendent. Beauvoir would express her answer in several literary forms: an essay, a novel and a play. But the essay and the play were not translated into English until the twenty-first century, and the novel was widely read as an 'existentialist' novel in which Beauvoir applied Sartre's ideas in fictional form. So it has been mistakenly assumed that Sartre developed the ethics of existentialism, one of the most popular movements in twentieth-century philosophy, when in fact, Beauvoir did – and in 1945 she said outright that that was what *she*, not Sartre, was doing.

Pyrrhus and Cinéas begins with a conversation between Pyrrhus and Cinéas. Pyrrhus is the king of Epirus, in the 4th century BCE; Cinéas is his advisor. They are discussing Pyrrhus' plan to conquer the world when Cinéas asks him: What difference did it make whether one conquered the world or rested at home?[27] Beauvoir agreed with Sartre that human beings make *projects*. They set goals and make limits for themselves, but those goals can always be surpassed or the limits redrawn. And even when we achieve the very thing we're after, we're often disappointed. Sometimes reaching our aim makes us realize we were in it for the pursuit; sometimes, once we achieve it, we no longer want it. So what is the point of acting, and why should we care whether we act ethically? *Being and Nothingness* ended on a note much like Cinéas' line above – that it doesn't make any difference whether one gets drunk alone or is a leader of nations.

But how could anyone think that? Beauvoir thought *it did make a difference*: the drunk has a different situation from that of the leader of nations, and different power to shape the worlds of others. Weaving scenes from life into paragraphs of philosophy, she wrote:

> I knew a child who cried because her concierge's son had died. Her parents let her cry, and then they got annoyed. 'After all, that little boy was not your brother.' The child dried her tears. But that was a dangerous thing to teach. Useless to cry over a little boy who is a stranger: so be it. But why cry over one's brother?[28]

Whatever else she had become, Beauvoir had not lost the incomprehension she felt when she saw her parents' indifference to the death of their concierge's child. But she knew there was a problem: if we open our eyes to the world's wrongs there's so much suffering and injustice that we can't cry for it all; we'd never stop. Our capacities are finite and we don't always know what to care about. If we identify with all the members of our sex or country or class, or with all of humanity, then we are increasing the scope of our care in words only.

The question is: what part of the world is ours to care for and cultivate? Our actions. That is Beauvoir's answer to the question – *why act?* – because your action is the only thing that is yours and yours alone, the means by which you become who you are. Only you can create or sustain the ties that unite you to others, for better or worse.[29] Your relationships with others are not givens: they have to be recreated, day by day, and they can be cultivated to flourishing or neglected and abused to death.[30]

For over a decade Beauvoir had been discussing the concept of freedom with Sartre, and attempting to *live* her life by the philosophy she believed in, just as she had formerly lived her life for the God she once loved. But it wasn't working: it wasn't liveable. The year that Sartre famously called other people 'hell' in his play *No Exit*, Beauvoir was publishing a philosophical rebuttal of his view. We are not alone in the world, and, contrary to Sartre, she thought that we would be miserable if we were, for it is only with others that our own projects can succeed. *Pyrrhus and Cinéas* returns to the themes of love and *devotion*, developing the lines of thought that she had sketched in her student diaries. Now Beauvoir wrote that everyone wants to feel at rest about the meaning of their lives. But the 'rest' that the devoted person claims for him- or – more commonly – *her*self is to live for another being. Some people claim to find that rest in God and some people find that rest in being devoted to other humans.[31]

But trying to justify one's existence through devotion is problematic. For one thing, the object of devotion may be irritated if your entire happiness rests on her acceptance of something she didn't ask for. Devotion to others can become tyrannical, if through devotion we limit the other's freedom against their desire. So Beauvoir wanted to know – since so many human beings seem to want to *be devoted* to another – is it possible to be devoted without being a tyrant?[32]

It was crystal clear now: she needed a different understanding of freedom from the one Sartre offered. She couldn't agree with him that freedom was limitless: our choices are constrained by the choices of others, and we constrain their choices too. Striving to be free, therefore, wasn't good enough – any person who valued freedom without hypocrisy had to value it in other people, to act in such a way that they exercised their freedom ethically.[33]

Beauvoir wanted her readers to come away with the point that our actions shape the worlds of the others in our lives, producing the conditions in which they act. She was disavowing her former political disengagement, certainly. But it is unclear how much to attribute this to her circumstances, and whether to assign greater weight to the historical moment of the Second World War or her own personal life. Even as a 'necessary' love Beauvoir suffered in her relationship with Sartre; and over time she realized that their relationship affected 'contingent' others in ways that were harmful. Years had passed since Beauvoir upbraided Sartre for the break-up letter he sent Bianca and she was now married to Bernard Lamblin – but Bianca had sought Beauvoir out again after the war: she was desperately unhappy. In 1945 Beauvoir wrote to Sartre again about their responsibility for her suffering. She had been talking with Bianca until midnight one night and was filled with remorse: 'she's suffering from an intense and dreadful attack of neurasthenia, and it's our fault, I think. It's the very direct, but profound, after-shock of the business between her and us. [...] we have harmed her.'[34] (Bianca's psychoanalyst, Jacques Lacan, would later agree.[35])

When *Pyrrhus and Cinéas* was published, it was a success. Indeed, in *Force of Circumstance* Beauvoir wrote that its reception was 'an encouragement to return to philosophy'.[36] She had subtly treated arguments from Benjamin Constant, Hegel, Spinoza, Flaubert, Kafka, Kant and Maurice Blanchot, rejecting them all. But she attributed her success to the French public's having been starved of philosophy during the Occupation, downplaying the significance of her own role in the development of existentialism.

Figure 7 *Simone de Beauvoir at work in* Les Deux Magots, *1944.*

Did she not see the significance herself? Fortunately for us, an interview from 1945 survives showing that she did. In *Les lettres françaises* Beauvoir expressed no concerns about the philosophical deprivation of the public but rather focused on the philosophical deficiencies of Sartre's system. In Beauvoir's own words: 'No ethics is implied in existentialism. I have sought, for my part, to extract one from it. I expounded it in *Pyrrhus and Cinéas*, which is an essay, then I tried to express the solution that I found in a novel and a play, that is to say in forms at once more concrete and ambiguous.'[37] So why would she omit this significant philosophical contribution from her account of her own life? In order to understand the answer to this question, we need to understand more of the path that led her to choose to become such a different self in public.

10

Queen of Existentialism

In January 1945 the United States State Department had sponsored eight French Resistance journalists to come to the United States and report on the American war effort, and Camus had invited Sartre. Sartre was elated: he had grown up watching westerns and reading thrillers and loved the idea of America. Some of the reality lived up to his expectations, but other parts fell woefully short. He was overwhelmed by its racism and the extremes he saw between the impoverished and the wealthy. He was also astonished by a woman he met at a New York radio station: a journalist by the name of Dolores Vanetti. Between the wars she had been an actress in Montparnasse, and had noticed the intellectuals in the Dôme and the Coupole. She had a low voice and – importantly, for Sartre – her mother tongue was French.[1] Before long, *amitié* became *amour*.

Beauvoir heard little from Sartre while he was away. She read his reports in *Combat* and *Le Figaro*, and she occasionally had news of him from Camus, who spoke to him by phone when he had a story to file. But she wasn't home to receive his letters anyway; in February Beauvoir went to Portugal for five weeks to visit Hélène and Lionel, now married. She gave lectures at the French Institute in Lisbon and wrote articles for *Combat*. It had been nearly five years since the sisters had last seen each other. Hélène was shocked to see her sister's worn clothes and Spartan shoes. The standard of living in Portugal was much higher than in France; so Simone returned with a new wardrobe for herself and gifts for 'the family'.[2]

In March Sartre wrote to say that he would stay a little longer in New York, until the end of May. On 29 April 1945 France held the first elections in which women had a right to vote. On 7 May Germany signed the act of military surrender in Reims; on 8 May it was signed in Berlin. In Europe, the war was over.

That June Sartre turned 40, and hated it. He decided to resign from teaching and throw himself wholly into writing. But he was feeling down for another reason, too: things were getting more serious with Dolores Vanetti, and despite the fact that she was a married woman she refused to be part of his life if Beauvoir was part of it too. There was no reason to write to her, Vanetti told him: it was over. By July Sartre couldn't bear to be at odds with Vanetti anymore and wrote to her. She replied encouragingly – maybe they could make things work after all. On 6 and 9 August the United States bombed Hiroshima and Nagasaki, and Japan surrendered.

After the war, the names Sartre and Beauvoir were everywhere.[3] Because of both her increased popularity and because her intellectual reputation became so firmly aligned with Sartre's and what they now, reluctantly, called 'existentialism', 1945 marked a significant turning point for Beauvoir's public image. That summer and autumn, between them, they released over half a dozen publications: novels, lectures, a play and a new periodical. In the space of a single week in October 1945 Sartre gave one of his most famous lectures (with the title 'Existentialism: Is it a Humanism?'), Beauvoir's play *Useless Mouths* opened, and the first issue of a new periodical, co-founded by Beauvoir and Sartre, was published. Paris news kiosks now sold monthly issues of their intellectual progeny, *Les Temps Modernes*. But the first issues bore only Sartre's name as 'Directeur'.

Named after Charlie Chaplin's 1936 comedy *Modern Times*, *Les Temps Modernes* was a literary, philosophical and political magazine. The magazine – which is still in existence as of 2019 – was heralded as a much needed 'third voice' between the Marxist and Christian discourses that dominated French politics. For Sartre and Beauvoir, it was a vehicle that enabled them to be 'engaged intellectuals' who focused on the pressing issues of the day. And it fed a hungry audience: In 1944, a law had been passed forbidding the publication of newspapers that had been published under Vichy occupation. Hundreds of periodicals were affected; only Resistance newspapers (such as *Combat* and *Libération*) and mainstream press from the Unoccupied zone (e.g., *Le Figaro* on the right, *Le Populaire* (socialist) or *L'Humanité* (communist)) survived. Collaborationist writers were tried and severely punished as part of a purge, which some writers described as a 'surgical operation' needed to restore France's 'social health'.[4] In addition to her editorial work on *Les Temps Modernes*, in the first years of its existence Beauvoir published several important essays on ethics and politics in it.

But there was a downside to launching so much with Sartre. Beauvoir's 1945 novel, *The Blood of Others*, tells two people's stories. But only one of them is described on the back cover of the Penguin edition:

> Jean Blomart, privileged *bourgeois* turned patriot leader against the Nazi Occupation, waits through the endless night for his lover Hélène to die. Flashbacks interweave the stories of both their lives until, with dawn approaching, Jean faces a momentous decision.
>
> *The Blood of Others*, written during the Occupation and published in 1945, portrays the agony of the French Resistance and the inner distress and awakening of a man impelled by anger and obsessed with family guilt. It remains one of Simone de Beauvoir's most gripping dramatizations of the existentialist's search to reconcile responsibility for others with personal happiness.[5]

According to this description, this is the story of *a man's* awakening. Hélène appears only to die, passively providing personal tragedy to heighten the drama of her hero's choice and action. But the novel is about more than one person's awakening: Hélène also discovers her responsibility to others – but the obstacles barring that discovery are not identical to the obstacles faced by her man.

Victor Brombert called it 'A breviary of existential beliefs' that Beauvoir 'dramatizes'. But the *The Blood of Others* does not just apply or dramatize Sartre's philosophy – it expresses Beauvoir's. It anticipates themes from *The Second Sex*, particularly concerning the ways women conduct themselves and the ways love is lived differently in the situations of individual men and women.

Early in the novel Hélène wants to love Jean because she thinks this will 'justify' her existence. However, as she ages – 'becoming a woman' – she is 'no longer content to love without hope of a return'.[6] Jean, too, realizes the fragility of Hélène's early love for him: he does not want to be the only thing she lives for because he could give her 'nothing but a wan tenderness'. He realizes that his love is a kind of imprisonment for her.[7]

This love is not satisfying for Jean or Hélène. For Jean, 'love is not the only thing' in life, and Hélène's demands are oppressive;[8] when Hélène 'awakens' to the reality of her responsibility for others she begins to see the place of love in her life differently.

Beauvoir later wrote that the mission of a writer is 'to describe in dramatic form the relationship of the individual to the world in which he stakes his freedom'.[9] But the world, for women, had different ideals and limitations from those it had for men. Beauvoir brought this disparity to life by telling the story of Hélène's awakening alongside Jean's, and also by weaving in ways women do not receive or demand the respect men are afforded. Jean's mother, for example, is always 'making excuses', apologizing and trying to take up less space;[10] Jean, by contrast, knows that he takes up space on earth.[11] In space and conversation, throughout the novel women are valued less than their male counterparts: Hélène notes that when Jean speaks to his friend Paul, he speaks 'man to man' and she is only a 'wayward, superficial little girl to them'.[12] She reproaches Paul for his hypocrisy: 'You have said to me so often that you respect other people's liberty. And you make decisions for me and treat me like a thing.'[13]

The novel also presents two men's approaches to sex, one that objectifies women and one that does not: Jean sees a full person in the lover who smiles in his embrace, and enjoys the mixing of his embodied consciousness with another's; Marcel, by contrast, 'can't bear to touch a body unless he sees it as an object – absolutely'.[14]

Beauvoir concluded the second volume of her memoirs with a paragraph of reflection on her work: she was dissatisfied with *She Came to Stay* because 'murder was not the solution'. In *The Blood of Others* and *Pyrrhus and Cinéas*, Beauvoir 'attempted to define our true relationship with other people': 'Whether we like it or not, we do impinge on other people's destinies, and must face up to the responsibility which this implies.'[15] *The Blood of Others* opens with an epigraph from Dostoevsky's *The Brothers Karamazov*: 'Each of us is responsible for everything and to every human being.' It was dedicated to Nathalie Sorokine.

In later life, when Beauvoir had begun to defend her own originality, she returned to the reception of *The Blood of Others*. In *Force of Circumstance* she wrote that its main theme was 'the paradox of this existence experienced by me as my freedom and by those who came in contact with me as an object'. Her intention was not, she says, 'apparent to the public; the book was labelled a "Resistance novel"' and an 'Existentialist novel'. It was bad enough that readers assumed her novels were 'thesis novels' – and worse that they thought that their theses could be found in Sartre's philosophy.

The word 'existentialist' was coined by the Catholic philosopher and playwright Gabriel Marcel to refer to Sartre's philosophy, and Beauvoir objected to the way people tried to stamp her with the same label: she had not even heard the term when she wrote the novel, and claimed that her inspiration 'came from [her] own experience, not from a system'.[16] In the *Wartime Diary* Beauvoir's early notes for *The Blood of Others* are explicit that she wanted the novel to show, among other things, a female character who fell prey to 'the illusion of the recognition of consciousness through love'.[17]

On 29 October, Beauvoir's one and only play, *Useless Mouths*, opened in Paris, with a benefit performance at the Théâtre des Carrefours. Set in medieval Flanders, the action unfolds in a fictional city-state called Vaucelles. Vaucelles has revolted against the Duke of Burgundy, and the play opens with a scene displaying the starvation of its inhabitants after a long siege. The leading aldermen decide that in order to preserve the city they must expel 'the useless mouths' – namely, women, children and the elderly. Food was scarce, they reasoned, so only workers and soldiers should have it. The town's name, pronounced 'vaut-elle' in French, is a homophone for the question: 'Does she have worth?'

Well before her better known political works *The Second Sex* (1949) and *Old Age* (1970), Beauvoir's play showed that some categories of people are considered useless simply for being what they are – child, woman, old. And, like so many of Beauvoir's works, the play also raises the question of whether all love or commitment is 'a prison'. One of its characters, Jean-Pierre, does not want to be 'given' a wife: 'Give her to me? Do you think that I would agree to lock her up and tell her that I alone am her portion of the world? I don't have the soul of a jailer.' Throughout the play, both Jean-Pierre and Clarice discover that another 'love' is possible. When he professes this love for Clarice, she asks him:

Clarice 'And how does one love on this earth?'

Jean-Pierre 'We struggle together.'[18]

Beauvoir dedicated the play to her mother[19] and the proceeds from opening night went to feed children who had been orphaned by their parents' deportation to Germany.[20]

Beauvoir later portrayed the critical response to *Useless Mouths* as hostile – 'the dailies tore me to pieces almost unanimously'.[21] And it is true that some reviews were critical, particularly about the production; others thought its message was too forced, that it was 'much less theatre than idea'.[22] But not all: 'How come in all Paris there wasn't to be found at least ten directors fighting for this manuscript? If there is any justice, if the public is still in a state to appreciate its worth, *Useless Mouths* will triumph on the boulevard de la Chapelle.'[23]

On the same night that *Useless Mouths* opened, 29 October 1945, Sartre was in another part of town giving a now-famous talk: 'Existentialism: Is it a Humanism?' The venue was a small one called Club Maintenant but even so the event's organizers were concerned it would be embarrassingly empty. When Sartre arrived there were crowds waiting to get in and he worried that he wouldn't be able to get in himself. When he finally made his way to the podium he said that 'existentialism' was a popular word but no one knew what it meant. The Christians thought it godless and immoral; the communists thought it nihilistic. But it was neither, Sartre said. People objected to his views because they preferred to be in bad faith than to face their freedom. 'Existence precedes essence,' he said: you are only what you make of yourself. That night's lecture (later published as *Existentialism is a Humanism*) became the *locus classicus* of French existentialism.

Shortly after Sartre's lecture the Club Maintenant had another, less well remembered existentialist evening: Jean Wahl gave a short talk on the history of existentialism, and other philosophers were invited to respond. Nikolai Berdyaev, Georges Gurvitch and Emmanuel Levinas discussed the ways it was indebted to Kierkegaard, Husserl and Heidegger.[24] And less remembered still is a lecture that took place there on 11 December – on 'The novel and metaphysics', by Simone de Beauvoir.[25]

Sartre's Club Maintenant lecture would become an iconic intellectual event of postwar Paris. Beauvoir's, by contrast, would not; she gave it less than a sentence in her autobiography. She was testing the limits between literature and philosophy, and defending her reasons philosophically. Others began to take note, and some to agree with her. Earlier in 1945 Merleau-Ponty had published an essay arguing that Beauvoir's *She Came to Stay* represented a new way of doing philosophy.[26]

But in the meantime, despite the initial success of *The Blood of Others*, like *Useless Mouths* it had begun to be accused of sacrificing literature for philosophy. In the press Maurice Blanchot had praised *She Came to Stay* for being philosophically rich but remaining virtuously ambiguous, not forcing a conclusion on the reader. But he condemned *The Blood of Others* as a thesis novel, and he was not the only one to do so. So in 'Literature and Metaphysics', Beauvoir responded to her critics, defending her attempts to reconcile philosophy and literature in personal and philosophical terms. 'When I was eighteen,' she began,

> I read a great deal; I would read only as one can read at that age, naively and passionately. To open a novel was truly to enter a world, a concrete, temporal world, peopled with singular characters and events. A philosophical treatise would carry me beyond the terrestrial appearances into the serenity of a timeless heaven. [...] Where was truth to be found? On earth or in eternity? I felt torn apart.

Beauvoir chose to write novels because of the capacity for literature to give us 'imaginary experiences that are as complete and disturbing as lived experiences'.[27] Philosophical works are often written in an abstract voice that wants to compel or persuade its reader to adopt their point of view, rather than inviting the reader to see different perspectives unfold in particular situations. A metaphysical novel, Beauvoir said, is an 'appeal' to the reader's freedom.

Beauvoir noted that she was in excellent literary and philosophical company in being accused of writing thesis novels – Dostoevsky had been accused of writing a philosophical treatise in *The Brothers Karamazov*, and she thought Kierkegaard demonstrated her point that the more a philosopher values the subjective side of human experience, the unique inner life of each person, the more likely they are to use a literary form that described the singular experience of individuals becoming themselves in time. Even Plato was torn between these two temptations: in one and the same dialogue he banished the poets from the Republic (because he was concerned that art would corrupt its citizens); and yet saw the power of art to encourage us to pursue the Good (after all, this giant of Western philosophy wrote dialogues – a literary form).[28]

After 1945 – the year she would later call their 'existentialist offensive' – neither Sartre nor Beauvoir could escape their celebrity. At home people stared at them in cafés and photographers snapped candid shots in the street. In America Sartre and Beauvoir appeared in the pages of *Vogue*, *Harper's Bazaar* and *Atlantic Monthly*. Sartre was an icon, but he was made all the more intriguing by the attractive and unconventional woman who was, in some sense, by his side. Beauvoir also published philosophical essays expounding existentialism that are 'more carefully considered and composed' than Sartre's.[29] But her intellectual contributions to this philosophical moment and her disagreements with Sartre have been relentlessly downplayed. In 1945

Figure 8 *Beauvoir on air in 1945, the year of the 'existentialist offensive'.*

the sensationalist postwar tabloid *Samedi Soir* called her 'la grande
Sartreuse' and 'Notre Dame de Sartre'.

In the public eye they were inseparable. But privately Beauvoir was
suffering through one of the most difficult of Sartre's 'contingent'
relationships, which had thrown her into 'great perplexity'.[30] In the 1970s,
in an interview with Sartre in which they discussed the other women in
his life, Beauvoir said that she was frightened of Dolores Vanetti because
Sartre was so attached to her. He dedicated the first issue of *Les Temps
Modernes* 'To Dolores' and instead of spending Christmas with Beauvoir
he left on 12 December 1945 to spend two months with Vanetti in
America. When Deirdre Bair asked Beauvoir about Vanetti in 1982, she
reported that Beauvoir became 'agitated and emotional'.[31] But this kind
of statement tells us very little: what kind of agitation, what kind of
emotion? Was it jealousy or grief that was still raw over thirty years
later? Or was it agitation or anger that she was still being asked about
this, still defined so much by Sartre and his other women?

In December 1945 Beauvoir published an essay in *Les Temps Modernes* entitled 'Existentialism and Popular Wisdom'. Existentialism continued to face accusations that it was a pessimistic philosophy with an unhealthy emphasis on human depravity and death, so Beauvoir wrote an essay wryly pointing out that it was hardly new of existentialism to notice human misery or mortality, nor to ask why we are born, what we are doing here, or what is the point of suffering.[32] She was beginning to tire of people asking her what they would gain by being an existentialist: it was a very strange question to ask a philosopher, she said. 'Neither Kant nor Hegel ever asked himself what one would gain by being Kantian or Hegelian. They said what they thought was the truth, nothing more. They had no other goal but truth itself.'[33]

The truth, as Beauvoir saw it, was that people took flight from their freedom in alibis. The pessimism Sartre expressed in *Being and Nothingness* was very like the pessimism of the French moralist tradition – a tradition including the celebrated writers Pascal and La Rochefoucauld. Pascal thought that humanity was capable of both great 'misery' and great 'grandeur', but tended towards the former. This gained him the nickname '*miserabiliste*' (miserabilist) and a literary afterlife in works like Victor Hugo's *Les Miserables* – The Miserable. La Rochefoucauld's similarly pessimistic *Maximes* describes the deceptions of human self-love as narcissistic delusions of epidemic proportions. Even in charity, he saw self-interest in disguise.

French readers well-versed in their nation's culture did not see much hope in Sartre's account of the human condition, in part because they recognized so much of these philosophies of misery and despair in it. What Beauvoir found surprising was that this should 'raise so much outrage': 'The theme of man's misery is not new,' she wrote. 'The Church fathers, Pascal, Bossuet, Massillon, preachers, priests, the entire Christian tradition has for centuries tried its best to fill man with the feeling of his abjection.' Secular moralists, too, have attacked propriety and convention: 'La Rochefoucauld, La Fontaine, Saint-Simon, Camfort, and Maupassant have vied with each other in denouncing baseness, futility, hypocrisy.'[34]

As Beauvoir saw it, both the Christian and moralist answers to the ambiguity of human existence were *alibis*. If human beings are *by nature* sinful, or *by nature* driven by self-interest, then they could comfortably consider themselves determined to their misery rather than free to resist the injustices that perpetuate it. If Sartre thought human beings were *by nature* doomed to desire domination, then there really was no exit from living with our own oppressors. Beauvoir's philosophy, by contrast, refused 'the consolations of lies and resignations' – it was an excuse to think that it's just human nature to dominate or submit.[35]

> People like to think that virtue is easy. [...] They also resign themselves, without much trouble, to believing that virtue is impossible. But they are reluctant to envisage that it could be possible and difficult.[36]

Determinism of any kind – Christian, secular, moralist, Marxist – relieved the human being of the burden of her freedom. Just as importantly, it relieved them of the weight of trying to use it ethically.

As Beauvoir gained prestige, she also gained opportunities to use it for the benefit of others. One day in the autumn of 1945 she was waiting to buy cinema tickets with a friend on the Champs Elysées when the friend saw an acquaintance who was an aspiring writer: Violette Leduc. A few days later Leduc gave Beauvoir her manuscript to read. Beauvoir read the first half in one sitting but the second half, she told Leduc, lost momentum. Leduc redrafted it and Beauvoir liked it so much she suggested the book to Camus for publication. He accepted the novel – *L'Asphyxie* – on her recommendation.[37] Beauvoir would go on to play an encouraging role in Leduc's life and work.

While Sartre was away she continued to work on her next novel, *All Men Are Mortal*, and also edited Sartre's lecture 'Existentialism: Is it a Humanism?' for publication under the revised title 'Existentialism is a Humanism'. Nathalie Sorokine was still at the Louisiane with Beauvoir; she was pregnant and preparing to move to California to be with her boyfriend, an American GI. 'She's gentle and nice and she's blooming,' Beauvoir wrote to Sartre, 'as is the child.'[38] Beauvoir and Bost were still lovers but his work as a journalist required frequent travel and he had begun to feel overshadowed by Sartre – even though the latter was almost as rarely present.

Beauvoir spent Christmas in Mégève with Bost, Olga and Wanda. Given the successes of the year, it is interesting that she described this skiing holiday as 'one of the best times [she]'d had this year'. She was already beginning to recognize that for her public success wasn't necessarily conducive to private satisfaction; she liked the well-worn intimacies of old friendship and the revitalising solitude of fresh air. When she returned to Paris in mid-January she found the change abrupt: one day she was in skis; 'Now I'm in town clothes, I've just had my hair done, and what's more I'm stunningly handsome because I've a magnificent complexion, all tanned and with my face all relaxed – which is quite out of keeping in Paris.'[39] Waiting for a plane to Tunisia, Beauvoir wrote to Sartre that her fame had followed her to the slopes: 'Did you know I'm really rather famous too? The good lady from the Idéal-Spirt asked Kos.: "Is she very well known, that Mlle de Beauvoir? Customers keep coming up to me and asking if that's really her."'[40]

After that, Sartre didn't hear anything from her for a month; he kept hoping for a letter and sent 'scads' of his own to Tunisia, but they had to rely on *postes restantes* and often missed each other.[41] In New York Beauvoir's novels were making trouble for him – Dolores had asked Lévi-Strauss if he liked Sartre. Lévi-Strauss feigned not to know that Dolores and Sartre were an item, and replied, 'How do you think I could like him after reading *She Came to Stay*?' He was such a 'filthy bastard'. ('Thanks a lot, little jewel,' Sartre wrote to Simone, 'for the portrait.'[42])

Beauvoir, meanwhile, gave lectures in Tunis and Algiers. She couldn't believe the 'wild success' of existentialism: in Algeria people came in droves. But she missed his letters, and when she got back to Paris, Bost was in Italy, Sorokine had left for America, Sartre was still in New York. Even so, people were starting to talk about Sartre and Vanetti. He was going around calling her the most wonderful woman: his biographer, Annie Cohen-Solal, wrote of this period that she didn't know whether to think his behaviour 'mad, perverse, cynical, opportunistic, cruel, sadistic, or simply clumsy'.[43]

Despite the fact that none of Sartre's books had been published in English, in New York Sartre had met with much-publicized fanfare. *TIME* magazine ran an article about 'the literary lion' of Paris who'd 'bounced into Manhattan'. It described *Being and Nothingness* as the 'Bible' of existentialism, and Simone de Beauvoir as its 'foremost disciple'.[44]

If Beauvoir had known what was happening on the other side of the Atlantic, she might have felt justified in fearing the worst. The face Sartre showed Beauvoir described him as enjoying New York and an American love affair but also finding himself 'scared' by Vanetti's love for him: he wrote as though he were keeping Vanetti's passion at arm's length.[45] But in fact Vanetti was pursuing a divorce. Columbia University had offered Sartre a two-year post and he had asked Vanetti to marry him.[46]

Sartre declined the post, and Vanetti's divorce was taking time, so she and Sartre agreed that he would return to France. They would spend more time together later in the year. And after that, who knew?

Back in Paris that February, Beauvoir started working on *The Ethics of Ambiguity* and published an article in *Les Temps Modernes* entitled 'An Eye for an Eye'. By this point after the War the Holocaust's horrors were no longer hidden, and 'An Eye for an Eye' is a subtle discussion of punishment and revenge, responsibility and forgiveness. She wrote that human beings are fundamentally ambiguous: both subject and object, both consciousness and matter. 'Absolute evil', she said, involves refusing to acknowledge that others are subjects, instead seeing them as objects that can be tortured and killed.[47]

On 15 March Sartre left New York for Paris. When he got back his conversation was peppered with 'Dolores-this' and 'Dolores-that'. Beauvoir found it hard to concentrate on her work; after a couple of hours she got a headache or felt distracted.[48] In April 1946 she was upset: did Sartre have a harmony with Dolores that she would never have with him? She wanted to rid herself of the uncertainty that plagued her, and the question burst out of her before she could choose her moment: 'Frankly, who means the most to you: Dolores or me?' They were on their way to lunch with friends, there wasn't much time. He replied that Dolores meant 'an enormous amount', but 'I am with you'.[49] She sat through the meal with her heart sinking. Was he with her out of faithfulness to the pact or because he wanted to be? After lunch Sartre explained: they had always taken actions to be more valuable than words, so why not do so now? He was with her.

She thought she believed him. But in May of 1946 Beauvoir was still working on *The Ethics of Ambiguity*, and after the shock of seeing Sartre infatuated with Vanetti she struggled. She continued to read philosophy, studying the concept of mediation in Hegel. She knew that she worked too hard sometimes, writing that there were days when she felt like a fish washed up on the rocks 'dying and drained'.[50] But drained or not, she delivered: on 14 May she handed over four articles for *Les Temps Modernes*; the introduction to *The Ethics of Ambiguity* was published on 1 June.[51]

The estrangement she felt from Sartre was made worse by the fact that they were now too famous to write in cafés. Sartre's stepfather had died the previous year while he was in America, and his mother had asked him whether he would consider sharing an apartment with her. He said yes, and in May 1946 he moved into the fourth floor of 42, rue Bonaparte. It had windows looking over the Place Saint-Germain-des-Prés; from his study he could see the terrace of Les Deux Magots and the intersection with the rue de Rennes.

Sartre had re-entered his mother's bourgeois world, fake Louis XVI furniture and all. But the apartment was comfortable, and for the first time ever he started to collect a library. Madame Mancy bought his clothes, and her maid, Eugénie, did Sartre's laundry. Beauvoir and Madame Mancy had still not exactly warmed to each other: now Sartre's mother was describing these new arrangements as 'her third marriage'.[52]

Soon after Sartre moved in they had word that Olga – who was due to perform in Sartre's play, *The Flies* – was ill. She had tuberculosis in both lungs. She was 29. She went to a hospital in Clichy, the Beaujon, where she had the operation that saved her life. Bost had just published a book of his own but he had little time to enjoy it; he visited Olga daily and Beauvoir often accompanied him.

Sartre's situation changed in another way shortly after his return from America. He had a letter from a keen student from the École Normale. Jean Cau was 21 years old and wondered: would Sartre like a secretary? Initially Sartre laughed at the idea. But then he came round to it and employed him for three hours each morning. Cau worked for Sartre for eleven years, writing the letters Sartre didn't want to and, eventually, managing Sartre's finances – an unenviable task. Madame Mancy let him in at 10 a.m. each morning and he began opening Sartre's mail. Sartre arrived at work around the same time – and then he worked 'like a mule'. At 1 p.m. Sartre would leave for lunch with Beauvoir or another woman and Cau would leave for the day. At 4.30 p.m. Sartre returned to the apartment with Beauvoir, who would set up to work on a bridge table in Sartre's study, and stay there until 8 p.m.

In the period from 1946 to 1949 Sartre – now with his mother managing his household, and domestic and secretarial staff – produced forty published works in less than four years. And Beauvoir, of course, was his editorial advisor; they still consulted each other about all of their books in progress. Beauvoir's labour was not exactly unpaid in these endeavours – she had her own income from her writing and editorial work, and her letters suggest that they related to Sartre's income as joint income (although once they had it they often gave it away).[53] But Beauvoir was supporting her family; she did not have the same means for private space and private staff.

For many readers of Beauvoir's autobiography, the Vanetti years have made it hard to resist wondering whether it would have been a relief for Beauvoir to end her 'necessary' relationship with Sartre. It was public knowledge that the pact had been made over fifteen years before. But it was not public knowledge that Beauvoir's relationship with Sartre was not conventional erotic love. When she wrote in *Force of Circumstance* that she 'possessed an incommunicable knowledge of [her] bond with Sartre' many simply assumed that this bond fitted the common narratives of women's lives – namely, the pursuit of a central place in a man's life, through licit marriage or illicit liaisons rather than an intense intellectual friendship.[54]

Beauvoir had started to see Merleau-Ponty again from time to time; he was going to take over the day-to-day editing of *Les Temps Modernes*, a role nominally held by Sartre. She had lunch with him on 6 May and they discussed Sartre's philosophy, which Merleau-Ponty thought failed to do justice to the intricacies of reality. This made her want to go back to writing her essay on ambiguity, Beauvoir wrote in her diary, but she felt too tired and didn't know why.[55]

In June of 1946 she published an early version of the 'Introduction' to *The Ethics of Ambiguity* in *Labyrinthe*. She criticized philosophers for fleeing reality in 'rational metaphysics and consoling ethics': 'as long as there have been men who live, they have experienced the tragic ambiguity of their condition, and as long as there have been philosophers who think, most of them have tried to mask it'.[56] What was needed was an ethics that looked the ambiguity of human life in the face instead of giving people alibis.

By the end of the month she had finished *The Ethics of Ambiguity* and she was wondering what to write next. She sat with blank paper, looking vacantly at it. A friend, the sculptor Alberto Giacometti, saw her and said she looked 'wild'; she explained that she wanted to write but didn't know what to write. He told her to 'write anything'. She had liked Michel Leiris's book *Manhood* and was inspired to write about herself: an idea began to take shape in her mind. So she made some notes and then chewed them over with Sartre. Her question was: 'What has it meant to me to be a woman?'

In Beauvoir's memoirs she described her conversation with Sartre as a revelation. At first, the account in *Force of Circumstance* says, she thought that being a woman hadn't meant much at all; she didn't feel inferior and she claimed that 'no one had ever said to me: "You think that way because you're a woman"; my femininity had never been irksome to me in any way'.[57] Sartre suggested that perhaps she should think about it further: she wasn't raised like a boy would have been. So she did look into the question, and it was then that she discovered just how much the world was a masculine world: her childhood was shaped by many myths, and those myths shaped boys and girls differently. So she put her autobiographical idea on a back burner and instead dived headlong into researching 'the myths of femininity', spending hours reading at the Bibliothèque Nationale. For this work she did not want to focus on her *own* experience of being a woman, but rather on the condition of 'woman'. Although *The Second Sex* contains passages that closely resemble the experiences of Beauvoir and some of her circle, and although she had already voiced criticisms of philosophers' pretensions to neutrality and universality in her diary in 1941, and her essays and novels throughout the 1940s, she had not fully come to see the extent to which the personal could become political. Philosophers wrote about 'man' and 'the human condition'. But what about 'woman'? Was there such a thing as 'the feminine condition'?

Some have taken this passage in Beauvoir's memoirs to give too much credit to Sartre for his role in the genesis of *The Second Sex*. Margaret Simons has pointed out that the idea that Beauvoir had never reflected on being a woman is patently false – it contradicts several passages in her diaries, letters, life and fiction. Given Beauvoir's deliberateness and her disposition to reflect, some have even argued that her telling of this story was *purposefully false*. After all, in her teenage years Beauvoir wanted to be one of the pioneers of philosophy so badly that she waged a campaign of silence against her parents; but she also acknowledged that fulfilling this desire meant estrangement from many of the roles traditionally reserved for women.[58] The teenage Beauvoir turned to her teacher, Jeanne Mercier, when she struggled to understand how philosophical rationality could coexist with her passionate side; her mentor urged her to see emotions as an integral part of life. In July of 1927 Beauvoir wrote that she wanted to 'remain a woman', but to be 'more masculine by her brain, more feminine by her sensibility'.[59]

A little over a decade later, during the war, she was about to turn 32 when she wrote: 'I feel myself to be a grown woman; I would like to know which one.'[60] She had just written to Sartre about an aspect of herself that truly interested her: her 'femininity', 'the manner in which

I am and am not of my sex'. 'This remains to be defined,' she said, 'as well as what I expect from my life, my thought, and how I situate myself in the world.'[61]

But the notorious passage in *Force of Circumstance* doesn't say that Sartre had the idea for the book; she said that her conversation with him was eye-opening. She had already read Leiris, made notes about the project, and then she discussed them with him as she worked on it.[62] He was, once again, not the source of her thoughts but their incomparable friend – a conversational catalyst. The concept of the *situation* is what Beauvoir would later say made *The Second Sex* so original. She did not see femininity as an 'essence' or a 'nature' but rather as 'a situation created by civilizations from certain physiological givens'.[63]

In summer of 1946 Beauvoir and Sartre travelled to Switzerland and Italy together. In Geneva Beauvoir gave a talk to students and in Lausanne she gave a public lecture. From Geneva they travelled to Fribourg, Neuchâtel, Basel. Beauvoir was finishing up her third novel, *All Men Are Mortal*, and Sartre was writing more plays. After their time together Sartre went to spend time with Wanda, and Beauvoir went walking in the Dolomites – again finding the retreat from city life and company restful and restorative. They went to Rome together in October, passing their days peacefully in writing.[64]

In December 1946 Beauvoir published *All Men Are Mortal*. It is very different from Beauvoir's other novels, with a sweeping historical plot rather than one driven by passionate interiority. It is less well known, perhaps because it lacks any character that could be presumed to be Jean-Paul Sartre. Like *The Blood of Others*, its narrator – Count Fosca – is male and recounts his story over the space of a single night. But unlike Jean Blomart, Count Fosca is immortal. He was born mortal – in Italy in 1279 – and has witnessed nearly six centuries of now indefinite life. Fosca chose immortality because he believed that with it he could orchestrate lasting changes in history: he would eliminate famine and war by becoming a world dictator, directing everything so that there was peace and prosperity for all on earth.

Fosca's own story is woven through significant moments in Europe's past: medieval Italy, sixteenth-century Germany (in the heat of disputes about Luther and the fallout of giving authority to individual conscience). Whether in the thirteenth century or the sixteenth, he finds war. He wants to reform society to help the poorest, but in each century he encounters resistance. After losing hope in Europe Fosca thinks perhaps the New World will not be tainted by the tradition-enforced savagery of the Old. But when he arrives there he discovers the destruction of the Incas and the exploitation of indigenous South Americans. He is told that 'the black people of Africa' and 'the savages in America' do not have souls, so their deaths and suffering should not stand between Europeans and their gold.[65] Seeing the misery that was justified in the name of the Good led him to doubt the existence of goodness itself.[66]

Fosca tells his history to an audience of one: Regina, a narcissistic twentieth-century woman who is enchanted by the idea that she can achieve immortality by being loved by an immortal man. She thinks being loved by Fosca will make her unique among women; when in fact his immortality reduces her to the place of one lover in a potentially limitless line. Mortal authenticity is found in neither Fosca nor Regina, but in another character, Armand, who is content with being committed to his own time. Beauvoir wanted *All Men Are Mortal* to express the morality of *Phyrrus and Cinéas*, but as an 'imaginary experience' rather than a lesson.[67]

The novel's immortal narrator and historical structure also expressed a theme that Beauvoir would go on to unpack in *The Second Sex*: 'that men have always kept in their hands all concrete powers'.[68] The women in *All Men Are Mortal* are, as Elizabeth Fallaize put it, 'an almost exclusively depressing demonstration of the marginality to which history has largely confined women'.[69] We see dependency, forced marriage, women left to die as expendable parts of society. But as history unfolds, in Fosca's later lovers, in later centuries, we also see women who want to fund science and found universities. With each of them, Fosca asks the question: What does it mean to love?

Beauvoir had been preoccupied with the problem of history since the early 1940s. After the end of the war, Beauvoir wondered where she should take her stand: with 'the nihilism of the false prophets' who declared that the third world war was already beginning, or with 'the giddiness of the good-timers'? Against contemporary Communists (politically) and against Hegel (philosophically), Beauvoir could not speak of the future of 'Humanity' as unified and progressive.[70] She had little optimism about history, and used Fosca's story to express this: 'Stupid wars, a chaotic economy, useless rebellions, futile massacres, populations unaccompanied by any improvement in the standard of living, everything in this period seemed to me confusion and marking time; I had chosen it for this very reason.'[71]

The question this novel asks is not 'what is to be done?', but 'can anything be done'?

11

American Dilemmas

On 25 January 1947 Beauvoir boarded a flight to New York for what would be a momentous four months in America. She had always loved English and American novels; after her childhood encounters with Alcott and Eliot she loved Hemingway, Woolf and too many others to list. So she was over the moon when Philippe Soupault, a French journalist and surrealist poet who was teaching at Swarthmore College, arranged a lecture series for her in the United States. Claude Lévi-Strauss, who was working for the French cultural embassy at the time, arranged to cover her expenses. Dolores Vanetti was going to Paris to be with Sartre while she was away.

When she got off the plane the immigration official asked her what the purpose of her stay was. Her visa said lectures; he asked 'On what?' Philosophy, she said. At the airport she was met by a woman from the French Cultural Services, who took her for a lobster dinner en route to her midtown hotel. Once the official welcome was over, Beauvoir set off into Manhattan, taking in the sights as she strode through the streets. She'd imagined them many times, but seeing them was surreal: Broadway, Times Square, Wall Street, Lady Liberty. She felt so free here; no one looked at her.[1]

She was amazed by New York: people dropped letters down chutes, bought things from machines, and spoke like characters in the movies she and Sartre so loved. Since the 1930s they had both developed a joint and dissonant affection for America and the USSR: they loved jazz, African-American spirituals, the blues, American movies, American novels. But they also thought that America sheltered the most hateful form of capitalist oppression and detested its exploitation of the poor – especially the segregation of blacks and whites. The USSR could not rival America's artistic attractions, but in the 1930s they admired its social experiment.[2]

Beauvoir was curious but wary about American ways. She went walking in Harlem by herself – defying the white locals' advice that it could be dangerous just as she defied her friends' warnings about hitchhiking in Marseille. She tried scotch because it seemed to her to be one of the 'keys to America'; at first she didn't like it but she quickly acquired the taste.[3] Gradually she overcame the knot in her stomach when she had to phone hotel reception or make an appointment in English, gaining confidence.

She set up a date with Dolores Vanetti, who hadn't left New York for Paris yet, because she wanted to meet her in the flesh and Vanetti had promised to put her in touch with some editors. So Beauvoir invited her for a drink at the Fifth-Avenue Sherry Netherland. They drank whiskey, a little nervously at first, and talked until 3 a.m.

After imagining this woman for months Beauvoir was happy to feel real pleasure to meet her.[4] She felt happy because she 'understood' Sartre's feelings, writing 'I could appreciate them, and honoured you for having them.' Soon after, Vanetti invited Beauvoir to a cocktail party, and even put her in touch with some American newspapers and magazines. Beauvoir wrote articles for extra income, on the topic of women writers and femininity. These show that two years before *The Second Sex* was published she was already tracing the contemporary situation of women to its roots in the First World War, which gave them greater access to paid work but not yet independence.[5]

While in New York Beauvoir became good friends with Ellen and Richard Wright, a mixed-race couple who would remain friends for decades. Richard was the author of the novels *Native Son* (1940) and *Black Boy* (1945); Ellen would go on to found a literary agency and Beauvoir would be her client for life.[6] Beauvoir had first read Wright in 1940, and *Les Temps Modernes* published one of his stories, 'Fire and Cloud', in its inaugural issue. Wright thought she and Sartre felt the human plight keenly, and that there was nothing quite like their writing. Before long Beauvoir was calling their Greenwich Village apartment – on Charles Street – her home. Their 5-year-old daughter liked her, which took Beauvoir a bit by surprise. And so did their friends: the Wrights introduced her to intellectuals like Bernard Wolfe, who had been Trotksy's secretary in Mexico and wrote books about the blues. She told him she wanted to hear real jazz, so he set her up with tickets to see Louis Armstrong at Carnegie Hall.[7]

Richard Wright also introduced Beauvoir to a book that would alter her intellectual course: *American Dilemma: The Negro Problem and Modern Democracy*. Published in 1944 by the Swedish sociologist Gunnar Myrdal, at the time it was the most prominent study of race and racism in America. (It would go on to be cited in the landmark desegregation trial *Brown v. Board of Education* (1954) and to sell 100,000 copies by 1965.) Myrdal thought that race relations in America were caught in not a vicious circle but resulted from something he called 'the principle of cumulation'. As he saw it, white people oppressed people of colour and then blamed them for performing poorly. Unless whites were cured of their prejudice, or the circumstances of black Americans were improved, the cycle would continue to take its toll on society. American political ideals – such as equality, meritocracy and opportunity – failed to take into account the ways in which black lives were, in the past and present, conditioned by oppression, prejudice and exclusion. Writing before the Civil Rights Movement,

Myrdal believed that many white Americans did not know about the situations faced by their black compatriots. So he thought that getting 'publicity' – consciousness raising – was crucial to improving the situation, because unlike a 'vicious circle' the principle of cumulation could work both ways: 'in an "upward" desirable direction as well as a "downward" undesirable direction.'[8]

America prided itself on being a country that welcomed new ideas, and Beauvoir was warmly received: *The New Yorker* interviewed Beauvoir and covered her visit. The write-up called her 'Sartre's female intellectual counterpart' and 'the prettiest Existentialist you ever saw'.[9]

In mid-February Beauvoir left New York for a 24-lecture cross-country tour on 'the ethical problems of the post-war writer'. Two articles on French women writers were published announcing the tour: 'Problems for women's literature' and 'Women of letters'. *France-Amérique* introduced their author as a 'philosopher, reporter, novelist'. What were the 'problems' of women's literature? Why had women achieved less literary success than men? Beauvoir argued that women's limitations were to be found in their situation rather than an inherent lack of ability:

> For centuries it has been men and men alone who have fashioned the world in which we live. That is to say that this world belongs to them. Women have their place in it, but are not at home there. It is natural that man seeks to explore the domain of which he feels himself the master; that he searches with curiosity to know it, strives to dominate it with his thought, and even claims, through the medium of art, to create it anew. Nothing stops him, nothing limits him. But, up until these last few years, women's situation was completely different.[10]

The situation of women had changed dramatically in recent years – not just in terms of winning the right to vote (which was a very fresh victory in France), but in terms of access to education and opportunity. And, as a consequence of this, women increasingly sought 'a deepening of their internal knowledge of themselves', leading them to 'turn toward philosophy'.[11] But Beauvoir thought that there was still much to overcome: because femininity was so often identified with modesty, women lacked audacity and they were afraid of the consequences of having it. In childhood, Beauvoir wrote, girls had some autonomy – but they were encouraged to forsake it as women in the name of happiness and love.[12]

One of her lectures was in Chicago, where she stopped for a day and a half. The streets were snowy and the Windy City lived up to its name. The cold felt inhospitable; she didn't want to explore this place alone. Her New York friends had given her a name to look up: Nelson Algren, a novelist with a tough guy veneer who wrote about the underbelly of American life – addicts and prostitutes.

She tried phoning him three times, but she couldn't pronounce his name and he kept hanging up on her. After the third time, she asked an American to try, and that evening they met at her hotel bar.[13] At 38, he was a year her junior, tall and trim. Beauvoir told him she was tired of seeing the shiny surface of America: her tour so far had taken her from one high-end hotel to the next. After so many luncheons, lectures and lobsters, could he please show her what Chicago really looked like?

He could and he did: he took her to the Bowery, which was well known for 'red lights, cheap liquor, wiggling dancers, and a variety of associated evils'.[14] They visited a burlesque club and listened to jazz in a black club. He spoke no French, and she was still struggling with English. But before the night was over he was telling her about his life. He was born in Detroit and raised in a poor part of Chicago's South Side. His father was Swedish and his mother was Jewish: he felt neither. He studied journalism at the University of Illinois and then travelled

around the American South by train. Once, he stole a typewriter in
Texas and ended up in prison for four months. He'd served in the
army in France, and stopped in New York on his way there and back.
Other than that he hadn't left Chicago much. But he loved writing,
and thought she should *really* see America.

At the end of the night they arranged to meet again the next day.
Beauvoir had lunch at the Alliance Française, but after that she asked
her hosts to drop her at Algren's. Her respectable escort was more
than a little surprised that she wanted to visit *this* neighbourhood.
They drove past vacant lots and abandoned warehouses. And then
they reached 1523 West Wabansia Avenue. Algren's house was a wreck,
strewn with newspapers and clutter. But there was a fire warming the
kitchen, and on his bed there was a colourful Mexican blanket.
Beauvoir didn't get too close to it on this visit: Algren wanted to show
her around. They wandered through the freezing cold, warmed up
with drinks, and then she had to leave for a dinner with the starchy
gentlemen of the French consul.

The next morning she was on a train to Los Angeles. Two days later
she arrived, and was greeted by Nathalie Sorokine (her former student
and lover) at the station. Nathalie and her husband, Ivan Moffat, were
living in Westwood with their little girl. They drove to the apartment,
where Moffat had breakfast ready. Moffat was having some success
as a screenwriter – later he would be nominated for an Academy
Award – and he had really liked Beauvoir's novel *All Men Are Mortal*.
He'd pitched it to a producer friend, George Stevens. They were talking
about Greta Garbo and Claude Rains in the leading roles, and a lot of
money. '$30,000,' she wrote to Sartre: 'Doesn't that make your head
spin?'[15] (She was hoping it would bring her back to America the next
year, but unfortunately the film never came off.[16]) Nathalie and
Beauvoir set off a few days later on an American road trip: Nathalie
drove Moffat's red Packard and Beauvoir navigated to San Francisco

and then to Lone Pine, a small town with a Sierra Nevada skyline, where Moffat and George Stevens met them.

When they got back to LA, Beauvoir and Sorokine got on a Greyhound bus to Santa Fe, New Mexico. They spent three weeks travelling together: Santa Fe, Houston, New Orleans, Florida and finally New York, with Beauvoir giving lectures all along the way. It was a tiring itinerary, but Beauvoir loved seeing, and learning, so much. While she went from city to city, she asked questions at drinks receptions and dinners, talking to her audiences, to university faculty and students. She read American books and made notes about American life. After her visit she published a travelogue, *America Day by Day* (1948). Parts of it were glowing: before New York, she said 'I didn't think I could love another city as much as Paris.'[17]

When she got back to New York on 12 March she sent Algren a letter – he had sent some books to her Chicago hotel but she hadn't received them when she checked out. He had also sent a note asking: Could she come back to Chicago? She replied that she didn't know – she had many lectures to give around New York – but it might be possible to visit in April.

Her tour was well-publicized, in fashion magazines and university papers. In mid-March *Vogue* published 'Femininity: The Trap', introducing Beauvoir as 'the leading disciple of Jean-Paul Sartre's *Existentialist* philosophy'. The irony of this is unlikely to have been lost on her, but did she find it irritating to be described this way? Or as 'a woman who thinks like a man'; 'a slender, handsome, thirty-eight-year-old Frenchwoman'? The same issue contained a profile describing André Malraux as a 'literary strong man', 'faithful DeGaullist and enemy of the communists'. (The reader is left to wonder whether he was slender or handsome.)

Beauvoir's article was advertised as a piece on 'the new role of women in France'. Some sections of it appear – almost verbatim – in

The Second Sex, although it is unknown whether they had already been written for the book or whether, in fact, Beauvoir later plundered her *Vogue* article.[18] All we know from her memoirs is that *Vogue's* editor, Jean Condit, threw a party in her honour soon after her arrival in New York, by 6 February she agreed to write for them, and on 12 February she dictated her work to a typist.[19]

In this article she clearly states one of the central claims of her mature feminism: 'there is no myth more irritating and more false' than 'the eternal feminine, which was invented, with the help of women, by men, who describe her as intuitive, charming, sensitive'.[20] The 'trap' of this femininity is that it often casts women as inferior to men and results in women feeling divided. Beauvoir thought that femininity gave women value in men's eyes, and that women therefore fear that if they lose it they will lose their value. She was beginning to think that when women gain value in their own eyes, through education or accomplishments, professional women often feel inferior to other women, on account of being less charming and sensitive – that is to say, less *feminine*. Men, by contrast, did not have to sacrifice success for masculinity, or accomplishment for feeling at ease: their professional gains were not personal losses. Only women were afflicted by this contradiction: 'Either they renounce in part the integration of their personalities, or they abandon in part their power of seduction over men.'[21] But why should success – or seduction – come at such a high cost?

While Beauvoir was in America she noticed things she wanted to remember for her book on women. Being in a different culture – and seeing it with foreign eyes – made her look at the way men and women related to each other from a different standpoint. She wrote in *America Day by Day* that she was surprised to find herself thinking that women were less free in the United States than they were in France. Before her visit, she took the words 'American woman' to be synonymous with 'free woman'. But to her shock she found that here unmarried women were less respected. At first, she wrote, American women's dress 'astonished me with its flagrantly feminine, almost sexual character. In the women's magazines here, more than in the French variety, I've read long articles on the art of husband hunting'. In the United States Beauvoir saw an antagonism between men and women; she felt they didn't like each other, which made their relationships struggles against each other. 'This is partly because American men tend to be laconic, and in spite of everything, a minimum of conversation is necessary for friendship. But it's also because there is a mutual distrust.'[22]

When Beauvoir got back to New York in the middle of April she stayed near Washington Square, in the Brevoort. She saw the Wrights again, and Bernard Wolfe. She was due to leave on 10 May and wrote to Sartre in Paris asking him to make arrangements for a 'nice return' for her: she didn't want to see anyone but him and Bost. Could they go away together just the two of them to catch up?

She had so much to tell him about: there were so many lectures around New York – Harvard, Princeton, Yale, Macon College, Oberlin, Mills College, Vassar, Wellesley and Smith. But even in the university papers she was described in ways that emphasized her appearance and relationship to Sartre: *The Daily Princetonian* reported that the 'elegant and attractive Simone de Beauvoir, the female ambassador for Existentialism in the United States' had told her audience that 'it is no longer permissible for the writer to stand apart and isolate himself in his ivory tower'.[23]

Outside the ivory tower, what she saw of America with Ellen and Richard Wright was eye-opening. When she was with them – that is, when two white women and a black man went out together – New York taxis passed them by. Wright took her to the Abyssinian Baptist Church to hear the political sermons of Reverend Adam Clayton Powell,[24] to see a poor church in Harlem.[25] Wright's novel *Native Son* had told the story of 20-year-old black man Bigger Thomas, which drew discussion about what it meant to be black – from the likes of James Baldwin and Frantz Fanon. The Wrights helped Beauvoir see segregation: 'From the cradle to the grave, working, eating, loving, walking, dancing, praying, he can never forget that he is black, and that makes him conscious every minute of the whole white world from which the word "black" takes its meaning.'[26]

It must have been strikingly dissonant to be snubbed on sidewalks by day and fêted by the famous by night. Once, after speaking at the New School (a new university and progressive hub), Beauvoir went to dinner with the Dadaist painter Marcel Duchamp before turning up at Erwin Piscator's for a huge party in her honour: the architect Le Corbusier was there, the composer Kurt Weill – even Charlie Chaplin. She had fun talking to Chaplin, but things got a little embarrassing – 'grotesque'! she wrote – when another guest suggested that she should acknowledge that Chaplin was an existentialist.[27]

America Day by Day was translated into English quite soon after, appearing in Britain in 1952. There, 'Mlle Gulliver en Amérique' met with dismissive reviews. A separate American edition appeared in 1953 – but Beauvoir's discussions of racial segregation were omitted. It wasn't the only time this would happen to Beauvoir's work: the English edition of *The Second Sex*, too, would cut swathes of her analysis of oppression. In 1953, the American public was deemed unready to hear what she had to say about race. More recent appraisals, however, have described it as 'one of the two best twentieth-century analyses of America'.[28]

On 24 April she wrote to Sartre saying she'd like to see Bost when she got back, before they went away together, and she put in a phone call to Nelson Algren: She had some time after all; could she visit? She flew back to Chicago and spent three – this time intimate – days with him. Four days later she got back to New York and a letter from Sartre; he had booked her 'her pink room' at the Hôtel Louisiane and would meet her from the airport bus.

On May Day Bernie Wolfe took her to a party where people were smoking joints. Did she want to try? The New Yorkers told her one would make her high, but even after six nothing happened. By then she was annoyed that she wasn't high, so she drank half a bottle of whiskey out of sheer irritation. The Americans were shocked: after all that, she was barely even tipsy.[29]

On 3 May she received a letter from Sartre at the hotel. Vanetti was making things difficult; please could she stay in New York for another week? It was a grey and rainy Saturday when she got it, and when she read it she had a 'breakdown', a return of the old anguish and tears. Beauvoir didn't reply for five days. When she did she said that she found the news 'devastating' but that the idea of returning earlier than Sartre wanted was 'unbearable'. She had some difficulties but managed to change her seat so that by Tuesday 6 May it was all arranged: she'd arrive at the Gare des Invalides on Sunday 18 May at 10.30. She didn't want to share Sartre during their first days back together so she asked him again to 'fix everything nicely so that we can be on our own for a long time'. She signed off with a postscript to Bost, saying that she was 'stupidly looking forward to seeing him' and thought of him much more than he deserved.[30]

Then she hopped on a plane to Chicago on 10 May, arriving mid-morning. Simone and Nelson would call this day their 'anniversary'. The next day he put a cheap Mexican ring on Beauvoir's finger; she said she would wear it all her life.

Simone and Nelson had a week together before she boarded the plane for Paris on 17 May; she wrote him her first letter from a layover at Newfoundland. She had cried in the taxi on the way to the airport but the tears were sweet. 'We shall never have to wake up, because it was not a dream; it is a wonderful true story which is only beginning.'[31] Her first letter was addressed to her 'precious, beloved Chicago man'.[32] Before long he would be 'her dearest American dilemma'.[33]

She hoped Paris's beauty would vanquish her sadness, and the day after she arrived she was happy to see it. But the day after that Paris was grey and dead – or maybe, she wrote to him, it was her heart that had died to it. Vanetti was still there. And Algren was not: she wrote to him entreating him to come, as soon as either of them got the money. She felt painfully at sea, with her body in Paris and her heart somewhere over the Atlantic.

On 21 May Beauvoir left the capital for the country, taking books and notebooks with her, to Saint-Lambert, a village in the Chevreuse valley. A mile away there were some ruins of a monastery, Port-Royal des Champs, where the philosopher Pascal lived for a while and the

Figure 9 *Simone de Beauvoir and Nelson Algren in Chicago, 1948.*

poet Racine was a pupil. In Paris she had none of Algren and half of Sartre; she needed solitude to regain her serenity. But Sartre had promised her two weeks – he, after all, wanted to see her too – so he divided his time between Paris and Saint-Lambert. Vanetti resented Beauvoir's presence, and after the two weeks Sartre went back to Vanetti in Paris. Beauvoir stayed on in the country. She made occasional visits to Paris for work for *Les Temps Modernes* or to see friends.

She was exhausted and probably depressed; she spent more time than usual sleeping. Sometimes she walked along the path to Port-Royal, which was decorated with a 'very bad' poem by Racine praising nature for its freedom, clarity and truth – and the 'fecund solitude' of this countryside. And she wrote to Algren, wearing his ring and using a red stylo he gave her. She didn't usually wear rings, she told him, and her friends had noticed: 'everybody in Paris was very amazed'.[34]

In Saint-Lambert at the end of May she re-read what she had written at the end of 1946 about women – the early material for *The Second Sex* – and had one of those days when she didn't understand why anybody bothered to write anything.[35] One of those days turned into a few days, and by 6 June she decided that she couldn't do 'the book about women' until she'd written about her travels. So she turned her mind to writing *America Day by Day* and slowly began to find her stride again.

Beauvoir's letters to Algren reveal much about her daily life: what she was writing, whom she saw at her publisher's cocktail parties, etc. She wanted him to learn French and included paragraphs of prose for him to translate: they were the best bits, she told him, so he had an incentive to learn. Beauvoir told Algren about the way Myrdal's *American Dilemma* and conversations with Richard Wright had inspired her book on women.[36] This book, she told Algren, made her 'begin again to think about the book I began about women's situation. I should like to write a book as important as this big one about

Negroes'.[37] She wanted to do for women what Myrdal had done for African-Americans, showing the ways that racism and sexism were rooted in the contingencies of culture – that with women, too, people were hiding behind alibis.

But her letters were rather quiet on the subject of Sartre, and even quieter on Vanetti. In July Vanetti left France by boat, from Le Havre. Once again Vanetti made an ultimatum: if Beauvoir came back a next time, it would be for good. Sartre felt torn, but Beauvoir was feeling divided, too; it had been two months since she got back to France and ever since she had had a lingering disquiet. By July Algren had written that when she came back to Chicago he wanted her to stay forever. So on 23 July she replied that she could not. She loved him but could not give her life to him. She didn't want to lie to him, and her heart had been aching with the question: 'Is it right to give something of oneself without being ready to give everything'?[38] Whatever happens, she said, she knew she couldn't give him everything, and although she felt torn and anxious about this she wanted it out in the open.

He wrote back with a proposal of marriage. He had been planning to ask her in flesh and blood, but her letter made him resort to pen and ink.

They wanted to be together but they both knew there was a problem: he didn't want to leave Chicago; she didn't want to leave Paris. He'd been married before and already felt as though she was more his wife than his 'real' wife of seven years had been. So they agreed on a less conventional approach as their next step: she would come to see him for a while and return to Paris. Then he would visit her in France.

In August she travelled to Copenhagen and Sweden with Sartre. And on 6 September she boarded a plane to Chicago. Sartre encouraged her to go, even offering her the money for the trip.

When she got there, Algren took her on a tour of the city:

I wanted to show her that the USA was not a nation of prosperous *bourgeois*, all driving toward ownership of a home in the suburbs and membership in a country club. I wanted to show her the people who drove, just as relentlessly, toward the penitentiary and jail. I introduced her to stickup men, pimps, baggage thieves, whores and heroin addicts. Their drive was downward, always downward. I knew many such that year. I took her on a tour of the County Jail and showed her the electric chair.[39]

Beauvoir took notes for her book; they sat in Chicago pizzerias and drank Chianti. When the visit came to a close they planned to see each other again in the spring of 1948, to travel for four months. But even so, after she left him she wrote to him in broken English that something 'broke up in her heart' when they said goodbye. He still wanted to marry her, but she told Algren that although she would give up much to be with him, she would not give up her work. 'I could not live just for happiness and love, I could not give up writing and working in the only place where my writing and work may have a meaning.'[40] Beauvoir's philosophy assigned pride of place to the concept of the *situation*: she thought the cultural context of individual lives and individual works mattered – possibly so much that she couldn't see that her insights were powerful enough to illuminate places other than France.

When Beauvoir got back to Paris at the end of September 1947 Sartre had found a new fling; Vanetti's grip on him was easing. The new interest was a 23-year-old American journalist called Sally Swing Shelley, who was in town to cover Princess Elizabeth's visit. When that affair fizzled out Swing would reflect that he treated women like drawers in a dresser, opening whichever one he wanted to whenever he wanted to. But at the time she was crazy about him.[41]

In November of 1947 Beauvoir published her second philosophical essay, *The Ethics of Ambiguity*, further developing her philosophy of freedom. In *Pyrrhus and Cinéas* she had written that everyone must decide which place they occupy in the world. In *The Ethics of Ambiguity* she returned to Sartre's idea of invulnerable, autonomous freedom and the theme of her essay 'An Eye for an Eye'. After the war she had learned about the atrocities of Buchenwald and Dachau; like so many in her generation she wondered how human beings were capable of such inhumanity. The Nazis, she said, systematically abjected the men they wanted to destroy so that their fellow men no longer saw them as human, as free, conscious subjects.[42]

In *Pyrrhus and Cinéas* Beauvoir had written that every person needs the freedom of other people, and in a sense we always want it because it is only the freedom of others that prevents us from atrophying into thinking of ourselves as things, as objects.[43] She argued that evil consists in denying freedom, whether one's own or another's. To fight evil, therefore, we have to recognize that affirming our own freedom entails responsibility to shape the present and future in such a way that we *and others* will be free.

This is not easy. It is much more comfortable to exist in a state of childlike dependence, taking our roles in the world to be foreordained. As children we don't know who we will become – and, for a time, this is developmentally appropriate. Young worlds are furnished with regular and reassuring features that we hardly notice enough to question: girls wear dresses, bedtime's at eight. But some adults relate to features of the world with the same passive acceptance: Jews wear stars, curfew's at nine.

Beauvoir thought that remaining childlike in this passive way is an act of bad faith. To become ethical we have to make what she called (like Sartre) an *original choice*. We have to choose what we want to be – not once and for all but over and over again, 'moment by moment for an entire lifetime'.[44] Again she criticized the concept of freedom put forward by Sartre in *Being and Nothingness* (although by now, under her influence, he was beginning to retreat from it). In Beauvoir's view, no one can be free alone: 'A man who seeks being far from other men, seeks it against them at the same time that he loses himself.'[45] To Sartre's slogan 'man is what he makes of himself', Beauvoir replied that we don't make ourselves alone or from scratch. 'We can only be who we are because of the others in our lives.'[46]

The Ethics of Ambiguity was published in English in 1976, at a time when there was no translation of *Pyrrhus and Cinéas* and only a partial translation of *The Second Sex*. So it is important to pause briefly on the way this work developed Beauvoir's earlier philosophy and laid foundations for what she would go on to do. She was still thinking about the idea of a 'situation', and how other people shape our lives. In *The Ethics of Ambiguity* she argued that in order to be free *ethically* you must use your freedom to embrace the ties that hold you to others. She calls this taking up the 'appeal' or 'call' of the other's freedom. Every human being longs for her life to be seen truly, and to matter not just because it is *a* life, but because it is *her* life. We all want to be 'justified', to feel that our lives have meaning. But to listen to the call of freedom in ourselves without hearing the call of freedom for others is solipsism: a kind of spiritual death, a refusal that stultifies our own becoming. Only with others can we bring certain projects, values – and a changed world – into being.

In *Being and Nothingness* Sartre included a footnote where he said that he would write an ethics of 'deliverance and salvation' as an antidote to its bleak and conflictual account of human existence. But although Sartre wrote notes for a book on ethics he never published it during his lifetime – and he was not a man who was reluctant to publish (the *Economist* once calculated his output at twenty published pages per day over his working life). Today, Beauvoir's ethics are beginning to be recognized as 'the fulfilment of Sartre's unkept promise'.[47] But in 1947, a book by Francis Jeanson appeared called *Sartre and the Problem of Morality*. One reviewer wrote that here 'for the first time' readers could see what an ethics of freedom could be for itself – 'if one disregards the interesting *Ethics of Ambiguity* of S. de Beauvoir'.[48] He gave no reason *why* it should be disregarded, so we are left wondering whether he had any.

In any case, it is clear that by 1948 Beauvoir was being dismissed in philosophical reviews, on the one hand, and irritated by the popularizing demands of 'incompetent' 'nonspecialists' on the other – how could they expect her to explain existentialism in a sentence? At one and the same time she was excluded by the philosophical elite and being philosophically elitist. Beauvoir wanted to be an engaged writer, which is why she wrote fiction and magazine articles as well as philosophy. But no one could reasonably expect to understand Kant or Hegel after reading a single slogan; why did they think this would be possible with existentialism?[49] In her view, understanding existentialism required understanding the long philosophical tradition on which it rested: at this stage, in her mind, existentialist *philosophy* was not something for everyone; existentialist *literature*, by contrast, could reveal to readers an existentialist perspective on the world and appeal to their freedoms by different means.

In January 1948 Beauvoir submitted *America Day by Day* to the publisher, with a dedication to Ellen and Richard Wright. And then it was time to focus on her essay on women. She and Algren were planning to travel together from May to September, so she wanted to write as much as she could before the trip. While Beauvoir was away with Algren Sartre had planned for Vanetti to come and stay in Paris (he would have to stop seeing Sally Swing for a while; Dolores didn't know).

But Beauvoir started having doubts about being away for so long – not just because of Sartre, but because she was planning to release instalments of *The Second Sex* between May and July. She talked to Sartre and decided to cut the trip down to two months, but she didn't have the heart to tell Algren by letter. Better to bring it up in person.

Beauvoir travelled down the Mississippi River to New Orleans and then South from there to the Yucatan, Guatemala, Vera Cruz and Mexico City. She and Algren made their way down the Mississippi on a riverboat, drinking whiskey on the deck. She loved the colours and textures of the cloth in Guatemala, buying blankets, curtains and fabric to take back to her dressmaker.[50] And she kept finding reasons not to tell Nelson that she was leaving early until one day, on the journey from Mexico City to Morelia, she clumsily made the announcement that she had to return on 14 July. 'Oh, all right,' he said. But the next day he didn't want to explore Morelia with her. At Cholula, Puebla and Taxco, too, he was withdrawn. What was wrong, she asked? Mexico was getting on his nerves.

Eventually he told her he didn't feel the same as he had. They got back to New York and one night Beauvoir blurted out, 'I can leave tomorrow.' But he didn't want her to leave, saying instead, 'I'm ready to marry you this very moment.'[51] It was an agonizing situation: neither of them felt ready for a transatlantic transplant and each of them regretted the other's reluctance. When Beauvoir left for Paris on 14 July 1948 she thought she might never see Algren again.

Back in Paris, she threw herself into work. She had not yet earned the means to have a private study of her own, so she often wrote at Les Deux Magots when she was not writing at Sartre's. The extracts of work in progress from *The Second Sex* were getting interesting reactions – the first one was on 'woman and myths', and in it Beauvoir discussed the way women were presented in the works of some respected novelists such as Henri de Montherlant, Paul Claudel and André Breton. She wrote to Algren that the book needed another year of work before it would 'be good'. But in the meantime, 'to her delight', she 'had heard that the portion published in *Les Temps Modernes*, has enraged some men. It's a chapter devoted to the stupid myths about women that men cherish and the ridiculous and kitschy poetry they produce from it. [These men] seem to have been affected at their most sensitive point'.[52]

The two of them still had their own sensitive point to resolve; Algren still wanted more of her. She wrote to him in August explaining that she'd always said she couldn't be his. She knew Sartre's role in her life bothered Algren. 'I told you already how I care for him,' she wrote:

> but it was rather deep friendship than love; love was not very successful. Chiefly because he does not care much for sexual life. He is a warm, lively man everywhere, but not in bed. I soon felt it, though I had no experience; and little by little, it seemed useless, even indecent, to go on being lovers. We dropped it after about eight or ten years rather unsuccessful in this way.[53]

Eventually Algren's letters grew warmer. He sent parcels with books and whiskey (hidden in a bag of flour). He was coming to Paris for a visit in May.

He read *The Blood of Others* and sent a long letter with a note from an American publisher who thought it wasn't hopeful enough, that it was full of characters 'who cannot be saved'. Beauvoir replied that the French papers also wanted existentialist novels to be 'heroical and smiling'. But for herself, she wrote: 'I like shadows in a book, as there is always a kind of dimness in life, but maybe I put in too much shadow?' Algren didn't comment on the quantity of shadows, but he did say that there was too much philosophy. Maybe he was right, she thought – but even so, she replied, 'that is my genuine way of feeling; when anything happens to me I am always ratiocinating about it inside myself [. . .] [F]eeling, events, and philosophy, it would be rather unnatural for me if I put it away'.[54] She was deep in the process of writing the book on women so couldn't think about writing another novel yet, but she knew already that she wanted to try.

She was working hard – reading and writing eight hours by day, eating too little and drinking too much by night. She wrote to Nelson that maybe she did things 'a little too crazily', whether it was work, travel, or love: 'But that is my way. I have [sic] rather not do things at all as doing them mildly.'[55] She had a way of weaving memories into her letters to show the way past moments lived on in the present, and wrote to Nelson to describe her excitement and impatience about some new clothes she was having made from the Guatemalan fabric they bought together:

I am having two beautiful things made with the Guatemala embroidered stuff: just the top of a dress, to wear with a black skirt. I stayed two whole hours standing up with five people around me to fix it nicely. I got mad, but I wanted it to be really pretty and I went to a good dressmaker. [...] (Remember when you bargained so cleverly the blue thing in Quetzaltenango?)[56]

In October of 1948 Beauvoir left hotel life behind her and moved into a small fifth-floor apartment on the rue de la Bûcherie. It was near the Seine, in the Latin Quarter, a fifteen-minute walk from Sartre's. She decorated it with red curtains and bought white armchairs; Giacometti had given her some bronze lamps he designed. And from the rafters she hung colourful decorations from Mexico and Guatemala. Now she had somewhere of her own to work in the mornings, she could cook her own meals at home, and she had somewhere to welcome Algren. She wrote to him in December that she was reading the Kinsey report, *Sexual Behaviour in the Human Male*, and wished that an equivalent work existed for women.[57]

By the standards of a conventional erotic relationship, Beauvoir and Sartre do not appear very 'necessary' to each other by this stage. Their accounts diverge on precisely *when* the sexual aspect of their relationship ended, with Sartre rather vaguely claiming that it lasted ten years longer than Beauvoir claimed – in 1970 he told an interviewer '1946, '47, '48, I don't remember'.[58] They never lived together unless adverse circumstances required it and always addressed each other with the formal second person, *vous*. But each day they spent hours working by each other's side, editing each other's work, and managing *Les Temps Modernes*. Was this the life that Valkyrie and Baladin had dreamed of?

The Bosts moved into the floor below Beauvoir's when another apartment became vacant, and the friends would often eat their evening meal together. But since Algren had come into her life Beauvoir had stopped sleeping with Bost. He never lacked for girlfriends, but even so, Bost was hurt by this at first. It was, to him, the least macho of the men she had known, that Simone would dedicate her next book: *The Second Sex*.

12

The Scandalous Second Sex

In *The Prime of Life* Beauvoir wrote that during the early 1930s 'feminism' and the 'sex wars' made no sense to her.[1] So how did she come to write the so-called 'feminist Bible'?

At the time of *The Second Sex*'s publication Beauvoir was 41 years old. She had seen her mother suffer an utterly unequal relationship with her father. As a girl she objected to being treated 'like a girl' when she knew boys and girls were equal in the eyes of God. Since the day the bookstore clerk flashed her she had often felt uneasy in the company of unknown men. She had lost Zaza, who died in the aftermath of arguments about the comparative value of dowries, propriety and love. She had seen her friends infected and hospitalized after illegal abortions. She had had conversations with women who were ignorant about their own bodies' functions and pleasures. She had visited other countries, which made her realize that customs can look like necessities just because they're common. She had read the opening pages of her friend Violette Leduc's novel *Ravages*, and felt shocked at her own shock to its frank discussion of female sexuality: it spoke about 'woman's sexuality in a way no woman ever did, with truth and poetry'.[2]

In *Pyrrhus and Cinéas*, Beauvoir had written that everyone must occupy a place in the world, but only some of us freely choose what place we will occupy. The human condition is ambiguous: we are both subject and object. As object, your world is restricted by the constraints others impose. And as a subject, your actions not only realize your own freedom but create new conditions in the world for others. The 18-year-old Beauvoir had written in her diary that there were 'things to hate about love'.[3] Her fiction from the 1940s had bridged the boundaries between philosophy and literature. But in *The Second Sex* she argued that what went in the name of 'love' wasn't actually love at all. She blended a different set of boundaries, between the personal, the philosophical and the political. And although she would be celebrated by some for doing so, Beauvoir would be severely ostracized by others first. It would be decades before the work gained recognition as a feminist classic. So what did it say that could provoke both strong disgust and – later – adulation?

In the first line of *The Second Sex* Beauvoir didn't conceal her hesitation and irritation with the subject of 'woman'. 'I hesitated a long time before writing a book on woman,' she wrote. But 'volumes of idiocies' had been published over the last century – mourning the loss of femininity and telling women that they must 'be women, stay women, become women' – and she could no longer stay passively on the sidelines.

Beauvoir's reticence makes better sense when understood in context. In 1863 Jules Verne wrote a novel called *Paris in the Twentieth Century*. Women would wear trousers, he predicted, and they would be educated like men. Jules Verne's other novels described fantastical human achievements: submarines, men travelling around the world in eighty days – even travelling to the moon! But despite Verne's reputation as a successful writer of science fiction, this was a step too far: his literary agent rejected *Paris in the Twentieth Century* as too far-fetched. In Beauvoir's generation Coco Chanel wore trousers and flapper fashion glamorized androgyny. Women had entered the workplace in unprecedented numbers. They had just won the right to vote. Some of them even outranked men on competitive national exams. They still couldn't open their own bank accounts – and would not be able to do so until 1965 revisions to the Napoleonic Code.[4] But by the late 1940s 'feminism' – a word that was, at the time, associated with the campaign for suffrage – had become *dépassé* in both America and France.[5] That decade they had won the right to vote. What more could they want?

When Beauvoir looked at history she saw that human beings have a habit of looking at others' bodies and creating castes, sometimes slave castes, based on their physical characteristics. No one doubted that this was true in the case of race. But, Beauvoir asked, what about sex? She argued that men have defined women as 'other' and relegated them to the status of a different caste: the second sex.

After her experiences in America and conversations with American feminists, Beauvoir knew that some feminists denied that the word 'woman' was even a useful term. But she thought they were in bad faith. Women like Dorothy Parker thought the inequality between the sexes could be resolved by defining women as 'human' instead of 'woman'. But the problem with the 'we're all human' point of view, Beauvoir said, is that women are not men. The equality they share at this level is abstract – and the possibilities open to men and women are different.

Each human being occupies a unique *situation*, and concretely the situations occupied by men and women are unequal. But why? Anyone can see, Beauvoir said, that human beings are split into two categories, with different bodies, faces, clothes, interests and occupations. But even so, the fact of the matter was that it wasn't enough to have certain reproductive organs to be considered 'woman' because some females had them and were still accused of being 'unwomanly'. When the novelist George Sand flouted conventional femininity, Gustave Flaubert tellingly called her 'the third sex'.[6]

So, Beauvoir asked: if being female is not a sufficient condition to be a woman, what *is* a woman?

Beauvoir's answer to the question 'what is a woman?' was that a woman is what a man is not. As Protagoras put it, 'man is the measure of humanity' – man is the norm by which 'the human' is judged. And throughout history, many men believed that women were inferior beings whose views were irrelevant to 'human' concerns. Even in the 1940s, Beauvoir found her opinions dismissed simply on the grounds that they were a woman's:

> I used to get annoyed in abstract discussions to hear men tell me: 'You think such and such a thing because you're a woman.' But I know my only defence is to answer, 'I think it because it is true,' thereby eliminating my subjectivity; it was out of the question to answer, 'And you think the contrary because you are a man,' because it is understood that being a man is not a particularity; a man is in his right by virtue of being man.[7]

In saying that woman is what man is not Beauvoir drew on Hegel's ideas about the 'Other'. Since human beings have a deeply rooted tendency to set themselves in opposition to what is Other to them, men set themselves as free 'subjects' and defined women by contrast – as objects. But Beauvoir was baffled by how this situation came to be so widespread, and why it persisted. Why, she wondered, didn't more women contest the demeaning ways that men defined them?

She knew the familiar arguments against feminism: It will ruin family values! It will lower wages! Women's place is in the home! We are 'separate but equal'! But she thought they were masks for pernicious bad faith, much like the Jim Crow laws in America.[8] George Bernard

Shaw had criticized white Americans for making black Americans shine their shoes, and then concluding that shoe-shining was all they were capable of. Beauvoir argued that the same invalid inferences were made about women's capabilities – because women are kept in *situations* of inferiority. The fact that they occupy an inferior situation in society does not mean that they *are* inferior innately. 'The scope of the verb *to be* must be understood,' she wrote; '*to be* is to have become.'[9]

The hopeful side of becoming is that situations can become better. For centuries men have spilt ink over the 'human' condition. But how, Beauvoir asked, 'in the feminine condition, can a human being accomplish herself'?[10]

That much she said in the introduction – a tiny fraction of the 972-page, two-volume tome. But it was not what her first readers would read first. In book form, *The Second Sex* was published in two volumes, in June and November of 1949. The material Beauvoir released in earlier issues of *Les Temps Modernes* was great from the point of view of publicity, and not so great from the point of view of myth-making and public censure. In 1963, when Beauvoir publicly evaluated the changing shape of her legacy in *Force of Circumstance*, she would write that the appearance of *The Second Sex* made her 'a target of sarcasm' like she had never been before.[11] The *ad feminam* dismissals of Beauvoir were about to begin – and sarcasm would not be the worst of it.

Beauvoir worked hard to finish parts of the book in the spring of 1949 because Algren was coming to Paris. Fortunately she found this book easier to write than a novel. For fiction she had to carefully craft viewpoints and develop characters, taking care with plots, dialogue and foreshadowing. For this she needed to research, organize and write. She wanted freedom for women. But there only seemed to be two possible reasons why they didn't have it: because they were oppressed, or because they chose not to be free. In both cases there was a moral problem; the question was, whose was it?

When Algren arrived in Paris Beauvoir was anxious at first: they hadn't parted well. She went to meet him in the white coat she'd worn in Chicago two years before. With him in town 'the family' couldn't believe the transformation they saw in her: she was soft and happy. Algren had been nervous about meeting Sartre, but their introduction was a success: Algren was at ease. He enjoyed meeting Olga and Sartre's latest lover, Michelle Vian: they spoke English with him and lapped up his stories of American sin.

Beauvoir had decided to publish parts of the second volume – on 'Lived Experience' – in instalments in *Les Temps Modernes* that summer. Her method in the second part was different: she compiled historical accounts and first-person descriptions of different stages of or possibilities in women's lives: childhood, being a girl, puberty, sexual initiation, lesbianism, marriage, motherhood, social expectations, prostitutes, old age.

When she published 'The Sexual Initiation of Woman' in May 1949 it provoked strong and revealing reactions. In it she described her vision of a non-oppressive, reciprocal sexual encounter where women enjoyed sex as subjects, not objects. Instead of being passive and submissive to non-reciprocal male desire, Beauvoir wrote about relationships where women, in 'love, tenderness, and sensuality', established 'a relationship of reciprocity with her partner. The asymmetry of male and female eroticism creates insoluble problems as long as there is a battle of the sexes; they can easily be settled when a woman feels both desire and respect in a man.'[12] Later she wondered whether it was a mistake to publish that chapter first.[13]

The esteemed Catholic novelist François Mauriac claimed that Beauvoir's writing 'literally reached the limits of the abject'. Was 'a serious philosophical and literary review really the place for the subject treated by Mme Simone de Beauvoir'?[14] This was the author whose steps Beauvoir had retraced as a student with Merleau-Ponty on her way to see Zaza: for decades she had admired his way with words and now he was using them to call her wayward.

The June and July issues of *Les Temps Modernes* flew off the newsstands. Beauvoir had published chapters on lesbianism and part of her section on maternity in these issues, and many readers were outraged. Her reputation was already scandalous in some quarters at this point – tied as it was to Sartre's – but now she attracted insults of a different order: 'unsatisfied, frigid, priapic, nymphomaniac, lesbian, a hundred times aborted, I was everything, even an unmarried mother'.[15] She was propositioned by 'sex maniacs' and 'active members of the First Sex'. The communists called her a *petite bourgeoise* whose analysis had nothing to say to the working classes. This time François Mauriac – that respectable pillar of the conservative establishment – wrote to one of the contributors to *Les Temps Modernes* that his 'employer's vagina has no secret from me'.[16] When these words were published Mauriac was horrified. Shortly thereafter he began a series in *Le Figaro Littéraire* condemning pornography in general and Simone de Beauvoir in particular.

When the first volume of the book appeared in June, it sold rapidly – 22,000 copies in the first week.[17] 'Biology is not destiny,' Beauvoir claimed – and neither is marriage or motherhood. Women like Marie Curie, she said, prove that it is not 'women's inferiority that has determined their historical insignificance: it is their historical insignificance that has doomed them to inferiority'. But culture – high and low – keeps perpetuating oppressive 'mythology' about women. 'Woman is not a fixed reality,' she wrote, 'but a becoming; she has to be compared with man in her becoming, that is her *possibilities*,' because 'when one considers a being who is transcendence and surpassing' – that is, conscious, changing, free – 'it is never possible to close the books.'[18]

If it were the case that women obviously had some biological, or psychological, or economic destiny, Beauvoir argued, there would be no problem: there would be a universal 'femininity' and those who had it would be 'woman'. In Part I she looked at 'woman' from the point of view of biology, psychoanalysis and history. But she found no satisfying explanation of women's secondary status in the sciences, or Freud or Marx, and demonstrated the ways in which she found their analyses wanting – why did Freud, for example, think he could base his views of female sexuality on male sexuality when he had no experience at all of the former?

The communist journalist Jeannette Prenant objected to the way that – she claimed – Beauvoir discouraged women from being wives and mothers. Another female reviewer, Marie-Louise Barron, called the first volume 'gobbledygook' and prophesied that the second would only offer 'trifles'.[19] Armand Hoog wrote that what Beauvoir really wanted to liberate was herself – she was humiliated to be a woman, but 'she was born a woman, and I do not really see what she could change about that [...] Destiny hardly lets itself be denied'.[20]

This newfound notoriety made it a little awkward showing Algren around Paris: she had been longing to show him her world for two years so they visited her beloved restaurants and cafés – but it bothered her that people whispered and stared. So after Bastille Day, she was relieved when they left for two months of travelling together: Rome, Naples, Amalfi and Pompeii – and from there to Tunis, Algiers, Fez, Marrakesh. On their way back from North Africa they visited Olga and Bost in Provence, where he was given the nickname 'Tough Algren'.[21]

When she escorted Algren to Orly airport in the middle of September, she felt that they had just had their best days yet. She would go to see him in Chicago next year. He was happy, too, and during his layover he discovered in a magazine that while he was away his novel *The Man with the Golden Arm* had been given the National

Book Award. His career was reaching its apex; in October Ernest Hemingway wrote a letter to his editor praising Algren as 'the best writer under 50 [...] writing today'.[22]

In October Beauvoir went back to Provence to be with Sartre and write. She'd been thinking about a new novel for a while but needed to get *The Second Sex* out of her system. She wanted the new novel to contain *her*, but once again she sat before blank paper wondering where to start. There would be a character loosely like herself: Anne. But where would this book take her? She took walks with Sartre, read, saw friends. One day they went to visit Sospel and Peira-Cava and they were surprised to read, in the next Sunday's paper, a full account of their afternoon. She found this relentless attention tiresome; but this was only the tip of it. She decided to translate one of Algren's novels, so she worked on that when she wasn't writing her own.[23]

The second volume of *The Second Sex*, published in November 1949, contained the famous line, 'One is not born, but rather becomes, a woman.'[24] Since every woman is a *becoming* and not a closed book, Beauvoir wanted to include women's own descriptions of their lived experience, showing some of the ways that they were made 'Other' throughout the courses of their lives. As an open book herself, she was still *Becoming Beauvoir*, and in the process of trying to understand her own experience she realized that some of the obstacles she faced were endemic threats to other women's becoming, too. Despite the passage of time, she was still the philosopher who had been inspired by Alfred Fouillée's idea that 'one isn't born, but rather becomes, free'. And now she argued that it was not biology, psychology and economics that determined women to live lives set apart from men, or submissive to them; 'civilization' played a significant role too. And with Simone de Beauvoir, 'civilization' was hard at work.

Although her candid treatment of female sexuality was scandalous, it was her treatment of motherhood that came under the most sustained attack. Beauvoir thought society was in extravagant bad faith: how could they not see the duplicity in showing contempt for women and respect for mothers? 'It is a criminal paradox to deny women all public activity, to close masculine careers to them, to proclaim them incapable in all domains, and to nonetheless entrust to them the most delicate and most serious of all undertakings: the formation of a human being.'[25]

With a population depleted by war France needed citizens – so Beauvoir was accused of being a traitor to her sex and her nation. After the war, French industry needed revitalization, and so in addition to more births they also needed more women to enter the workforce.[26] Beauvoir's language was and still is shocking in places, and in hindsight there are passages that seem ill-judged given the political context and the experience of women who did not feel 'enslaved' by motherhood. Beauvoir referred to pregnant women as hosts to 'parasites' and slaves to the species. (So did Schopenhauer, but for some reason he did not provoke the same reaction.) Beauvoir was interested in pregnancy as it is experienced by women subjectively, 'from within' – with their loss of bodily autonomy, and the anxiety they experienced about who they would become when they became mothers. She claimed that women should not be reduced to their reproductive function. She also said (though few seemed to notice) that this was not a rejection of motherhood altogether. Beauvoir wanted to show that even pregnancy, childbirth, and caring for the young – supposedly the epitome of uniquely female embodied experience – was experienced differently depending on a woman's *situation*.

Clearly, Beauvoir was not a mother herself, and she acknowledged this, drawing on other women's voices, including letters, diaries and novels, to show that, 'Pregnancy and motherhood are experienced in very different ways depending on whether they take place in revolt, resignation, satisfaction, or enthusiasm.'[27] She wanted to address two dangerous misconceptions about being a mother: (1) that it was 'enough in all cases to fulfil a woman' and (2) that a child was 'sure to find happiness in his mother's arms'.[28] Her research showed that while many women enjoyed motherhood they did not want it to be their life's only project. Children were unlikely to be happy, she thought, if their mothers were frustrated and unfulfilled; 'it would obviously be better for the child if his mother were a complete person and not a mutilated one'.[29]

But many men objected: *How dare she* approach that sacred subject when she wasn't a mother herself?

It had never stopped them, she said.

In addition to accusing society of bad faith with respect to motherhood, Beauvoir returned to the theme that had preoccupied her for decades: the ethics of love and devotion. In *The Second Sex* she claimed that the word 'love' has different meanings for men and women – and that these differences are responsible for many of the disagreements between them.

Beauvoir believed that men remained 'sovereign subjects' in love – that they valued their beloved women alongside other pursuits, as an integral part – but only a part – of their whole life. By contrast, for women love was presented as life itself, and ideals of love encouraged women to live lives of self-sacrifice or even complete self-forgetting for the sake of their beloved. Men were raised to expect to be active in the world – to love but also to be ambitious and to act in other domains. Women were taught that their value was conditional – that they needed to be loved by a man to have worth.

One of the barriers to authentic love is that women have been objectified so much that now they objectify themselves, attempting to identify with their beloved man and become more desirable in his eyes. The woman in love tries to see through his eyes, shaping her world and herself around him: she reads his preferred reading,

interests herself in his art, his music, his ideas, his friends, his politics
– and so on. Sexually, too, Beauvoir objected that many women are
used as 'instruments' for male pleasure rather than as subjects whose
desires and pleasure are also taken into account.

The problem with the dominant paradigms of love, as Beauvoir
saw them, was that they were *not reciprocal*. Men expected women to
give themselves in love in ways that were not mutual. Consequently,
love was dangerous for women in ways that it was not dangerous for
men. She did not lay the blame for this exclusively at the feet of men.
Women, too, perpetuated the oppressive structures of non-reciprocal
love through participating in it. But it was hard not to, Beauvoir wrote,
because the world was structured in a way that enticed them to
consent to their own oppression.

Although Beauvoir's account in *The Second Sex* largely frames the
discussion in heteronormative terms, she herself had faced this
tension in life in her own relationships with women. In 1940, following
a conversation with Bianca Bienenfeld about Bienenfeld's desire to
occupy a more central role in Beauvoir's life, Bienenfeld wrote to
Beauvoir:

> You don't give yourself, you take.
> It's *false* that I'm your life – your life is a mosaic.
> For me, though, you are my life – I'm all yours.[30]

Beauvoir thought authentic love was possible in reciprocal
relationships – and she hoped it would become more widespread. 'The
day when it will be possible for the woman to love in her strength and
not in her weakness, not to escape from herself but to find herself, not
out of resignation but to affirm herself, love will become for her as for
man the source of life and not a mortal danger.'[31] It was possible for
women to love their beloved *and* themselves as subjects in their own
right. But it was hard: because non-reciprocal myths of love

perpetuated women's secondary status, promising them salvation and delivering a living hell.

Like Beauvoir's fiction, *The Second Sex* raises the question of how much autobiography to read into Beauvoir's philosophy – and which autobiography? For in addition to Beauvoir's early encounters with Bianca, in a letter from Beauvoir to a later lover she identified 'true reciprocity' rather than sex, as the quality she found lacking in her relationship with Sartre. This raises the question: when she described 'reciprocal love' in 1949 did she believe herself to have lived it? There are other passages in the book that closely resemble Beauvoir's own becoming – including an 'older sister' who resents participating in 'maternal chores', and grandparents who 'poorly hide' the fact that they would have preferred a male grandchild. Was she drawing on her research on 'woman' here, or on the lived experiences of Simone and Hélène?[32] Her chapter on lesbianism also provoked speculation. Prior to the posthumous publication of her letters to Sartre there were only novels and suspicions to compare it with – what did she mean when she wrote about feeling 'obscure longings' for women in *Memoirs of a Dutiful Daughter*?[33] – but even so people wondered: was it rooted in her own experience, or even in suppressed desire? Was she in bad faith about her own sexuality? In the book she claimed that there is 'no sexual destiny that governs an individual's life' and that homosexuality is 'a choice made from a complex whole, contingent on a free decision.'[34]

At the end of *The Second Sex* Beauvoir did what her Grasset rejection letter said she failed to do when they declined *When Things of the Spirit Came First* in the 1930s. Henry Müller had written: 'You are content to describe a disintegrating world, and then to abandon your readers on the very threshold of the new order, without giving any precise indication of what its benefits will be.'[35]

So in the final chapter she presented 'The Independent Woman', whose freedom came at a cost, but not at the cost of love.

There Beauvoir said that men are at an advantage in a society that 'Others' women, not just for the benefits they reap (those are easy enough to see from 'without') but also 'within' themselves. Men, from boyhood onwards, can enjoy their vocations as human beings without anyone telling them that their vocation contradicts their 'destiny' as a lover, husband or father, or that their success lessens the likelihood that they will be loved. But for a woman to be *feminine* she must renounce her claims to what Beauvoir calls 'sovereignty' – to have a vision for *her* life, to pursue her own projects – because this is perceived to be unfeminine. This places women in a lose–lose situation: should she become herself if that means becoming unlovable? Should she renounce herself to succeed at love? Sartre had written that in the human condition we are 'condemned to be free'. Beauvoir now wrote that in 'the feminine condition' women were condemned to feel divided, to become 'split subjects'.

The root of the problem is that 'the individual is not free to shape the idea of femininity at will'.[36] For centuries men benefited from the myths of femininity, and it was understandable that they were afraid to lose both the myths and their benefits. It was understandable that they told women that they didn't need vocations apart from marriage and family; that it was against nature to want them; that they would be 'happy' if they succeeded in the life cycle of being desired as sexual objects before sacrificing themselves as loving wives and mothers. But men should feel uneasy about doing so, since 'there is no way to measure the happiness of others, and it is always easy to call a situation that one would like to impose on others happy'.[37]

When Volume II of *The Second Sex* was published in November 1949 the reviewers redrew their weapons – Beauvoir would later refer to the coverage of this volume as 'the scandal'. The *Figaro* columnist André Rousseaux expressed 'embarrassment' for this 'female follower of Bacchus' who had written about 'sexual initiation', who wanted to ruin love in order to claim the freedom of pleasure. After all, he said, women were already emancipated![38] A surprising quantity of his words were dedicated to ridicule and attacks on her person: he wrote that 'woman, relegated to the level of the Other, is exasperated in her inferiority complex', that Beauvoir argued with 'such tenacity' that he wondered if she needed existentialism to 'deliver her from a veritable obsession'. Emmanuel Mounier, writing in *L'Esprit*, lamented the 'tone of *ressentiment*' that he found in the book. If it had been better controlled, he said, perhaps it 'would have less impeded the lucidity of the author'.[39] They called her life sad, neurotic, frustrated. Camus accused her of 'making the French male look ridiculous'.[40] The philosopher Jean Guitton expressed pain at seeing between its lines 'her sad life'. *L'Epoque* published a prediction that in ten years no one would be talking about 'this nauseating apology for sexual inversion and abortion'.[41]

The Vatican put the book on its list of forbidden books.

Beauvoir had made a philosophical argument about the oppression of women, drawing on the lived experience of women – including herself – to say that many women's situations must be changed if they were to be truly 'human'. She claimed that women's desires should shape sex; that their projects should shape family life; and that their agency should shape the world.

But the reception it met was largely *ad feminam*. In many quarters Beauvoir was mocked, derided and dismissed. But not in all. There was another, much more welcoming readership: the next generation. They read the book as something without precedent – something which talked frankly about female experiences that had been taboo. Some, desperate for information about their own bodies, read it as a sex manual. *Paris Match* published excerpts in August, introducing their author as 'Jean-Paul Sartre's lieutenant and expert in existentialism, [who] is without doubt the first woman philosopher to have appeared in men's history. It fell to her to extract a philosophy of her sex from the great human adventure.'[42]

Since its publication, Beauvoir's 'philosophy of her sex' has often been summarized by the claim that there is a distinction between the concepts of 'sex' and 'gender', with the former being biological (i.e., male, female) and the latter acquired socially through acculturation (e.g., masculine, feminine). But there are significant problems with reducing *The Second Sex* to this claim. First, the word 'gender' never appears in the book. Second, the idea that there is a biological and cultural dimension to the concept 'woman' and the perpetuation of women's oppression was not an original one, even in 1949. For centuries before Beauvoir (as she discusses in *The Second Sex*), philosophers and writers have claimed that women's inferior status in society resulted from their lack of concrete educational, economic and professional possibilities – not from any innate inferiority. In the eighteenth century (to give one example) Diderot had already written that women's inferiority was 'largely *made* by society'.[43]

It is important to dwell on this because to reduce *The Second Sex* to the claim that gender is a social construct risks divorcing it from one of its most powerful and unpopular claims: that the sexual objectification of women's bodies plays a large part in the perpetuation of their oppression. In the first volume, 'Facts and Myths', Beauvoir studied the ways in which 'femininity' had been construed as a destiny for women – over and over again, she found that the ideal woman was the object of men's desires.

The second volume, 'Lived Experience', was much longer. Here Beauvoir adopted a different method of analysis and considered the question 'what is a woman?' from the point of view of women themselves, at different stages in their lives. In doing this Beauvoir reversed the philosophical perspective on power: instead of analysing 'woman' from the point of view of those who dominated, she turned to the everyday lives of those who were expected to submit. To do this she had to discuss topics that the philosophical elite did not consider to be worthy of the title 'philosophical': how household work was divided, how managers appraised work, how women experienced sexual initiation and practices. These were not elevated questions about the nature of reality or the possibility of knowledge.[44] Rather, they were questions about who gets to say what parts of reality matters – and whose knowledge is worthy of the name.

She knew all too well that it was difficult to let women speak for themselves: one of the features of their oppression was that they did not have the means to leave records of their lives in the same quantity and quality that men did. Women's voices were less public, and when they became public their testimony was often dismissed as partial or false, malicious or immoral. To analyse the submission of women Beauvoir cited particular women's experiences of the private sphere, a situation that was, structurally and systematically, reduced to silence.[45]

One of Beauvoir's childhood inspirations, George Eliot, once wrote that 'if we had a keen vision and feeling of all ordinary human life, it would be like hearing the grass grow and the squirrel's heart beat, and we should die of that roar which lies on the other side of silence'.[46] On the other side of silence, Beauvoir heard a restless refrain of confusion, resignation and despair – a chorus of women's voices, asking: what have I become?

When she researched *The Second Sex* Beauvoir was dismayed by her own discoveries. But she found reasons to hope in them, too. Yes, in 1949 women *were* inferior to men, 'because their situation opened fewer possibilities to them'. But they didn't have to be. If men and women stopped hiding behind alibis, things could be different.

The Second Sex is often described as a book that 'applied' Sartre's philosophy to 'the woman question'. And at this stage Beauvoir did still agree with Sartre about some things – the importance of freedom, for example. But she was doing what philosophers do – agreeing with what she thought was true, and dismissing what she thought was false, inconsistent or unethical, even if it was someone she loved who thought it. She rejected Sartre's conception of the 'situation', drawing instead on Heidegger's characterization of human beings as 'thrown' into a world that always already has meanings that we have not made ourselves. She was returning in full force to the question she had asked Sartre in the 1930s: what kind of freedom can a woman in a harem achieve?

But by now she had seen more clearly that women don't have to be kept in harems to be told that their value comes from magnifying men's greatness or satisfying their pleasures. Even in 1949, even in America or France, a woman could not simply escape the ways that sexual difference structures the possibilities available to her simply by claiming to be human. Philosophers like Husserl, Sartre and Merleau-Ponty were beginning to write philosophy about the body (a topic that Western philosophers have a long history of ignoring, in favour of the mind). But Beauvoir claimed that they failed to take into account women's bodies, and in particular the alienation that a woman can feel *from her own body* when she recognizes the way it is reduced to a sexual object by a certain kind of male gaze – a gaze that sees her as '*prey*' to be hunted and possessed rather than a person in the process of becoming.

Beauvoir wasn't satisfied with what she saw of women through this distorted lens. So she used an original philosophical method that consisted of presenting multiple first-person perspectives, describing her task as 'describing the world that is *proposed* to women from the point of view of women'. If it were the case that women *by nature* submitted to men, then there would be nothing immoral about a hierarchy between men and women. But if that hierarchy were perpetuated by culture, and women's submission was experienced by them as the 'degradation' of their freedom, then the problem was a moral problem, and both the oppressors and the oppressed were responsible for redressing it. In Volume II, Beauvoir combined women's voices describing their experiences of becoming a woman under the hegemony of man-made myths, to show the ways that girlhood is an 'apprenticeship' in the feminine condition, a preparation to renounce autonomy and submit to the expectation that to become a woman is to *be for men*.[47]

Because Beauvoir published sections of the book in advance the earliest readers couldn't follow her argument from start to finish. But it is not just piecemeal readings that led to the *ad feminam* reception she received. Many readers had strong reasons to want her to be wrong, unread or misheard. After all, alibis are a great way to get off the hook. If Beauvoir's readers could reject her as an unoriginal thinker, a failure of a woman, or an immoral person, then they could rest untroubled by her account of human suffering in 'the feminine condition'. They could tell the silence to shut up again.

In a 1949 radio interview about *The Second Sex* Beauvoir was asked about the attacks she received after its publication. She said that it wasn't her fault that in France, when one speaks of women, 'people immediately think of sex'. It didn't escape her notice that, despite relatively few of the 1,000 pages of *The Second Sex* being dedicated to sex, it was these pages that drew the most comment. She thought it was problematic that sexual matters weren't taken seriously, as matters deserving philosophical scrutiny. It was as if people didn't think philosophy could be something living, something that could illuminate even this dimension of human life.[48]

The Second Sex didn't gain momentum immediately – it was ahead of its time and, quite frankly, for many it was also too intimidating. Beauvoir's extensive classical, philosophical and literary education is reflected in this work: she cites ancient Greek playwrights, Roman philosophers, the Bible and the Qur'an, centuries' worth of philosophical and theological writing on women, swathes of literature, letters and diaries, psychoanalytic accounts, and more, as well as employing a phenomenological method and existentialist perspective in her analysis. As Marine Rouch's research has shown, many of Beauvoir's readers wrote to reproach her for making *The Second Sex* so difficult. One reader asked outright:

> Why did you write such a book? For a little literary club of a few hundred (or thousand) people initiated into esoteric jargon of metaphysics and its existentialist category? Or for any public that has the common sense and understanding to usefully address such problems? Couldn't it be expressed in familiar language, without this pedantic algebra used by professional 'philosophers'?[49]

Encouraged by her work, feminists in the 1960s and 1970s would continue to confront some of the 'real idiocies uttered against women by the most eminent minds'.[50] But in 1949 Beauvoir didn't know that *The Second Sex* would be recognized as a classic and inspire political movements. When the time came, feminists would criticize Beauvoir for her 'unconscious misogyny', claiming that she separated herself from women while writing about them.[51] Some thought that she was blind to the privileges of her class, race and education; others thought that she had been conscientious about these privileges but nevertheless made the misstep of universalizing about the experiences of women. She was accused of writing from 'the personal to the general'; and also praised for using her personal experience as an 'energetic anger' that propelled the book forward.[52] Some feminists objected that Beauvoir excluded women of colour and appropriated their suffering as a rhetorical strategy in the interests of white feminism.[53] After decades of hearing from her readers, Beauvoir would admit that aspects of her attitude towards men and her own experience was naïve. She was a 'token' woman, protected from the daily realities of many kinds of oppression.[54] But in the immediate aftermath of the book's publication she paid a high price for being such an outspoken token. She had emerged from Sartre's shadow, only to find herself in the scorching light of scandal – the *ad feminam* target of ridicule, spite and shame.

Toril Moi, in *Simone de Beauvoir: The Making of an Intellectual Woman*, writes that by the end of 1949, 'Simone de Beauvoir had truly become Simone de Beauvoir: personally and professionally, she was "made".'[55] She declares that Beauvoir's work after 1949 was 'retrospective', that she produced 'almost nothing but autobiography'. But, professionally, Beauvoir still had not written her prize-winning novel *The Mandarins*, two further volumes of fiction, any of her life writing, her book on old age, or supporting materials for massive changes to French legislation; *The Second Sex* had not yet played its role in the genesis of second-wave feminism; and Beauvoir's career as a feminist activist had not even begun. Personally, life still held the promise of reciprocal relationships. There was much more for Beauvoir to become.

13

Putting a New Face on Love

In early 1950, Beauvoir's days had once again settled into a reassuring routine: writing, working on *Les Temps Modernes*, doing interviews on *The Second Sex*. But one day that February, entirely by chance, Beauvoir ran into someone she hadn't seen for a long time: her cousin Jacques. He was a shadow of his former self: ruined, alcoholic, penniless – he had been rejected even by his own wife and five children. Whether out of timeworn tenderness or sheer generosity, she arranged to see him again and gave him financial support.[1]

Beauvoir wanted to see the Sahara, so in March she left Paris again with Sartre. They crossed the desert for four days in a truck, saw Tamanrasset, and passed caravans on their way to El Goléa before flying across the Sahara to Mali.

Alongside her larger projects Beauvoir continued to write short articles and in 1950 she published a magazine piece in *Flair*, an American style magazine. *Flair* was short-lived – only publishing a year's worth of issues – but in that time it included works by Jean Cocteau, Tennessee Williams, Eleanor Roosevelt, Salvador Dali and Margaret Mead. Beauvoir's article – entitled 'It's About Time Women Put a New Face on Love'[2] – discussed sexual desire in light of her view that human beings are both free and conscious, and incarnate in different bodies. Sexual attraction, she wrote, thrives on difference: 'the other sex has the fascination of an exotic country'.

The problem, as Beauvoir saw it, was that men thought of love in terms of inequality and submission and many women were resisting love because 'it evoked ancient slaveries'. The difference between the sexes, as Beauvoir saw it, was too often that of superior and inferior, subject and object, giver and exploitative taker: but domination was not love, and neither was devotion. Women were becoming increasingly active in the world, independent and responsible. Now that women had entered public life some were dismayed, wondering: would love be ruined? Would it lose its poetry and happiness? Beauvoir didn't think so: 'Is it not possible to conceive a new kind of love in which both partners are equals – one not seeking submission to the other?'[3]

She had caught partial glimpses of this new love in famous writers; Nietzsche, Tolstoy and D. H. Lawrence recognized that 'true and fruitful love' included both the physical presence of the beloved and the beloved's aims in life. But they proposed this ideal to *woman*, since love was her purpose and she had no other. In 'equalitarian' love, by contrast, Beauvoir thought that women would still aspire to be their lover's ally in this way – that they would aim for reciprocity and friendship – but that the same ideal would be shared by men:

> The man, instead of seeking a kind of narcissistic exaltation in his mate, would discover in love a way of getting outside himself, of tackling problems other than his own. With all the twaddle that has been written about the splendour of such generosity, why not give the man his chance to participate in such devotion, in the self-negation that is considered the enviable lot of women?[4]

 If each partner thought 'simultaneously of the other and the self', both would benefit.

It is interesting, given the non-sexual nature of her relationship with Sartre, that she is explicit in this piece that such love can be platonic (although she acknowledges that sexual attraction is 'the more usual instrument'). Returning to the theme of 'Femininity: The Trap' and to ground she covered in *The Second Sex*, Beauvoir wrote about widespread fear she saw in women, that losses of 'femininity' would cost them their desirability in men's eyes. She knew that women want to be desired – but she did not think their desirability could be so easily eradicated: 'the physical need that each [sex] has for the other will maintain their mutual magic'.[5]

In June Beauvoir went to Chicago to see Algren. She had asked to come in June because Sartre was going to see Vanetti a final time – he was trying to let her down gently – and both she and Sartre liked it if she was away at the same time he was, so they could be together more. She made no secret of the fact that she was scheduling her trip around Sartre when she wrote to arrange it.

Nelson agreed. But his letters became fewer and fewer. She started to wonder: should she even go? Sartre encouraged her to give it a try. On the plane it was surreal to see the person next to her reading *The Second Sex*. After visiting Stépha and Fernando Gerassi in New York, in September 1951, she flew to Chicago. It took less than twenty-four hours to recognize that things had changed. She asked Algren what was the matter. He was happy to see her, he said, but he didn't like it that she came only to leave again. She wrote to Sartre that his detachment now bordered on indifference.[6] Algren's ex-wife wanted to re-marry him, but after Beauvoir, Algren said, wasn't sure he'd ever love another woman.

Even so, he told her, something had died. The next night they tried to make love but neither of their bodies would cooperate. When she and Algren moved to a cottage on Lake Michigan at the beginning of August they slept in separate rooms. Beauvoir started to worry that she would never experience passion again. She took corydrane, an amphetamine Sartre took in high doses to sustain his huge output, and worked on her novel – the one she would dedicate to Nelson. Their days settled into a peaceful rhythm, passionless but productive: writing in the morning, swimming, reading in the afternoon. Once, she nearly drowned in the lake – she never was a very good swimmer. And then Nathalie Sorokine came to visit, and things went south. Algren disliked her intensely, and told Beauvoir that Sorokine had shocked his friends with her 'lesbian side'.[7] Beauvoir felt torn between the two of them – Sorokine wasn't easy to live with, but Algren hadn't exactly handled himself well. She was looking forward to being back with Sartre, her 'dear little absolute'.[8]

In *Force of Circumstance* Beauvoir described that visit as one in which despair drained her of all feeling. She glosses over its end, moving on to the insults Sartre was receiving in abundance in Paris at the time.[9] But her letters show that at the end of October, just before she left Chicago for New York, her hope for the relationship with Algren was rekindled. At the visit's end, Beauvoir told Nelson that she was glad to have his friendship. To which Algren replied, 'It's not friendship. I could never give you less than love.'[10]

She wrote to Nelson the same night, saying that she cried all the way to and from the airport, and on the plane too: 'In this "introduction" you made me read yesterday, Thomas Mann says that before each fit Dostoevsky had a few seconds of bliss which were worth ten years of life. Certainly you have the power to give me in a few minutes, at times, a kind of fever that is worth ten years of health.'

It was fair, she said, that he wanted to evict her from his heart. But, as her not-quite-fluent English put it: 'thinking it is fair did not prevent it to be hard'.[11] She loved him, she said, 'for the love you gave me', 'for the great new sexual longing and happiness you had aroused in me'. But even in the absence of those things, she loved him 'because of who you are'.[12]

When she got back to Paris Sartre was writing plays and reading about Marxism; he seemed distant and far away but she attributed this to his having become a public figure: he no longer wanted to sit in cafés and stroll through Paris, or join her skiing trips. He invited her to read the things he was reading, to follow his intellectual path, but she had her novel to finish and – although she was interested in politics – she did not want to spend her time following his. He wanted to create a new ideology that would solve humanity's problems; she didn't share these ambitions. Some days their growing distance loomed like a thin veil of sadness; on other days despair gnawed away at her like a corrosive.[13]

The Second Sex had made Beauvoir money as well as earning her a largely unwanted reputation, so she bought a record player and some records; Sartre came to the rue de la Bûcherie a couple of nights a week to listen to jazz or classical music. And in November 1951 Beauvoir wrote to Algren with excitement: she'd found a new passion: 'As love is forbidden, I decided to give my dirty heart to something not so piggish as a man: and I gave to myself a nice beautiful black car.'[14] She was taking driving lessons three times a week.

Since the war Paris had blossomed into one of Europe's leading cultural centres. Miles Davis played in Left Bank clubs, and intellectuals, artists and writers – including anticolonial activists – gathered for meetings and events. In 1950 the Martinican poet Aimé Césaire published *Discourse on Colonialism*, in which he likened European Nazism to colonialism on account of their shared pursuits of domination and control. India had won its independence from the British in 1947 and anticolonialism was gaining ground. In 1952 Frantz Fanon's *Black Skin, White Masks* was published, passionately describing the effects of racism on the oppressed. But many in France were reluctant to relinquish their empire, despite the growth of anticolonial and Algerian nationalist movements since the 1930s.

During this period, Beauvoir's work was becoming one of France's leading cultural exports. The first translation of *The Second Sex* appeared in West Germany in 1951 under the title *Das andere Geschlecht* – 'The Other Sex'. It sold so quickly it had to be reprinted three times: 14,000 copies in five years.[15]

Meanwhile, Beauvoir's correspondence with Algren played more variations on the same melancholy theme. She started to call him her 'pang collector'. He wanted to be with her, but he wanted her to stay with him in Chicago, which meant that they might be together a month a year instead of the three or four they might manage if he would come to Paris. And he was angry about her New York letter. But what was she supposed to do? He charged her with wanting to keep his life without giving her own, but she felt this was unfair. 'You could not expect me to react like an obedient machine,' she wrote.[16] Her claim in *The Second Sex* that women were expected to see love as life – and to sacrifice everything for it – became painfully personal. For her, it could only ever be part of life. In *Force of Circumstance* she would write that 'Even if Sartre hadn't existed, I would never have gone to live permanently in Chicago.'[17]

Over 1952 the letters between Beauvoir and Algren became fewer; the intervals between them stretched from near daily, to weekly, to monthly. Beauvoir was 44 now, and worried that she had been 'relegated to the land of shadows'.[18] In *The Second Sex* she had described it as a tragedy of women's sexuality that they lose their desirability long before they lose their desire, becoming 'objects without assets'. She thought women reached their sexual peak in their mid-thirties. But soon afterwards, she said, they were haunted by ageing. Beauvoir's fictional women – especially in her later novels – frequently embody the lonely dissatisfaction of listless desire.

Early in 1952 Beauvoir felt that she and Sartre had grown apart on account of his public prominence and political engagement; there was now a third person in their relationship: Beauvoir, Sartre and 'Jean-Paul Sartre'. She told him that she wished he were an obscure poet. Although he had adopted some of her views about ethics and the importance of cultural values by this point, pressures on their time and diversions of their interests exacerbated her feelings of loss and isolation, which made her feel very low. In *Force of Circumstance* she described her sadness becoming 'a universal despair' that 'crept into my heart until I began to long for the world to end'.[19]

Beauvoir's typist Lucienne had died of breast cancer in January and not long afterwards Beauvoir discovered a lump in one of her own breasts. She told Sartre, who encouraged her to go to a doctor if she was worried about it. By March of 1952 it had grown painful, so she made an appointment and in April she went to the specialist. The surgeon reassured her: she was young, it was unlikely to be too bad, but even so they should operate and do a biopsy. The worst case scenario was that the breast would have to be removed: would she agree to this?

She did. But she emerged from the consultation feeling shaken; she had seen these waiting rooms with Lucienne, and she had also seen women who'd lost one breast come back ten years later to lose the other, or dying from infection. When she told Sartre what the doctor had said he replied with Cold War sardonicism: in the worst case scenario she had twelve years to live, and by then the atomic bomb would have killed everyone.[20] She spent the day before her operation visiting a beautiful abbey with Bost.

In Rome in May 1952 Sartre heard that the French government had violently suppressed a demonstration of the French Communist Party. He did not join the party but he became an outspoken public sympathizer just at the time when most Western intellectuals were beginning to distance themselves from Stalin. Whatever its political savvy, Sartre's conversion to communism brought Beauvoir one unexpected benefit. The *Les Temps Modernes* people had a regular meeting on Sunday afternoons at the rue Bonaparte. Sartre wanted the journal to reflect his new political zeal, so he invited some young Marxists onto the editorial board. One of them was a quick-witted friend of Sartre's secretary. Claude Lanzmann was 27, funny and had magnificent blue eyes.

One day Sartre's secretary, Jean Cau, told Beauvoir that Lanzmann found her attractive. She shrugged it off: she had started to have anxiety attacks about ageing and believed dusk had fallen on her sexual life.[21] But sometimes she noticed that his gaze lingered on her during meetings. After a party one evening in July her telephone rang: Lanzmann invited her to see a movie. Which one? She asked. 'Anything you like,' he said. They fixed it for the next day, and when she put the phone down she burst into tears.[22]

Although it would be clearer in her later work on *Old Age* (published when she was 62) than in the autobiographical account given in *Force of Circumstance* (published when she was 55), the young Beauvoir was disgusted by mature female sexuality. As a young woman she 'loathed' what she called 'harridans' who had the gall to dye their hair, wear bikinis and flirt when their place was, to use Beauvoir's image, 'on the shelf'. Beauvoir promised that she would 'dutifully retire to the shelf' when her time came. At 44, she thought her time had come. But it had come too soon.[23]

At their first meeting Lanzmann and Beauvoir talked their way through the afternoon into the evening, and at the end of that they agreed to have dinner the next day. When he flirted she protested: she was 17 years older than he was. It didn't matter to him, he said: in his eyes she was not old. That night he didn't leave her apartment on the rue de la Bûcherie, nor the next.

A few days later she left for Milan – she drove her Simca Aronde, Sartre went by train – where they met on the Piazza della Scala. She wanted to see museums, churches, art; he just wanted to work. So they compromised: sightseeing for the morning, and working in the afternoon. For him, it was *The Communists and Peace*, and for her, more work on the novel that never seemed to end. Sartre read it in autumn 1952 and found much to praise, but he was still not satisfied that it was finished. She was fed up, and wondered about ditching it. But then Bost and Lanzmann read it and encouraged her to keep going. When it was finished, Sartre would cite it as the reason he stopped writing novels – even leaving his 'Roads to Freedom' series unfinished. There wasn't any point finishing it, he said, *The Mandarins* had already 'explored the problems of the time much better than I could have ever done', 'maintaining freedom, uncertainty, and ambiguity throughout'.[24]

From Italy Beauvoir wrote letters to Lanzmann. Five letters, in fact, before he replied. She had promised that she would still love him when she returned to Paris. Only until then, he asked? He had more confidence than that.[25]

Beauvoir visited her sister en route to Paris, but she had to wait two weeks for Lanzmann to come back from his own travels in Israel before 'their bodies met each other again with joy'.[26] They began to share stories of their pasts: he was Jewish, and his reflections on Jewishness helped her understand it in ways she hadn't imagined. (In later life many would say the same of him; he went on to – with sustained support from Beauvoir – direct the acclaimed Holocaust documentary *Shoah*.)

Conversations about the past segued into conversations about the future. He had little money after his travels so Beauvoir invited him to move in with her. It was the first time she had ever lived with her lover, and she was nervous about giving up her solitude, but they would live like this for seven years. He was also the only lover Beauvoir ever addressed in the familiar second person, *tu*. Sartre commented on this in later interviews, claiming that he had never been closer to any woman than he was to the Beaver. But even so, they had never said 'tu'.[27] In 2018, Beauvoir's letters to Lanzmann became available to researchers. Interspersed throughout discussion of what Beauvoir was writing, reading and seeing when she was away from Lanzmann, there are tender professions of love and practical details of daily life. For someone who wanted to be alone as much as Beauvoir did, it is significant that she was willing to share her life with him in this way.

In Josée Dayan's film portrait of Simone de Beauvoir, Simone asked Lanzmann about his first impression of her:

Lanzmann   I found you very beautiful, you had a smooth face and I wanted to see what lay behind your impassivity.

Beauvoir   And then you found that I was less impassive then I looked.

Lanzmann   Oh absolutely. [...] I don't know if I ought to talk about that.... What was striking about you right from the beginning, was your taste for life, your constant projects. You always wanted to do something, to travel, to see things in detail [...]. It was most surprising to discover the world with you, which is in effect what I did.[28]

The past two years, for Beauvoir, had brought her a bitter end to a love affair and seemed to signal the end of her sexual era. But with Lanzmann, Beauvoir said, 'I leapt back enthralled into happiness.'[29]

Beauvoir continued to see Sartre, but their habits changed.[30] She did not want to leave Lanzmann for two months, as their usual annual vacations would have required. So they agreed that Lanzmann would come too, for ten days at least. Lanzmann was writing about the recently established State of Israel; he was deeply impressed by the fact that there, Jews were not outsiders. So he and Beauvoir wrote together in the mornings, and then in the afternoon she kept her custom of going to work with Sartre.

But although she and Lanzmann shared an apartment as well as a bed their relationship was conducted on the same, non-exclusive terms as Beauvoir's others. She expected him to see other women and to tell her everything; she expected to see Sartre and tell him everything. Lanzmann became part of 'the family': they spent New Year's Eve with Olga, Bost, Wanda and Michelle. With time she came to appreciate the long, shared history of these people more and more: 'there was so much understood between us that a smile conveyed as much as a whole oration'.[31]

Lanzmann was a passionate man, spontaneously expressing his emotions and reactions for others to see; early in their affair he expressed gratitude that Beauvoir could love him despite his 'madness'. He had a tempestuous past, but that was not the only thing that shaped his temperament. He was griefstruck by the postwar discovery of France's complicity with the Jewish genocide. And his childhood – in addition to academic excellence at thc Lycée Louis le Grand and friendships with Jean Cau and Gilles Deleuze – had included violence between his parents so severe that his mother left his father, and their three children, with no indication of where she could be found.

But he wasn't the only one with darkness to reckon with, and Lanzmann – as the only lover she ever lived with – saw Beauvoir's own storms at close quarters. Lanzmann thought that that one of the important things that Beauvoir shared with Sartre was an existential angst on the verge of depression or despair. In Sartre, they manifested as 'gloom and inactivity', and he fought them off with corydrane, writing and seduction. In Beauvoir, they manifested as what Lanzmann called 'explosion':

Sitting, standing, or lying down, in the car or on foot, in public or in private, she would burst into violent, convulsive sobs, her whole body racked with gasps, with heartrending cries punctuated by long howls of incommunicable despair. I don't remember the first time, it happened many times during the seven years we spent together, but thinking about it now as I write, it was never associated with some wrong done to her nor some misfortune. On the contrary, she seemed to break on the rocks of happiness, to be crushed by it.

Lanzmann tried to reassure Beauvoir but he was 'utterly helpless' in the face of her 'excruciating awareness of the fragility of human happiness'.[32] But just like the 'Mlle de Beauvoir' of her student days, the explosions would pass; Beauvoir and Lanzmann passed peaceful hours living and working together in the rue Schoelcher, sometimes writing for as long as five hours without speaking to each other.[33]

In 2018 Claude Lanzmann sold a selection of his letters from Beauvoir to Yale University.[34] On announcing the sale *Le Monde* published one letter from 1953, in which Beauvoir wrote that while she 'certainly' had loved Sartre, it was: 'without true reciprocity; and without our bodies ever amounting to anything'.[35] This revealing claim shows that by 1953, Beauvoir clearly did not take Sartre to be central to her life in a romantic sense, and moreover, that her criticism of their relationship was not just sexual, but ethical. If history were to repeat itself, readers of these letters would focus only on the sex. They would rehearse their surprise that 'the greatest love story' of the twentieth century was not what they were led to believe. But the sex was not the only thing Beauvoir found wanting. She objected to its lack of reciprocity – something she believed to be necessary for romantic love to be authentic. Since generations of Beauvoir's readers have wondered whether she was in bad faith about her relationship with Sartre, it is very significant that she admitted outright (to those closest to her) that it had serious imperfections. Yes, she loved Sartre. But in important respects, from her point of view, their relationship did not succeed.

What she told the public was a different story, but it was also complicated by what the public said about her. In spring 1953 the first English translation of *The Second Sex* was published. Blanche Knopf, the wife of the publisher Alfred Knopf, had heard people talking about it when she was in Paris. Her French wasn't good enough to assess the work herself; she thought it was some kind of intellectual sex manual so she asked a professor of zoology to write a reader's report. H. M. Parshley wrote back praising it as 'intelligent, learned, and well-balanced'; it was 'not feminist in any doctrinaire sense'.

The Knopfs wrote back: would he like to translate it? And please could he cut it down a bit? (Its author, Knopf said, suffered from 'verbal diarrhea'.[36]) In French, *The Second Sex* was 972 pages long. In correspondence with Knopf, Parshley said he was cutting or condensing 145 of them – deleting nearly 15 per cent of what Beauvoir said. Parshley had no background in philosophy or French literature, and he missed many of the rich philosophical connotations and literary allusions of Beauvoir's original French, making her look much less rigorously philosophical than she was. He also cut sections and translated material in less-than-innocent ways. The hardest hit section was the one on women's history, where he deleted seventy-eight women's names and almost every reference to socialist forms of feminism. He cut references to women's anger and oppression but kept references to men's feelings. He cut Beauvoir's analysis of housework.[37]

When she saw what Parshley had cut, Beauvoir wrote back that 'so much of what seems important to me will have been omitted'. He wrote back saying that the book would be 'too long' if he didn't cut it, so Beauvoir asked him to state outright in the preface that he had made omissions and condensed her work. But he was not as forthright as she hoped.

In America the book was not billed as an 'existentialist' work because Blanche Knopf thought existentialism was a 'dead duck'; she had, in fact, asked Parshley to play it down in his preface.[38] When Parshley's preface appeared he said that since 'Mlle de Beauvoir's book is, after all on woman, not on philosophy'[39] he had 'done some cutting and condensation here and there with a view to brevity.' '*Practically* all such modifications,' he writes, 'have been made with the author's express permission.'[40] In a 1985 interview Beauvoir said that she begrudged Parshley 'a great deal.'[41] (A new English translation, with the missing pieces restored, would not be published until 2009 in Britain, 2010 in America.)

When *The Second Sex* went on sale in the United States, it leapt onto the bestseller lists. Some of the early evaluations were very positive about Beauvoir's style and originality, simultaneously pointing out that she falsely universalized challenges that really only pertained to artistic or intellectual women.[42] Others concluded that this author (as a reviewer in *The Atlantic* put it) clearly had 'the extreme feminist personality type.'[43] A reviewer in the *New Yorker* and the anthropologist Margaret Mead called it 'a work of art' and 'a work of fiction', respectively.[44] It has sold well since publication, reputedly passing the million-copy mark in the 1980s. In the 1950s, it was one of the few books women who wanted to think about their status in the world could turn to.[45]

Because of *The Second Sex* Beauvoir would be referred to as the 'mother' of second-wave feminism. Curiously, however, some of the best-known feminist pioneers of the 1960s failed to acknowledge her influence until later. Kate Millett's *Sexual Politics* owed a great deal to *The Second Sex*, prompting Beauvoir to comment that Millet's book, while 'very good', had taken 'it all, the form, the idea, everything', from her.[46]

In America, it was Beauvoir's ideas about sexuality, the 'independent woman', and maternity that would draw the most sustained attention.[47] And although reactions weren't as vitriolic as the ones she'd had in France, it still managed to ruffle feathers in some quarters and provoke fury in others. After a trip to Saint-Tropez with Sartre and Lanzmann, in April of 1953 a parcel arrived for her at Les Deux Magots, in Paris. It was postmarked Chicago so she thought it was from Nelson and opened it excitedly. But in fact it was an anonymous gift: 'laxative pills to help evacuation of bile'.[48]

She was still writing to Algren monthly, regularly updating him on *The Mandarins*. When Beauvoir wrote to him she called it 'his' book – although it was Lanzmann who found her the title (from the beginning, Lanzmann said, their rapport was both 'intellectual and carnal'[49]). *The Mandarins* was taking shape slowly, more slowly than she wished, so by August 1953 her letters to Algren were calling it 'his damned book'. By December it was her 'damned dirty novel'.

In June 1953 Beauvoir and Lanzmann travelled to Switzerland and Yugoslavia before going to Venice for a 'joint session' vacation with Sartre and Michelle. Lanzmann drove the Simca Aronde, while Beauvoir planned eight-hour hikes with gruelling itineraries. At Trieste they discovered that they could get visas to enter Yugoslavia. Beauvoir had never been behind the iron curtain: they packed the car with supplies and into communist territory they went.

In Amsterdam that August Beauvoir kept working on *The Mandarins*. She was enjoying the rhythm of working there, alongside Sartre, when she received distressing news from Lanzmann: she had planned to meet him in Basel, but he had been hospitalized in Cahors after a car accident. She got in the car immediately, and drove to his side.[50]

Meanwhile, Sartre went back to Paris. He was going to meet Beauvoir and Lanzmann in Cahors but he had a few matters to attend to for the Beaver – errands, mainly – and a new lover to woo for himself. He had fallen for Lanzmann's sister, Evelyne. And although Michelle knew nothing about it, Evelyne had fallen for Sartre, too. So Sartre now had three 'mistresses': Wanda, Michelle and Evelyne, some of whom were more in the know than others, and all of whom he supported financially and lavished with literary gifts.

In February of 1954 Beauvoir got a letter from Algren asking if she still had 'magic' in her life. Despite the presence of Lanzmann she replied that she would never love a man like she had loved Nelson. She had become disenchanted with the world and blamed her age; now she lived 'a magicless life'.[51] But at the end of April she wrote to him again, jubilant – she'd finished the book. It was 1,200 pages of typescript, and Sartre, Bost and Olga thought it was her best novel ever. It was an American story, about a man and a woman, and although she hadn't yet given 'the monster' to Gallimard she was already feeling the relief of completion.

Beauvoir was worried about Sartre's health: he'd been pushing himself too hard for years, taking corydrane at several times the recommended dose. He had high blood pressure so the doctors had recommended rest. He made no changes, except to increase his stimulant intake when he started to feel slow. Beauvoir and Lanzmann both told him he was killing himself, but he didn't want to stop.

In May 1954 Sartre left on a trip for the USSR. His visit was covered in the French papers, and Beauvoir followed it in the press, but he hadn't sent letters. The same month Hélène came to Paris to show her paintings, and in June Simone and Lanzmann travelled to England, (where she was decidedly unimpressed by the English 'summer'). They got back to find a note from Bost under her apartment door, asking her to come and see him immediately. They went downstairs (Bost and Olga were still living on the floor below) to see what the matter was: he told them that Sartre had been hospitalized in Moscow. It was his high blood pressure, Jean Cau said, nothing serious.

Beauvoir phoned Moscow and was reassured to hear Sartre's voice. He spent ten days recovering before flying back to France. But in addition to his health Beauvoir began to find his principles disquieting. On this trip he'd written an article for *Liberation* claiming that in the USSR there was complete freedom of expression. Everyone knew that that wasn't true; what was he thinking? Sartre was stubborn, and wouldn't publicly criticize the USSR until the Soviet invasion of Hungary.

When he got back from Russia he went to Rome to convalesce. Michelle went with him, but all he felt like doing was sleeping. In August, he joined Beauvoir for a trip to Germany and Austria, and Beauvoir was surprised by his low mood and physical state: she thought his fatigue had brought on mental disgust. He was irritable and dismissive, even calling literature – the vocation to which both of them wanted to dedicate their lives – 'horseshit'.[52] He was dysphoric and questioning his life's purpose. No number of women could deliver him from this despair.

October 1954 saw the publication of *The Mandarins*. Beauvoir was apprehensive after the reception of *The Second Sex*: 'I could almost hear the unpleasant gossip in advance.' It was extremely well received, and what astonished her most is that it was well received everywhere: the right wing and the left found things to like about it. The first print run of 11,000 copies was not enough; by the end of the first month it had sold 40,000.[53] She wrote to Nelson that his book was the biggest success she'd ever had. It was even a contender for the Prix Goncourt, a prestigious French prize awarded annually in November. Lots of people said the novel deserved it but she wondered if her reputation as the author of *The Second Sex* would work against her.

The convention was for the nominees to go to a special Goncourt lunch to hear the winners announced and then – if you were the lucky one – thank the jury. After that the publisher had a cocktail party where the press could ask questions and take pictures. Many writers enjoyed the fanfare and public attention, and wanted to do this. Simone de Beauvoir did not.

She didn't like the way the newspapers wrote 'dirt' about her and Sartre, or, more recently, about her as the author of *The Second Sex*. Nor did she relish public appearances since, in her view, 'publicity disfigures those who fall into its hands'.[54] So she decided to play the game her own way, and stay out of its hands – she hid.

Two days before the prize was announced reporters started to watch the door of her apartment building from a bar across the street. But she slipped out the back door and went to stay elsewhere. So on the day itself she had a small party with Sartre, Olga and Bost, listening on the radio to hear who won while the journalists sat waiting all day at the rue de la Bûcherie. They got impatient and tried several ruses, including phoning her flat and impersonating Sartre.

But the joke – and the Goncourt – was hers.

The literary power brokers were angry; she had successfully conveyed her message that she could do without them. One newspaper spitefully published an artificially aged photo, making dark shadows under her eyes. A TV feature showed video clips of her empty place at the white-linen table, before showing the 'less shy' winner of the Renaudot prize, Jean Reverzy, signing books (fulfilling 'the little obligations of glory', as the announcer put it).[55] But despite Beauvoir's refusal to play by the rules, *The Mandarins* sold well – better than usual even for a Goncourt winner – and she received more letters. Their tone was softer than the disdainful deluge that followed *The Second Sex*. She heard from old friends, old pupils. But she wanted to know what Algren thought. This American love story was not exactly theirs, she told him; but she tried to put something of them in it.[56]

Beauvoir was the third woman to receive the Goncourt since its inception in 1903. A month after she won it, her friend Colette Audry explained that Beauvoir 'had chosen for herself the life of an intellectual', and that her novel showed the 'wounds of individual maturing and the seriousness of collective experience'. Beauvoir's work, Audry wrote, 'asks readers to reflect on themselves and their own situation'.[57] Her aim as a writer was still to appeal to the reader's freedom, and in a 1963 interview Beauvoir expressed frustration at the insistence of some readers that *The Mandarins* was autobiographical: 'in reality, it was truly a novel. A novel inspired by circumstances, by the postwar era, by people I knew, by my own life, etc., but really transposed on a totally imaginary plane widely straying from reality'.[58]

Despite Beauvoir's protest, even today the book is sold as a true-to-life an account of the left-bank intellectuals in their famous circle. The Harper Perennial edition published in 2005 describes it as 'an epic romance and philosophical manifesto' that will give readers insight into the lives of famous men:

> In wartime Paris, a group of friends gather to celebrate the end of the German occupation and to plan their future. [...] Punctuated by wickedly accurate portraits of Sartre, Camus and other intellectual giants of the time, this is a love story that you will never forget.

Although *The Mandarins* was prize-winning, its reception also demonstrates the trope that Beauvoir was a self-centred woman whose literature lacked imagination and drew only from her own life. According to this reading, Anne Dubreuilh is Beauvoir, her husband Robert is Sartre, Henri Perron is Camus, his lover Paule is sometimes thought to be Violette Leduc (although as Beauvoir noted, several women saw themselves in this character[59]). There is also an American man called Lewis Brogan – a man with whom Anne has an affair.

We have already seen that Beauvoir acknowledged that the novel was inspired by her life. But from her point of view it was neither autobiography nor a thesis novel, and since people accused it of being both she explained her own intentions in *Force of Circumstance*. The theme of *The Mandarins* is what Kierkegaard called 'repetition', which Beauvoir understood to mean that 'truly to possess something, one must have lost it and found it again'.[60] She did not want to impose a thesis on the novel, instead showing 'the perpetual dance of conflicting points of view'.

Here Beauvoir says two rather shocking things, from the point of view of her legendary relationship with Sartre: first, that she deliberately used a philosophical technique called 'indirect communication', in which the reader is presented not with a direct imperative to live a certain way, but with a choice. Kierkegaard used this technique in his writings – sometimes publishing under pseudonyms, and sometimes creating pseudonyms within pseudonyms to provoke reflection in his readers about what was true, and about what way of living they should choose for themselves. Such writing, when penned by Kierkegaard, is called philosophy – so why not hers? Is the answer simply that Kierkegaard was a man, and she a woman? Time and time again, she was dismissed as a superficial and imaginationless thinker, as incapable of being a 'true' philosopher. And when she defended the depth and originality of her own philosophy, she was rarely believed.

Second, Beauvoir says outright that this novel is a reworking of the philosophical questions she asked in her diary *before* she met Sartre: 'The basic confrontation of being and nothingness that I sketched at the age of twenty in my private diary, pursued through all my books and never resolved, is even here given no certain reply. I showed some people, at grips with doubts and hopes, groping in the dark to find their way; I cannot think I proved anything.'[61]

In *Force of Circumstance* Beauvoir defended both the philosophical nature and originality of her work forthrightly and firmly. By the early

1960s she had nearly two decades' experience of her own thinking being dismissed as 'applied existentialism', and her intellect and creativity being described as parasitic on Sartre's. She now knew all too well that tensions could arise not only because of what an author said, but between what was said and who said it. So she stated, unequivocally but quietly, that she had had her own ideas.

But a critical legend developed according to which Beauvoir had 'written an exact and faithful chronicle',[62] a *roman-à-clef*:

Études, 1955
'Yes, it is the story of "Sartre's band" that we are told.'[63]
Informations sociales, 1957
'The sale of 185,000 copies of *The Mandarins* is not only explained by Simone de Beauvoir's Prix Goncourt but also by all the legend that proliferates around Saint-Germain-des-Prés. Simone de Beauvoir is considered the muse of Jean-Paul Sartre, the icon of existentialism, and many readers have hoped to have, by reading this novel, new light on a movement that seems full of mysteries.'[64]

American reviews, too, claimed that, 'As expected, we find Simone de Beauvoir herself in the novel.'[65] For Beauvoir, this was not only a frustrating reception but it led to personal difficulty: 'this legend turned my inventions into indiscretions or even into denunciations.'[66]

Doris Lessing praised *The Mandarins* above all for its 'brilliant portraits of women'.[67] Its women are told that women are all the same.[68] And yet we see some suffering on account of unreciprocal love;[69] others frustrated that men do not take them seriously enough to discuss serious matters with them. An intergenerational dimension is brought into the story through Anne's daughter Nadine, who objects to her lover that: 'You discuss things with other people [...] But with me you never want to. I suppose it's because I'm a woman, and women are only good for getting laid.'[70]

One problem with indirect communication is that it leaves so many possible interpretations open. Although Beauvoir claimed that there was as much of herself in Henri as there was in Anne, one part of *The Mandarins* – the posthumous publication of Beauvoir's letters to Algren revealed – resembled life quite closely:

The Mandarins
'Oh! You're already in bed!' Brogan said. His arms were laden with clean sheets and he looked at me questioningly. 'I wanted to change the sheets.' 'It's not necessary' [. . .] 'Anne!' 'The way he said it moved me deeply. He threw himself on me and for the first time I spoke his name. 'Lewis!'

Letters (SdB to Algren)
'Don't forget to change the sheets when I come and sleep there. I'll always remember you so puzzled with the sheets in your arms, when you saw me already lying in the bed, the first, first night. It seems to me I began to really love you this very minute, never to stop.'

Once such lifelikeness was established after the publication of Beauvoir's letters, readers speculated about what other examples the book contained. Where should they draw the line between the real and the imaginary?

On 9 January 1955 Beauvoir turned 47 and felt 'really middle-aged'.[71] Birthdays had the unfortunate effect of reminding her of death, which she still couldn't think about with equanimity.

That year, with her Goncourt prize money, she bought a studio flat on the rue Victor Schoelcher, a small road off the boulevard Raspail that bordered the southeast side of the Montparnasse cemetery. It was a nine-minute walk from the apartment she was born into, near the Dôme and the Coupole. She and Lanzmann moved in in

August. Lanzmann remembered crossing the threshold together, commemorating the occasion with a 'sexual housewarming'.[72] But Beauvoir barely had time to unpack before she left with Sartre to visit China at the beginning of September. They had a month in Peking and then travelled around the country, curious about the kind of lives people led under Mao's communism. On this trip they felt their foreignness and their privilege keenly: here there were no luxuries, and no one had heard of them. They travelled back via Russia.

In the spring Violette Leduc's novel *Ravages* was published. In an earlier draft it had included a lesbian relationship that had offended Gallimard's readers and was therefore – in Beauvoir's word – 'amputated'.[73] Leduc was so upset that they wanted to cut it that she became physically ill. Beauvoir spent time with her while she recovered, writing to Sartre about the 'hard day' they had together.[74] The missing scenes were not restored when the book was published. But, even so, she and Leduc strolled through hyacinths and tulips discussing their hopes for it. Among other literary friendships, Beauvoir still saw Ellen and Richard Wright when she could; they often entertained her with her American publisher. They were working on a translation of *The Mandarins* but would have to cut some of the sex, he told her, since, 'In the States, it's all right to talk about sex in a book,' 'but not about perversion.'[75]

That June Merleau-Ponty published *Adventures of the Dialectic*; reviewers announced that it had dealt Sartre's philosophy a death blow. Beauvoir thought it had not – so she wrote a reply contradicting Merleau-Ponty's reading of Sartre point by point. Her contemporaries were critical of her for doing this – why did she defend him? In *Force of Circumstance* Beauvoir discussed the way her response drew attack. Some said that she should have left the replying to Sartre since it was his philosophy being condemned, others that she was too 'virulent'. To the former criticism she said that anyone who sees the defects of a philosophical argument can reply to it. And as to the latter, her friendship with Merleau-Ponty 'was great': 'our differences of opinion were often violent; I would often get carried away, and he would smile'. Beauvoir's acerbic wit comes through in her description of this episode. To the claim that the tone of her philosophical essays would benefit from being more temperate – a charge rarely levelled against male philosophers in those days – she said 'I don't think so. The best way to explode a bag of hot air is not to pat it but to dig one's nails into it.'[76]

By the autumn of 1955 the Algerian War was raging and France was divided over questions of race and colonialism. Morocco and Tunisia were about to gain their independence. Algeria wanted independence too, however the French had just suffered a defeat in Indochina in May and the government was humiliated. French empire – and French pride – had to be defended, and it would be defended by keeping Algeria. Beauvoir was deeply discomfited – even disgusted; she thought France's actions were indefensible. She struggled to sleep and felt ashamed of her nation's torture of innocents. *Les Temps Modernes* came out in support of Algerian independence early, and once again she faced the accusation that she was a traitor to her nation, anti-French.

In 1955 she published a collection of three essays under the title *Privileges*. The question that linked them together was: how can the privileged think about their situation? The ancient nobility ignored this question altogether: they used their rights without worrying about whether they were legitimate. So the first essay examined the Marquis de Sade because, she said, he illustrates the point that if one wishes to contest unjust hierarchies, the first condition of doing so is not to be ignorant of them. Sade failed to do what Beauvoir thought writers should: to reveal the world's possibilities and appeal to the freedom of their readers to work for justice. Instead, Sade took flight into the imaginary, and developed justifications for cruelty and perversion. Sade's so-called eroticism missed the truth of the erotic, which can only be found by those who abandon themselves to their vulnerability to and emotional intoxication with their beloved. But nevertheless, she said, Sade has enduring merit: he showed 'with brilliance that privilege can only be desired egotistically, that it cannot be legitimized in the eyes of all'.[77]

In the second essay she examined the processes by which some conservatives justify inequality: usually by conflating 'general interests' with their own. It is impossible to defend privilege philosophically, she says. So those people who think it defensible have succumbed either to 'forgetfulness' – a kind of lack of attention to the world – or to bad faith. The third essay analysed a particular case: culture. Here she wrote that culture is a privilege, and that many intellectuals are guilty, like other privileged classes, of forgetting the lives of less fortunate people.

Just eight years before, Beauvoir had written an article for *France-Amerique* about the 'incompetence' of 'nonspecialists' who wanted to understand existentialism, saying that it could not be summarized in a sentence or even an article:

> No one would dream of demanding that the system of Kant or Hegel be dispensed in three sentences; existentialism does not lend itself to popularization any easier. A philosophical theory, like a physics or mathematical theory, is accessible only to the initiated. Indeed, it is indispensable to be familiar with the long tradition on which it rests if one wants to grasp both the foundations and the originality of the new doctrine.[78]

Even then she recognized that the wider public was interested in existentialism because it was 'a practical and living attitude toward the problems posed by the world today'. It spoke to people. But in America, this led some critics to doubt that existentialism was, in fact, philosophy. In France philosophy was not so narrowly defined.[79] But even so, she must have wondered: had she forgotten that it wasn't just intellectuals who need answers?

After the essays on privilege, Beauvoir decided to write a book about China. She wanted a break from novel writing, but she also wanted to challenge her Western readers' prejudices about communism. *The Long March* (published in 1957) drew on Beauvoir's reaction to her travels in 1955; this trip challenged her not to take the wealth of Europe and the United States as her norm. 'Seeing the masses of China upset my whole idea of our planet; from then on it was the Far East, India, Africa, with their chronic shortage of food, that became the truth of the world, and our Western comfort merely a limited privilege.'[80] She wanted her first-hand experiences, her sights and conversations, to be available to others, so they too could see that the Chinese were 'fighting hard to build a human world'.

She wrote an account of the transition from 'a democratic to a socialist revolution' because she wanted to do justice not to their abstract philosophical definitions but rather to what she called 'the most concrete of all truths: the present is nothing but evolution, a becoming'. Whatever she saw during her time in China, she told her reader, it was 'simultaneously a survival from the past' and 'something in the throes of being born'.[81] Although her optimism about Mao proved ill-founded, she found much to praise in what she saw.

In 1956 *The Mandarins* joined *The Second Sex* on the Catholic Church's index of forbidden books, and Beauvoir joined Sartre for what would become a routine they followed until death did them part: autumn in Italy. They had hotel rooms next to each other in the centre of the Eternal City, and their days followed a harmonious rhythm of solitude and companionship, work, whiskey and gelato. Now that she had found her literary stride again, Beauvoir especially liked the period between the 'vertigo' of the blank page and the 'minutiae' of the final draft; after comments by Sartre, Bost and Lanzmann she described the process as one where 'she cut, amplified, corrected, tore up, began again, pondered, made decisions'.[82]

That year Beauvoir resumed the project she shelved a decade before, in 1946: her memoirs. A lot had changed since she first had the idea: she'd written *The Second Sex*, met Algren, struggled with 'the monster' that became *The Mandarins* and won the Prix Goncourt. She had travelled to America and China and many other places, and she had developed the conviction – as she put it in her final essay of *Privileges*, that culture was a privilege and that intellectuals should not forget the people whose lives did not afford it.

In Italy that autumn Beauvoir read Sartre passages she had written about her cousin Jacques, which would become part of the *Memoirs of a Dutiful Daughter*. She wrote to Lanzmann regularly, describing her days, and the books she found interesting, including C. Wright Mills' *The Power Elite*. Its opening sentence describes the way that 'the powers of ordinary men are circumscribed by the worlds in which they live, yet even in these rounds of job, family and neighbourhood they often seem driven by forces they can neither understand nor govern'. Mills thought that men and women in mass society felt 'without purpose in an epoch in which they were without power'.[83] How, Beauvoir must have wondered, could people recognize the power they did have?

It is striking that Beauvoir's turn to autobiography coincides with increasing criticism of intellectual privilege and involvement in politics.[84] This may be simple coincidence, but it seems more likely to me that Beauvoir's life writing was one of the ways she put her politics in action. Margaret Simons has argued that Beauvoir's trip to China – and more specifically, her encounter with a very popular book by Ba Jin entitled *The Family* – was what inspired Beauvoir to write her life in a way that might serve to liberate her readers from convention. *The Family* was about two brothers, one who accepted arranged marriage and one who rebelled; it sold by the tens of thousands and Beauvoir thought it 'gave voice to the resentments and hopes of an entire generation'.[85]

The Second Sex had articulated many of Beauvoir's objections to 'conventions' constraining women and her hopes for their liberation, but she had not written it with the ordinary woman in mind – the book's language, style and length were characteristic of works of the 1940s Parisian philosophical elite, employing and adapting concepts from philosophers who are not exactly known for being accessible: Hegel, Marx, Husserl, Sartre, Merleau-Ponty. By the mid-1950s Beauvoir knew that many people weren't buying – let alone reading – both volumes of it. By May of 1956, volume I of *The Second Sex* had gone through 116 editions in French. Volume II was selling more slowly (reaching 104 editions by 1958) – and that was the volume where women spoke, in their own voice, about their experiences of becoming women; that was where she wrote about love, independence and dreaming one's own dreams.[86] She must have wondered why the second volume sold more slowly than the first – perhaps even feeling disappointment that the one that talked about love and liberation was less read. Did she also wonder whether she had done enough to share her privilege with other women, whether she had shared it in the best ways?

When Beauvoir wrote her New Year's greetings to Algren in 1957 she told him that she'd finished the book about China (saying with characteristic self-deprecation that it was 'not too good'), and that now she was beginning something different: 'memoirs of childhood and youth, trying not only to tell a tale but to explain who I was, how it came to make me who I am, in connection with the way the whole world in which I lived was and is'.[87]

Like *The Second Sex*, *Memoirs of a Dutiful Daughter* flowed out of her, taking eighteen months to write. She read through old diaries; checked old newspapers at the Bibliothèque Nationale. And she thought about what to do about *people*. She was happy to share her life – or her persona, at any rate – with the public; but would the others she wrote about be content for her to share theirs? She gave pseudonyms to Merleau-Ponty (for the part of the book where he was Zaza's beau, but not for the part of the book where he was her fellow philosopher) and to Maheu, and to Zaza's family. But she worried about what her mother would think.

In January of 1958 Beauvoir turned 50 and hated it – with much greater force than her usual discomfort at the thought of life ending. The Algerian War had intensified and Beauvoir became so obsessed with it, so disgusted to be French, that she couldn't sleep and even literature felt 'insignificant'; she worked on *Les Temps Modernes* to publish the testimony of Algerians and soldiers. Sartre, too, was intensely disturbed about politics, although not for the same reasons. On 4 November 1956, Soviet tanks had entered Budapest, killing over 4,000 Hungarians. He had wanted so much to believe in the Soviet Union, but there was no way to overlook this. Sartre denounced the Russians' action in an interview in *L'Express*, but between the USSR and the worsening situation in Algeria, he was using so much corydrane that by evening his speech was affected and he had to drink to relax. Beauvoir wanted him to stop, and told him it was enough – sometimes angrily breaking glasses for emphasis.[88] He almost always took her advice about literature but on this she couldn't make herself heard: he didn't want to listen.

In May, Pierre Pflimlin became Prime Minister of France. He was a Christian-Democrat known to be in favour of negotiating a settlement with the Algerian nationalists. On 13 May riots broke out in Algiers; right-wing members of the French army, led by General Massu, seized power in order to defend 'French Algeria'. The next day, General Massu demanded that Charles de Gaulle should be returned to power, threatening to attack Paris if he was not. The government reorganized with Charles de Gaulle at its head and de Gaulle developed a new constitution. A few centre-left politicians and the communists opposed this coup – Sartre included – but the constitution would be put to a vote in September.

On 25 May, Claude Lanzmann was in North Korea, and Beauvoir, after taking refuge in Virginia Woolf – 'read as an antidote, to return to myself' – started to conduct another 'appraisal' of her life. She had finished the memoirs of her childhood; what should she write now? More fiction? Essays in the vein of *Privileges* (1955) and *The Long March* (1957)? She wanted to write a book that would be 'more than the rest of [her] work', that would compare 'the confused "vocation" of her childhood with what she had achieved, by the age of 50'.[89]

Beauvoir and Sartre went to Italy earlier than usual in 1958, in June. *Memoirs of a Dutiful Daughter* was due to be published in October, and she was already starting to feel nervous about how people would react.[90] From the very first volume of her life writing Beauvoir had been explicit that she was not making the usual autobiographical 'pact' with her reader.[91] In the publicity blurb for the book she said that 'one could perhaps say that I have reconstructed my past in the light of what I have become; but it is my past that made me, so by interpreting it today I bear witness to it'.[92] In a piece in *France Observateur* on 4 June 1958, she overtly said that she used the style of a narration or story (*récit* in French) in order to avoid using theoretical terms from philosophy and psychoanalysis, but that she didn't want to falsify it. She wanted to take the theme of *becoming* a woman, so central to *The Second Sex*, and write about how she became herself. Although she didn't come out and say it in *France Observateur*, by 1956 she knew very well that her life was interesting to her readers (whether they agreed with how she lived it or not). Given her past history of writing philosophical texts and then 'imaginary experiences' in different literary forms, it is hardly a wild speculation to consider the possibility that she explicitly chose to write the philosophy of *The Second Sex* in a different literary form – about her own life.

While volume one of the memoirs was receiving a warm reception, the as yet untitled next volume was resisting a definite shape in her mind. She knew that the next period of her life would require a different literary form and treatment from that of *Memoirs of a Dutiful Daughter*. It raised dissimilar questions, questions that were difficult intellectually and personally. Intellectually, she realized that she had always revered novels above other literary forms. 'But now,' she wrote in her journal, 'I'm asking myself why.' 'With the benefit of hindsight,' she wrote, 'I must also speak about philosophy: why I didn't do it.' Personally, she wanted to write about ageing, loneliness and Sartre. How much should she say about him? Or, for that matter, about Bost, Olga, Bianca and Nathalie? Throughout May and June she hesitated between two options: fiction or a continuation of the autobiographical project that would take the form of an 'essay about the writer'. In an interview in *France Observateur* she called it an 'essay about herself'.[93]

Beauvoir returned to Paris in the middle of August, travelling with Sartre to Pisa and then driving back alone. She found it harder to say goodbye to him and wondered if her age was to blame; separations were becoming more difficult. Soon she was back in the Bibliothèque Nationale working on her memoirs, but her mind was already wandering on to another project. She wrote in her diary on 24 August that more and more she wanted 'to write about old age'.[94]

While Beauvoir wrote and spent time with Lanzmann, back in Italy Sartre discovered that for ten years Michelle Vian had been having an affair with another man, André Rewliotty – she was leaving Sartre for him. Despite his own history of two- or even three-timing, he was distraught. He preferred playing the liar to being deceived. Lanzmann had also met someone else, and tried to hide it: she was an aristocratic woman, younger than Beauvoir. One night he returned to the rue

Schoelcher later than usual. He crept up to their bedroom and found Beauvoir sitting upright in bed, her face sullen: 'I want to know,' she said.[95]

Lanzmann told her everything. She was immediately relieved, and he was surprised by her acceptance. Beauvoir proposed an 'arrangement': three nights with her one week, four with the other woman, and then the reverse on alternate weeks. Lanzmann thought his aristocrat would find this an appealing prospect – no more sneaking around, no more curtailed nights. But the aristocrat would have none of it: she wanted Lanzmann to herself.[96]

On the evening of 14 September Lanzmann took Beauvoir to dinner; the next morning she went to meet Sartre at the station. They spent the day talking; she already knew Sartre was exhausted because she'd seen his most recent newspaper article – it was clearly uninspired. The referendum – which would pass or reject de Gaulle's constitutional changes – was just around the corner and Sartre was eager to get back to work but within days he came down with a liver infection. He worked himself for a 28-hour stretch even so: he had promised an article to the newspaper *L'Express* on Thursday 25 September and didn't want to miss his filing deadline.

He collapsed and she edited his piece, re-writing parts to prepare it for publication. In the run-up to the election the police and North Africans regularly exchanged machine gun fire in the streets of Paris. In Algeria, 'ten thousand Algerians had been herded into the Vel' D'Hiv', like the Jews at Drancy once before'. Beauvoir was exhausted: her neck was constantly tense and she struggled to sleep and to concentrate. One night she was visited by her 'old horror', despair, feeling that 'only evil in this world is bottomless'.[97] But she kept trying to fight it.

On 27 September, the night before the referendum vote, Beauvoir addressed a crowd of 2,400 people at the Sorbonne. But the next day, it was defeat. On 28 September the new Constitution was approved by 79.25 per cent, and France entered the Fifth Republic. The new constitution expanded the executive powers of the presidency. Algeria was still French, but Algerians were given some of the political rights that they had been promised for over a century. Algerian workers were also given a curfew.

It was a rejection of everything they believed in, but it was the kind of defeat that spurred them into further action. However, it was also a serious blow to Sartre's health. When Beauvoir finally persuaded him to see a doctor, the doctor said that Sartre had just avoided a heart attack. While they were in Rome Sartre was popping corydrane nonstop to work on a play. And now he still wanted to work on it, despite the fact that his body was sending him multiple warning signs: vertigo, headaches, verbal dyspraxia.

The doctor prescribed some medicine – prohibited drinking and smoking – and told him to rest. Beauvoir sat and watched him across her table in the rue Bonaparte: he didn't know how to stop. She told him to rest, and occasionally he would accede. But the play, he protested – he had promised it by October, it needed to be done. So Beauvoir went to the doctor again, concerned that Sartre was going to kill himself right before her eyes. He spoke frankly with her, saying that Sartre was an emotional man who needed moral calm, and that if he didn't slow down he wouldn't last six months.

Calm! In the Fifth Republic? Beauvoir left the doctor and went straight to see the woman to whom Sartre owed his play: she agreed to postpone it – *The Condemned of Altona* – to the following year. Then she went home and told him what the doctor – and director – had said. He was not to overwork himself. She expected him to be incensed that she'd done all of this without consulting him; instead he took the news with unnerving passivity. The hardest thing about watching Sartre's decline, she was beginning to realize, was that she was losing her thought's 'incomparable friend'; she couldn't discuss her worries with Sartre because he was their subject.

Once Sartre was out of danger she let herself enjoy the reception of *Memoirs of a Dutiful Daughter*, which was published on 6 October – it affected her more personally than her previous books had. Some critics complained that her recounting of daily life included too much tedious minutiae (who wants to hear the other side of silence?). Others compared her to Rousseau and George Sand – like her, writers who had taken to autobiography in their fifties.

Beauvoir had received letters following the publication of her other works, but this was different. Research by Marine Rouch has shown, based on the archive of over 20,000 letters Beauvoir received, that the publication of the memoirs dramatically changed Beauvoir's readership and her relationship with her readers. From now on she would receive much more correspondence from 'ordinary Frenchwomen', who wrote effusive and sometimes intimate letters because they felt that the Simone of the memoirs was close to them: 'You have descended from a pedestal [...] you have become more human and your intellectual and cultural superiority no longer makes you so distant.'[98]

From these letters we learn that Beauvoir's readers were surprised to imagine her cooking, hungry or cold, that her books were more expensive than those of her male contemporaries, and that it took longer for them to appear in inexpensive paperback formats than it took Sartre's.[99] Hundreds of readers wrote to her about how they, too, longed for a 'justification' of their existence or felt emptiness in their lives despite their 'success' as comfortably off wives and mothers. One reader even wrote about her attempt to kill herself.

Beauvoir's memoirs also prompted women to return to *The Second Sex*, and to write to her about their experiences of reading and recommending it:

There are two kinds of women who read *The Second Sex*, and in lending it I have always been a little afraid: those who wake up, feel afraid and ... go back to sleep and those who wake up, feel afraid, and can't go back to sleep! The latter read all of your books and try to understand.[100]

Over time, the letters from Beauvoir's readers also reveal that her care for women extended to replying to her readers individually. In some cases, she corresponded with individual readers for ten years or more, encouraging them to see the world through their own eyes, to find projects for their lives; some of these letters led to her supporting women's literary careers, and meeting them in person. Her daily schedule was as rigorously disciplined as ever, but it included an hour a day for this correspondence.

Beauvoir had concluded *Memoirs of a Dutiful Daughter* with the story of Zaza's death, writing that together they had fought the 'revolting fate' that awaited them and that, for a long time, she 'believed that I had paid for my own freedom with her death'.[101] And it was now – only now – that she learned the real reason behind Merleau-Ponty's fall from grace.[102]

After publication, one of Zaza's sisters, Françoise Bichon, wrote to Simone to explain the reasons behind the Lacoins' refusal. They met in November, and Zaza's sister showed Simone certain letters that she had received from Zaza. The truth of the matter was that the family had hired a detective to investigate their potential son-in-law – after all, in addition to their daughter's life a dowry of a quarter of a million francs was involved – and the detective discovered that Merleau-Ponty was illegitimate. From the Lacoins' Catholic perspective adultery was a mortal sin, and any alliance between their daughter and Merleau-Ponty was therefore untenable.

Merleau-Ponty promised to withdraw his suit if the Lacoins would keep their discovery discreet – his sister was engaged and he did not want a scandal to prevent her marriage. Zaza, however, was unaware of the investigation and its consequences. It was only when she was upset and confused by Merleau-Ponty's sudden disinterest that her mother finally told her the reasons why. Zaza had tried to reconcile herself to her parents' wishes. But by the time they realized how disastrous this decision was for their daughter, it was too late.

Nothing could rewrite Zaza's story with a happy ending – but finally Beauvoir knew the truth. She wanted her writing to appeal to the freedoms of her readers, opening up new possibilities in their imaginations and paths in their lives. Who would have guessed that readers, too, could shine liberating light on her own?

14

Feeling Gypped

At the end of 1958, and the beginning of Beauvoir's sixth decade, Claude Lanzmann left her. There is little material to draw from about the end of the relationship from her point of view; in Beauvoir's published *Letters to Sartre* there is only one letter after 1958, dating from 1963; and there is a gap in letters from Sartre in the published collections as well, although we know that they didn't switch to using the telephone during times apart until 1963.[1] Her letters to Algren from this period only mention that she 'felt the need of living like a bachelor again'.[2] In the public account in *Force of Circumstance* her remarks are brief; she comments that they 'drifted apart', and that 'the business of separation was difficult'.[3] We know from Lanzmann that they allowed some space between them after separating, and then began the work of rebuilding a different kind of friendship. Lanzmann recalled that 'there was never the least trace of bitterness or resentment between Castor and me, we ran the publication just as we always had, we worked together, campaigned together'.[4]

They went to see Josephine Baker and again Beauvoir was overcome by the effects of age: she could see in Baker's face the wrinkled reflection of her own. That year she published an essay on 'Brigitte Bardot and the Lolita Syndrome' in *Esquire*.[5] She had recently read Nabokov's *Lolita* and she was struck by how differently Brigitte Bardot was treated in America and in France. Bardot's film *And God Created Woman* made a pittance in French cinemas, and a fortune on the other side of the Atlantic. She was convinced that it wasn't just prudery that put off the French (since, she said, it wasn't particular to them to 'identify the flesh with sin').

It wasn't the real Brigitte Bardot that mattered, she said, but the *imaginary creature* she was on screen. Beauvoir thought that the director Roger Vadim had recreated the 'eternal female', by introducing a new eroticism that helped the myth survive the challenges of the time. Over the 1930s and 1940s the social differences between the sexes decreased. Adult women now lived in the same world as men, working and voting. So the 'dream merchants' of cinema had to improvise: they created a new Eve, she said, by mixing the 'green fruit' with 'femme fatale'. Men could see that full-grown women were subjects in the world, so their fantasies adapted, shifting focus to younger women who did not challenge their object-state. It had not escaped her notice that Nabokov's *Lolita* was 12 years old; one of Vadim's films focused on a girl of 14. Beauvoir attributed the success of the sexualization of younger and younger women to men's unwillingness to give up their role as 'lord and master'. They still wanted to see women as things – 'to do with as he pleases without worrying about what goes on in her mind and heart and body'.

Beauvoir thought that society had spiritual pretensions about sex, and liked that Vadim tried to 'bring eroticism down to earth'. But he overshot: he dehumanized it.[6] He reduced bodies to objects for visual consumption. In real life people are defined by more than their sexuality; our bodies have histories and our erotic lives unfold in situations – situations that include our emotions and our thoughts. But, for some reason, Beauvoir wrote, 'the male feels uncomfortable if, instead of a doll of flesh and blood, he holds in his arms a conscious being who is sizing him up'.[7]

Beauvoir's *Lolita Syndrome* was critical of the ways that women's sexual autonomy was denied – and of the ways that men still pursued 'lordship and mastery' over women instead of reciprocity. Despite these criticisms, however, this work has been cited in places as prestigious as *The New York Times,* as recently as 2013, to claim that Beauvoir offered 'an evangelical defence of the sexual emancipation of the young', that she herself was an apologist for the pursuit of 'Lolitas' to be discussed in the same breath as Jimmy Savile and Nabokov's Humbert Humbert. It is surprising that anyone who had read the book in full could come to this conclusion. It is also rather ironic. After all, her point was that men do not like it when women size them up and find them wanting – and so choose younger women, in their dreams and on their screens, to avoid confronting the gaze of a freedom who was confident enough in herself to be 'the eye that looks' and speak her mind. The fact that Beauvoir has been misconstrued in this way raises the question: whose interests does it serve to cast her as a sexual libertine who had neither reservations nor regret about the consumption of 'Lolitas'?

Being sized up by a conscious being can be uncomfortable even when you're doing it to yourself – and Beauvoir was still hesitating about how to handle the second volume of her autobiography. In January of 1959 she told Nelson that she didn't feel like writing 'in this kind of France'.[8] During the height of her turmoil about Algeria in 1958 Beauvoir had started keeping journals again – something she hadn't done since 1946.[9]

In her private diaries in May 1959 Beauvoir wrote that as a 20-, 30-, and even 50-year-old woman she had 'never stopped saying thank you to, and asking forgiveness from' the 5-year-old girl she once was. Her life, she thought, had a certain 'admirable harmony'. She was doing another of her 'appraisals', and under the heading 'Essential' she asked the question that had concerned her for decades: what does it mean to love? It perplexed her that at times she had preferred Sartre, 'his happiness, his work before mine':

> Is there something in me that makes this way the easiest? Is it for me, and for those who *love*, easiest to love? [...] This is the true key, the only, the only problem and crucial point in my life. And precisely because I have never been questioned or questioned myself about it. If anyone was interested in me, whom I would nickname divine: that's the question, the only one.[10]

Even pioneers have to walk a long way down some paths before discovering they're dead ends. In her letters to lovers, Beauvoir used the same effusive language that some Christian mystics used to describe their union with God – 'union totale' (with Lanzmann), 'my absolute' (with Sartre). But no man could fill the place emptied by God: it was a tall order to expect someone to see her completely – from birth until death, or first sight until final breath – with a gaze of pure love. Even so, by the age of 51 she had made and remade the choice of her 21-year-old self many times, and she decided once more: 'Sartre is for me the *incomparable*, the *unique* one.'[11]

Again they spent a month together in Rome; Sartre was better now, finishing the play that had nearly killed him the year before. One evening he gave Beauvoir the last act to read. Neither of them minced their words with each other's work. But this she really didn't like. Whenever she was disappointed by one of his works she tried first to convince herself that she was wrong not to like it. This made her angry, and led to her becoming even more firmly convinced that she was right. That evening in the Piazza Sant' Eustacchio she was in a bad mood when he came to join her: she felt let down. He changed it, making the final scene a dialogue between father and son – and she ended up thinking it was the best scene in the play.[12] (Once staged, the reaction to the play was much more positive than Sartre expected;

after the reviews came in he wrote to Beauvoir 'Many thanks, my sweet, thanks very much.'[13])

Now that Michelle Vian was out of the picture Sartre had reallocated Michelle's time to another young woman, Arlette Elkaïm. Instead of two hours on a Sunday Arlette had been promoted to two evenings per week. They had had a brief sexual relationship but on the whole his feelings were more paternal than passionate. Before long she became his contingent holiday companion. In September 1959 he left Beauvoir in Milan and travelled with her, but he kept in touch with Beauvoir by letter, reassuring her that he wasn't drinking *too* much.[14]

Lanzmann was coming to meet Beauvoir a week later, on friendly terms. They spent ten days at Menton, where he read her work too and made comments. When she first met him, she reflected, she wasn't yet 'ripe for old age' and felt she could hide from it in his presence. But like it or not, she was becoming older – so she reluctantly came to terms with it. 'I still had the strength to hate it, but no longer to despair.'[15]

After Beauvoir delivered the second volume of her memoirs to the publisher, at first untitled, she went back to the Bibliothèque Nationale to start work on the next part. She had already written about much of it in *The Mandarins*, but she felt that novels didn't show the contingency of life in the way that autobiographical writing did. Novels are crafted into an artistic whole; life is full of unpredictable and gratuitous events that are not held together by any overarching unity.[16]

In autumn of 1959 Beauvoir continued working on her own books and spent hours working on Sartre's *Critique of Dialectical Reason*.[17] She wrote prefaces to books on family planning and birth control – she was starting to become a pre-eminent voice on these issues. One preface – to a book entitled *The Great Fear of Loving* – opens with the question, 'How do other women do it?' The 'it' in question is not getting pregnant. And Beauvoir's preface challenges the optimistic claim that women's rights and possibilities were equal to men's. They could still not legally and safely control their fertility. So how, Beauvoir asked, 'in the current economic circumstances, can you succeed in a career, build a happy home, joyfully raise children, be of service to society and achieve self-realization, if at any moment the crushing burdens of a new pregnancy can come upon you?'[18]

Over the winter she rediscovered music: when she'd had enough of words for the day she spent evenings on her divan with a glass of Scotch and a symphony. She and Sartre often went walking together on Sunday, and lamented the diminishing effects of age on their curiosity. They now had invitations to travel all over the world. Sartre recoiled at the idea of being resigned to anything, so to reassure himself he accepted an invitation to Cuba. They left in the middle of February of 1960; Batista had been ousted scarcely a year earlier and relations between Cuba and the United States were strained. Sartre and Beauvoir wanted to see what the revolution had done for Cuban people. They spent three days with Fidel Castro and watched Sartre's play, *The Respectful Prostitute*, at the National Theatre in Havana.[19] He took them to see happy crowds, sugar cane, palm fronds, Havana. The atmosphere was hopeful, even joyful. Sartre called it the 'honeymoon of the revolution'.[20]

When Beauvoir got back from Cuba on the 20 February Nelson Algren was staying in her apartment.

She was nervous about seeing him; *The Mandarins* had been published in America in May of 1956, at the same time as his last novel, and the press had hounded him. He said some blunt things, in public, in *Time* magazine: he was angry, and said that a good novelist 'should have enough to write about without digging up her own private garden. For me, it was just a routine relationship, and she's blown it up'.[21] In private, however, he apologized for saying these things – he wanted to come to Paris to see her again.[22] He was low: he had remarried his ex-wife but the marriage was foundering for a second time. He told Beauvoir that the best days of his life were days spent with her; but he still didn't want to compromise his terms and neither did she. He felt like he had lost whatever it was that gave him the ability to write.

For a long time the US government had refused to give Algren a passport because he had previously sympathized with communists, so he could not travel to Paris. But Beauvoir encouraged him not to give up on that or writing: he was too hard on himself, she said: 'the little light inside you could not die; it never will'.[23] For a few years afterwards their communication followed the holiday conventions of America and France: Christmas cards from him, New Year's greetings from her.

But in July 1959 he was finally given a passport. He wrote more, sent her packets of books and made plans to visit – to stay for six months. So when she got back from Cuba in March 1960 and rang her doorbell he answered it. When her eyes lit on his face she didn't see the effects of time: all she saw was Algren. Age didn't stop them feeling 'as close as during the best days of 1949'.[24]

He had just come from Dublin and told her about his travels in Irish mists was well as his disillusionment with American politics. His last visit had fallen during the publication furore of *The Second Sex*. Her life was quieter now, so they spent time together in the rue Victor Schoelcher and with 'the family': Olga and Bost, Sartre and Michelle (who were on again) and Lanzmann.

In Paris they worked together in the mornings in her flat; then she went to Sartre's in the afternoon as usual. They walked to the rue de la Bûcherie to revisit the past, and spent evenings at the Crazy Horse and other strip joints, where Algren was confused by the presence of strippers of both sexes. They travelled together, to Marseille, Seville, Istanbul, Greece, Crete.

In the spring of 1960 Beauvoir received a letter from a baccalaureate student in Rennes. Her name was Sylvie Le Bon. Born in 1941 in Rennes, Sylvie enjoyed philosophy and admired Beauvoir's books enough to write expressing her appreciation. Beauvoir replied and when Le Bon visited Paris a few months later Beauvoir took her out for dinner. Sylvie wanted to study at the École Normale, and went on to do very well there, becoming an *agregée* in philosophy. In time, she would also come to occupy a central place in Beauvoir's life.

In August Beauvoir flew to Brazil with Sartre, leaving Algren in her apartment. He stayed until September. She wrote to him from Rio, and regularly for the rest of the year. Her epithets were back to the endearing heights of their earlier relationship: he was the 'subversive beast' of her heart. Beauvoir and Sartre were celebrated with honours and invited to give several talks and interviews: on 25 August she gave a talk at the national faculty of philosophy, 'Simone de Beauvoir speaks of the condition of women'. In early September she gave two interviews that were published in *O Estado de Sao Paulo*, and in October Beauvoir and Sartre took some time for private travel. She became ill in Manaus, a town on the Amazon River, and ended up in a hospital for a week in Recife with suspected typhoid fever.

Even when they weren't in France, their actions caused a stir. In August and September of 1960 Beauvoir and Sartre both put their names to the 'Manifesto of the 121', demanding Algeria's independence – and they published it in *Les Temps Modernes*.[25] Before they left Brazil Lanzmann phoned to tell them that it wasn't safe for Sartre to fly into Paris. In addition to signing the Manifesto, Sartre had supplied a letter for the defence of Francis Jeanson, who was under trial for his support of the Algerian National Liberation Front.[26] He was being accused of treason, and 5,000 veterans had marched down the Champs Elysées yelling 'Shoot Sartre!' Thirty of the manifesto's

Figure 10 *At a book signing in Sao Paolo, Brazil, 6 September 1960.*

signatories had been charged with treason and many had lost their jobs. There were threats of prison.

They changed their flights and were met in Barcelona by Bost. They drove to Paris and Lanzmann joined them outside the city, so they could make a quiet entrance by back roads.[27] When Beauvoir got back to Paris in November there were no letters from Algren.

Sartre was getting death threats, and friends worried that both he and Beauvoir were in danger if they stayed in their homes. So for the next few weeks they lived together in separate rooms in a large, elegant flat that was lent to them by a sympathizer, a M. Boutilier.[28] It was one of the only times they lived like this, and in a letter to Algren dated 16 November Beauvoir wrote teasingly of the strangeness of it: 'I *cook* for him.' There wasn't much to work with: ham, sausages, things that could be kept in tins. Sometimes Bost came with fresh things and made meals.[29]

Beauvoir hadn't testified in Jeanson's trial but her support was soon courted for another: the trial of Djamila Boupacha, an Algerian Muslim member of the Liberation Front who was cruelly – including sexually – tortured by French soldiers. Many Algerian women had been raped and tortured before her. But Boupacha was willing to testify, and she had the support of a Tunisian-born lawyer, Gisèle Halimi, who had been involved in the trials of many Liberation Front fighters. Halimi asked to meet Beauvoir and told her Boupacha's story. Like many of her compatriots, Boupacha joined the independence and helped underground networks by exploiting French assumptions about the 'traditional' and 'passive' roles played by North African women. Algerian women were considered to be apolitical by default. But in November 1956 and January 1957, Boupacha planted bombs in Algiers. She was discovered, arrested, tortured and tried – but she contested the legitimacy of the court.

Halimi convinced Boupacha to sue the French authorities on account of the torture she underwent. Would Beauvoir publicly support her cause? The consequences could be serious: Boupacha could be given the death penalty. Beauvoir agreed to support it in one of the most powerful ways she could: by pen. She wrote a defence of Djamila Boupacha, which was published in June in *Le Monde*, and helped set up a committee for her defence. Their aim was to publicize the case and, with it, reveal the shameful behaviour of the French during the war. In *Le Monde* Beauvoir wrote that the most scandalous thing about this scandal was that people had become so used to it. How could they not be appalled by their own indifference to others' suffering?

In 1946 Beauvoir had written about the trial of Robert Brasillach; then the French demanded justice for this collaborator who had betrayed the values of France. In 1960, she described the actions of the same nation: 'men, women, old people, children, have been gunned down during raids, burnt down in their villages, shot down, their throats cut, disembowelled, martyrized to death; in internment camps entire tribes have been left to suffer from hunger, the cold, beatings, epidemics'. Every French person was complicit in this torture, she said: did it reflect their values? The collective action of those who said it did not carried Beauvoir into the future with more hope. It also renewed the strength of a long friendship: Bianca Lamblin (formerly Bienenfeld) campaigned alongside her.[30]

On 25 October 1960 the second volume of Beauvoir's memoirs was published – *The Prime of Life*. It was a huge success: many critics thought that the subject of her own life brought out Beauvoir's best writing. Carlo Levi described it as 'the great love story of the century'. In it, commentators celebrated the fact that Beauvoir had made Sartre appear as a human being: 'You revealed a Sartre who had not been rightly understood, a man very different from the legendary Sartre.' Beauvoir replied that that was exactly her intention. At first, he didn't want her to write about him. But 'when he saw that I spoke about him the way I did, he gave me a free hand'.[31]

With the benefit of hindsight, it is easy to see many reasons why she 'simplified' the 'legend of the couple', Sartre and Beauvoir.[32] Olga, it seems, still didn't know about her nine-year-long affair with Bost – but whether she kept it secret out of a desire to protect Olga, Bost or herself is unclear. And as for her relationships with women, in addition to reasons of Beauvoir's own privacy and the privacy of the women she slept with, the reception of *The Second Sex* gives some insight into why she might have considered it wise not to be forthright. There were also reasons of law to consider – although the 1970 French law on private life (*la loi sur la vie privée*) was still a few years away, article 12 of the UN's 1948 Universal Declaration of Human Rights still held:

'No one shall be subjected to arbitrary interference with his privacy, family, home or correspondence, nor to attacks on his honor and reputation. Everyone has the right to the protection of the law against such interference or attacks.' Olga, Nathalie and Bianca were all living their own lives: they were still Beauvoir's friends and, in Bianca's case at least, we know that Beauvoir promised never to reveal her identity.

Given the frequency with which Beauvoir has been accused of prudishness or deception, it is important to bear in mind that she never promised her readers that all would be revealed. Her exclusions may have been motivated by modesty, privacy or fear – or simply to abide by the law. But it is also possible that she told her story the way she did because of the message she wanted to convey to her readers, and a desire not to muddy that message with the full truth about the messenger.

Reviewers praised Beauvoir's autobiography as her best writing, but for feminists this has raised several suspicions: Was it because she was writing something more conventionally feminine? Because it gave readers unprecedented access to a hidden side of Jean-Paul Sartre? There is something to this suspicion – after all, *The Mandarins* was her most successful novel, and it was also considered to be her most autobiographical. But whether or not Beauvoir was praised for writing 'more feminine' works, it is highly unlikely – given the audacious risks Beauvoir had already taken – that she chose to write in this form because it was *more proper* for a woman to write about her life with 'a great man' than to express her ideas about politics and philosophy. After all, that conclusion flies in the face of both her politics and her philosophy.

Intellectuals, she said, should not forget those who lacked access to culture. That meant writing things they would read – stocking their minds with new possibilities through story. Whether or not she had these exact thoughts, the memoirs were reaching a new audience. *The*

Prime of Life sold 45,000 copies before it was even in the shops, and in the first week it sold 25,000 more.[33] It was amazing! She wrote to Nelson in December – it had already sold 130,000 copies.[34]

It was in this volume that Beauvoir wrote that she was 'not a philosopher'. She did not think of herself as the creator of a system, like a Kant or Hegel or Spinoza – or a Sartre. The English translation of her explanation describes her <u>rejecting philosophical systems as 'lunacy' because they made universal claims that didn't do justice to life and 'women' 'are not by nature prone to obsessions of this type'</u>.[35] These claims have perplexed English-speaking readers of Beauvoir – what does she mean, not a philosopher? Why does she, of all people, make such huge generalizations about women? The truth is, she didn't – her translator did. In French she wrote that philosophical systems arise from the stubbornness of people who want to find 'universal keys' in their own rough judgements. And she said that 'the feminine condition' did not dispose one to this kind of obstinacy. Her scepticism made it through the translation, but nuanced sarcasm did not.[36]

By now Beauvoir was under few illusions about the ways in which she was dismissed as Sartre's derivative double, and misunderstood by people who had a vested interest in not understanding her. So she got straight to the point: She did not want to be anyone's disciple, and was not content with developing, collating or criticizing someone else's views instead of doing her own thinking. In *The Prime of Life* she asked outright: how could anyone 'bear to be someone else's follower?' She admitted that at times in life she did 'consent' to play such a role, to an extent. She did not give up on 'thinking life' as she put it in her student diaries, but rather decided to think life in literature because she deemed it the best vehicle for communicating 'the element of originality' in her own experience.[37]

Because the English translation of this passage has so often been interpreted as internalized sexism on her part, it is important to emphasize that being a woman is not the only reason one might feel excluded from the title 'philosopher'. In fact reading Beauvoir's story in this way distracts us from the philosophical reasons underpinning her denial. Many well-known 'philosophers' have denied that title – including Albert Camus, who criticized philosophy's confidence in reason as overblown, and Jacques Derrida. It is important, therefore, not to shoehorn Beauvoir into a single trope about what women can and can't be: the issue of what philosophy can and can't be was also in play.

For Beauvoir, whether she was 19 or 50-something, philosophy had to be lived. But now she had come to the view that being committed to the freedom of others meant participating in concrete projects of liberation. As the conflict over Jeanson's trial intensified, Sartre decided to use his position to protest the way the signatories of the Manifesto of the 121 were being treated. He called a press conference in Beauvoir's apartment and defended the thirty signatories who had been charged with treason: if they were found guilty, he said, then all 121 were. And if not, then the case should be withdrawn. The government dropped the charges. Sartre's reputation spared all of them since, in de Gaulle's words, 'One does not imprison Voltaire.'

This was good news, but they were not out of the woods; in July 1961 Sartre's rue Bonaparte apartment was bombed with a plastic explosive. The damage was limited, but even so he moved his mother out and went to live at Beauvoir's. In October 1961 30,000 Algerians demonstrated against the curfew imposed on them in Paris: it was a peaceful march with a clear purpose – they wanted to be allowed to stay out past 8.30 p.m. But the French police reacted violently, with guns and clubs, even throwing some Algerians into the Seine. Eyewitness accounts reported policemen strangling Algerians, and at least 200 Algerians were killed that day.

The French press covered it up. But *Les Temps Modernes* did not.

In July 1961 Beauvoir met C. Wright Mills, the author of *White Collar* and *The Power Elite* – she was interested in his work and its popularity in Cuba. Then she left for her summer trip to Italy with Sartre. They spent evenings in the Piazza Santa Maria del Trastevere and she tried to work on the third volume of her memoirs. But it was hard to think about the past when she felt 'hounded by the present'. Lanzmann had recently brought Sartre a manuscript by Frantz Fanon – *The Wretched of the Earth* – passing on a request for a preface to it. Sartre agreed, and all three of them were delighted when Fanon said he would visit them in Italy. After the Algerian revolution began in 1954, Fanon joined the Algerian National Liberation Front. He had been expelled from Algeria in 1957, but kept fighting even so – even after being diagnosed with leukaemia early in 1961.

Lanzmann and Beauvoir went to meet him at the airport. Beauvoir caught sight of him before Fanon saw them. His movements were jumpy and abrupt: he kept looking around and seemed agitated. Two years earlier he had arrived in Rome for medical treatment after being wounded on the Moroccan border, and an assassin had come for him in his hospital room: when he landed, Beauvoir said, this memory was 'very much on his mind'.[38]

On this visit Fanon talked about himself with unusual frankness, prompting his biographer David Macey to comment that Beauvoir and Sartre must have been 'both skilful and sympathetic interrogators. There is certainly no other record of Fanon speaking as openly as this to anyone'.[39] He told them that when he was a young man in Martinique he thought education and personal merit were enough to break the 'colour barrier'. He wanted to be French, served in the French army, and then studied medicine in France. But no quantity of merit or quality of education stopped him being 'a Negro' in the eyes of the French.[40] Even as a doctor, people called him 'boy' – and much worse. His life story opened up conversations about Frenchness, blackness and colonization.

Beauvoir suspected that Fanon knew more than he was telling them about Algeria. He was open and relaxed when they talked about philosophy, but then they took him to see the Appian Way and he couldn't understand why. As Beauvoir tells the story Fanon told them outright that 'European traditions had no value in his eyes'. Sartre tried to move the conversation along to Fanon's experiences of psychiatry. But Fanon pressed Sartre: 'How can you continue to live normally, to write?' As he saw it, Sartre wasn't doing enough to denounce France. Fanon left her with a strong impression, long after they said goodbye. When she shook his hand she 'seemed to be touching the very passion that was consuming him', a 'fire' that he communicated to others.[41]

That autumn Sartre wrote the preface to Fanon's *The Wretched of the Earth* while Beauvoir wrote the preface to a book by Gisele Halimi, *Djamila Boupacha*, which told the story of the woman behind the trial. Just as she'd criticized the Marquis de Sade for fleeing the horrors of reality for the illusory safety of the imagination, Beauvoir wanted the French state to look the ugliness of their actions in the face. Its publication brought her a death threat.

On 7 January 1962 there was another attack of plastic explosives at the Rue Bonaparte. It had been placed on the fifth floor by mistake – Sartre's apartment was on the fourth – but when Beauvoir went to see it the next day the door of the apartment had been torn off. An armoire had disappeared, too, and its contents – manuscripts and notebooks of Sartre *and* Beauvoir – had been stolen.[42] Sartre's mother was now living in a hotel permanently, for her safety. By 18 January the owner of the Saint-Germain apartment evicted Sartre, so Sartre moved to 110, quai Blériot, in the 14th arrondissement.[43]

By February, the reaction to Beauvoir's stance on Djamila Boupacha made her realize that her own apartment was at risk so some students from the University Antifascist Front stayed with her as guardians.

That spring she attended antifascist meetings and walked in marches protesting state violence. After the United Nations passed a resolution recognizing Algeria's right to independence, de Gaulle began negotiating with the Liberation party, and in March 1962 they signed the Évian Accords – it went to a vote in France in 1962 and the French electorate approved it.

On 1 July there was a referendum in Algeria: 99.72 per cent voted for independence. But when Beauvoir and Sartre boarded a plane for Moscow on 1 June they were disillusioned by the way France had desperately clung to colonialism: in their eyes it was bad faith on a national scale. Sartre was also surprised to have received an invitation to Russia after what he wrote about Hungary in 1956. But under Nikita Krushschev, Russia was thawing. The abuses of Stalin were condemned. Was the thick Western wall wearing thin?

When Sartre and Beauvoir arrived they were amazed at what they saw: Russians were hearing jazz and reading American novels. Krushchev had even allowed the publication of Solzhenitsyn's *One Day in the Life of Ivan Denisovich*. The Soviet Writers Union had provided Sartre and Beauvoir with a guide, Lena Zonina.[44] She was a literary critic and translator – in fact, she was hoping to translate them. It didn't take long for Sartre to follow what his biographer has called 'the unwritten rule by which Sartre fell in love in every country he visited'. Sartre fell for her – and he fell hard.[45]

Sartre had come to life again after meeting Zonina. He wrote to her daily, and she wrote back, but they couldn't use the post because of Soviet censors. This meant that they had to rely on messengers to deliver letters, waiting for long periods with no way of communicating. It was not an easy way to conduct a courtship, and when Sartre told Zonina about his 'medical round' (that was what he now called the rotation of women in his life) she was unimpressed. He still saw Wanda twice a week; and Evelyne, and Arlette Elkaïm, as well as

Michelle. Why should she believe he'd have time and attention for her too? That December Sartre and Beauvoir flew to Moscow to spend Christmas with her, and went to Leningrad to see the white nights. As an employee of the International Commission of the Writers Union, Zonina was an official representative of the Soviet government. Over the next four years Sartre and Beauvoir made nine trips to the USSR.

By the early 1960s Sartre had distanced himself from existentialism, which was beginning to be seen as a philosophy of its time, for its time. In the late 1950s Sartre wrote that Marxism was really 'the unsurpassable philosophy of our time', and in the 1960s he was criticized by Claude Lévi-Strauss and others for focusing too much on the conscious subject and not enough on the unconscious.[46] Sartre's philosophical star was waning, but feminist interest in Beauvoir was on the rise. In her sixth decade Beauvoir was well practised at using words subversively and skilled at creating imaginary experiences that appealed to her readers' freedom. But she wanted more than subversive words and imaginary freedoms – she wanted legislation that would make concrete differences in the situations of real women's lives.

During this decade second-wave feminism was gaining momentum. Until the 1960s, family planning was taboo and legislation restricted the sale of contraceptives. In 1960 the pill was approved for sale in the United States; in the UK the National Health Service made it available in 1961 – but only for married women. It would not be legalized for sale in France until 1967 (when unmarried women in Britain also gained legal access), and Beauvoir would play a significant role in advocating for this change. But *The Second Sex* continued to inspire women and feminist writers around the globe. In 1963 Betty Friedan published *The Feminine Mystique* – a work that is often seen to have inaugurated the feminist movement in the United States, and that was deeply influenced by *The Second Sex*.[47]

In the summer of 1963 Sartre and Beauvoir went back to the USSR, visiting Crimea, Georgia and Armenia with Lena Zonina. All the hopes of 'the thaw' had hardened into disappointment. There were food shortages again and Krushchev was back to defending Stalin and attacking the West. Sartre spoke to Beauvoir: should he propose to Zonina? It was far from clear that they would be able to see each other if he did not. If a man with his international intellectual reputation asked to marry her the Russian government would probably say yes, and she and her daughter would be allowed to come to France. But Zonina did not want to leave her mother, or become Sartre's dependent, another stop on his 'rounds'. She said no. But accepted or denied, Sartre's proposal to yet another woman shows how far removed from romance his relationship with Beauvoir had become.

After Russia it was time for Rome again. They stayed in the Minerva, a hotel in the centre of the city on a Piazza of the same name. Beauvoir was taking a break from writing to enjoy reading and seeing Italy – they took the car to Sienna, Venice, Florence. When in Rome Sartre had a letter from Zonina. The more she read Beauvoir's memoirs, Zonina said, the more she realized that she could not change the bond between them – and she did not want to be a second-tier woman in his life. She admired Beauvoir as a friend and respected her. 'But you and the Beaver together have created a remarkable and dazzling thing which is so dangerous for people who get close to you.'[48]

At the end of October, just before they were supposed to return to Paris, Bost called Beauvoir: her mother had had a fall and broken her femur. By the next month it was hopelessly clear: she was dying.

After the fall Françoise was taken to a clinic and while there they discovered a terminal cancer. When Beauvoir heard the news Sartre accompanied her in a taxi to the nursing home; she went in alone.[49] The doctors had told Simone and Hélène the diagnosis, but not Françoise. The daughters decided it was wisest not to tell her. After the operation there were two optimistic weeks when Simone and Hélène were with her in her room, peacefully. It wasn't love that made her stay, Simone wrote to Nelson, but 'a deep and bitter compassion'.[50] The night of her mother's operation, Beauvoir went home, talked to Sartre, and listened to Bartók before bursting out into 'tears that almost degenerated into hysteria'.[51] The violence of her reaction took her by surprise; when her father died she hadn't shed a single tear.

A few weeks after the operation Françoise began to experience more pain, and to be exhausted by it. So they asked the doctors to give her more morphine – even if her life would be foreshortened, so would her suffering. After that she spent most of her days sleeping. She never called for a priest or any of her 'pious friends', as Beauvoir called them. During that November Beauvoir felt closer to her mother than she had since early childhood. The night after the operation Beauvoir had been overcome by a tidal wave of emotion: she was grieving for her mother's death, but also for her mother's life – she had sacrificed so much to the suffocating straitjacket of convention.

After her mother died, Beauvoir threw herself into writing *A Very Easy Death*, an account covering the final six weeks of her mother's life and her own aching experience of love, ambivalence and bereavement. She had never felt so compelled to write something, to think life with her pen. And she knew to whom it would be dedicated: Hélène. She had been keeping a journal during the months of her mother's decline (when she gave it a title she called it 'My Mother's Illness'; she didn't know it would be Death). It chronicled the companionship of Bost, Olga and Lanzmann in a way that *A Very Easy Death* did not. Her days were punctuated with helpless and unsuccessful attempts to hold back tears, and at several points she mentions taking tranquillizers before seeing Sartre so that she could be sure 'not to annoy Sartre by crying'.[52]

In *A Very Easy Death* Beauvoir recorded her mother saying 'I have lived for others too much. Now I shall become one of those self-centred old women who only live for themselves.'[53] She described Françoise's loss of inhibition, and how it jarred Beauvoir to see her mother's naked body in the hospital, a body that had filled her with love as a child and repulsion as an adolescent.[54]

I had grown very fond of this dying woman. As we talked in the half-darkness I assuaged an old unhappiness; I was renewing the dialogue that had been broken off during my adolescence and that our differences and our likenesses had never allowed us to take up again. And the early tenderness that I had thought dead for ever came to life again, since it had become possible for it to slip into simple words and actions.[55]

When it was published some journalists accused her of capitalizing on her mother's suffering and her own grief; they even got a surgeon on the record stating that Beauvoir sat at her mother's bedside callously taking notes because she wanted to get 'material'. Once again, the view from without was casting her in a sinister light. From within, she said, writing gave her 'the same comfort that prayer gives to the believer'.[56] As she saw it, there was no such thing as a 'natural' death.

Since meeting Sylvie Le Bon in November 1960 Beauvoir had kept in touch with her, and they met occasionally. By 1964 their meetings had become more regular; Sylvie was a huge support to her during the time of Françoise's death. Beauvoir wrote that she appreciated the reciprocity of their relationship; Sylvie was intellectually capable and shared many of her passions. Beauvoir felt a connection to her, and the more she got to know her the more like her she felt. Sylvie listened well, she was thoughtful, generous and affectionate.[57] *All Said and Done*, the last volume of Beauvoir's autobiography, would be dedicated to her.

Beauvoir described their lives as mutually intertwined, and she was grateful that life had brought her this new companionship. She was wrong, she said, when she had said in 1962 that she'd already had her life's most significant relationships. Both women denied that the relationship was sexual, but it was physically affectionate – Sylvie called it 'charnel' in French, which many have chosen to translate as 'carnal'. It can also mean 'embodied', encompassing non-sexual forms of physical affection.

On 30 October 1963 *Force of Circumstance* was published in French, just over five months after she submitted it to the publisher.[58] In it Beauvoir continued to self-consciously evaluate her legacy, denying implications that her works were intellectually parasitic on Sartre and owning her own philosophical interests and insights. It was in this volume of autobiography that Beauvoir discussed the shift in treatment she experienced after the publication of *The Second Sex*: 'I was never treated as a target of sarcasm until after *The Second Sex*; before that, people were either indifferent or kind to me.'[59] She could see for herself that this book in particular provoked *ad feminam* reactions, and she wanted her readers to see it too.

In *Force of Circumstance* she wrote that *The Second Sex* was 'possibly the book that has brought me the greatest satisfaction of all those I have written'.[60] In hindsight, of course, there were things she would have changed. But the letters she received showed her that she had helped women 'become aware of themselves and of their situation'.[61] She was now 55 years old, and aware that (despite not claiming to be a model) her life had become an idealized example that others turned to for inspiration. Even after twelve years she was still receiving letters thanking her for *The Second Sex*, telling her that she had helped women overcome the myths they felt crushed by. In the decade after *The Second Sex* was published, other feminists published works she described as more daring than her own. Too many of them focused too much on sexuality; but, she said, at least now women could 'present themselves as the eye-that-looks, as subject, consciousness, freedom'.[62]

And yet, it is also in this book that Beauvoir wrote the famously perplexing statement that she had 'avoided falling into the trap of "feminism"' in *The Second Sex*.[63] Three years earlier, in a 1960 interview, she explained that she wanted readers to know that she was not partisan or anti-men because, if viewed through that lens, her point of view would be undermined: 'I would like it to be known that the woman who wrote *The Second Sex* did not do it [...] in order to avenge a life that had [...] embittered her. If one interprets the book in that way, one [...] repudiates it.'[64]

It was at this point, in the epilogue of *Force of Circumstance*, that Beauvoir wrote that her relationship with Sartre was the 'one undoubted success' of her life. The epilogue confused readers: it opened by claiming her success with Sartre, celebrating their unending interest in each other's conversation. But it ended with an intriguing line: 'The promises have all been kept. And yet, turning an incredulous gaze towards that young and credulous girl, I realize with stupor how much I was gypped.'[65]

What did this mean? Reviewers speculated: Did 'la grande Sartreuse' regret her 'romance of the century' with Sartre? Did the 'dutiful daughter' regret becoming an atheist? Was she disappointed by the doublespeak of a France that claimed to stand for *liberté, egalité, fraternité* – but not if it was liberty, equality and fraternity for Algerians?

Readers, too, wrote to her in shock: she had been a beacon of hope in their lives; how could she, with such accomplishments, such lovers, such a life, feel cheated? Françoise d'Eaubonne wrote that there was no more-discussed phrase at the time than Beauvoir's 'I was gypped'; even de Gaulle's most famous words hardly rivalled this sentence: she remembered people going 'back to the dictionary to know the exact sense of the term, to try to discern whether it was authorial teasing or the drama of an authentic disillusionment'.[66]

Beauvoir knew it was a provocative way to end the book. Sylvie Le Bon de Beauvoir has said that the 'misunderstanding' provoked by these words was 'in part, deliberate' and 'is about the very nature of literature'.[67] In a 1964 interview with Madeleine Gobeil (published in in *The Paris Review* in 1965) Beauvoir was asked about her autobiographical project and what it was that led her to pursue a vocation as a writer. Her answer was that she wanted her books to 'move readers'. She wanted to write characters that spoke into her readers, charting paths in their imaginations that transformed their possibilities in life – like Jo March in *Little Women* and Maggie Tulliver from *The Mill on the Floss* had for her.[68]

She *had* moved her readers, but many did not like it. After reading Beauvoir's claim that she had been 'gypped' some even wrote to reassure her, saying 'you are unjust to yourself, because it is false that your experience has produced nothing': how could she think that when she had lit a 'luminous hope in the heart of millions of women'?[69] Had she fought myths of woman only to become one herself?

Beauvoir had downplayed the roles of Bost and Lanzmann in her life. She had excluded what looked like a serious love affair in Sartre's life from the unfolding of her story because his lover was Soviet. Clearly, concerns of privacy affected them both. But in Beauvoir's case it was starting to look like age seemed to condemn her to celibacy; in Sartre's case, it did not.

She knew people were fascinated by her relationship with Sartre: it was an interesting story. But why not show, in multiple volumes, that becoming a woman can involve valuing different things at different times in life? Or that you may understand your own situation

differently in hindsight? Or, indeed, that having the audacity to voice
what many leave silent might make you subject to attack by those who
don't want you to be heard?

There is a passage in *Force of Circumstance* in which Beauvoir
returned to Nelson Algren and the challenges of 'the pact' because she
recognized a problem that her younger self had taken to be too easily
resolved: 'Is there any possible reconciliation between fidelity and
freedom? And if so, at what price?'[70]

> Often preached, rarely practiced, complete fidelity is usually
> experienced by those who impose it on themselves as a mutilation
> [...]. Traditionally, marriage used to allow the man a few
> 'adventures on the side' without reciprocity; nowadays, many
> women have become aware of their rights and of the conditions
> necessary for their happiness: if there is nothing in their own lives
> to compensate for masculine inconstancy, they will fall a prey to
> jealousy and boredom.

In hindsight, Beauvoir told her readers, their approach had many
risks. One partner may begin to prefer a new attachment to the old
one, leading the other to feel betrayed; 'in the place of two free persons,
a victim and a torturer confront each other'. Some couples, on
Beauvoir's view, were impregnable. But there was one question she
and Sartre 'deliberately avoided: How would the third person feel
about our arrangement?' On this point, she wrote,

> an unavoidable discretion compromised the exact truthfulness of
> the picture painted in *The Prime of Life*, for although my
> understanding with Sartre has lasted for more than thirty years, it
> has not done so without some losses and upsets in which the
> 'others' have suffered. This defect in our system manifested itself
> with particular acuity during the period I am now relating.[71]

◦   When this volume appeared it got bad reviews and some quite spiteful ones. It sold well. But once again Beauvoir objected to the way the media treated her. They called her 'complacent', 'desperate';[72] the embodiment of the 'mutation' of the feminine world. She was accused of attention-seeking, of doing 'everything to shock gratuitously, uselessly', of breaking 'more appearances than was necessary to her message'.[73]

Esprit's review, by Francine Dumas, was entitled 'A tragic response'. For women who had chosen to live traditional lives of faith, motherhood and marriage, it was ungenerous and unjust to find the absence of these things responsible for Beauvoir's 'internal trembling':

> For the greatness of her destiny is precisely that deliberate abandonment of a traditional background (which was not without price in her eyes) and the will to replace it with the perilous way of ever-changing choices. The rope is so stiff that it may break, and Simone de Beauvoir refuses any safety net.[74]

In the press, one paper had selectively translated parts of Nelson Algren's *Who Lost an American* to make it look like Algren resented Sartre and Beauvoir: she objected that they had taken away all the humour, the 'little friendly words'. At this point she and Algren were still corresponding, so she wrote to him expressing her frustration: 'these dirty people know nothing about nothing, chiefly when it comes to friendship and love'.[75]

By the mid-1960s, the second and third volumes of Beauvoir's autobiography had cemented the Sartre–Beauvoir legend. Some of those close to them thought she had a personal agenda: putting herself in control of their public image. Sartre was happy with how Beauvoir portrayed him, but Sartre's other women were unsettled – or worse. Wanda hated Beauvoir's memoirs; she thought the Sartre–Beauvoir they portrayed was an imaginary ideal that bore little resemblance to reality. But they also made her worry about Sartre: after all these years, to Wanda he still denied that he was romantically close to Beauvoir.

In later life Sartre continued to conduct multiple relationships simultaneously, and he did not convert to the point of view that saw truth-telling as something everyone deserved. Beauvoir, by contrast, was open about her relationship with Sartre and the terms in which she was available to others – which was more honest, but not necessarily less hurtful.

Force of Circumstance was published in America in the spring of 1965, which brought Beauvoir's friendship with Algren to an abrupt halt. She had already given a fictionalized account of their romance in *The Mandarins*, but what she wrote in *Force of Circumstance* provoked his fury. When asked about the accuracy of the account in the memoir for *Newsweek*, he said that 'Madame Yackety-Yack' had written a middle-aged spinster's fantasy.[76] He reviewed the book in two magazines – *Ramparts* and *Harper's* – with sarcasm and spite. And the next summer he published a poem dedicated to her in *Zeitgeist*: its subject was a blabbermouth he wanted to banish to a dank basement. Beauvoir had published two excerpts from *Force of Circumstance* in *Harper's* in November and December 1964, entitled 'A Question of Fidelity' and 'An American Rendezvous'. In Algren's May riposte, he wrote:

> Anybody who can experience love contingently has a mind that has recently snapped. How can love be *contingent*? Contingent upon *what*? The woman is speaking as if the capacity to sustain Man's basic relationship – the physical love of man and woman – were a mutilation; while freedom consists of 'maintaining through all deviations a certain fidelity!' What she means, of course, when stripped of its philosophical jargon, is that she and Sartre created a façade of petit-bourgeois respectability behind which she could

continue to search for her own femininity. What Sartre had in mind when *he* left town I'm sure I don't know.[77]

Beauvoir wrote her last surviving letter to Algren in November of 1964. She hoped to visit him in 1965, but her trip to the United States was cancelled because of the Vietnam War. However, it is unclear if anything of their intimacy was salvageable after Algren's reaction to the publication of *Force of Circumstance*.[78] Algren would go on to be elected to the American Academy of Arts and Letters in 1981. In an interview about the award, a journalist asked him about Beauvoir; and described Algren responding with emotion that was still raw. He'd been having heart trouble so the interviewer redirected the conversation. The next day Algren was having a party at his cottage to celebrate, but when the first guest arrived he found Algren dead.

When Beauvoir's letters to Algren were published in 1997 it provoked an uproar about the truth of her memoirs. Her long correspondence revealed that her passion for him, though hidden, was profound. The memoirs succeeded in forging the Sartre–Beauvoir myth; but they had misinformed the public spectacularly. Now it seemed that Algren was the most ardent love of her life; some even charged her with bad faith concerning her relationship with Sartre.[79] Their relationship too would have a fantastical literary afterlife: Kurt Vonnegut wrote a lengthy section on Algren in *Fates Worse than Death*, where 'Miss de Beauvoir' appears as 'Madame Yak Yak', whom Algren 'helped achieve a first orgasm'.[80]

A year before *Force of Circumstance* was published in America, Beauvoir wrote a very short preface to *The Sexually Responsive Woman*, a study of another misunderstood phenomenon: female sexuality. 'In this realm as in so many others,' Beauvoir wrote, 'male prejudice insists on keeping women in a state of dependency. In contrast to this, the authors grant women autonomy – both physiological and psychological – equal to that of men.' The review is comical and touching at the same time: she says she is 'not qualified to pass definite judgment' on all of the claims of Drs Phyllis and Eberhard Kronhausen, but it was 'absorbing and fascinating reading.'[81]

It is interesting that in the reception of *Force of Circumstance* as in other domains Beauvoir was accused of not having a sense of humour.[82] Feminists are often accused of being killjoys, and many episodes in Beauvoir's life illustrate what is now a well-documented dynamic: when Beauvoir expressed unhappiness her unhappiness was discussed as though the issue at stake was *her unhappiness* rather than *what her unhappiness was about*.[83] For decades Beauvoir had been unhappy about the ways in which society mistreated women, Jews, Algerians – why couldn't she just lighten up? And now she was becoming increasingly unhappy about the way society mistreated the old. It wasn't good enough to make light of dark situations – the point was to make the situations themselves less dark.

In May of 1964, after finishing *A Very Easy Death*, she decided that she wanted to distance herself from autobiography and write a novel again. This time she would write about protagonists who were unlike her in almost all respects, save that they were women – ageing women.[84] Throughout the 1960s Beauvoir continued to use her writing to support projects that she thought would improve women's situations – whether academic studies or magazine articles like 'What Love Is – And Isn't'. She wrote that love only appears to 'those who openly or secretly wish to change. For it is then that you anticipate love and what love brings: through another person, a new world is revealed and given to you.'[85]

As 1965 drew near Sartre was approaching his 60th birthday so he decided that, as a childless man whose future was growing shorter, he needed an heir and literary executor. There was no point, he thought, in giving that task to Beauvoir since she was almost as old as he was.

So Sartre legally adopted Arlette Elkaïm the year she turned 30, on 18 March 1965. The witnesses were Simone de Beauvoir and Sylvie Le Bon. It was covered in *France Soir* but most of his friends had no forewarning – Wanda, Evelyne and Michelle were beside themselves.

After the bombing of North Vietnam by the United States in February 1965 Beauvoir refused an invitation to speak at Cornell University. She gave interviews on ageing, on writing, on literature, on autobiography. Sartre, too, was interviewed about her: in July 1965 American *Vogue* published an interview with him, entitled 'Sartre Talks of Beauvoir'. Sartre thought she was 'a very good writer':

> She has achieved something which has manifested itself particularly since *The Mandarins*. It's apparent in the memoirs and in her book *A Very Easy Death*, which I consider the best thing she's written. What she has achieved is immediate communication with the public. Let's put it this way: there's a difference between her and me. I don't communicate emotionally, I communicate with people who think, who reflect, who are free in relation to me. That may or may not be a good thing. But Simone de Beauvoir communicates emotionally at once. People are always involved with her by virtue of what she says.[86]

In Beauvoir's notes for *All Said and Done*, written in 1965–1966, Beauvoir wrote that the published 'story' of her life had only conveyed a 'mutilated truth' because it was not exhaustive; a 'deformed truth, since time is not exactly restored'. But it had delivered a 'literary truth'.[87] She thought that her life was an example of what it meant to *live* an existential choice: there was no 'decree' from on high about who she should be, no predetermined path or Epicurean *clinamen* by which she swerved away from it. Instead, there was a blueprintless becoming – a project that she pursued throughout her life, which sometimes branched off into secondary projects along the way.[88]

Sometimes, the weight of past choices weighed heavily on her. She still regretted the way she treated 'Lise' (Nathalie Sorokine), and felt 'imprisoned' by the way her projects had 'petrified', accumulating behind her an 'ineluctable past'.[89] But, on the other hand, her ineluctable past was part of the way she became who she was, and being a public figure opened up new possibilities – and responsibilities. She could not in good conscience have written what she wrote about the world and not *act* to make it better. So how could she refuse to respond to letters and sign petitions? Her situation had the power to transform the lives of others: she had to make the most of it.

In August 1965, Sylvie and Simone went to Corsica. After that Beauvoir and Sartre went for their annual dose of Rome. Sartre left Italy for Paris on 12 October by train; Beauvoir was driving the car back. They planned to meet on the evening of the 14th, at 7 p.m., at hers. But at lunchtime that day the phone rang; it was in the news that Beauvoir had had a car accident in the Yonne and had been hospitalized in Joigny. Lanzmann and Sartre set out at once, driving at breakneck speed to be with her. She had four broken ribs. Her face was swollen, with stitches and a bruised eye. She had taken a bend too fast.

Sartre stayed the night in a hotel nearby and then escorted her back to rue Victor Schoelcher in an ambulance. He helped her to her apartment and said he would stay with her until she was able to walk; she was in so much pain even undressing was a challenge. She was bedridden for three weeks, during which Sartre, Lanzmann and Sylvie Le Bon cared for her, supplemented by daily visits from a nurse.

She made a good recovery; in June of 1966 Sartre and Beauvoir went back to the USSR, and in September they took off for Tokyo. They had never been to Japan. They knew that their works were read there – it was one of the best markets for Sartre's work and *The Second Sex* had just been translated into Japanese. But when they got off the plane they were not expecting to be blinded by the flash of journalists' cameras. Their interpreter took them to a room to take questions from the press; young people tried to touch them as they passed. In her memoirs Beauvoir wrote about Sartre's engagements and her voracious reading about Japanese history and culture without elaborating on the contents of her own lectures.[90] But she was not there as Sartre's plus one: she gave three lectures on 'The Situation of Women Today'. Once again, it is unclear whether she omitted this out of self-deprecation, some convention of modesty, or in order not to write her life in a way that would render it too distant to her readers.

This question is only intensified by knowing what her memoirs left unsaid. In her 20 September lecture she said that feminism was 'far from being outdated', and not only worthwhile to women: It is 'a cause that is common to men and women, and men will only come to live in a more just, better-organized world, a more decent world, when women have a more just and more decent status. The acquisition of equality between the sexes is the business of both'.[91] Beauvoir expressed hope that *The Second Sex* would become outdated because, once women achieved equality, its analyses of women's alienation would be redundant. She thought that women's exploitation could be abolished without abolishing sexual difference. But she was concerned by what she saw as an antifeminist 'regression' in her and other cultures. In France women were claiming that their true vocation was to be a wife and mother: a homemaker.

Part of Beauvoir's concern was that women who were 'confined' to private life lived precariously, in economic dependence on someone who could stop loving them at any time, leaving women without means and without the meaning around which they built their life. But Beauvoir did not hide the fact that she thought this kind of life 'inferior' to 'real participation in social life', to 'helping to build the world in which we live'.[92] She thought that women were 'victims' of the regression to being housewives: partly because women suffered from comparing themselves with other women, and also because working women were still expected to be housewives when they got home. The result was guilt and exhaustion about their decisions: 'If a woman has put in an eight-hour day at work and works five or six hours more at home, at the end of the week she finds herself in an absolutely terrifying state of exhaustion. It is not yet at all customary for the man to really help the woman.'[93]

What Beauvoir found valuable in countries where she had seen a greater number of women in the workforce was their 'self-rapport', their relation to themselves; she thought this self-understanding was derived from participation in public life. She had always been interested in what it meant to become a self, and in *The Second Sex* she had identified a common challenge facing women: the possibility of being 'split subjects', torn between the selves they want to be as lovers and mothers and the selves they want to become in the wider world. Beauvoir's second lecture in Japan returned to 'the divided character of women's condition'. Since working women also want a happy life, love, and a home, many opt to sacrifice their ambition: 'she finds it prudent to be self-effacing on the professional plane'.[94]

Three years later, in 1969, when *The Second Sex* was published in Japan, it appeared on the bestseller list. On the way back from Tokyo, Beauvoir and Sartre stopped in Moscow. It was Sartre's eleventh visit to the USSR, but he now realized he had lost his reason to return: it was over with Lena Zonina.

In November 1966 Beauvoir's return to fiction, *Les Belles Images*, was published – in English this title could be rendered 'Pretty Pictures' or 'Beautiful Images'. A review in *La Cité* described it as a 'short novel about contemporary morals entirely impregnated with existentialist morality', again reinforcing the narrative that Beauvoir belonged in the same intellectual category with Sartre and taking no note of the ways Beauvoir's depictions of women questioned society's treatment of them. The review dismissively said it was unsuccessful satire; a list of 'all of the clichés read in weeklies presented in a sort of collage'.[95] But the sales told a different story: 120,000 copies sold fast.[96]

Beauvoir later described its protagonist Laurence as 'disgusted with life to the point of anorexia'.[97] She is a successful advertising agent, wife, and mother of two daughters. She enjoys extramarital sex at work before coming home to put the kids to bed and spend the evening with her successful architect husband. She drinks, but she doesn't eat.

Laurence's equilibrium (if it can be so-called) is disrupted by her child's questions – Why do people exist? Why are some unhappy? What do you do for the unhappy ones? – provoking her to reflect on what she values. She is in the business of marketing beautiful images, writing sleek slogans; she has honed the skills required to present a very pretty picture of herself. But maintaining the appearance of the beautiful life – with its beautiful cars, beautiful home, beautiful clothes, beautiful food, beautiful vacations – leaves her dissatisfied with the status quo. Laurence was 10 years old in 1945; she can remember the Holocaust. And she starts to wonder why there is so little sadness over Algeria; to notice that images of civil rights protesters in America are forgotten as soon as they fade from the TV screens.

The book criticizes capitalism and consumerism, explicitly asking whether money makes one happy.[98] Implicitly, it can be taken to respond to shifts in feminism and women's situations, and the equation of money with independence. It also satirized Michel Foucault, who was becoming known as a leading thinker in France. In a 1966 interview, Beauvoir claimed that Foucault's works, and the journal *Tel Quel*, provided 'bourgeois culture' with 'alibis'. Whereas the message of *Les Belles Images* was that progress 'must be at once material, intellectual and moral, or it will simply not be progress at all', in Beauvoir's view Foucault's thinking lacked commitment to social change.[99]

Beauvoir's novel concludes with Laurence reflecting on her children: 'To raise a child is not to make a beautiful image.' Beauvoir had said in *The Second Sex* that raising a child is an ethical undertaking, the formation of a human freedom – and that, too often, for women and children, it was a schooling in indifference. In the novel's final scene Laurence looked in the mirror and thought that for her, the chips were down. Her children would have their own chance. But what chance?[100]

The next February Beauvoir, Sartre and Lanzmann travelled to the Middle East, to Egypt and Israel. *Les Temps Modernes* was running a special issue on the Arab–Israeli conflict. In Egypt they were welcomed by Mohamed Hassanein Heikal, the director of the newspaper

Figure 11 *Claude Lanzmann, Simone de Beauvoir and Jean-Paul Sartre at Giza.*

Al-Ahram and friend of Egypt's second president Gamal Abdel Nasser. *Al-Ahram* ran an interview with Beauvoir entitled 'The Philosopher of *The Second Sex* in Cairo'.[101] From Egypt they visited Palestinian camps at Gaza on 10 March, and on the 11 March Beauvoir gave a talk on 'Socialism and Feminism' at the University of Cairo.

Because of the Arab–Israeli conflict there were no airlines flying direct from Egypt to Israel, so they had to travel via Athens.[102] When they got to Israel they visited Jaffa and Tel Aviv, and some kibbutzim. They stayed for two weeks, and Beauvoir again gave lectures, this time on 'The Role of the Writer in the Contemporary World' at the Hebrew University in Jerusalem. Beauvoir was fascinated by women's status in this society, and wanted to understand how young people felt about the competing claims of the Israelis and Palestinians. That June, the Six-Day War remapped territories and divided political opinion in the world and 'the family'. Beauvoir supported Israel; Sartre supported Palestine. Once Beauvoir's support of Israel was public, her works were banned in Iraq – two days before the Six-Day War. Closer to home, Lanzmann felt betrayed by Sartre. He had read Sartre's book on anti-Semitism in the 1940s and found it hugely inspiring; was its author now an anti-Semite?

The previous month Sartre and Beauvoir had taken part in the Russell Tribunal. The British philosopher Bertrand Russell – then 94 years old – led a group intended to raise public awareness and condemnation of the atrocities Americans were committing in Vietnam (Russell's age made his chairmanship honorary; he stayed in England). In May the group met in Stockholm for ten days of discussion; in November they reconvened in Copenhagen.[103] They heard eyewitness reports, which made for exhausting days. Many members of 'the family' were there – Lanzmann, Bost (reporting for *Le Nouvel Observateur*), Sylvie Le Bon and Arlette Elkaïm.

After *Les Belles Images* Beauvoir began to work on a collection of three novellas, which appeared in 1967 as *The Woman Destroyed*. For a long time she and Hélène had wanted to produce something written by Beauvoir and illustrated by Hélène, and this was the perfect thing: Hélène made some engravings for the title story and to publicize it Beauvoir arranged to have the book serialized in *Elle*.[104] It flopped so badly some people asked Hélène why she'd agreed to produce illustrations for her sister's worst book.

Beauvoir's earlier fiction included both male and female protagonists, but each novella in *The Woman Destroyed* is written only from the point of view of a single woman's consciousness – in each case, an ageing woman's consciousness – and treats the themes of isolation and failure. Beauvoir wrote that in this work she attempted 'to depict the critical moments of three female existences: the encounter with old age, the exasperation of solitude, and the brutal end of a love affair'.[105]

'The Age of Discretion' describes the heartbreak of a writer, wife and mother of an adult son. She is keenly conscious of growing old, experiencing her own body with a mixture of disgust and resignation.[106] She has just published a book and is worried that she will never live up to the heights of her previous works, that she no longer has anything worth saying. Her son has made a choice that she vehemently disapproves of, so she threatens never to speak to him again if he will not acquiesce to her wishes. Her husband defies her by continuing to speak to their son, forcing a thick wedge of alienation deeper into an already wounded marriage: she was grieving the loss of its physical intimacy. The novella includes a reconciliation of kinds: together its protagonist and her husband face up to their diminishing future, learning to live 'a short-term life'.[107]

The second story's prose is unlike anything else Beauvoir wrote – it is the stream of a consciousness hovering on the edge of madness.

This protagonist's child has been taken away from her, she is isolated and outcast, an ugly mirror to the reality that people can be 'despicable' when you're down.[108]

The title story, 'The Woman Destroyed' is written in diary form; it is the devastating chronicle of a woman's descent into depression. Monique's marriage is in decay and she desperately wants to revitalize it. Her happily fulfilled 'vocation' was to be a wife and mother. But her children have recently reached adulthood and she now wants to live 'for herself a little'.[109] Devotion and self-giving – Beauvoir's student diary themes – were fulfilling for her and experienced as a free choice. But then her husband Maurice embarks on an affair. And without his fidelity the edifice that they built together crumbles, burying her under paralysing anxiety and self-doubt.

Monique's story raises the familiar themes of judgement and suffering – the judgement that women face when they 'do nothing' but stay home with children, and the suffering that they undergo when they commit to a joint project with a partner who accepts this self-giving and then renounces it for a younger giver. Monique challenges her husband but he gaslights her for making a 'scene', trying to make her feel guilty for producing an uncomfortable situation that pales in comparison with her own suffering. He succeeds in turning the moral spotlight so it blinds her conscience instead of burning his. Several times she thinks she has hit rock bottom, only to sink deeper into unhappiness.

When *The Woman Destroyed* was published, it provoked harsh criticism, even by the standards of reactions to Beauvoir's other books. The literary critic Henri Clouard wrote that Beauvoir had never before 'put her talent so much to the use of demoralizing propaganda'. Was this nuisance of a woman now suggesting that all women who build their lives around men will fail? Once again, Clouard said, Beauvoir was 'administering' a 'lesson' to the public.[110] What about Maurice's character, the man's point of view? It wasn't well enough developed. Really, he protested, one expected more 'clarity of mind', 'more freedom', in her art. 'Truly, she is out of date'; 'Madame de Beauvoir is continuing her campaign for the emancipation of women as if our contemporaries still needed it'.[111]

Beauvoir herself would not so hastily have argued from a particular case (or rather, in this case, three particular short stories) to a universal conclusion. She had taken care to make Monique's *situation* ambiguous: her authorial intention was to make the book a detective story, a post-mortem investigation of a marriage in which the reader is invited to ascertain who or what is the culprit. But Jacqueline Piatier wrote in *Le Monde* that 'There are lessons everywhere, no matter what she says'.[112] In *All Said and Done*, Beauvoir lamented the way the book was read; as ever, she was accused of writing autobiography, of including the voices of Simone and Jean-Paul as if they spoke for all humanity. She was asked whether Sartre had left her.[113] Ironically, others objected that this book wasn't 'real Simone de Beauvoir' because the fiction wasn't based in the world they thought she inhabited. Where was Sartre? Why was this all about wives and mothers?

In *All Said and Done* Beauvoir wrote that she did not understand why the book provoked so much hatred. Condescension did not surprise her: she had serialized it in *Elle*, so *Figaro littéraire* claimed it was a novel for shop girls. But the reactions she experienced were venomous, personal, gendered and ageist:

> Ever since I caught a glimpse of Simone de Beauvoir in the rue de Rennes I have been very sorry I wrote that article: she was creeping along, looking faded and haggard. One should pity the aged. That is why Gallimard goes on publishing her, by the way.
> Oh yes, Madame, It is sad to grow old![114]

Beauvoir knew she was ageing, and she was honest enough to admit that she did not like it. But she saw no reason to hide from it. Instead, she confronted it head-on, as a subject lacking philosophical analysis and in need of political action. She had already been thinking about her book on old age for a few years; later she would call it *The Second Sex*'s counterpart. But when she started her research in earnest and started looking for books on old age she was surprised by how few she could find. In the catalogue room of the Bibliothèque Nationale she discovered essays by Emerson and Faguet, then slowly compiled a bibliography. She read gerontological periodicals from France; ordered enormous American volumes in English from Chicago.[115] Her former colleague, Claude Lévi-Strauss, gave her access to the comparative anthropology material at the Collège de France, so she could study monographs that discussed the status of the elderly in several societies.

Day by day she worked away at her research. As the events of May 1968 unfolded – with student protests and general strikes so massive that France's economy ground to a halt – Sartre and Beauvoir gave a brief statement supporting the students' cause in *Le Monde*. The political upheaval of this year led Sartre to reconsider his position on what role intellectuals should play in society; he was increasingly interested in Maoism.

The committee for *Les Temps Modernes* now met fortnightly at Beauvoir's apartment. At 10.30 a.m. on Wednesdays they arrived and set to work. Sylvie Le Bon was a new member of the crew, and Bost and Lanzmann were also involved (Lanzmann hadn't yet started work on his epic Holocaust documentary, *Shoah*). But Sartre came less and less often. *Les Temps Modernes* had been ground-breaking in the 1940s. But now it had acquired the dust of an established institution.

Sartre wanted to be part of something revolutionary, and he had become friendly with some Maoists, including a young man named

Pierre Victor. Victor asked Sartre if he would assume the editorship of the French Maoist newspaper, *La Cause du peuple*, since if he were the editor it might not encounter so much government censure. In April 1970, Sartre was named editor in chief. That June he and Beauvoir handed out issues on the streets of Montparnasse and were arrested for it. They were just as quickly released, but the arrest gave Sartre a platform from which to call out double standards and demand true freedom of the press.

Beauvoir did not share Sartre's latest political enthusiasm. In fact, politically their battles had been diverging dramatically over recent years. While Sartre's Maoism marginalized him from the intellectual mainstream, Beauvoir's feminism gave her a leading role in the international women's movement. In 1969 alone the paperback edition of *The Second Sex* had sold 750,000 copies.[116] By 1970 it had gained the status of a 'classic' in North America; The Canadian activist Shulamith Firestone dedicated her 1970 book *The Dialectic of Sex* to Beauvoir, and in an interesting reversal of the 1949 'scandal' (after the publication of *The Second Sex* in France), Firestone and many other feminists expressed appreciation for Beauvoir's life as well as her work: the dedication in *The Dialectic of Sex* read: 'To Simone de Beauvoir, who kept her integrity'. In 1971 Elizabeth Janeway's *Man's World, Woman's Place* made connections between Beauvoir's theory of woman as 'Other' and the behaviours of subordinate groups. Even in France, in 1971 a prominent cultural magazine included it with Kafka's *The Trial* and the first (male) Kinsey Report as one of the most significant books of the time.[117]

Over the previous year, the women's liberation movement in France had been gaining political momentum. In the spring of 1970 there were women's demonstrations at the University of Vincennes. But it was in Paris, deserted during the August holidays, that the MLF (the Mouvement de Libération des Femmes) was born. A wreath of flowers was placed below the Arc de Triomphe to honour the memory of the wife of the Unknown Soldier. Their banners read: 'One man in two is a woman'; 'More unknown than the Unknown Soldier is his wife'.

In October, a special edition of *Partisans* was published under the title 'Women's liberation, year one'.[118] Shortly thereafter, Beauvoir met with the activists who initiated it – although in print neither Beauvoir nor they acknowledged having made the first move.[119] Anne Zelinsky, Christine Delphy and others wanted to mount a serious campaign to lift the restrictions on abortion. Contraception had been legalized in France in 1967, but abortion was still illegal. The weekly paper *Le Nouvel Observateur* agreed to publish a manifesto – but on the condition that some celebrated names endorsed it. Simone de Beauvoir had such a name, and she agreed to lend it to this cause. They needed space to meet, too, so she offered her apartment.

For the next few months' Sundays the campaign was organized on her sofas. It was a triumph: they gathered 343 signatures and the 'Manifesto of the 343' was published on 5 April 1971 in *Le Nouvel Observateur*. Its message was simple:

> One million women get abortions each year in France. They do it under dangerous conditions because of the secrecy to which they are condemned, although the procedure, when carried out by medical professionals, is extremely simple. These millions of women are silenced. I declare that I am one of them. I declare that I've had an abortion.

The signatories said that they had each aborted (although we don't know for sure whether Beauvoir did and many other signatories had not[120]); they signed because they wanted women to have the right to do so freely and safely.

The word abortion had never before been pronounced on French radio or TV. But now Colette Audry, Dominique Desanti, Marguerite Duras, Gisèle Halimi, Catherine Deneuve and Jeanne Moreau all claimed to have done the unspeakable. In addition to Beauvoir, many members of 'the family' signed too: Olga, Arlette, Michelle and Hélène all supported the cause. Unsurprisingly, the signatories were slurred as the '343 sluts'.

15

Old Age Revealed

When Sartre and Beauvoir returned from Rome in September of 1970 Beauvoir was waiting for *Old Age* to come out and thinking about what should come next. Sartre's health had not worried for her a while, but one Saturday evening in October when Sartre was at her flat with Sylvie – his Saturday nights were spent with them – he drank a lot of vodka and then fell asleep. The next morning he went back to his own apartment. But when Sylvie and Beauvoir took him for Sunday lunch (a weekly date at La Coupole) he was bumping into furniture. He'd had very little to drink at that point, so why couldn't he walk well?

When Beauvoir got back to her place she felt despair: she had had feelings of foreboding since the scare in Moscow in 1954, and Sartre was still smoking two packs of Boyards per day and drinking heavily. The next day Sartre seemed to have recovered his balance and he went to see his doctor, who recommended tests. The encephalogram came back normal. But he was on medication for vertigo, which made him dizzy, and their side effect was sleepiness. She tried not to fear the worst, but what if this was it?

When *Force of Circumstance* was published in 1963 Beauvoir was 55 years old, and many readers were offended that she had not censored her discomfort with old age. She thought she understood why: people turned her into an image because they wanted to identify

Figure 12 *Beauvoir with Sylvie Le Bon and Sartre in the Piazza Navonna, Rome, August 1970.*

with the Simone de Beauvoir of their imagination, an icon unworried by mortality, untroubled by decline. They preferred not to face the reality of ageing and death; how dare she admit that she was afraid of it?[1]

She had felt 'Other' as a woman, which contributed to her analysis in *The Second Sex*. But in the 1960s she began to feel 'Other' in another way: she began to feel old. Once again, her own experience made her wonder about the experiences of others. But it was taboo to talk about ageing and the old. The novelist André Gide, too, had wondered about this question, and asked (through his character La Pérouse) why books had so little to say about the elderly. His answer was that 'it is because the old can no longer write them and because when one is young one does not bother'.[2]

So Beauvoir decided to bother while she could. She started working on this question in the middle of 1967, going back to the Bibliothèque Nationale to study. She read biological and ethnological and historical accounts for the first half of the book, and in the second half – just like she had done in *The Second Sex* – she wanted to include lived experience. She went to retirement homes, she read memoirs written by people of advanced years and, as always, she read literature. The finished product drew on sources ranging from Alain's philosophy to Sophia Tolstoy's diaries, including Louis Aragon, Samuel Beckett, Charles Baudelaire, the Buddha, Chateaubriand, Confucius, Winston Churchill, Dickens, Diderot, Dostoevksy, Marguerite Durand, Ralph Waldo Emerson, Erasmus, James Fraser, Judith Gautier, Gide, Mme de Grafigny, Hegel, Kant, Mme de Maintenon, Nietzsche, Proust, George Sand, Schopenhauer, Mme de Sévigné, George Bernard Shaw, Valéry, Voltaire – and Virginia Woolf.

When Virgina Woolf was 58 she wrote in her diary:

I loathe the hardness of old age. I feel it coming. I creak. I am embittered.

The foot less quick to tread the dew
The heart less feeling to emotions new
Crushed the hope less quick to rise again

I have just opened Matthew Arnold and I have copied out these lines.[3]

In *Old Age* Beauvoir argued that not all ageing is equally hard, creaking or bitter because 'old age' does not refer to a single universal experience. Like becoming a woman, becoming old varies a great deal depending on the physical, psychological, economic, historical, social, cultural, geographical and family context of the individual in question. The *situation* of ageing dramatically affects the experience of it.

Like being female or being pregnant, old age has an obvious biological component. But Beauvoir argued that it is also a cultural phenomenon. She was perplexed by the way society ignored age. In the case of women, she said, only half of the species have to live the secondary status they are assigned by sexism. But age is a fate that affects everyone, so long as they live a long life. Age as a biological fact is a universal human destiny – for those whose lives last long enough. But age as marginalization and loneliness is not.

She used philosophy borne out of actual, lived experience to make her argument, as she did in the *The Second Sex*. She also demonstrated how ageism and sexism frequently work in tandem. The aged of both sexes are often barred from new projects and possibilities. But for men, age does not seem to have the same diminishing effect on erotic prospects.

Her analysis in this work differed from *The Second Sex* in that it focused on economic scarcity much more than the first book had. It is not by chance, Beauvoir said, that people speak of both children and old men as extraordinary for their age: 'the extraordinariness lies in their behaving like human beings when they are either not yet or no longer men'. The child, however, represents the future, whereas the aged person is 'no more than a corpse under suspended sentence'.[4]

When seen in this way from without, it is little wonder that ageing can feel like incarceration from within. Beauvoir wanted to show the reader how the experience of becoming shifts with the passage of time. The past, Beauvoir said, became 'heavier' with age; it became more difficult to break free from past choices and make new projects. In youth we are full of dreams and possibility; with age, she wrote, we realize that some of the dreams we dreamt are 'infinitely remote from the dream made real'.[5] But we also realize that what gives life meaning – even at its bittersweet end – is 'reciprocal relationships'.[6]

Old Age was published in January of 1970, and quickly climbed the bestseller list. Once again, Beauvoir had tackled a taboo, drawing on a diverse range of experience that 'old age' can entail. She cited people who had experienced and reflected on growing old in writing, which meant her research drew mainly from privileged people's experiences of ageing. But she thought she was justified in including literary sources because that enabled her to emphasize the role of subjective experience in her discussions of age as a social and political category. Age is such a category when viewed from without. But it must be lived *from within*, in situations that can be made better or worse.

Again Beauvoir was accused of being unoriginal, writing a 'second-hand' book, a 'compilation'[7] that said nothing new, a 'grandiose attempt at devising a thoroughly sophisticated philosophy of the aged individual based on the principles of Sartre's existentialism'.[8] One reviewer went so far as to claim that 'Beauvoir does not have a subtle or original mind. [...] She has apparently devoured whole libraries, but has digested them incompletely. [...] she has swallowed the work of three men in particular (Marx, Freud and Sartre) uncritically.'[9]

She had, as a matter of fact, been publishing philosophical criticisms of all three since the 1940s. It is little surprise, then, that in her fourth volume of memoirs, *All Said and Done* (1972), she defended her originality in *Old Age*: In part I, 'The analysis of this material, the reflections it aroused, and the conclusions I drew – all this was work that no one had done before me.'[10] And part II, was 'an entirely personal piece of work', guided by her own questions: 'what is the relationship between the aged person and his image, his body, his past and his undertakings?' She read letters, diaries and memoirs, she interrogated herself; but, she said, 'drawing the conclusions was entirely original work'.[11]

Once again, she had drawn attention to behaviour that she thought was unethical. And once again, she was called unoriginal, derivative of Sartre, and incapable of understanding great men. So she defended herself in print, and decided to try to raise her ideas through other media, too. In 1974 she agreed to participate in a documentary film on old age. She rarely agreed to do anything on radio or TV, but she made an exception to discuss society's treatment of the old and her own experience of ageing. In scenes in nursing homes she left viewers in no doubt that she considered this way of ending life inhumane. Sterile institutional settings were juxtaposed with scenes in her own flat in Paris, where she was surrounded by the material remains of her illustrious life – books, artefacts from around the world, photos of friends. The worst thing about death, she said, was that the future was closing before her eyes. In the final scene she is walking around a cemetery: death, she says, no longer horrifies her like it did when she was young. At 30 she could not imagine disappearing from the earth without horror. Approaching 80, she found herself more disgusted by the unknown life before her than the thought of it coming to an end.[12]

In the early 1970s Beauvoir drew a tremendous amount of attention from 'without', and she had begun to draw criticism from some feminists for being 'Sartre-fixated' and for writing for a male periodical (*Les Temps Modernes*).[13] She found these conclusions hasty and

Figure 13 *Beauvoir at home.*

irritating, and it's not hard to imagine why. Professionally, despite the fact that her work took different philosophical positions from those of Sartre she was still cast as his puppet, shadow or accomplice. Personally, the public knew little about her relationship with Bost, a fraction of the story with Algren, and next to nothing about her relationships with Lanzmann and Sylvie (not to mention her relationships with women during the war). She was dismayed by the ease with which people jumped to conclusions. And although this may come across as disingenuous given the way she presented their lives, the way that many readers and reviewers tended to define and dismiss Beauvoir looks not so much bothersome as punishing. When she called out the hypocrisy of her society, she was called sad, unoriginal and worse.

In 1971 Sartre had to have his teeth replaced with dentures, which he struggled with symbolically and practically: would he be able to continue his public speaking or would his own mouth be the end of it?[14] For Beauvoir, it was an unavoidable reminder of his decline. By May, Sartre was staying with her more than usual because her flat was on the ground floor and the elevator in his building was out of order – he found it too tiring to climb ten flights of stairs. He turned up on the evening of Tuesday 18 May with the feeling that his legs were giving out. His words were not distinct and his mouth did not settle in its usual way. It was obviously a stroke, but she tried not to panic, reminding herself that she had seen friends make a full recovery. He agreed to see the doctor on Wednesday morning, but insisted on having his nightly whiskey. By midnight he struggled to take himself to bed; Beauvoir struggled to hold herself together.

When they were finally seen by the doctor he said it was worse than October, and worrying to see these symptoms again so soon. Sylvie drove them back to Beauvoir's flat that evening, and Sartre had fruit juice instead of whiskey. He was shocked and still not in control of his body: his Boyard cigarette kept tumbling from his mouth. Sylvie retrieved it and handed it back to him. But then he dropped it again. So the same cycle recurred, with wrenching repetition, throughout the evening. The next day his prescription was changed and the doctor advised rest and company; he shouldn't be left alone. If he followed the doctor's instructions, they said, he could recover within three weeks.

By the following Wednesday he was walking and talking normally, but he still couldn't play the piano or write. Beauvoir made it her mission to keep him off alcohol, caffeine and stimulants. He reacted to his decline with detached indifference, morbidly making light of his condition because he knew it wouldn't last that long. Beauvoir took no solace from this. Her dread of her own death may have abated, but her dread of his had not.

That summer he was due to spend five weeks travelling – three with Arlette and two with Wanda – while Beauvoir was with Sylvie. Beauvoir loved her travels with Sylvie, but leaving Sartre in this condition was difficult: each night in Italy she cried herself to sleep.

But she remained politically active. She continued her feminist advocacy, becoming president of the movement 'Choisir' (Choose) in July 1971. She had co-founded it with Gisèle Halimi, Jean Rostand (an academic), Christiane Rochefort (a novelist) and Jacques Monod (a Nobel-prize winning doctor). The group had three objectives: to educate women about sex and contraception; change the French law on abortion, which had been in place since 1920; and to provide women who had had abortions with free legal defence.

The same month, while in Switzerland, Sartre had a relapse – but forbade Arlette to tell Beauvoir. When Simone met him at the Termini station in Rome, his face was swollen because of an abscessed tooth but he seemed full of life; they stayed up until 1 a.m. talking. He had energy again and enjoyed Rome. He was taking his medicines and had restricted his alcohol intake to a glass of wine with lunch, beer with dinner and two whiskey *digestifs*. He was working on his biography of

Flaubert, *The Family Idiot*, and talking about life as if there were decades left to live. Back in Paris he regained his interest in people and world events. He read and criticized the manuscript of Beauvoir's fourth volume of memoirs, *All Said and Done*. By mid-November she had almost stopped worrying. The timing was good, from the point of view of her activism – the MLF was growing at a fast pace, and on 11 November 1971 she marched through Paris with thousands of women demanding the legal right to abortion.

Proving Beauvoir's point in *Old Age* that age affects men's and women's erotic possibilities differently, in 1972 Sartre started his last romance: with Hélène Lassithiotakis, a woman in her twenties. The same year *Old Age* was published in English. It had a scathing review in the *Los Angeles Times*, which dismissed it as careless and overly general – the reviewer was Nelson Algren.

Now that Beauvoir was campaigning for abortion rights, she began to receive letters from women who claimed that they were fulfilled by motherhood and housework. Some were written in tones of aggressive rebuke; others encouraged her to see motherhood as more than servitude. So on 6 March 1972 Beauvoir published an article in *Le Nouvel Observateur* entitled 'Response to Some Women and a Man', writing that she was aware that motherhood could be chosen deliberately, and that she was 'aware of the joy that children can bring when they are wanted'. She did not want to impose her way of life on all women, she said, since she was 'actively fighting for their freedom: freedom to choose motherhood, contraception, or abortion'.[15]

But she also thought that the respect motherhood was afforded was suspect, and that the reality was still beset by myths that damaged both women and children. Beauvoir pointed out that it was difficult in France, in 1972, to be an unwed mother. Many women chose to marry because they thought it the safe option; but 'a child without a father is often happier than one whose parents don't get along'.[16]

Beauvoir declared boldly that she was for the dissociation of motherhood and marriage: 'I am for the abolition of the family.' This is the kind of sentence that, out of context, played well into the hands of Beauvoir's conservative and *ad feminam* readers, who dismissed her as anti-maternal, unfeminine and even unfeminist. But in the same paragraph she defines the term 'family' in the following way: 'the family is the intermediary by which this patriarchal world exploits women, extorting billions of hours of "invisible work" from them each year. In France, in 1955, forty-three billion hours were devoted to paid work, compared to forty-five billion hours devoted to unpaid work in the home'.[17]

Beauvoir thought that women must be *conditioned* to accept this work as their lot. Since it does not come naturally to accept that one's vocation in life is to wash dishes and do laundry, she said, something better must be found:

> Maternity is exalted because maternity is the way to keep women at home and make them do housework. Instead of telling a little two-, three-, or four-year-old girl, 'You will be destined to wash dishes', she is told, 'You will be destined to be a mommy.' She is given dolls, and maternity is exalted so that when she becomes a young woman she thinks of one thing: to get married and have children. She has been convinced that she will not be a complete woman if she does not have children.

But the same is not said of men: no one says of a man without children 'he is not a true man'.[18]

Abortion law (as it was) penalized the poorest women in society. If a woman could plan her pregnancies 'according to her desires and her interests', then she could be reconciled with a life that included studying and a career. Beauvoir took men's resistance to this possibility to be rooted in fear – 'fear that women would discover and reclaim their autonomy in all domains by taking their destiny into their own hands.'[19]

To put this in context, prior to 1965 married women in France had no legal recourse to work – or to their own bank accounts – without their husbands' permission. In 1970 French law instituted 'parental authority' in the place of 'paternal power'. And in 1972 a filiation law granted equal status to children born in or out of wedlock.

Beauvoir wanted to make 'abortion irrelevant by making more available the contraceptive methods that are officially authorized, but that only 7% of French women are using'; she believed that, 'Realizing this reform will at the same time surpass it.'[20] Beauvoir's defence of abortion raised issues of power, responsibility and justice – not just 'choice'. In October 1972 Beauvoir wrote that it was 'a great responsibility to bring a human being into this world', asking, 'How can one consent to this if one is incapable of helping him find his place on Earth'?'[21] The worst-off women were most disadvantaged by lack of access to contraception and safe abortion, and it was these women who were charged with breaking the law while rich, bourgeois women had the means to escape these consequences.

Autumn of 1972 saw the publication of the fourth and final volume of her memoirs, ominously entitled *All Said and Done*. This volume departs from the chronological order followed by its three predecessors, instead offering a compilation of Beauvoir's thoughts about things she valued: writing, reading, films, politics, music, art, being engaged in the world. Since the publication of *Force of Circumstance* in 1963 she had seen that readers wanted to take the conclusion of *Force of Circumstance* as 'an admission of failure and a disavowal of my life, in spite of all the statements that fundamentally denied any such interpretation.'[22] On publication of *All Said and Done* a review in *Esprit* asked: 'Why did she write it? What did she want to tell us?' It was 'neither history nor legend', but rather 'application exercises (as one says at school) of Sartre's thought, which are a little annoying'. It was disappointing to find her 'total lack of reflection on a commitment that was punctuated by so many failures'.[23]

But it wasn't an *application* of Sartre's philosophy and, although she did not show the world all of them, she was a woman who reflected on her failures. Among the things Beauvoir included were defences of her originality and descriptions of her methodology in *Old Age*, as well as the changing role of writing in her life. Between 1963 and 1970 she had written the memoir of her mother's death, two works of fiction, two prefaces and *Old Age*. But she experienced periods when the idea of holding a pen made her feel sick. She had become someone who felt that her life's public work had been accomplished: 'my work is complete, even though it may go on'.[24]

At the outset of the book Beauvoir also marks the deaths and illnesses of those near her: Giacometti had been ill, his mother died; Sartre's mother's death is also recounted.

She memorialized Violette Leduc. Since meeting the aspiring novelist in a cinema queue in the mid-1940s, Beauvoir's life had been 'closely mingled' with Violette's, especially for the ten years leading up to Violette's sudden death from cancer in May 1972.[25] Leduc always considered Beauvoir her literary mentor, and made Beauvoir the guardian of her unpublished writings. She would go on to oversee the 1973 publication of Leduc's *La chasse à l'amour* (*Hunting for Love*).[26]

Beauvoir continued to take pleasure in reading, which enabled her to see the world through others' eyes. In *All Said and Done* she chronicled some of her interests, Solzhenitsyn's *Day in the Life of Ivan Denisovich*, Artur London's *On Trial*, ethnological studies, Bettelheim's *The Empty Fortress*, biographies. She read Oscar Wilde, George Sand, Anais Nin, Hannah Arendt, psychoanalysis and detective novels. She re-read the Bible.[27] She did crosswords; time was no longer a commodity she wanted to hoard.

She was still interested in the question 'how does a woman adjust herself to her womanly state, her female condition?' But her views had evolved, and she wanted to tell her readers how the process of living had led her to see new perspectives. If she were to write *The Second Sex* again, she said, she would take a more materialistic approach rather than basing her analysis on the opposition between self and other. She had not, in hindsight, given enough weight to the economics of scarcity and the situations in which men become men. Her claim that one was 'not born a woman, but becomes one' was correct, she said, but it needed to be completed by the statement that one is 'not born a man, one becomes one'.[28]

She regretted that since the publication of *The Second Sex* there had been a backlash of books encouraging women to accept traditional feminine 'vocations', with false prophets declaring feminism out of date. What the new generation of feminists (Millet, Firestone, Morgan, Greer) demanded was the 'decolonization of women', since women have been 'colonized from within' to see unreciprocal unpaid work in the home and discrimination and exploitation in the workplace as just the way things are.[29] At the end of *All Said and Done* she wrote: 'This time I shall not write a conclusion to my book. I leave the reader to draw any he may choose.'[30] As ever, the writer's vocation was to appeal to the freedom of her reader – even when writing about her own life.

In 1972 Simone de Beauvoir publicly adopted the label 'feminist' in an interview with the German journalist Alice Schwarzer. Given her writings and political campaigns between the 1940s and early 1970s it is very hard to believe that Beauvoir was making a ground-breaking admission – but it was big enough news to be bought by a newspaper. For although in 1949 Beauvoir declared that she, like the suffragists, was a feminist,[31] and in a 1965 even called herself 'radically feminist' (in an interview with Francis Jeanson, a colleague at *Les Temps Modernes*),[32] in the much more widely read *Force of Circumstance*

Beauvoir claimed that she had 'avoided falling into the trap of "feminism"' in *The Second Sex*.[33]

With increased political momentum, in the early 1970s debates about feminism in France (and elsewhere) had become diverse enough to require precise definitions of allegiance. Beauvoir and Schwarzer did the interview for two reasons: because they wanted the public to know that Beauvoir had 'converted' to a particular kind of political feminism and because they needed to raise funds for a feminist 'Tribunal' to be held that February at the Paris Mutualité. An interview like this would sell, they thought: and the *The Nouvel Observateur* bought it.

Schwarzer presented this interview as 'historic'; that in it Beauvoir proclaimed 'loud and clear, "I am a feminist"'.[34] Schwarzer asked her the obvious question: why was the author of *The Second Sex* only calling herself feminist twenty-three years later? Beauvoir's answer was that the situation in France hadn't changed enough in those years. Only 7 per cent of women were taking the pill, and women were still barred from interesting careers and progression. She claimed that she had not identified with the reforming and legalistic feminisms she saw in France before the MLF, and liked the latter's radical approach because it seemed better for tackling the radical inequality that persisted between the sexes. Even within political groups whose aim was to liberate everyone, Beauvoir still saw women doing the tedious, creditless, powerless jobs while men were given interesting roles of public responsibility. She made it clear that she did not repudiate men – she rejected the conflation of feminism and misandry, and acknowledged that the men of her day did not set up the patriarchal structures of society. But they still profited from them, and for that reason she thought it was important to have a 'cautious attitude'.[35]

Other feminists had criticized *The Second Sex* for being a middle-class document, written by an elite woman who was blind to her own privilege. And in this interview Beauvoir acknowledged that she had overlooked many questions of class in her earlier work. But she didn't think the class struggle would emancipate women because they were not a different *class* but a different *caste*. People can rise or fall into different classes. But once you are born into a caste you stay there: a woman cannot become a man, she said, and the way they are treated economically, politically and socially is as an inferior caste.[36]

Rather than confessing a conversion from non-feminist to feminist outlooks, in her interviews Beauvoir publicly rejected her previous belief that economic independence and socialism would deliver the changes needed to emancipate women. Instead, she endorsed women-only movements that gave voice to 'anonymous' women's voices rather than those of male 'specialists'.

The MLF had a homosexual undercurrent, and Beauvoir thought this disadvantaged it to a certain degree because it perpetuated the image that they were, in Beauvoir's words, 'hysterical shrews and lesbians'.[37] Her words are shocking to modern readers, particularly in the knowledge of the ways she herself was the target of gendered slurs and had lesbian relationships. Her relationships were still not public knowledge, but in her interview Schwarzer asked Beauvoir whether female homosexuality could be a 'political weapon'. Beauvoir's reply, and the ensuing conversation, shows that she associated lesbian feminists with the imposition of 'sexual dogmas': she thought that homosexuality can play a useful role politically, but 'when they allow themselves to be obsessed with their biases, they run the risk of driving heterosexuals away from the movement':

Alice Schwarzer Their first argument is that, in the current circumstances, any sexual relationship with men is oppressive. They therefore refuse it. What do you think of this?

Simone De Beauvoir Is it really true that any sexual relationship between a man and a woman is oppressive? Couldn't one work toward, not refusing this relationship, but making it so that it isn't oppressive? The claim that all coitus is rape shocks me. I do not believe this. When they say all coitus is rape, they are taking up masculine myths again. That would mean that the man's sexual organ is a sword, a weapon. The issue is inventing new sexual relations that are not oppressive.[38]

In May of 1972 Beauvoir went to Grenoble to give a lecture for *Choisir*, for whom she was actively campaigning, and on 8 November there was a trial at the Court of Bobigny that attracted national attention to their cause. A young woman of 16 years, 'Marie-Clare C.', had had an abortion with the complicity of her mother. She had broken the law, and she was tried along with three other women. Gisèle Halimi defended them, drawing on several prominent scientific and cultural authorities (including Beauvoir) in her defence. She argued that these women were being tried by another age. The 1920 law especially penalized the poor. Each year millions of women who were ill informed about contraception resorted to this option. And in doing so they endangered their lives and risked irreversible mutilation.

The trial shifted the tide of public opinion – in 1970, only 22 per cent of French people favoured lifting restrictions on abortion; a year later support had risen to 55 per cent.[39] Although there were still a few years to wait, in 1974 the Minister of Health, Simone Veil, developed new legislation, making access to contraception easier in December 1974 and championing what became known as 'la loi Veil' (the Veil law), legalizing abortion from January 1975.

Meanwhile, in March 1973 Sartre suffered another stroke. This time it was worse; he was not remembering things and not recognizing people. The doctor said he had asphyxia of the brain, and again advised no drinking or smoking. Sartre was 67 now, and he made a half-hearted attempt to forego his vices. But then he wholeheartedly embraced them again.

In addition to her writing and feminist work, Beauvoir continued to be dedicated to her editorial role in the management of *Les Temps Modernes*, and with Sartre ill she assumed the task of chairing its Wednesday morning meetings. Claire Etcherelli, a novelist Lanzmann had introduced her to in the late 1960s, remembered the scene:

> 11:00. She welcomed everyone, seated on her yellow divan. Next to her was a pile of articles [. . .] conscientiously read and annotated. The small group which constituted the committee took their places in a semi-circle around the divan.[40]

Etcherelli described witnessing Beauvoir's rejection phone calls to aspiring authors, during which she could be 'frank and brutal' in her criticism. But Beauvoir did not use her status as director to publish anything without the support of the committee.[41]

That summer Beauvoir and Sylvie Le Bon were travelling in southern France before meeting Sartre to travel together to Venice. (He had already had his summer holiday with Arlette, and was on the way to having his holiday with Wanda.) Beauvoir and Le Bon stayed in Venice for a couple of days but then left: Beauvoir did not want Sylvie to be bored in Venice, and both women had an appetite for seeing new places. But Beauvoir had begun to feel a 'double-edged guilt': guilty if she left Sartre that she was letting him down, or guilty if she stayed that she was letting Sylvie down instead.[42]

The three of them reconvened in Rome in mid-August. Sartre's sight had deteriorated; he had had a haemorrhage behind his left eye and now neither eye could see clearly. They had always followed strict schedules at home and now the routine shifted to accommodate Sartre's new needs: Beauvoir read to him in the mornings; then lunch; then Sartre would sleep while Beauvoir and Sylvie went for walks or read quietly. When Sartre woke up Beauvoir read him the newspapers, in French or Italian, and then all three of them went to dinner together.

Mealtimes showed the depths to which he'd fallen. He was prediabetic, and Beauvoir worried about his careless consumption of pasta and gelato. As an effect of his dentures and his stroke his lips were beyond his full control, so he did not eat cleanly.[43] When Olga and Bost met them in Rome that year they were taken aback to see him so much in decline.

Not long after they returned to Paris Sartre decided to hire a new secretary, not to do the correspondence (he already had someone for that) but to read to him and talk. The secretary was Pierre Victor, the Maoist who had asked him to take over *La Cause du peuple*. At first, Arlette was suspicious. She phoned Beauvoir, saying that she didn't want to have a 'Schoenman' situation on their hands. (Ralph Schoenman was the general secretary of the Russell Tribunal, who had made quite an impression in Stockholm and Copenhagen by claiming to speak on behalf of Bertrand Russell, whose age prevented his being there himself.) But Sartre wanted this, Beauvoir thought, and she didn't want to infantilize him. It also meant that Beauvoir would have a little time to herself in the mornings, because Pierre would do the reading aloud.[44] It was a decision she would come to regret.

Sartre was no longer doing the rounds of his women; they now attended him. He was 68 and completely dependent. In October 1973 he moved to a tenth-floor apartment in a modern building, 22 boulevard Edgar Quinet, near the Montparnasse Tower. It was just across the cemetery from Beauvoir's. In Rome in the summer of 1974 Beauvoir recorded a series of conversations with Sartre that she said would be an oral sequel to his autobiography, *Words*. By the end of that summer he realized that his eyesight was not going to improve: he would never see again.

But he was still trying to work, planning a book with Pierre Victor that they had provisionally entitled *Power and Liberty*. Victor was, like many of his generation, interested in the thought of Foucault and Deleuze, and he told Sartre that their collaboration was a kind of dialectical, in which they thought in opposition to each other. Beauvoir was convinced, even after the events that unfolded, that Victor took the job out of sincere care for Sartre. It wasn't easy: Victor often felt like quitting. When he arrived Sartre was often sitting in his flat, dozing or listening to music. It was 'a constant struggle against death', Victor wrote, and he had been employed to fight 'sleep, lack of interest, or, more simply, torpor [. . .]. What I was really involved in was a sort of resuscitation'.[45]

During the winter of 1973–1974 the feminist movement in France was at a turning point. With the battle for abortion nearly won, divisions emerged between different tendencies, and strategies, in the movement. Simone de Beauvoir wanted a law against sexism, like existing laws against racism. Sexism could not be legislated out of existence any more than racism could, but Beauvoir believed a law against it would be a useful tool. So with Anne Zelinsky she co-founded the League of Women's Rights, an association with anti-sexist legislation as its objective.

The League met with opposition from fellow feminists, who saw it as a concession to – or even collaboration with the bourgeois and patriarchal framework of the legal system. The League took the view that social subversion was no longer the right course of action; instead, they pursued the reform of existing structures. Beauvoir was the League's president, but she used her power in other domains to give voice to its opposition, too. In 1973 she offered a permanent column in *Les Temps Modernes* to those who wanted to denounce sexism. Called 'Everyday Sexism', its contributors deployed humour, lived experience and reflection to expose and challenge sexism rather than pursuing legal redress. The preface to the column is powerfully direct:

An individual who calls another a 'dirty nigger' in front of witnesses, or who prints insulting remarks about Jews or Arabs can be brought to trial and convicted of 'racial slander'. But if a man publicly shouts at a woman, calling her 'a whore', or if in his written work he accuses *Woman* of treachery, foolishness, fickleness, stupidity, or hysterical behaviour, he runs absolutely no risk. [. . .] We [the League of Women's Rights] will demand that 'sexist slander' also be considered as a crime.[46]

The next year she published a preface to a book that passionately pleaded for divorce reform. Again, Beauvoir's analysis includes philosophical nuances that are easily overlooked in the heat of political debate. To the objection that divorce was bad for the children, she replied that 'a child can be "assassinated" by parents who insist on living side by side in disunion'. Divorce, according to Beauvoir, 'is not a panacea'; 'It only liberates women if they know how to put their freedom to use in a positive way. But in order to discover their own possibilities, divorce is often a necessary condition.'[47]

During the 1970s, Beauvoir increasingly used her voice to amplify the voices of others. In the introduction to a special issue of *Les Temps Modernes* entitled 'Women Insist', she wrote that the struggle against sexism, 'attacks within each of us what is most intimate to us and what seems most sure. It questions our very desires, the very forms of our pleasure'.[48] Feminists made people uncomfortable; but if their words were in fact powerless they would not be subject to ridicule, treated like shrews, and gaslit. In this piece she acknowledged that in the past she had 'more or less played the role of the token woman', believing that the best way to overcome the barriers to her sex was to ignore them. But younger feminists helped her see that this stance made her complicit in perpetuating inequality, so now she was calling it – and herself – out.

Beauvoir's acknowledgement of her own complicity was admirable: she had become a woman who could see the failings of her former self. But could she see all of them? When she wrote that the struggle against sexism 'attacks within each of us what is most intimate to us and what seems most sure', what were the constraints and desires that held her back from telling the full story about her love of philosophy and her loves other than Sartre? Was she motivated by self-preservation, concern for others in 'the family', or delusion? Or was she motivated, as she herself put it in *All Said and Done*, by giving her life an 'artistic necessity' that would infuse it with the potential to liberate her readers, to show them new possibilities like Louisa May Alcott's Jo and George Eliot's Maggie had done for her?[49] (She had said that that's what she was doing in the middle of the 1960s in an interview for *The Paris Review*. Saying it again in *All Said and Done* might imply that she meant it.)

Given Sartre's deserved reputation as a womanizing man – and the ongoing lies he told his contingent women – it is a little surprising to find him telling their story in ways that emphasized Beauvoir's intellectual centrality to his life first and foremost. But when Sartre gave interviews in the 1970s, that is exactly what he did. He wrote that 'You have her version in her memoirs,' but that 'For me, I think our relationship developed intellectually at first.'[50] To this, his interviewer John Gerassi – the son of Beauvoir's friend Stépha – asked outright, 'were you not in love with each other?'

Sartre's reply was that they loved each other, but not in the way that love is commonly understood:

we fell in love with each other's intuition, imagination, creativity, perceptions, and eventually for a while bodies as well, but just like one cannot dominate a mind (except through terror, of course), one cannot dominate taste, dreams, hopes, etcetera. Some things Castor was better at, some I was. Do you know that I would never allow any writing of mine to be published, or even made public to anyone, until Castor approved?'[51]

Sartre had always been conscious of posterity, and determined to defeat mortality by having a long afterlife as a great writer. In June 1975, to mark the occasion of Sartre's 70th birthday, *Le Nouvel Observateur* commissioned an interview. Among other things, his interviewer, Michel Contat, asked him about all of his women. Sartre admitted that there were several. But he said that 'in a sense', Simone de Beauvoir was the only one. He mentioned two others by name – Michelle and Arlette. But Beauvoir, he said, had played a role that no one else could:

J.-P. S.   I have been able to formulate ideas to Simone de Beauvoir before they were really concrete [. . .]. I have presented all of my ideas to her when they were in the process of being formed.

M.C.   *Because she is at the same level as you, philosophically?*

J.-.P. S.   Not only that, but also because she was the only one at my knowledge of myself, of what I wanted to do. For this reason she was the perfect person to talk to, the kind one rarely has. It is my unique good fortune . . .

M.C.   *Still, you have had to defend yourself against Simone de Beauvoir's criticisms, haven't you?*

J.-P. S.   Oh, often! In fact we have even insulted one another. [. . .] But I knew that she would be the one who was right, in the end. That's not to say that I accepted all her criticisms, but I did accept most of them.

M. C.   *Are you just as hard on her as she is on you?*

J.-P. S.   Absolutely. As hard as possible. There is no point in not criticizing very severely when you have the good fortune to love the person you are criticizing.[52]

The same year Beauvoir decided to interview Sartre herself for *Les Temps Modernes* (although they didn't call it an interview when they published it, they called it an 'interrogation'). She got straight to the point: 'Sartre, I want to ask you about the question of women.' Why is it, she asked, that he claimed to be on the side of the oppressed, speaking out for them when they were 'workers, blacks, Jews – but not women? How do you explain this?'

His childhood, probably, he said.

'But you became an adult!' She pushed him, asking whether it might not be possible that many men have a blind spot where women are concerned (like she herself had, for a long time). Couldn't their blindness to women's suffering be like the blindness of the ancient Athenians, who talked about ideals like justice and democracy while the slaves worked their land and cooked their dinners? Wasn't it possible that his indifference would look as shocking to later generations as the apathy of the Athenians?[53]

Beauvoir continued to engage with feminist writers and campaigns, taking part in many interviews herself. In 1976, as she looked back on her life in conversation with Alice Schwarzer, she commented that she had escaped women's 'slave labour' because she was neither a mother nor a housewife. But for over two decades she had been receiving letters from women all over the world, telling her about their struggles, which made her realize that the other side of silence was even worse than she thought. Many women who wrote to her were between 35 and 45 and married. They married young, for love, and were happy to do so at the time, but later in life they found themselves facing dead ends: their children no longer needed them and they had no professional training, no projects of their own to pursue.

In 1976 Beauvoir thought marriage and motherhood were still – too often – traps. If a woman wanted to have children, she said, she should seriously consider the conditions in which she would raise them, since it was *she* who would be expected to give up her work, to stay home when the children were ill. And it was she who would be blamed if they did not succeed.[54] The problem wasn't with house and care work in themselves, Beauvoir said, because no work is degrading in itself; but that everybody – not just women – should be doing the work needed to maintain life because that way they would still have enough time to do things that were life-giving. She called herself an 'activist for voluntary motherhood'.[55]

The same year, across the Atlantic, Adrienne Rich published *Of Woman Born*, a book that began with Beauvoir's discussion of motherhood in *The Second Sex* to develop an account of maternal power. In March 1976 an International Tribunal on Crimes Against Women was held in Brussels with a letter by Beauvoir as part of its proceedings – she found it laughable that the event opened just after the 'Year of the Woman' – another thing 'organized by male society for the mystification of women'.[56]

In March 1977 Sartre was experiencing pain in his leg; the doctors warned him that if he didn't stop smoking they may have to amputate his toes – or more. Two days later he gave his Boyards and his lighters to Sylvie Le Bon. But alcohol was harder to give up, and he began to play deceitful games with the women in his life in order to have it. He told Beauvoir that he would have only a glass of whiskey each night. But he had Michelle smuggle bottles in, hiding them behind books in his bookshelf. The Beaver didn't have to know *everything*, he said.

One day Beauvoir caught him hungover, and she was furious. When she discovered that he was still drinking whiskey by the half-bottle at Michelle's, she was irate. She phoned Michelle and fired her from his Saturday nights.[57] Arlette was pleased about this: she had always been jealous of Sartre's other women. But over time, Arlette Elkaïm Sartre had overcome her dislike of Pierre Victor, who was, like her, North African and Jewish. By 1978 they had begun to learn

Hebrew together, since Victor had developed an interest in Jewish theology and messianism. In February of 1978 Beauvoir was worried that they were taking advantage of his weakness, co-opting his reputation for their own political ends: Sartre, Victor and Elkaïm were going to Jerusalem. Sartre was taken to the plane in a wheelchair and he stayed in a luxury hotel; he returned in one piece. But when they got back Victor tried to publish a piece on the peace movement in Israel in *Le Nouvel Observateur* with Sartre's name as a co-author. Beauvoir had a telephone call from Bost, who was working on the paper at the time, telling her the piece was bad and Sartre should withdraw it. Beauvoir read it and agreed, and persuaded Sartre not to publish it.

Beauvoir was clearly one of Sartre's carers by this point. But there were several people who wanted to be his intellectual custodian, and conflicting accounts about what he himself wanted. Sartre never told Victor why the piece didn't run. But at an editorial meeting for *Les Temps Modernes* (which Victor attended in Sartre's place) Beauvoir mentioned it, assuming that he knew. He was irate, stomping out of the meeting and calling his colleagues 'putrefied corpses'.[58] He no longer attended the meetings of *Les Temps Modernes* and now referred with disdain to the members of the old guard as 'the Sartreans'. Arlette took Victor's side.

Meanwhile, Sartre gave more interviews in which he said that he never let anyone but Simone de Beauvoir read his manuscripts before publication, claiming even in July 1978 that her role in his life was 'essential and unique'.[59] According to Sylvie Le Bon, the last five years of Sartre's life were particularly hard on Beauvoir. She had to watch his blindness develop, and found it harder to be stoical for him than for herself. She drank and took Valium, but that didn't stop her from regularly breaking down in tears. She took solace in other friendships when she could. Claude Lanzmann lived in rue Boulard, five minutes away, and when he was in Paris they saw each other twice a week. But he was directing *Shoah* – a film that Beauvoir had lent him the money to kickstart – and was often away travelling.

In 1978, a film adaptation of *The Woman Destroyed* was made and reviewed in *Le Monde*, which again declared Beauvoir's work outdated, and her feminism inferior: 'Today, the argument and the tone of the book seem especially to have archaeological value. They make it possible to measure the accelerated evolution of a feminism for which this type of problem is more a question of *Elle* or *Marie-Claire* than, for example, of 'Women on the move' [Femmes en mouvement].'[60]

By the late 1970s, Beauvoir was exhausted by Sartre's decline and no longer inclined to write lengthy new material, but in 1979 she published *When Things of the Spirit Come First* (the novel she'd written during the 1930s, which Gallimard and Grasset had rejected). It contains a fictional couple based on Zaza and Merleau-Ponty, Anne and Pascal, written before Beauvoir discovered the truth about Merleau-Ponty's courtship. Anne's mother persecutes her daughter, criticizing her ideas, her book-reading, and her friendship with the Simone character 'as though they were so many sins'.[61] The book's execution is not as accomplished as Beauvoir's later works, but it reveals that Beauvoir's preoccupations in the 1930s included questions of love and self-sacrifice, happiness and what it means to become a woman. It also shows that she was not afraid, even then, to pepper her prose with philosophy: her characters discuss Duns Scotus, Bergson, Leibniz and Hobbes, alongside Racine, Baudelaire, Claudel and Péguy.

That autumn she participated in a film about her work by Josée Dayan and Malka Ribowska: it was called 'Simone de Beauvoir' and the opening credits called it 'a documentary on our only woman philosopher'.[62] In interviews about the film she was asked why she agreed to make it, given that she had already spoken about herself so much in her life-writing. She answered that she wanted to 'rectify' certain things, to tell the truth, to give 'a more just image of herself'.[63]

In 1979 she also became Publication Director for *Questions feministes*, a feminist magazine whose relaunch she would oversee in the early 1980s, and won the Austrian Prize for European Literature. *Le Figaro* announced this honour under the headline: 'A perfect bourgeoise: Simone de Beauvoir', explaining that 'Simone de Beauvoir, the first woman to receive the Austrian Prize for European Literature, owes everything to a man.'[64] It is little wonder that, when asked why she continued her feminist advocacy, she said it was because even in 1980, women were 'given the illusion that a woman can achieve anything today, and that it is her fault if she does not'.[65]

The following March Beauvoir heard that *Le Nouvel Observateur* was going to publish interviews between Sartre and Pierre Victor, over three Sunday issues. Sartre hadn't published anything in a long time (by Sartre's standards, at any rate); it would draw a lot of attention. She had asked to see what they were working on several times over recent years, but nothing prepared her for what it was: Sartre and Elkaïm had both evaded her questions. When Sartre let her see the extracts they'd selected for publication she was horrified.

Pierre Victor was going to use his real name – Benny Lévy – in print. (He had not had the legal right to be in France until Sartre took up his cause and got him leave to remain.) The tone was dismissive of much of what Sartre had stood for, rejecting the meaning of literature and political engagement that he'd dedicated his life to. In the last interview, Lévy even got Sartre – who had been a lifelong friend of secular Jews – to claim that the only 'real' Jews were religious ones. Sartre had even conceded ground to messianism. Beauvoir begged Sartre not to publish it, but he refused to be dissuaded. Was her incomparable friend losing his capacity for thought?

She was deeply upset – tearful and anxious. Lanzmann and Bost both rang the editor of *Le Nouvel Observateur* to try to stop the publication. But the editor, Jean Daniel, received a call from Sartre himself saying that he wanted the interview published: if the *Nouvel Observateur* wouldn't have it, another paper would. The interviews appeared on 10, 17 and 24 March 1980.

Between the second and the third Sundays, on Wednesday 19 March, the atmosphere between them was still tense when Beauvoir arrived for her turn on the rota, staying over at Sartre's apartment. When she entered his room to wake him the next morning at 9.00 a.m. he was sitting in his bed, panting for breath. He had been there for hours, unable to speak or call for help. She went to call the doctor but there was no dial tone: the secretary had not paid the phone bill.

So she ran downstairs to the concierge's phone: the doctor came quickly and called for an ambulance. Beauvoir watched anxiously as they administered an emergency treatment, and then took him to the Broussais hospital. She went back up to the apartment and got dressed, and then went to lunch with Jean Pouillon as she had planned. She asked if he would go with her to the hospital; she didn't want to go alone. At first it looked hopeful. They made another rota of readers and visitors to keep Sartre company; for a few weeks Beauvoir regularly attended her afternoon slot. On Sunday, 13 April, Sartre held her wrist and told her he loved her very much. On 15 April, he went into a coma. Beauvoir spent the day next to him, listening to him breathe, and then went back to her flat and started drinking. At 9.00 p.m. the phone rang. It was Arlette Elkaïm – it was over.

16

The Dying of the Light

Beauvoir went back to the hospital with Sylvie Le Bon. She called Bost and Lanzmann, Jean Pouillon and André Gorz, who came to the hospital immediately. The hospital staff said they could stay with the body until 5 a.m., then it would be moved.

How could they call him 'it'?

Elkaïm went home, while the old 'family' drank and reminisced until the early hours of the morning. Journalists were already circling the area but Bost and Lanzmann told them to beat it. Then Beauvoir wanted to be alone with him. After the others left she crawled up on Sartre's bed. She was about to get under his sheet when the nurse stopped her – his bedsores were gangrenous. So she climbed up on top of the sheet, lay down beside him, and fell asleep.

At 5.00 a.m. they came for the body. She went to Lanzmann's to sleep, and stayed there on Wednesday. She couldn't bear the phone in her apartment, let alone the stake-out of journalists, so after Lanzmann's she went to Sylvie Le Bon's. Hélène came to be with her from Alsace and she was flooded with cards, letters, telegrams. Lanzmann, Bost and Sylvie took care of the funeral arrangements: it would be Saturday, 19 April.

When the day came Beauvoir got into the hearse with Sylvie, Hélène and Arlette. Behind them followed tens of thousands of people, paying their respects to Sartre. But Beauvoir could see nothing. No quantity of Valium and whiskey could restrain her tears, but she took both anyway. When they arrived at Montparnasse Cemetery she asked for a chair. Later that week *The Times* of London would report that 'Mme de Beauvoir' 'was on the verge of collapse and supported by two friends' when she stood before the coffin.[1] There were swarms of people around her, but her mind was blank. She didn't remember what happened after that: she went to Lanzmann's and then they had dinner in a private room, but she drank too much and she had to be helped down the stairs. Sylvie tried to stop her drinking, but now she would not be stopped.[2]

After that she stayed at Sylvie's. The following Wednesday the cremation took place at Père Lachaise, but Beauvoir was too tired to go. When Sylvie and Lanzmann returned they found her on the floor, delirious. She had pneumonia.

She was hospitalized in the Hôpital Cochin for a month; at first the doctors didn't think she would ever recover, after the binge on pills and whiskey she had cirrhosis of the liver and some motor-neuron damage. When she returned to the rue Victor Schoelcher the pneumonia was gone but the depression wasn't. Throughout June and July Sylvie stayed with Beauvoir as much as she could during the week and, when Sylvie was teaching, Lanzmann and Bost came to be with her. She had always said that her life would end when Sartre's did; they were worried that she would enforce this literally. At weekends Sylvie took her away from Paris in the car. In August, when it was time for her annual trip to Rome, she said to Sylvie that they needed to leave Paris: 'I want to live and I need to go somewhere far away to do it.'[3]

They went to Norway, on a fjord cruise. Slowly she began to resurface, to remember that there were other meaningful relationships in her life that were still worth living for. But she also began to see that some relationships would never be the same. Three days after Sartre's cremation, Arlette had emptied his apartment. This was surprising from a legal point of view, because the law required that his property be untouched until an evaluation was made for tax purposes. Arlette told different stories about why she had done it: she couldn't pay the rent until the end of the probate period; she feared a break-in. But Beauvoir felt certain that she had done it to prevent Beauvoir taking things that were rightfully hers. It was an unpleasant dispute: other friends wanted mementos of Sartre, and when Lanzmann asked Arlette to give something to Bost, given their 40-year-long friendship, she gave him Sartre's old slippers.

Sylvie, who had never particularly liked Arlette, was furious. Sartre had Beauvoir's father's books in his apartment: these were not his for her to inherit. He also had a drawing Picasso had given to them both, and a painting by Riberolle with the same provenance. Both Sylvie and Lanzmann asked Arlette for them on Beauvoir's behalf but Arlette said she could ask for them herself if she wanted them so much.

Sylvie got Georges Bertrand de Beauvoir's books back. But there was only one thing Beauvoir herself asked for: the manuscript to Sartre's *Notebooks for an Ethics*. When Sartre had finished *Being and Nothingness* he gave Beauvoir the manuscript as soon as it was published; it was her most treasured possession. And at the end of *Being and Nothingness* Sartre had promised to publish an ethics, which he started in the late 1940s, around the same time Beauvoir wrote her own *Ethics of Ambiguity*. Arlette knew that Beauvoir wanted this manuscript, since one of the first things she did when released from the hospital was to 'humble' herself to ask Arlette for it. But Arlette said no. And in 1983, she published it.

When Beauvoir was released from the hospital in May 1980 the doctors told her to stop taking Valium and drinking, and to have massage and therapy to help her body recover. She followed most of their advice – apart from giving up whiskey and vodka. During these weeks she realized that she wanted her doctors to be able to discuss her condition with Sylvie. According to French law her nearest blood relative, Hélène, was her legal guardian and heir. Sylvie could not even drive Beauvoir to her treatments without her sister's permission.

Beauvoir did not want to move to Alsace to live with Hélène and Lionel, and it would not have been practical for them to uproot themselves to Paris to care for her. So Beauvoir decided to ask Sylvie if she could legally adopt her. She told Lanzmann and Bost first, and they were both in favour. They had learned from the Arlette case what problems could arise when all parties were not equally in favour of new arrangements, so she raised the issue carefully with Sylvie first and then Hélène. Initially Hélène felt the discomfort of displacement, but she realized that her life would not last much longer than her sister's, and it was already full enough.

Sylvie, on the other hand, was a little reluctant. She had always detested Arlette's willingness to live as Sartre's kept woman. Sylvie Le Bon was an independent woman who had her own professional life – she was an *agrégée* and taught philosophy – and she did not want her relationship with Beauvoir to be considered alike to Arlette's with Sartre. She also knew that scholarly research had begun to concentrate on the role of mothers and daughters in Beauvoir's writing, and she thought adoption would provide a 'feast' of speculation.

But by this stage Beauvoir had had decades to get used to people making imaginary characters out of her life. She encouraged Sylvie to see their friendship from within, where it wasn't defined by their ages or traditional roles. Beauvoir confided to Sylvie that over the course of her life she made several attempts to find another friendship like the one she had with Zaza. But until Sylvie, none of them succeeded. In Sylvie, Beauvoir said, it was as if she had found Zaza's reincarnation. Sylvie accepted, later writing that her relationship with Beauvoir was one of 'unique and incomparable intimacy'.[4] Beauvoir told Deirdre

Bair during an interview that she was fortunate 'to enjoy a perfect relationship with both a man and a woman'.[5]

The year of Sartre's death bore all the wounds of grief: tears, depression, wondering what she could have done otherwise. Again Beauvoir turned to literature as catharsis: she decided to write an account of Sartre's death. *Adieux* was published in 1981: it chronicled Sartre's decline and death, focusing on the changing situation of his life as age and illness restricted his possibilities. It also included the interviews she had done with Sartre in Rome in the mid-1970s as a testament to their friendship of thought, their constant conversation. Friends worried about her working on the project, but this was the only way she could come to terms with his death. Writing had been catharsis with Zaza, and with her mother, so she persisted. Her opening words read:

> This is the first of my books – the only one no doubt – that you will not have read before it is printed. It is wholly and entirely devoted to you; and you are not affected by it. [. . .] When I say *you*, it is only a pretense, a rhetorical device. I am speaking to no one.[6]

Some readers have called *Adieux* her fifth volume of memoirs. But it is more elliptical than the others, describing Sartre's decline with little focus on her own life beyond it. And it is a mixture of two forms: memoir and dialogue. Beauvoir believed that *Adieux* was a tribute to Sartre and an extension of *Old Age*. In 1970 *Old Age* had described the way old people are marginalized and treated by some as subhuman. In *Adieux* readers saw that this fate awaited even Jean-Paul Sartre.[7]

She thought it would be harshly received, and she was right: once again she was accused of indiscretion, or of speaking for Sartre when he could not speak for himself. Pascal Bruckner described the book as a mix of 'homage and vengeance' in *Le Point*.[8] (Among other things, she had asked him why he thought men had 'a certain pride', whether he had always felt free, since childhood.[9]) Her defenders were primarily

English-speaking women. The translator of Sartre's *Being and Nothingness*, Hazel Barnes, condemned the gossip that painted *Adieux* as Beauvoir getting her own back 'in return for having to put up with Sartre's infidelities. This is slander. The narrative is both factual reporting and a tribute'.[10] Sartre's biographer Annie Cohen-Solal thought it elicited the usual reactions to this mythical couple: 'utter respect or radical rejection'.[11]

One of her harshest critics was, of course, Arlette Elkaïm Sartre. She published an open letter in *Libération* attacking Beauvoir, disparaging her relationship with Sartre, her claims to centrality in his life, and her conduct in the Benny Lévy affair. Both women thought the other had reduced Sartre to an inferior being, and claimed to be the pre-eminent witness to Sartre's life. Beauvoir refused to reply in print because she did not want to dignify Arlette's claims with a response, or to be a public spectacle. Privately she was full of disdain.

In 1981 Beauvoir began her conversations with Deirdre Bair, her first biographer: she liked American women, and Beauvoir and Bair developed a habit of 4.00 p.m. interviews over neat scotch. She had been thinking about the image she would leave to posterity for over twenty years now, with the benefit of decades of experience of how 'publicity disfigures those who fall into its hands'.[12] She did not want Arlette to have the last word concerning her relationship with Sartre. So she decided to publish Sartre's letters to her, and made a public announcement of this intention, so the world could see for themselves what Jean-Paul Sartre thought of Simone de Beauvoir. She did not have the legal right to do so, since in France the literary executor has rights to any word Sartre penned, regardless of to whom he wrote them or who held the texts in question. So Beauvoir consulted her publisher, Robert Gallimard, who told her to leave the talking to Arlette to him.

There was much more at stake here than two of Sartre's women arguing over whom he loved more. It was not a question of romance, for Beauvoir: she had been dogged all her life by people who denied her independence as a thinker, even claiming that Sartre wrote her books. And she thought the letters would show 'my critical influence on him, as well as his critical influence on me'.[13]

When Sartre died, some Paris obituaries did not mention Beauvoir once. *Le Monde* mentioned the thousands of people at his funeral. But it did not mention her.[14] A long article in *L'Express* includes a timeline which mentions the date when they met, and Beauvoir taking second place in the *agrégation*; but the rest of their relationship does not receive a single comment.[15]

In English *The Times* of London made no mention of Beauvoir in their initial article announcing Sartre's death;[16] the full obituary introduced her as one of his 'closest friends' who 'became his mistress and life-long political, philosophical, and literary ally'.[17] *The Guardian*'s death announcement didn't mention her either, declaring that he had 'lived his last years alone in Paris, visited and helped by friends and disciples'.[18] In their full obituary she is not included in the 'group of gifted intellectuals' with whom he studied; rather she is mentioned for their 'life-long union' in which she 'helped him in his various intellectual enterprises'.[19]

The New York Times was slightly more inclusive: 'Mr. Sartre was scarcely less well known as a writer and thinker than Simone de Beauvoir, his stanch and close companion of many years. Their relationship persisted through numerous phases, but their basic attachment to each other, their fortification of each other, was never seriously doubted'.[20] But the *Washington Post* introduced her as a 'liaison'[21] – could no one see her as an intellectual interlocutor, an active participant or even inspiration in the development of his thought?

This woman-as-man's-disciple trope did not only affect her in relation to Sartre, either. During the early 1980s, Beauvoir continued to see Bianca Lamblin (née Bienenfeld) for lunch regularly. When the subject of Israel came up their discussion became heated. Lamblin criticized Beauvoir for being 'unconditionally pro-Israel', not even trying to see the Palestinian point of view. Lamblin was unsettled enough by their conversation to write to Beauvoir after it, further explaining her position. Like her review of Merleau-Ponty's *Adventures of the Dialectic*, Beauvoir's reply to Lamblin shows both her temperament in conflict and her frustration with the assumption that her views are derivative of Sartre's or any other man's:

> I'm answering your letter so that you don't think I read it indifferently, but it's stupid. Since the situation is 'ambiguous', as you say, why would I bear any sort of grudge or scorn towards someone who doesn't share my opinions? [...] As for Lanzmann [...], I'm sorry you subscribe to the chauvinist prejudice that a woman is able to form her ideas only from a man's.[22]

When Beauvoir published her correspondence with Sartre it cost her some friendships – for the first time, Olga and Wanda would see the reality of her role in Sartre's life. The Bosts had separated several times in recent years and Beauvoir saw less of Olga because she was closer to Bost; they still worked together on *Les Temps Modernes*. According to Deirdre Bair, Beauvoir warned Olga that she was going to publish the letters, and ignored Olga's requests to exclude anything about her and her sister, causing a permanent rift in their relationship.[23] But if it cost them their illusions it was worth the price, in Beauvoir's view, to show the rest of the world the truth. By now she was back to giving lectures and broadcasts on feminism, more cognizant than ever of the way even her prizes were attributed to Sartre's genius. It took a lot of time to organize their voluminous correspondence. But in November 1982 she gave the manuscript to Gallimard. It was dedicated 'To Claude Lanzmann, with all my love.'[24]

The path to publication was not easy: before it could be published Arlette wanted to establish herself as the legitimate heir of Sartre's philosophical legacy, and she published not only the *Notebooks for an Ethics* (the manuscript she had refused Beauvoir) but also Sartre's *War Diaries*.

When the letters finally appeared readers could see what Sartre had said, yes. But then they asked: why did she not publish her own part of the story? In their 1974 interviews Sartre said he wanted his letters to be published after his death, so she said that she was following his wishes. As for her own letters, she told Bair that they were nobody's business but her own.[25] In an interview in 1985 Margaret Simons asked Beauvoir if she had read Michèle Le Doeuff's review of Sartre's letters; did she know that Le Doeuff claimed that Sartre was 'the only speaking subject' in their relationship?[26] Beauvoir replied that these letters were Sartre's letters: naturally it was Sartre speaking in them. 'If I published my own, I would be the one speaking. But in my lifetime, I won't publish my letters.'[27]

After the publication of Sartre's letters Beauvoir dedicated her time to the two things that gave her pleasure: working for women's liberation and spending time with Sylvie and other friends. In one of her interviews with Beauvoir Alice Schwarzer said that 'such great friendships' between women were uncommon. But Beauvoir replied that she was 'not so sure': 'Many friendships between women endure, whereas love fades. Real friendships between men and women are very, very uncommon, I think.'[28]

The year 1980 also heralded the end of '1970s' feminism in France, not just in the sense that a new decade was marked on the calendar, but in that a new association was formed, calling itself Mouvement de Libération des Femmes (MLF; The Movement for the Liberation of Women) – it claimed this name as a commercial trademark, and was officially registered with the National Institute of Industrial Property. Anyone who used the name without consent could be sued. Whereas the MLF of the 1970s was an organic movement with three simple criteria of belonging – that one was a woman, aware of the oppression of women, and committed to fighting it – this new MLF claimed to speak for women rather than letting them speak for themselves. This was no longer feminism, in Beauvoir's view; it was 'tyranny'.[29]

But there was good news, too: in 1980, the first Cabinet-level ministry for women in France came into existence. Its first Minister for Women, Yvette Roudy, asked Beauvoir for support in campaigning for François Mitterrand.

In 1981, Beauvoir gave an interview to publicize the relaunch of *Nouvelles questions féministes* in which she discussed how much a new anti-sexist law meant to her. Yvette Roudy, then Secretary of Women's Rights, was working on legislation concerning professional equality, and she wanted to complement this with a bill against sex-based discrimination. This would extend the anti-racist legislation to sexism and make it possible to fight against public advertisements that attacked women's dignity.

Beauvoir wanted it to be against the law to insult women, although she realized that legislation 'would not prevent women from leading struggles of their own against sexism'. She had seen, through her life, letters and editorial work, that women suffered a great deal of violence at the hands of men. But though this was the fact of the matter she was convinced that there was no 'unchangeable given' that made men violent. Rather, she claimed that, 'One is not born, but rather becomes, a man' – violence takes root in individual men in societies that tolerate sexism and discrimination.

Beauvoir did not like it that '[p]arts of our bodies are displayed on the city streets for the glory of this profit-driven society'. The manifesto of the League of Women's Rights claimed that women's bodies should not be used as merchandise; physical pleasure and sexual initiative should not be the preserve of men; that they would fight for the application of rights already won for women and pursue new ones. Advertisers, claiming to be heralds of freedom, denounced Beauvoir's proposal dismissively: she was at once a Puritan and a hypocrite. Didn't she realize that if her rules were implemented literature itself would have to be banned? – including her own?

Beauvoir's reasoned response was ignored: she was not attacking literature. She thought there were good grounds for attacking advertisements because 'instead of being *offered* to [individual] freedoms', they 'are *imposed* upon all eyes that are subjected to them, willingly or not'.[30] Some claimed that the anti-sexist law was revenge on men. But Beauvoir argued that its motivation was rather to change the cultural environment in which men became men so that there was less legitimation of their violence against women. She wanted to achieve this by prohibiting degrading images of women in: 'advertisements, pornography, literature. An anti-sexist law would allow us to publicly denounce each case of sexist discrimination'.[31] It would also, Beauvoir thought, help women develop reflexes against sexism, helping them to stand up against injustice and ill-treatment instead of taking it as 'just how it is', as just how men are – as women's lot.

Beauvoir and her fellow feminists were accused of being 'intellectuals with no contact with reality'. But they were doctors, lawyers, engineers, mothers – was this not reality? Underlying the public outcry Beauvoir saw two motivations: money and manipulation. The money argument is familiar enough in late capitalism not to require rehearsal. As for the manipulation, in Beauvoir's view, many men remained 'deeply convinced that woman is an object to manipulate and that they are the masters of this manipulation'.[32] She wanted women to be 'the eye that sees', for their perspective on the world to be articulated, heard and respected.

When Roudy founded the Commission on Women and Culture, Beauvoir was made its honorary chair. She was an active participant, and the group informally called itself 'the Commission Beauvoir'. She attended monthly meetings at the ministry headquarters, where they studied the structure of society in order to make concrete proposals to the government to improve women's situations. In 1982 François Mitterrand offered her the Legion of Honour, but she refused it. She was an engaged intellectual, not a cultural institution.

After twelve years, Claude Lanzmann was finally coming to the end of his film *Shoah*. It was a difficult film to make, and he relied heavily on Beauvoir's companionship and support: 'I needed to talk to her, to tell her of my uncertainties, my fears, my disappointments.' He came away from his conversations 'strengthened' on account of 'the unique and intensely moving way she had of listening, serious, solemn, open, utterly trusting'.[33] In the early years after the death of Sartre, Lanzmann saw her weariness of living. Several times during the making of the film he invited her to the studio where *Shoah* was being edited – she still liked to be involved in his projects, to see sections of the film in progress.

In 1982, President Mitterrand asked Lanzmann for a private screening of the first three hours. Beauvoir went with him to the Elysée Palace, watching the not-yet-subtitled scenes as Lanzmann shouted translations from the aisle. She wrote to Lanzmann the next day: 'I don't know if I'll still be alive when your film is released.' She would go on to write a front-page article in *Le Monde* when it was, and later the preface for the book *Shoah*. But the day after the presidential screening she sent Lanzmann her thoughts, in case she did not live to see the film released:

I have never read or seen anything that has so movingly and so grippingly conveyed the horror of the 'final solution'; nor anything that has brought to light so much evidence of the hellish mechanics of it. Placing himself on the side of the victims, of the executioners, of the witnesses and accomplices more innocent or more criminal than the others, Lanzmann has us live through countless aspects of an experience that, until now, I believe, had seemed to be inexpressible. This is a monument that will enable generations of mankind to understand one of the most malign and enigmatic moments of their history.[34]

Apart from notes like this one (which were written with half an eye on posterity) little private material is available from the end of Beauvoir's life. But over the 1980s she participated in several interviews. In one of them Alice Schwarzer asked her how she had succeeded in remaining independent alongside her relationship with Sartre. Her answer was that she always wanted her own career: 'I had dreams, not fantasies, but very bold dreams, things I knew I wanted to do, long before I met Sartre! To be happy, I owed it to myself to fulfil my life. And to me fulfilment meant work.'[35] In these interviews she revealed that she did have doubts about her relationship with Sartre during the affair with Dolores Vanetti, and she regretted that their relationship had caused so much suffering for the third parties in their lives. She had already readily admitted, in a public interview, that Sartre did not treat women well. He made her an exceptional case, a token – like she herself had when she was younger. But he also encouraged her like no one else – believing in her own potential even in times when she struggled to see it for herself. Neither of them would have become who they were if it weren't for their dialogue with each other – if it weren't for the sum of both their actions.

Large portions of her days were still dedicated to writing: she wrote prefaces and introductions for books she believed in, and wrote tenure references, encouraged activists, replied to correspondence. She gave financial support to feminist publishers and donated to women's shelters. At times she felt that her public reputation had become that of a 'sacred relic', she said, whose words were commands to younger generations of women who had the energy to take the next steps for change.[36]

Two years after Sartre's death, she was satisfied with her work, past and present, and her desire to travel had been rekindled. When she was still recovering Sylvie had suggested a trip to New York as a dangling carrot: and it worked. Since the 1940s Beauvoir had had ambivalent feelings about America: she found so much to adore about it and so much to detest. When she received the Sonning Prize for European Culture in 1983, it carried a cash award of $23,000 and she was ready for another adventure. So in July of that year she and Sylvie boarded the Concorde for New York. She did not want to be in the public eye, so careful precautions were made by her American editor at Pantheon Books. She met Stépha Gerassi and her son John, and some more recent friends like the feminist Kate Millett, but she wanted the trip to be restful and personal. She would give no lectures, take no notes.

Despite their efforts, when they checked in to the Algonquin Hotel in New York they were spotted almost immediately by a journalist from *The New Yorker*. He phoned her room and she told him in no uncertain terms that she did not do phone interviews. So he backed off and she and Sylvie visited museums unharassed: the Metropolitan, the Guggenheim, MOMA, and – Beauvoir's favourite – the Frick. They went to the top of the World Trade Center. They had dinner at Elaine's one night, and were introduced to fellow diners Woody Allen and Mia Farrow. After that they travelled through New England for six weeks, and she visited Kate Millett's Christmas-tree farm in Poughkeepsie, where Millett had started an all-female artists' commune. This farm was the setting for the only professional engagement of the trip: the filming of a conversation with Kate Millett for a TV series on *The Second Sex*. They returned to France in time for Sylvie to go back to teaching. Beauvoir brought back hordes of books.

In December of 1983 Beauvoir had a fall: Sylvie found her lying on her floor, and she had been there so long that she caught pneumonia.

She spent Christmas and most of January in the hospital, but was well enough at Easter to go to Biarritz. By summer she had recovered enough to travel further afield, so she and Sylvie flew to Budapest and drove around Hungary and Austria.

Beauvoir was still the head of *Les Temps Modernes* in 1985, although Claude Lanzmann was managing more and more of it. They met in her apartment and she read submissions, selected articles, and edited and proofread like she always had – she continued to attend meetings until a few weeks before her death. Claire Etcherelli remembered Beauvoir's 'physical presence, her strength, her authority, which inspired her to keep the journal alive'[37] as holding the committee together despite many storms, personal and political.

She was still engaging in feminist activism and giving interviews, expressing her hope that a new translation of *The Second Sex* would be released in English, 'An honest translation, with the philosophical

Figure 14 *A scene from Beauvoir's activist life: at the Women and the State Debate in Paris, 15 May 1984.*

dimension and with all the parts that Mr. Parshley judged pointless and which I consider to have a point.'[38] In conversation with Margaret Simons she clarified the sense in which she meant the confusing claim in *The Prime of Life* that she was not a philosopher:

> I'm not a philosopher in the sense that I'm not the creator of a system, I'm still a philosopher in the sense that I've studied a lot of philosophy, I have a degree in philosophy, I've taught philosophy, I'm infused with philosophy, and when I put philosophy into my books it's because that's a way for me to view the world and I can't allow them to eliminate that way of viewing the world.[39]

Centuries before Beauvoir, thinkers like Pascal and Kierkegaard rejected 'systematic' philosophers like Descartes and Hegel for forgetting that part of what it means to be human is that each person must live their life without knowing their future – craving a meaning that cannot be known in advance. Beauvoir, too, was committed to the view that because life can't be understood forward we feel anxiety about who we will become, for ourselves and in the eyes of others.[40] But for many of Beauvoir's French contemporaries, even Pascal and Kierkegaard were considered 'subphilosophical', not because they were female, clearly, but because they were religious. Beauvoir's early philosophical insights – and her concern to avoid the Scylla and Charybdis of egoism and devotion – were written in dialogue with many thinkers who might not be called 'philosophers' today for the same reason.[41]

In 1985 Beauvoir's health deteriorated. She put it down to the upcoming election in March 1986, but everyone could see that the whiskey was taking its toll. Her cirrhosis had made her belly so distended that she could not stand upright. Walking was painful, and friends stood by in agony as she pretended not to notice. Sylvie tried to dilute Beauvoir's whiskey, but now Beauvoir was the patient who rejected moderation: she just kept pouring more. Bost was not a virtuous influence in this respect so Sylvie appealed to Lanzmann, who thought it might distract Beauvoir to write the preface to the book version of *Shoah*. She agreed with pleasure – and she wrote the preface to another book, too – but she did not stop drinking.

At the beginning of 1986 Beauvoir was still conducting her meetings with friends, scholars and writers. Her only concession to age was that she now conducted them in a red bathrobe.

In February of 1986 she saw Hélène: Simone was walking poorly, but they went around a gallery together. She was characteristically encouraging of her sister's artistic endeavours: that year Hélène was looking forward to an exhibition of her art in California – at Stanford University, funded by the French Ministry for the Rights of Women. But the legislative elections of 16 March dictated otherwise: the minister for women, and the funds, were no longer available. Simone refused to countenance the idea that her sister wouldn't attend her own exhibition, and insisted on paying her way.[42]

On the evening of 20 March Simone de Beauvoir had stomach cramps. She thought it was the ham she ate for dinner, but the pain persisted long enough that Sylvie insisted on a visit to the hospital. After several days with no clear diagnosis they performed an exploratory surgery: apart from diabetes and damage to her arteries she had everything Sartre had: cirrhotic damage, fluid retention and pulmonary edema. After the surgery she developed pneumonia and was moved into intensive care. She was there for two weeks, during which she tried to convince her masseuse not to vote for the far-right nationalist Jean-Marie Le Pen.

Hélène and Lanzmann were both in California – she at her exhibition, he to receive an award – when they received the news. Simone was dead.[43] It was 4 p.m. on 14 April, eight hours short of the anniversary of Sartre's decease. She was 78 years old.

The next day, when her death was announced in *Le Monde*, its headline proclaimed: 'Her works: more popularization than creation.'[44]

17

Afterwords: What Will Become of Simone de Beauvoir?

We owe respect to the living; to the dead we owe only truth.[1]

VOLTAIRE

Le Monde was not alone in announcing Beauvoir's death – and setting the tone for her terrestrial afterlife – in sexist, disparaging, false terms. Obituaries in global newspapers and literary reviews noted that even in dying she followed Sartre, dutifully taking her proper place: second. Whereas some obituaries of Sartre made no mention whatsoever of Beauvoir, obituaries of Beauvoir never fail to mention him – sometimes at great length, dividing the column inches dedicated to her work into shockingly diminutive fractions.

The Times of London declared that Sartre was 'her guru'; that as a philosophy student Beauvoir was 'nominally the pupil of Brunschvicg, but in practice she was coached by two fellow students with whom she had *liaisons*, first René Maheu and then Sartre.'[2] In fact, she was *actually* the pupil of Brunschvicg, achieved her first philosophical successes without either of these men, coached Maheu and Sartre on Leibniz before their oral exam, and provided critical feedback on almost everything Sartre ever wrote.

In the *The New York Times* we read that 'Sartre encouraged her literary ambitions and was credited by her with pushing her into the investigation of women's oppression that led to the rage and accusation of "Le Seconde Sexe."' Sartre did encourage her literary ambitions; it is beyond dispute that she valued the 'incomparable friend of her thought'. But in fact, her book was called *Le deuxième sexe*, and she had been developing her own philosophy and analysis of women's oppression for years before writing it. *The Washington Post* got the title right, but also described her as Sartre's 'nurse', Sartre's 'biographer', Sartre's 'jealous' woman.[3]

One might hope for better justice in specialist literary reviews, but there too such hope is disappointed. The entire seven-page entry from the 1986 *Dictionary of Literary Biography Yearbook* on 'Simone de Beauvoir' is dedicated to both Sartre's and Beauvoir's lives. Sartre is the agent in this narrative, credited with making her feel 'intellectually dominated' and suggesting the idea for *The Second Sex*.[4]

In the *Revue de deux mondes* we read that, even in death, 'The hierarchy is respected: she is number two, behind Sartre'; 'because she is a woman, Simone remains a fan of the man she loves'. She is a fangirl, an empty, imaginationless receptacle: 'she had as little imagination as her inkwell'. Nor were these her only vices. Through her role in 'the family' she limited and impaired a great man: 'Sartre's life would have been different without this impermeable wall built little by little around their couple, without this carefully maintained revenge.'[5]

When Beauvoir's letters to Sartre were published in English in 1991, including the passages in which Beauvoir recounted her sexual encounters with Bienenfeld and Sorokine, she was called 'a vindictive, manipulative woman', not so much 'scandalous as vapid and self-centred.'[6] Claude Lanzmann objected to the letters' publication at the time, writing that Beauvoir and Sartre had been 'arrogant and competitive' letter writers in their youth, and

> that while Beauvoir might at times have thought ill of those closest to her, the idea of hurting them was unbearable to her: I never knew her to miss an engagement with her mother, with her sister, with interlopers if she had agreed to meet them, or with pupils she had known long ago out of loyalty to some shared idea of the past.[7]

Lanzmann's fears proved well founded; Beauvoir's words proved hurtful. After Deirdre Bair's biography made her identity public, Bianca Lamblin wrote a memoir of her own, *A Disgraceful Affair*, accusing Beauvoir of lifelong lies. Beauvoir was, in Lamblin's words, 'a prisoner of her past hypocrisy'.[8]

But it is utterly dissatisfying to reduce Beauvoir's life to its worst moments, to mummies of dead selves that she herself deeply regretted. She may have been a hostage to her own past, but she was also a prisoner of society's prejudice; her life is a testament to double standards that beset women in 'the feminine condition', and especially to the ways that women are punished when they dare to speak the truth as they see it – when they claim the power of being the 'eye that sees' and to find men's actions wanting.

Personally, philosophically and politically, Sartre did not escape her criticism: she thought he had blind spots, and published some of them for world to see too.[9] But, even so, she chose to love him.

Beauvoir was buried next to Sartre in the Montparnasse Cemetery, in her red turban, red bathrobe and Algren's ring. She was honoured by groups around the world, from the Socialist Party of Montparnasse to universities in America, Australia, Greece and Spain. At her funeral the crowd chanted the words of Elisabeth Badinter: 'Women, you owe her everything!'

They may have spoken with the hyperbole of grief, but Beauvoir was the first to admit that some women found her ideas 'upsetting'.[10] Within days of her death, Beauvoir's last preface was published: it opened a novel, *Mihloud*. The book was a love story between two men which raised questions about sexuality and power. Like many others Beauvoir lent her name to in this way, it told a story that was dangerous to make public: the Holocaust, the torture and rape of Algerian women, the struggles of feminism, or the alienation of a gifted lesbian – these were facets of humanity that many found difficult to look in the face.

At the time of her death Beauvoir had been a celebrity for forty years; loved and hated, vilified and idolized.[11] Then and since, famous chapters of her early life with Sartre have been used, *ad feminam*, to undermine her moral integrity as well as the philosophical, personal and political challenges of her work – especially *The Second Sex*. She had claimed that if men wanted to be ethical, they needed to acknowledge the ways that their actions contributed to the oppressive conditions for others in the world, and do better. And she had challenged women, too – to stop consenting to submit to the myth that to be a woman is to be for men. It is hard to flourish, as a human, when you're so relentlessly defined from without.

From within Beauvoir never saw herself as 'an idol'. In an interview with Alice Schwarzer Beauvoir said, 'I am Simone de Beauvoir for other people, not for myself.'[12] She knew that women were hungry for positive models to emulate; they often asked her why she hadn't created more positive heroes in her novels, instead of writing women who failed to live up to her feminist ideals. When readers claimed to see Beauvoir in her female characters,[13] they wondered: Did they fail to live up to her feminist ideals because Beauvoir herself had not?

Beauvoir responded that she found positive heroes 'horrifying' and books with positive heroes uninteresting. A novel, she said, 'is a problematic'. And, in Beauvoir's own words, so was her life:

The history of my life itself is a kind of problematic, and I don't have to give solutions to people and people don't have a right to wait for solutions from me. It is in this measure, occasionally, that what you call my celebrity – in short, people's attention – has bothered me. There is a certain demandingness that I find a little stupid, because it imprisons me, completely fixing me in a kind of feminist concrete block.[14]

During her lifetime readers rejected Beauvoir's ideas because of the way she lived her life: because she loved too many men, the wrong man, the right man in the wrong way (they didn't know about the women yet). They accused her of giving too little of herself or too much of herself, of being too feminist or not feminist enough. Beauvoir admitted that the way she treated others was not always above reproach. She clearly expressed regret at the suffering her relationship with Sartre caused *les tiers* – the contingent 'thirds'.

When Schwarzer asked Beauvoir about her claim that her relationship with Sartre was the greatest success of her life, she asked whether they had succeeded in having a relationship based on equality. Beauvoir said that the problem of equality never arose between them, because there was 'nothing of the oppressor' in Sartre.[15] It is curious here that she says, 'If [she] had loved someone other than Sartre', she would not have let herself be oppressed. Some have interpreted this comment to attribute her escape from domination to her professional autonomy; feminists have wondered if she is guilty of bad faith, if Sartre was 'the one sacrosanct area of her life to be protected even against her own critical attention'.[16]

There is no doubt, now, that she was critical of him – although many may not find her critical enough.

In the mid-1980s an American philosopher told the Beauvoir scholar Margaret Simons that she was angry at Beauvoir because she wrote 'we, we, we' in her autobiography. Where was *she*? 'She had completely disappeared.' But she hadn't disappeared. She used her voice. She said 'we' with it, and she said 'I', too – because she believed that 'one can be close to a man and be a feminist'.[17] One could, in fact, be close to several – men and women. She thought that the most important thing about her was her thoughts, and that Sartre was their incomparable friend. Beauvoir's reviewers called her derivative and imaginationless from without; even lovers told her her books were boring or too full of philosophy;[18] but Sartre was, for much of her life, her 'main source of encouragement',[19] an interlocutor in a matchless meeting of minds.

We will never know what it was like to be Beauvoir from within: the life lived cannot be resurrected from the life recounted. But from without, we must not forget the agency with which she struggled to become herself. In some cases, she chose to write overlooked instances of the word 'I'. In *Force of Circumstance*, she claims that she had a philosophy of being and nothingness before she met Sartre, the man who would become famous for writing *Being and Nothingness*. There was a 'basic confrontation of being and nothingness that *I* sketched at the age of twenty in my private diary, pursued through all my books and never resolved'.[20] And she also said that after *She Came to Stay*, something changed: 'I always had "something to say"'.[21]

In *All Said and Done* (1972) there is a passage in which Beauvoir says explicitly that she preferred sharing life with someone who mattered 'a great deal to her – usually with Sartre, sometimes with Sylvie'. She says outright that she would not distinguish between 'I' and 'we' because 'in fact, apart from a few short periods, I always had someone with me'.[22] In later life she described solitude as a 'form of death', and herself as coming back to life as she felt 'the warmth of human contact'.[23]

Beauvoir loved philosophy, but she wanted it to express 'palpable reality', to tear 'aside the cleverly woven web of our conventional self'.[24] In many cases, she chose literature as the best means of doing this because her characters could be brought to life in their contact with each other. Nietzsche thought that 'it is impossible to teach love',[25] but Beauvoir thought that she could *show* it. In her novels she gave concrete examples in which women and men suffered from a lack of reciprocity. And in *The Second Sex* she made explicitly philosophical claims: that to be ethical love must be reciprocal – lover and beloved must *both* be recognized as conscious and free, committed to each other's projects in life, and, in cases where their love was sexual, seen as sexual subjects – not objects.

When Rousseau scrutinized the history of 'civilization' for political purposes in his work *Discourse on the Origin of Inequality*, he did so in order to better outline the inequalities that existed between men. When Nietzsche turned to the past to illuminate the morality of the present in *On the Genealogy of Morality* he thought a 'revaluation of values' was needed in the wake of the 'death of God'. Beauvoir thought that a philosophical revaluation of *woman* was necessary, and that concrete freedom for women wouldn't be achieved without a revaluation of what 'civilization' called love.

When a philosopher like Plato uses a literary form, it is philosophy. When he speaks of love, it is philosophy – even when it comes from a context where pederasty is a cultural norm and discusses something as absurd as the story that all humans were once quadrupeds, that we have been divided from our other half, and now long to be reunited with our missing pair.[26]

Simone de Beauvoir's life became a symbol of success for generations of women who were no longer content to 'dream through men's dreams'.[27] She was 'the feminist voice of the twentieth century'[28] – a philosopher whose thinking demonstrably altered the course of legislation and many lives. And yet, on the centenary of her birth in 2008, *Le Nouvel Observateur* decided to honour her – a woman whose work included campaigning to make explicit images of women illegal – by publishing a photograph of her naked.

From within Beauvoir saw herself as a becoming that never stopped. She didn't believe that any single point in her life showed 'the' Simone de Beauvoir because 'there is no instant in a life where all moments are reconciled'.[29] All action carries the possibility of failure – and some failures only reveal themselves as failures after the fact. Time passes; dreams change; and the self is always beyond reach. The individual moments in Beauvoir's becoming were dramatically diverse. But if there's one thing to learn from the life of Simone de Beauvoir, it's this: No one becomes herself alone.

Notes

Introduction

1 DPS 266, 28 May 1927.

2 See Toril Moi, *Simone de Beauvoir: The Making of an Intellectual Woman*, 2nd edn, Oxford: Oxford University Press, 2008, p. 26.

3 Claude Jannoud, 'L'Œuvre: Une vulgarisation plus qu'une création', *Le Monde*, 15 April 1986.

4 Moi, *Simone de Beauvoir*, p. 27.

5 Beauvoir, 'Existentialism and Popular Wisdom', PW 218.

6 Sandrine Sanos, *Simone de Beauvoir: Creating a Feminist Existence in the World*, Oxford: Oxford University Press, 2017, p. 118.

7 SS 3.

8 DPS 57, 7 August 1926.

9 FC 288.

10 Henri Bergson, *Time and Free Will: An Essay on the Immediate Data of Consciousness*, New York: Dover, 2001, p. 178.

11 Ovid, *Tristia* III.iv.25, cited in Descartes (Descartes, Letter to Mersenne), April 1634, *Oeuvres de Descartes*, ed. Charles Adam and Paul Tannery, volume I, Paris: Cerf, 1897, pp. 285–6.

12 PL 22.

13 Annie Cohen-Solal, *Sartre: A Life*, London: Heinemann, 1987, p. 86.

14 http://www.bbc.com/culture/story/20171211-were-sartre-and-de-beauvoir-the-worlds-first-modern-couple

15 Quoted by Madeleine Gobeil in an interview with Simone de Beauvoir, 'The Art of Fiction No. 35', *Paris Review* 34 (Spring–Summer 1965).

16 Hazel Rowley, *Tête-à-tête: The Lives and Loves of Simone de Beauvoir and Jean-Paul Sartre*, London: Vintage, 2007, p. ix.

17 MDD 344.

18 Beauvoir, cited in Simone de Beauvoir, Margaret A. Simons and Jane Marie Todd, 'Two Interviews with Simone de Beauvoir', *Hypatia* 3(3) (1989): 13.

19 Alice Schwarzer, *Simone de Beauvoir Today: Conversations 1972–1982*, London: Hogarth Press, 1984, p. 13.

20 All publication dates given in this paragraph refer to the first French editions.

21 As Margaret Simons has noted, the English translation of Beauvoir's letters to Sartre did little to help this: it deleted a third of the material available in French. From November and December 1939 alone, thirty-eight references to Beauvoir's work on the novel *She Came to Stay* were cut. (See Margaret Simons, 'Introduction', PW 5.)

22 The letters are available for consultation at the Beinecke Rare Book & Manuscript Library at Yale University.

23 PL 8.

24 Robert D. Cottrell, *Simone de Beauvoir*, New York: Frederick Ungar, 1975, p. 95.

25 'Elle est incapable d'inventer, de s'oublier.' P. de Boisdeffre, 'LA REVUE LITTERAIRE: Deux morts exemplaires, un même refus: Jean Genet et Simone de Beauvoir', *Revue des deux mondes* (1986): 414–28.

26 SS 166.

27 DPS 77, 21 August 1926.

28 Bianca Lamblin, *A Disgraceful Affair*, trans. Julie Plovnick, Boston: Northeastern University Press, 1996 [Fr. 1993], p. 161.

29 *CJ*, 758, 2, 3, 4 September 1929, 'l'ami incomparable de ma pensée' (italics added).

30 SdB to Nelson Algren (NA), 8 August 1948, TALA 208.

31 Virginia Woolf, *A Room of One's Own*, in *A Room of One's Own/Three Guineas*, London: Penguin Classics, 2000, p. 32.

32 William Barrett, *Irrational Man: A Study in Existential Philosophy*, New York: Doubleday, 1958, see pp. 231–2.

33 'Simone De Beauvoir', *The Times* [London, England] 15 April 1986: 18. The Times Digital Archive. Online 24 March 2018.

34 Deirdre Bair, *Simone de Beauvoir: A Biography*, London: Jonathan Cape, 1990, p. 514.

35 https://www.the-tls.co.uk/articles/private/sartres-sex-slave/

36 Moi, *Simone de Beauvoir*, pp. 44–5.

37 Moi, *Simone de Beauvoir*, p. 39.

38 bell hooks, 'True Philosophers: Beauvoir and bell', in Shannon M. Mussett and William S. Wilkerson (eds), *Beauvoir and Western Thought from Plato to Butler*, Albany, NY: SUNY Press, 2012, p. 232.

39 Rowley, *Tête-à-tête*, p. 13.

40 Elizabeth Bachner, 'Lying and Nothingness: Struggling with Simone de Beauvoir's Wartime Diary, 1939–41', *Bookslut*, November 2008.

41 Richard Heller, 'The Self-centred Love of Madame Yak-yak', *The Mail on Sunday*, 1 December 1991, 35.

42 To the 1978 edition of *le Petit Robert*. See Preface to 'Everyday Sexism', Notes, FW 241.

43 bell hooks, 'Beauvoir and bell', p. 231.

44 Sarah Churchwell, *The Many Lives of Marilyn Monroe*, New York: Picador, 2005, p. 33.

45 François Mauriac, 'Demande d'enquête', *Le Figaro* (1949), 30 May. See Ingrid Galster, *Le Deuxième Sexe de Simone de Beauvoir*, Paris: Presse universitaire Paris-Sorbonne, 2004, p. 21. Beauvoir discusses the reaction to this chapter's publication in FC 197.

46 E.g., in Mill's discussion of impartiality and the command to 'love your neighbour as yourself' in chapter 2 of *Utilitarianism*, or Kant's discussion of the same command in section I of the *Groundwork for the Metaphysics of Morals*.

47 Laurie A. Rudman, Corinne A. Moss-Racusin, Julie E. Phelan and Sanne Nauts, 'Status Incongruity and Backlash Effects: Defending the Gender Hierarchy Motivates Prejudice against Female Leaders', *Journal of Experimental and Social Psychology* 48 (2012): 165–79.

48 For the psychology, see Z. Kunda and R. Sanitioso, 'Motivated Changes in the Self-concept', *Journal of Experimental Social Psychology* 25 (1989): 272–85; R. Sanitioso, Z. Kunda and G. T. Fong, 'Motivated Recruitment of Autobiographical Memories', *Journal of Personality and Social Psychology* 59 (1990): 229–41; R. Sanitioso and R. Wlordarski, 'In Search of Information that Confirms a Desired Self-perception: Motivated Processing of Social Feedback and Choice of Social Interactions', *Personality and Social Psychology Bulletin* 30 (2004): 412–22.

49 Voltaire, 'Première Lettre sur Oedipe' in *Oeuvres* (1785) vol. 1.

50 Carolyn Heilbrun, *Writing a Woman's Life*, London: The Women's Press, 1988, p. 30.

51 For example, psychoanalytic or Marxist biographies seek to achieve understanding of human beings through significant childhood experiences or economic and other social structures. See James Conant, 'Philosophy and Biography', lecture given at a symposium on 'Philosophy and Biography', 18 May 1999.

52 BO 39.

53 EA 20.

54 SS 88.

55 PC 120.

56 Bair, p. 13.

57 SdB to S, 24 April 1947, LS 451.

58 'A story I used to tell myself', UM 159.

59 DPS 297, 29 July 1927.

60 Schwarzer, *Simone de Beauvoir Today*, p. 86; DPS 296, 29 July 1927.

61 Virginia Woolf, 'Not One of Us', October 1927, CE IV, p. 20, cited in Hermione Lee, *Virginia Woolf*, London: Vintage, 1997, p. 773 n. 42.

Chapter 1

1 The original spelling on her birth certificate was 'Simonne'.

2 Although the family address was on the 103 boulevard du Montparnasse, according to Hélène de Beauvoir the apartment was on the Raspail side of the building. See HdB to Deirdre Bair, cited in Bair, p. 620 n. 18.

3 Bair wrote that the Bertrand de Beauvoirs could trace their history to the twelfth century, to a co-founder of the University of Paris and disciple of Saint Anselm, and that they considered themselves minor nobility. In my interview with Sylvie Le Bon de Beauvoir she denied this, corroborating the version Hélène de Beauvoir gives in *Souvenirs* (HdB p. 14). For Beauvoir's childhood we rely on MDD, VED, Bair, Hélène de Beauvoir's memoir, *Souvenirs*, Paris: Séguier, 1987, and Sylvie Le Bon de Beauvoir's 'Chronologie' in MPI.

4 MDD 37.

5 See Sylvie Le Bon de Beauvoir, 'Chronologie', MPI lv; for Bair's account (reliant on interviews with SdB and HdB) of the parents' meeting, see Bair, pp. 27–30.

6 Simone de Beauvoir, cited in Bair, p. 620 n. 19.

7 MDD 37.

8 MDD 42.

9 HdB, *Souvenirs*, p. 13.

10 MDD 75, 24, 25.

11 HdB, *Souvenirs*, p. 16.

12 MDD 23.

13 MDD 36, 51.

14 HdB, *Souvenirs*, p. 44.

15 HdB, *Souvenirs*, p. 58.

16 MDD 43.

17 SLBdB, 'Chronologie', 1915, MPI lvii. In *Memoirs of a Dutiful Daughter* she did not mention this story, instead writing that the 89-page *La famille cornichon* was her first (October 1916, at age 8). Other stories from childhood survived but have not been published, including one she dedicated to her sister, *Histoire de Jeannot Lapin* (written in 1917–18, fifty-four pages in Beauvoir's handwriting); 'contes et histories variées' (1918–19, nineteen pages); *En vacances. Correspodance de deux petites amies* (June 1919, twenty-three pages).

18 MDD 61.

19 In MDD she was referred to as Elisabeth Mabille to protect her identity.

20 Hélène de Beauvoir, cited in Bair, p. 133.

21 MDD 114.

22 DPS 67, 16 August 1926.

23 VED 33.

24 MDD 38.

25 MDD 41, 82.

26 MDD 41.

27 Quoted in Bair, p. 47.

Chapter 2

1 MDD 72.

2 MDD 106.

3 MDD 16.

4 MDD 71.

5 Bair, p. 51.

6 Hélène de Beauvoir, cited in Bair, p. 58.

7 MDD 97.

8 MDD 131.

9 VED 35.

10 Thion de la Chaume, cited in HdB, *Souvenirs*, p. 27.

11 MDD 66.

12 MDD 29.

13 MDD 30.

14 MDD 55.

15 *Entretiens avec Simone de Beauvoir* [1965], in Francis Jeanson, *Simone de Beauvoir ou l'entreprise de vivre*, Paris: Seuil, 1966, cited in Deguy and Le Bon de Beauvoir, *Simone de Beauvoir: Ecrire la liberté*, Paris: Gallimard, 2008, p. 99.

16 MDD 121.

17 MDD 36.

18 SLBdB, 'Chronologie', MPI lix. Françoise de Beauvoir gave Simone a copy in July 1919.

19 1965 Paris Review interview. https://www.theparisreview.org/interviews/4444/simone-de-beauvoir-the-art-of-fiction-no-35-simone-de-beauvoir

20 MDD 85.

21 MDD 109.

22 When Beauvoir read the sequel in which Laurie married Amy she threw the book across the room; when Jo March married an old professor and 'corked up her inkstand' in order to start a school, Beauvoir wrote that 'his intrusion' upset her (MDD 104–5) [she refers to it in SS too].

23 DPS 63, 12 August 1926.

24 MDD 140.

25 See VED 36–7.

26 MDD 166.

27 MDD 131.

28 BO 10–11.

29 HdB, *Souvenirs*, p. 29.

30 Bair, p. 55.

31 VED 35.

32 MDD 57.

33 SS 320.

34 MDD 92.

35 See Bair, pp. 79–80.

36 SS 378.

37 HdB, *Souvenirs*, p. 36.

38 MDD 176.

39 MDD 121.

40 See, e.g., CJ 744, 3 August 1929.

41 See MDD 152.

42 Félicien Challaye to Amélie Gayraud, in Amélie Gayraud, *Les Jeunes filles d'aujourd hui*, Paris: G. Oudin, 1914, pp. 281–3.

43 Bair, p. 90.

44 MDD 157.

45 MDD 158.

46 See MDD 101–2, 107.

47 MDD 160.

48 MDD 160.

49 Claude Bernard, *Introduction to the Study of Experimental Medicine*, 85, cited in Margaret Simons and Hélène N. Peters, 'Introduction' to 'Analysis of Bernard's *Introduction*', Beauvoir, PW 18.

50 Bernard, *Introduction to the Study of Experimental Medicine*, 37, 38, 39, 73, cited in Margaret Simons and Hélène N. Peters, 'Introduction' to 'Analysis of Bernard's *Introduction*', Beauvoir, PW 18.

51 In French, 'On ne naît pas libre, il le devient'. These words are cited in Beauvoir's textbook: Charles Lahr, S.J., *Manuel de philosophie résumé du cours de philosophie*, Paris: Beauchesne, 1920, p. 366. The same phrase ('one isn't born, but rather becomes, free') is often attributed to the poet Rimbaud, and taken to pithily summarize Spinoza's philosophy of freedom. See, e.g., Alain Billecoq, 'Spinoza et l'idée de tolérance', *Philosophique* 1(1998): Spinoza, pp. 122–42.

52 See Alfred Fouillée, *La Liberté et le déterminisme*, 3rd edn, Paris: Alcan, 1890. Beauvoir wrote in her *Mémoires* that Fouillée's *Les Idées-forces* was assigned reading in her philosophy class, but it is unclear which book she is referring to: Fouillée published three essays on 'idées-forces' between 1890–1907: *L'Évolutionisme des idées-forces* (1890), *La psychologie des idées-forces* (1893) and *La Morale des idées-forces* (1907). See MDD 157; MPI 146.

53 MDD 160.

54 Moi, *Simone de Beauvoir*, p. 42; HdB, *Souvenirs*, p. 67.

55 See SLBdB, 'Chronologie', MPI lxi.

56 MDD 208.

57 See DPS 58–61, 66, especially 16 August 1926.

58 Simone de Beauvoir, *Carnets* 1927, unpublished holograph MS, Bibliothèque Nationale, Paris, 54–5; cited in Margaret A. Simons, 'Introduction' to 'Literature and Metaphysics', PW 264.

59 PL 265–6.

60 DPS 55, 6 August 1926.

61 DPS 55, 6 August 1926.

62 DPS 63, 12 August 1926.

63 DPS 63, 12 August 1926.

64 See DPS 65, 63.

65 DPS 67, 16 August 1926.

66 SLBdB, 'Chronologie', MPI lxi.

67 DPS 68, 17 August 1926.

68 See DPS 112, 12 October 1926.

69 DPS 162, 5 November, 1926.

70 DPS 164, 5 November 1926.

71 See Bair, p. 112.

72 See Elizabeth Fallaize, *The Novels of Simone de Beauvoir*, London: Routledge, 1990, p. 84.

73 MDD 171–3.

74 DPS 232, 20 April 1927.

75 MDD 195.

76 DPS 246–8, 6 May 1927.

77 DPS 246–8, 6 May 1927.

78 MDD 82. See Isaiah 6:8. In Genesis 22:1 Abraham also uses the same words, in the passage famously discussed by Kant and Kierkegaard about the ethics of the Akedah.

79 MDD 188.

80 MDD 193.

81 DPS 265, 28 May 1927.

82 DPS 277, 7 July 1927.

83 DPS 279, 10 July 1927.

84 DPS 274, 29 June 1927.

85 MDD 158.

86 See Bair, p. 119.

87 DPS 163, 5 November 1927.

88 The category that Sartre is thought to have 'added' to the Hegelian in-itself and for-itself, the *pour autrui*, is in fact found in the works of Alfred Fouillée, whom both Sartre and Beauvoir read in their teens. (See Herbert Spiegelberg, *The Phenomenological Movement: A Historical Introduction*, volume 2, The Hague: Springer, 2013, 472–3.) And Beauvoir's 'within' and 'without' distinction may be indebted to Bergson's metaphysics, which employs a similar distinction (see *The Creative Mind: An Introduction to Metaphysics*, trans. Mabelle L. Anderson, New York: Citadel Press, 1992).

89 See Bair, p. 124.

Chapter 3

1   CJ 255–62, 4 January 1927.

2   See George Pattison and Kate Kirkpatrick, *The Mystical Sources of Existentialist Thought*, Abingdon: Routledge, 2018, especially chapters 3 and 4.

3   MDD 234–43.

4   MDD 239.

5   See Bair, p. 124.

6   MDD 262.

7   DPS 277, 7 July 1927.

8   MDD 314. The 'personality' was a concept discussed by Henri Bergson and others Beauvoir was reading during this period. In *Time and Free Will*, Bergson wrote that 'we are free when our acts spring from our whole personality, when they express it, when they have that indefinable resemblance to it which one sometimes finds between the artist and his work'. Beauvoir would go on to write a thesis on the philosophy of Leibniz for the Diplôme d'Études Superieures under the supervision of Léon Brunschvicg.

Leibniz had written that the *place of the other* [*la place d'autrui*] is the true point of perspective in politics and in ethics. See 'La Place d'autrui est le vrai point de perspective' in Jean Baruzi, *Leibniz : Avec de nombreux textes inédits* (Paris: Bloud et cie, 1909), p. 363.

9 MDD 265.

10 DPS 277, 7 July 1927.

11 To my knowledge, the thesis did not survive; this was confirmed in conversation by Sylvie le Bon de Beauvoir and Jean-Louis Jeannelle.

12 MDD 295.

13 Bair, p. 124.

14 MDD 137.

15 MDD 138.

16 MDD 138.

17 CJ 771, 'résumé de ma vie'.

18 MDD 74.

19 MDD 125.

20 MDD 132.

21 MDD 161.

22 HdB, *Souvenirs*, p. 39.

23 HdB, *Souvenirs*, p. 43.

24 MDD 41.

25 MDD 138.

26 MDD 141.

27 DPS 262, 21 May 1927.

28 DPS 284, 18 July 1927.

29 It is strange that Beauvoir associates 'reason' with men here, and 'heart' with women, because in French philosophy there is a tradition according to which the 'heart' is a separate faculty of knowing. The 'heart', as Blaise Pascal famously put it, 'has its reasons which reason does not know', namely, reasons that move us by intuition or desire, not deduction.

30 Jules Lagneau, *De l'existence de Dieu*, Paris: Alcan, 1925, pp. 1–2, 9. Lagneau claimed that rational arguments for God's existence were bound to be less successful than a 'moral proof' rooted in the human desire for perfection.

31 DPS 289, 20 July 1927.

32 DPS 299, 1 August 1927.

33 See CJ 733, 20 July 1929.

34 DPS 303, 304, 5 and 6 August 1927.

35 DPS 311, 7 September 1927.

36 See 'Notes for a Novel', a manuscript dated to 1928, in UM 363–4.

37 'libre de se choisir', 'Notes for a Novel', UM 355.

38 Cited by Jean Lacroix, *Maurice Blondel: Sa vie, son oeuvre, avec un exposé de sa philosophie* (Paris: Presses Universitaires de France, 1963), p. 33.

39 'Notes for a Novel', UM 367.

40 DPS 315, 3 October 1927.

41 This letter is quoted in Bair, p. 137.

42 See MDD 349–60.

43 Cited in MDD 354.

Chapter 4

1 MDD 323.

2 MDD 313.

3 In French, 'la douceur d'être femme'. Résumé de September 1928–1929, CJ 766.

4 Sheila Rowbotham claims that Beauvoir 'began an affair' ('Foreword' to SS 12); Fullbrook and Fullbrook (2008) draw inferences about their sexual intimacy that I do not take to be warranted by Beauvoir's texts. See Edward Fullbrook and Kate Fullbrook, *Sex and Philosophy: Rethinking de Beauvoir and Sartre*, London: Continuum, 2008.

5 Bair, p. 129.

6 MDD 321.

7 SLBdB, 'Chronologie', MPI lxv.

8 CJ 704, 22 June 1929.

9 CJ 709, 25 June 1929.

10 Cited in MDD 331. The original, in her diaries, can be found in CJ 707, 25 June 1929.

11 MDD 331–2.

12 Bair, pp. 144, 142–3.

13 HdB, *Souvenirs*, p. 90.

14 A 245.

15 Sartre, Jean-Paul, with Michel Contat and Alexandre Astruc, *Sartre by Himself*, New York: Urizen Books, 1978, pp. 21–2.

16 MDD 334.

17 See CJ 720, Monday 8 July 1929.

18 See CJ 721, 10 July 1929.

19 Sartre, Jean-Paul, with Michel Contat and Alexandre Astruc, *Sartre by Himself*, New York: Urizen Books, 1978, p. 23. See also CJ 723, Thursday 11 July 1929.

20 MDD 337.

21 CJ 724, 12 July 1929.

22 CJ 727, 14 July 1929.

23 CJ 730–1, 16 July 1929.

24 MMD 339.

25 CJ 731, 17 July 1929.

26 CJ 731, 17 July 1929.

27 *Le Nouvel Observateur*, 21 March 1976, 15; cited in Gerassi, *Jean-Paul Sartre: Hated Conscience of His Century*, vol. 1, London: University of Chicago Press, 1989, p. 91.

28 14 July 1929 journal entry, *Zaza: Correspondence et carnets d'Elisabeth Lacoin (1914–29)*, Paris: Seuil, 1991, pp. 304, 367.

29 CJ 731, 17 July 1929.

30 CJ 734, 22 July 1929.

31 CJ 738–9, 27 July 1929.

32 See Jean-Paul Sartre, *Écrits de jeunesse*, Paris: Gallimard, 1990, 293 ff.

33 CJ 740, 29 July 1929.

34 CJ 731, 17 July 1929; MDD 343–4.

35 MDD 344.

36 Bair, pp. 145–6; FF 16.

37 CJ 734, 22 July 1929.

38 Maurice de Gandillac, cited in Cohen-Solal, *Sartre*, p. 116.

39 Moi, 2008, p. 37.

40 Moi, 2008, pp. 44–5.

41 MDD 343.

42 Moi, 2008, p. 71.

43 Ralph Waldo Emerson, 'Considerations by the Way', from *Complete Works*, vol. 6, 'The Conduct of Life', 1904.

44 CJ 734, 22 July 1929.

Chapter 5

1 CJ 744, 3 August 1929.

2 Bair, p. 148.

3 CJ 734, 22 July 1929.

4 CJ 749, 8 August 1929.

5 Letter from Hélène de Beauvoir, cited in Bair, p. 148.

6 See CJ 749–50.

7 CJ 753.

8 CJ 756.

9 CJ 757.

10 CJ 757.

11 CJ 757.

12 CJ 758, 2, 3, 4 September 1929, 'l'ami incomparable de ma pensée'.

13 CJ 759. 2, 3, 4, September 1929.

14 DPS 76, 21 August 1926.

15 CJ 760, 6, 7, 8 September 1929.

16 CJ 762, 10 September 1929.

17 Gerassi, *Jean-Paul Sartre*, p. 90. Maheu confirmed that he had been Beauvoir's first lover in another interview with Gerassi; see Bair, p. 628.

18 PL 62.

19 CJ 763.

20 Alice Schwarzer, *After the Second Sex: Conversations with Simone de Beauvoir*, trans. Marianne Howarth, New York: Pantheon Books, 1984, p. 84.

Chapter 6

1 VED 40.

2 PL 12. SLBdB, 'Chronologie', MPI lxvi.

3 WT 50.

4 PL 14.

5 CJ 789.

6 CJ 795.

7 CJ 788, 24 September 1929.

8 CJ 783, 20 September 1929.

9 The distinction is attributed to Sartre in PL 19; for its use in the diaries see CJ 801–2, 14 October 1929.

10 DPS 274, 29 June 1927.

11 PL 22.

12 PL 24.

13 PL 27.

14 PL 25.

15 CJ 801–2.

16 CJ 807.

17 CJ 808, 23 October 1929.

18 CJ 808, 814.

19 PL 15–16.

20 CJ 815, 3 November 1929.

21 CJ 825, 12 December 1929.

22 CJ 824, 12 December 1929.

23 CJ 828, 13 December 1929.

24 Maheu, copied in SdB to Sartre, 6 January 1930, LS 3.

25 CJ 824, 12 December 1929.

26 PL 52–3.

27 CJ 839, 9 June 1930.

28 CJ 839, 9 June 1930.

29 HdB, *Souvenirs*, pp. 71, 96.

30 For Beauvoir's debt to Schopenhauer see Christine Battersby, 'Beauvoir's Early Passion for Schopenhauer: On Becoming a Self', forthcoming.

31 PL 52.

32 CJ 839.

33 CJ 842, 6 September 1930.

34 CJ 842, 6 September 1930.

35 CJ 814–15.

36 Sartre to Simone Jollivet, undated (1926), in *Witness to My Life*, pp. 16–17.

37 PL 40.

38 PL 41.

39 PL 42. See also MDD 343–5.

40 MDD 145.

41 CJ 827.

42 SS 710.

43 PL 70–74.

44 PL 47.

45 PL 61.

46 CJ 848–9, 31 October 1930.

47 CJ 848–9, 31 October 1930.

48 PL 59.

49 PL 51.

50 PL 54.

51 FC 287.

52 Cohen-Solal, *Sartre*, p. 43.

53 PL 82.

54 PL 71.

55 PL 56.

56 PL 57.

57 PL 76.

58 PL 78.

59 PL 88.

60 Bair, p. 177.

61 PL 94.

62 PL 95.

63 PL 80, 101.

64 PL 106

65 Bair, p. 176.

66 Colette Audry, 'Portrait de l'écrivain jeune femme', *Biblio* 30(9), November 1962: 3–5.

67 Bair, p. 173, citing an interview with Audry.

68 PL 128.

69 PL 128.

70 Cited in Bair, p. 201.

71 PL 16.

72 PL 134.

73 PL 129.

74 Jean-Louis Viellard-Baron claims outright that what would later be called the 'phenomenological approach' in French philosophy and the study of religion is what Bergson called 'concrete metaphysics'. See 'Présentation' to Jean Baruzi, *L'Intelligence Mystique*, Paris: Berg, 1985, p. 16.

75 See DPS 58–61, 66 especially 16 August 1926.

76 Anon. 'Views and Reviews', *New Age* 1914 (15/17): 399. My thanks to Esther Herring for bringing this to my attention.

77 PL 143.

78 PL 145.

79 PL 17, 18.

80 PL 15.

81 SLBdB, 'Chronologie', MPI lxx. On the Nozière affair, see Sarah Maza, *Violette Nozière: A Story of Murder in 1930s Paris*, Los Angeles: University of California Press, 2011.

82 PL 149.

83 PL 181.

84 SLBdB, 'Chronologie', MPI lxxii–lxxiii.

85 See Cohen-Solal, *Sartre*, pp. 99–100. Jean-Pierre Boulé, *Sartre, Self-formation, and Masculinities*, Oxford: Berghahn, 2005, p. 165.

86 PL 184.

87 PL 186.

88 Cohen-Solal, *Sartre*, p. 100.

89 PL 153.

90 PL 162.

91 WD 87.

92 Jean-Paul Sartre, *War Diaries*, trans. Quintin Hoare, London: Verso, 1984, p. 76, quoting Rodolphe Töpffer.

93 Nicolas of Cusa and many others called God 'the Absolute'; see WD 77; PL 207.

94 PL 107.

95 PL 206–9.

96 PL 210.

97 PL 213.

98 SdB to Sartre, 28 July 1935, LS 6–7.

99 PL 212.

100 PL 222.

101 See Eliane Lecarme-Tabone, 'Simone de Beauvoir's "Marguerite" as a Possible Source of Inspiration for Jean-Paul Sartre's "The Childhood of a Leader"', trans. Kevin W. Gray, in Christine Daigle and Jacob Golomb, *Beauvoir & Sartre: The Riddle of Influence*, Bloomington: Indiana University Press, 2009.

102 See Jean-Louis Jeannelle and Eliane Lecarme-Tabone, 'Introduction', MPI x.

Chapter 7

1 HdB, *Souvenirs*, p. 115.

2 Julia Kristeva and Philippe Sollers, *Marriage as a Fine Art*, trans. Lorna Scott Fox, New York: Columbia University Press, 2016, p. 6.

3 Although she changed the date to 1917 on her marriage certificate at the *mairie*. See Hazel Rowley, *Tête-à-tête*, p. 59.

4 PL 165.

5 PL 166.

6 WML 249, SdB to Sartre, 24 January 1940.

7 John Gerassi interview with Olga Kosakiewicz, 9 May 1973, Gerassi collection at Yale.

8 PL 218–19; WML, S to SdB, 3 May 1937.

9 PL 220.

10 PL 220.

11 Beauvoir, 'Jean-Paul Sartre', PW 232.

12 PL 221.

13 Simone de Beauvoir, interview with Madeleine Gobeil, 'The Art of Fiction No. 35', *Paris Review* 34 (Spring–Summer 1965).

14 Simone de Beauvoir, cited in Bair, p. 194.

15 Cited in Rowley, p. 357: SdB to Olga, 6 September 1935; Sylvie Le Bon de Beauvoir archives.

16 PL 226.

17 PL 239.

18 PL 261.

19 PL 246.

20 PL 260.

21 PL 260.

22 DPS 267, 3 June 1927.

23 Interview with Deirdre Bair, cited in Bair, p. 200.

24 PL 276–7.

25 Bair, p. 203.

26 PL 288, 290.

27 PL 315.

28 PL 316.

29 SdB to S, 10 September 1937, in LS 9.

30 Quoted in *Nouvelle Revue Française*, January 1970, p. 78.

31 Sylvie Le Bon de Beauvoir, 'Avant-propos' to *Correspondences croisées*, p. 8.

32 Cited in PL 327.

33 Bair, p. 197.

34 See Sarah Hirschman, 'Simone de Beauvor: professeur de lycée', *Yale French Studies* 22 (1958–9), cited in Jacques Deguy and Sylvie Le Bon de Beauvoir, *Simone de Beauvoir: Ecrire la liberté*, Paris: Gallimard, 2008.

35 Lamblin, *A Disgraceful Affair*, p. 18; Jacqueline Gheerbrant and Ingrid Galster, 'Nous sentions un petit parfum de soufre …' *Lendemains* 94 (1999): 42.

36 SdB to Bost, 28 November 1938, CC 136.

37 SdB to Sartre, 19 January 1940, LS 262.

38 Lamblin, *A Disgraceful Affair*, p. 25.

39 Bianca wrote a book about their relationship, *A Disgraceful Affair*, under her married name, Bianca Lamblin, after her agreement with Beauvoir (never to reveal her name) was broken by the publication of Deirdre Bair's biography (see pp. 8–9 for Lamblin's reasons for writing after so many years).

40 In an interview with Alice Schwarzer, see Schwarzer, *Simone de Beauvoir Today*, p. 112.

41 See Lamblin, *A Disgraceful Affair*, pp. 6, 25.

42 Lamblin, *A Disgraceful Affair*, pp. 6, 9.

43 Lamblin, *A Disgraceful Affair*, pp. 8–9.

44 Lamblin, *A Disgraceful Affair*, p. 171.

45 Lamblin, *A Disgraceful Affair*, pp. 6–7.

46 WML, undated, Sunday July 1938, p. 145.

47 SdB to Sartre, 15 July 1938, LS 16.

48 SdB to Sartre, 27 July 1938, LS 21 (translation modified).

49 Bost to SdB, 6 August 1938, CC 52.

50 CC 74 and passim.

51 Bost to SdB, 3 August 1938, CC 47.

52 SdB to Bost, 30 July 1938, CC 33.

53 SdB to Bost, 22 August 1938, CC 57.

54 SdB to Bost, 21 September 1938 CC 86; SdB to Bost, 27 August 1938, CC 62.

55 Sylvie Le Bon de Beauvoir, Avant-propos to CC 12.

56 SdB to Sartre, 6 July 1939, LS 30.

57 SdB to Bost, 28 August 1938, CC 64.

58 Bost to SdB, 13 September 1938, CC 79.

59 SdB to Bost, 21 September 1938, CC 84.

60 SdB to NA, 8 August 1948, TALA 209.

61 SdB to Bost, 25 August 1938, CC 59.

62 SdB to Bost, 2 September 1938, CC 69.

63 SdB to Bost, 28 November 1938, CC 136.

64 See Lamblin, *A Disgraceful Affair*, p. 5.

65 Lamblin, *A Disgraceful Affair*, p. 39.

66 SdB to Bost, 5 February 1939, CC 233.

67 'what kind of reality does the consciousness of another have', SdB to Bost, 24 May 1939, CC 373.

68 Bost to SdB, 25 May 1939, CC 376.

69 SdB to Bost, 4 June 1939, CC 386.

70 Bost to SdB, 7 June 1939, CC 391.

71 SdB to Bost, 8 June 1939, CC 397.

72 PL 319–20.

Chapter 8

1 WD 40, 2 September 1939.

2 Bair, p. 201.

3 WD 51, 5 September 1939.

4 WD 85, 3 October 1939.

5 André Gide, *The Journals of André Gide*, trans. Justin O'Brien, New York: Knopf, 1948, vol. II: 1914–27, p. 91, 16 October 1914.

6 WD 61, 14 September 1939.

7 WD 63–70, 16–19 September 1939.

8 WD 73, 20 September 1939.

9 WD 75, 22 September 1939.

10 WML 275, 2 October 1939.

11 Jean-Paul Sartre, *Carnets de la drôle de guerre*, Paris: Gallimard, 1995, pp. 116–21, 10 and 11 October 1939. This 1995 edition includes the first notebook, covering September–October 1939, which was omitted from the first French and English editions.

12 WD 105, 15 October 1939.

13 WD 120, 20 October 1939.

14 WD 86, 4 October 1939.

15 WD 98, 11 October 1939.

16 WD 119, 29 October 1939.

17 Sartre to SdB, 30 October 1939, WML 322–3 .

18 WD 129–30, 2 November 1939.

19 SdB to Algren, 8 August 1948, TALA 208.

20 WD 132–3, 3 November 1939.

21 See WD 109 for the commendation.

22 WD 143, 147, 9–12 November 1939.

23 See Annabelle Martin Golay, *Beauvoir intime et politique: La fabrique des Mémoires*, Villeneuve d'Ascq: Presses Universitaires du Septentrion, 2013, p. 147.

24 WD 144, 10 November 1939.

25 WD 147, 11 November 1939.

26 See WD 147–9.

27 WD 157, 16 November 1939; WD 159.

28 WD 176–7, 2 December 1939.

29 WD 192, 14 December 1939. For Marie Ville's comments see WD 187. Marie Ville is called Marie Girard or 'the Moon Woman' in the memoirs and diaries.

30 SdB to Sartre, 11 December 1939, LS 206.

31 SdB to Sartre, 14 December 1939. *Lettres à Sartre*, p. 351 (French edition).

32 WD 192, 13 December 1939.

33 Note that in this letter there is no mention of having been loved this way by Olga. SdB to Sartre, 21 December 1939, LS 223.

34 WD 210, 30 December 1939.

35 WD 210, 30 December 1939.

36 SdB to Sartre, 14 December 1939. *Lettres à Sartre*, p. 350. In her diary the same day she wrote: 'I don't know how he is going to give a content to his ethics' (14 December 1939, WD 192).

37 Beauvoir, cited in Bair, p. 270.

38 SdB to Sartre, 12 January 1940, LS 252.

39 See Lamblin, *A Disgraceful Affair*, p. 90.

40 See WD 217–20.

41 Sartre to SdB, 12 January 1940, QM 25.

42 SdB to Sartre, 14 January 1940, LS 255.

43 Sartre to SdB, 16 January 1940, QM 31.

44 Sartre to SdB, 17 January 1940, QM 33.

45 SdB to Sartre, 19 January 1940, LS 261.

46 Sartre to SdB, 18 February 1940, QM 61.

47 Sartre to SdB, 19 February 1940, QM 64.

48 SdB to Bost, 5 February 1939, CC 234.

49 SdB to Sartre, 18 February 1940, LS 277.

50 Sartre to SdB, 29 February 1940, QM 87–8.

51 SdB to Sartre, 4 March 1940, in LS 285.

52 Lamblin, *A Disgraceful Affair*, p. 9.

53 Lamblin, *A Disgraceful Affair*, p. 86.

54 SdB to Sartre, 27 February 1940, LS 279.

55 Sartre to SdB, 28 February 1940, QM 85.

56 SdB to Sartre, 1 March 1940, LS 282.

57 SdB to Sartre, 4 March 1940, LS 285.

58 See LS 311.

59 SLBdB, 'Chronologie', MPI lxxix.

60 Sartre to SdB, 29 May 1940, QM 206.

61 SdB to Sartre, 11 July 1940, LS 312.

62 SdB to Sartre, 11 July 1940, LS 315.

63 For more see Ursula Tidd, *Simone de Beauvoir*, London: Reaktion, 2009, p. 70.

64 Bair, pp. 242–3.

65 Sandrine Sanos, *Simone de Beauvoir*, p. 88.

66 Simone de Beauvoir, *La Force de l'âge*, Paris: Gallimard, 1960, p. 549.

67 PL 456–7.

68 PL 456–8. See also WD 304–9.

69 WD 304, 6 July 1940.

70 Lamblin, *A Disgraceful Affair*, p. 89.

71 Lamblin, *A Disgraceful Affair*, pp. 94, 92.

72 WD 318, 19 November 1940.

73 WD 320, 9 January 1941.

74 WD 320, 21 January 1941.

75 VED 104.

76 VED 31.

77 VED 15.

78 VED 42.

79 Sylvie Le Bon de Beauvoir, 'Chronologie', MPI lxxxiii.

80 Homosexuality was decriminalized in France in the 1790s. But on 6 August 1942, the Vichy Government introduced a law in the Penal Code increasing the age of consent for homosexual relations to 21 – it was 13 for heterosexual ones but this would be increased to 15 in 1945. (Penal Code article 334 [moved to article 331 on 8 February 1945], ordonnance 45–190, Provisional Government of the French Republic.)

81 See Ingrid Galster, *Beauvoir dans tout ses états*, Paris: Tallandier, 2007.

82 Although she may have begun earlier, at least by the 1942–43 academic year at the Lycée Camille Sée, Beauvoir taught her students phenomenology. One of her students, Geneviève Sevel, described her courses as 'united by the perspective of phenomenology', and expressed gratitude to Beauvoir 'for having introduced [her] so early and with such an intellectual talent to the thought of Husserl and Heidegger', which was not yet taught in French universities. Geneviève Sevel, 'Je considère comme une grande chance d'avoir pu recevoir son enseignement', *Lendemains* 94 (1999): 48.

83 See SdB to Sartre, 20 January 1944, LS 380.

84 Ingrid Galster, 'Simone de Beauvoir et Radio-Vichy: A propos de quelques scenarios retrouvés', *Romanische Forschungen* 108. Bd. H. 1/2 (1996): 112–32.

85 See LS 384 n. 320; 'Chronologie', MPI lxxxi.

Chapter 9

1 WD 320, 21 January 1941.

2 PL 434.

3 SCTS 343.

4 PL 340.

5 SCTS 6–7.

6 Angela Carter, 'Colette', *London Review of Books* 2(19) 2 October 1980: 15–17.

7 Edward Fullbrook and Kate Fullbrook, *Sex and Philosophy*, London: Continuum, 2008, 79 & passim.

8 PL 434.

9 See VED 68.

10 SCTS 108.

11 SCTS 17.

12 SCTS 16.

13 SCTS 158.

14 SCTS 159.

15 See SCTS 124, 207, 297, 337.

16 SCTS 244.

17 Claude Francis and Fernande Gontier, *Les écrits de Simone de Beauvoir*, Paris: Gallimard, 1979, p. 16. See SCTS 371.

18 SdB to Sartre, LS 21.

19 SCTS, chapter 8.

20 'Introduction', MPI: xii.

21 'Notes' autour de *Tout compte fait*, MPI 984.

22 See LS 381 n. 318.

23 The scholarly sources indicate that there were seven such articles; it is unclear whether he asked her or she volunteered. Ursula Tidd, 'Some Thoughts on an Interview with Sylvie le Bon de Beauvoir', *Simone de Beauvoir Studies* 12 (1995): 22–3.

24 PL 46.

25 Jean-Paul Sartre, *Being and Nothingness*, trans. Hazel Barnes, London: Routledge, 2003, p. 647.

26 Sartre, *Being and Nothingness*, 627.

27 PC 90.

28 PC 92, altered translation. The French noun 'enfant' is masculine so this passage was translated with male pronouns in English; but the story matches the story from Simone's own childhood, later recorded in *Memoirs of a Dutiful Daughter* in 1958, so I have used 'her' instead of 'his'.

29 PC 93.

30 PC 107.

31 Although she says here that 'I don't know if God exists' (PC 116).

32 PC 118.

33 It was not 'freedom from the self' that mattered, as Sartre's 'transcendence of the ego' suggested, but rather the freedom to become an ethical self. Many Beauvoir scholars have written excellent material on this topic, including Karen Vintges, 'Introduction' to 'Jean Paul Sartre', PW 223–8 and 'Simone de Beauvoir: A Feminist Thinker for the Twenty-First Century' in Margaret Simons (ed.) *The Philosophy of Simone de Beauvoir*, Bloomington, IN: Indiana University Press, 2006; Sonia Kruks, *Situation and Human Existence: Freedom, Subjectivity, and Society*, London: Unwin Hyman, 1990; Nancy

Bauer, *Simone de Beauvoir, Philosophy, and Feminism*, New York: Columbia University Press, 2001.

34 LS 389, SdB to Sartre, 13 December 1945.

35 Lamblin, *A Disgraceful Affair*, p. 170.

36 FC 75.

37 'Dominique Aury,'Qu'est-ce que l'existentialisme? Escarmouches et patrouilles', *Les Lettres françaises*, 1 December 1945, p. 4, cited in Simons, 'Introduction', PW 11 n. 14.

Chapter 10

1 See Cohen-Solal, *Sartre*, p. 237.

2 SdB to S, 26 July 1945, LS 386 n. 321.

3 FC 46.

4 Jean Lacroix, 'Charité chrétienne et justice politique', *Esprit* 1945 (February).

5 BO, back cover.

6 BO 128.

7 BO 129.

8 BO 174.

9 UM 3.

10 See BO 9.

11 BO 17.

12 BO 51.

13 BO 102.

14 For Jean, see BO 106; for Marcel, BO 126.

15 PL 607.

16 FC 44, 45.

17 WD 322, 29 January 1941.

18 UM 66.

19 SdB to her mother, in Bair, p. 267.

20 A. Collingnon, 'Bouches inutiles aux Carrefours', *Opéra*, 31 October 1944.

21 FC 59.

22 Jean-Jacques Gautier, writing in *Figaro*, cited in Maragaret A. Simons, 'Introduction' to 'Literature and Metaphysics', PW 263.

23 Cited in UM 25.

24 Emmanuel Levinas, in Jean Wahl, *Petite histoire de 'l'existentialisme'*, Paris: Éditions Club Maintenant, 1946, pp. 84–6.

25 It would be published in 1946 with the title 'Literature and Metaphysics'.

26 Maurice Merleau-Ponty, 'Metaphysics and the Novel', trans. Hubert Dreyfus and Patricia Allen Dreyfus, *Sense and Nonsense*, Evanston, IL: Northwestern University Press, p. 28. First published as 'Le roman et la métaphysique', *Cahiers du sud* 270 (March 1945).

27 'Literature and Metaphysics', PW 270.

28 'Literature and Metaphysics', PW 274. In 'Literature and Metaphysics' Beauvoir distinguished between philosophers who expressed their metaphysics (that is, the way they grasped the world) into two groups: 'system' philosophers and 'subjectivity' philosophers. She wrote that it would be absurd for the former (such as Aristotle, Spinoza or Leibniz) to write novels, because they were not interested in subjectivity or temporality. But philosophers like Kierkegaard were attracted to using literary forms that communicated truths about individuals in their singularity, as they unfolded in time.

29 See Jonathan Webber, *Rethinking Existentialism*, Oxford: Oxford University Press, 2018, p. 3.

30 FC 164.

31 Bair, p. 302.

32 'Existentialism and Popular Wisdom', PW 210.

33 'Existentialism and Popular Wisdom', PW 214.

34 'Existentialism and Popular Wisdom', PW 204, 205.

35 'Existentialism and Popular Wisdom', PW 216.

36 'Existentialism and Popular Wisdom', PW 213.

37 FC 27. See also LS 390 n. 350.

38 SdB to JPS, 25 January 1946, LS 400.

39 SdB to Sartre, 18 January 1946, LS 395.

40 SdB to Sartre, 18 January 1946, LS 397.

41 Sartre to SdB, February 1946 (n.d.), QM 274.

42 Sartre to SdB, February 1946 (n.d.), QM 275.

43 Cohen-Solal, *Sartre*, p. 279.

44 *TIME* (1946) 'Existentialism', 28 January, 28–9.

45 Sartre to SdB January 1946 (n.d.), QM 274. He reiterates a similar sentiment in February 1946, too.

46 See Jean-Pierre Boulé, *Sartre, Self-Formation and Masculinities*, p. 168.

47 Beauvoir, 'An Eye for an Eye', in Margaret Simons, ed., *Philosophical Writings*, Urbana: University of Illinois Press, pp. 245–60, here p. 257.

48 FC 87.

49 FC 78.

50 FC 84.

51 In *Labyrinthe*, see Sylvie le Bon de Beauvoir, 'Chronologie', xc. FC 92.

52 ASD 105.

53 For an example, see *Letters to Sartre*, 25 January 1946, 'we've just had 300,000F out of the blue'. In the 1950s, too, letters referred to 'our finances' (see SdB to Sartre, 20 August 1950, LS 472).

54 FC 171.

55 See FC 70, 84.

56 'Introduction to an Ethics of Ambiguity', PW 290.

57 FC 103.

58 DPS 259, 19 May 1927.

59 DPS 284, 19 July 1927.

60 WD 3 November 1939.

61 WD 133.

62 See SdB, in SdB, Simons and Todd, 'Two Interviews with Simone de Beauvoir', *Hypatia* 3:3 (1989): 17.

63 *La Force de l'âge*, p. 417, cited in Simons, 2010, p. 921.

64 Sartre to SdB, QM 277–8.

65 AMM 187.

66 FC 72.

67 FC 75.

68 SSP 187.

69 Elizabeth Fallaize, *The Novels of Simone de Beauvoir*, p. 83.

70 FC 73.

71 FC 72.

Chapter 11

1 SdB to Sartre, 26 January 1947, LS 412.

2 PL 138–41.

3 ADD 15.

4 SdB to Sartre, 30 January 1947, LS 415.

5 See Margaret Simons, 'Introduction' to FW 2.

6 See Bair, p. 389.

7 SdB to Sartre, 11 February 1947, LS 425.

8 Gunnar Myrdal, with Richard Sterner and Arnold Rose, *An American Dilemma: The Negro Problem and Modern Democracy*, New York: Harper, 1944, Appendix 3.

9 'The Talk of the Town', *The New Yorker*, 22 February 1947.

10 Beauvoir, 'Problems for Women's Literature', 23 February 1947, *France-Amérique* 14. Translated by Véronique Zaytzeff and Frederick Morrison, in FW 24.

11 Beauvoir 'Problems for Women's Literature', FW 25.

12 'Women of Letters', in FW 30.

13 SdB to Sartre, 28 February 1947, LS 433.

14 'Chicago's Bowery', *The Chicago Tribune*, 13 November 1910.

15 SdB to Sartre, 28 February 1947, LS 433.

16 See SdB to NA, 12 March 1947, TALA 13.

17 ADD 72.

18 See Nancy Bauer, 'Introduction' to 'Femininity: The Trap', in FW 39.

19 See ADD 40; and LS 419, 423, 427, 430.

20 'Femininity: The Trap', FW 43.

21 'Femininity: The Trap', FW 46.

22 ADD 330–34.

23 *Daily Princetonian*, 22–24 April 1947, cited in Francis and Gontier, *Les écrits de Simone de Beauvoir, Textes inédits ou retrouvés*, Paris: Gallimard, 1979, p. 147.

24 ADD 57.

25 ADD 272.

26 ADD 58.

27 SdB to Sartre, 24 April 1947, LS 451.

28 Simons 182. See Diane Rubenstein, '"I hope I am not fated to live in Rochester": America in the Work of Beauvoir', *Theory & Event* 15:2 (2012).

29 SdB to Sartre, 8 May 1947, LS 454.

30 SdB to S, 8 May 1947, *Lettres à Sartre*, p. 355.

31 SdB to NA, 17 May 1947, TALA 15.

32 SdB to NA, 18 May 1947, TALA 16.

33 SdB to NA, 17 January 1954, TALA 490.

34 See SdB to NA, 23 May 1947, TALA 18.

35 SdB to NA, 24 May 1947, TALA 19.

36 See ADD 236–48; see also Margaret Simons, *Beauvoir and* The Second Sex: *Feminism, Race, and the Origins of Existentialism*, New York: Rowman & Littlefield, 2001, p. 177.

37 SdB to NA, 1 December 1947, TALA 113.

38 SdB to NA 23 July 1947, TALA 51.

39 Nelson Algren, 'Last Rounds in Small Cafés: Remembrances of Jean-Paul Sartre and Simone de Beauvoir', *Chicago*, December 1980, p. 213, cited in Bair, pp. 335–6.

40 SdB to NA, 26 September 1947, TALA 66.

41 See Isabelle Grell, *Les Chemins de la liberté de Sartre: genèse et écriture (1938–1952)*, Bern: Peter Lang, 2005, p. 155. On Swing's later recollections, see Hazel

Rowley, *Tête-à-tête*, p. 187. Rowley interviewed Swing in 2002. Sixty-two pieces of correspondence from Sartre to Swing are held by the Morgan Library in New York. Sartre refers to Swing as 'the little one' in correspondence to SdB; see QM 282.

42 EA 101.

43 EA 71.

44 EA 40.

45 EA 66.

46 EA 71.

47 Jean-Louis Jeannelle and Eliane Lecarme-Tabone, 'Introduction', MPI xl. In English, see Webber, *Rethinking Existentialism*.

48 A. de Waelhens, compte-rendu de Francis Jeanson, *Le problème moral et la pensée de Sartre*, *Revue Philosophique de Louvain* 1948 (10): 229.

49 See Beauvoir, 'What is Existentialism?', PW.

50 SdB to NA, Friday, 20 August 1948, TALA 213.

51 FC 170.

52 SdB to NA, 3 August 1948, TALA 206.

53 SdB to NA, 8 August 1948, TALA 208.

54 SdB to NA, Friday, 20 August 1948, TALA 210, 212.

55 SdB to NA, Friday, 20 August 1948, TALA 214.

56 SdB to NA, 26 August 1948, TALA 216.

57 SdB to NA, 31 December 1948, TALA 254.

58 Sartre, quoted in interview with John Gerassi, *Talking with Sartre: Conversations and Debates*, New Haven: Yale University Press, 2009, p. 32.

Chapter 12

1 PL 62.

2 TALA 184. The novel was *Ravages*, but the early section Beauvoir read was too scandalous to be published with the rest of the book in 1954 – it wouldn't appear in French until 2000 as *Thérèse et Isabelle*.

3 DPS 77, 21 August 1926.

4 Gisela Kaplan, *Contemporary Western European Feminism*, London: UCL Press, 1992, p. 163.

5 Rosie Germain, 'Reading *The Second Sex* in 1950s America', *The Historical Journal* 56(4): 2013: 1041–62, p. 1045.

6 Gustave Flaubert, cited in Allison Guidette-Georis, 'Georges Sand et le troisième sexe', *Nineteenth Century French Studies* 25 (1/2): 41–9, p. 41.

7 SS 25.

8 SS 32.

9 SS 13.

10 SS 37.

11 FC 199.

12 SS 475, 476.

13 Schwarzer, *Simone de Beauvoir Today*, p. 71.

14 François Mauriac, 'Demande d'enquête', *Le Figaro*, (1949), 30 May. See Ingrid Galster, *Le Deuxième Sexe de Simone de Beauvoir*, Paris: Presse universitaire Paris-Sorbonne, 2004, p. 21. Beauvoir discusses the reaction to this chapter's publication in FC 197.

15 FC 197.

16 See Ingrid Galster, *Le Deuxième Sexe de Simone de Beauvoir*, p. 45 n. 33, for the full note, which mentioned her clitoris, too.

17 FC 196.

18 SS 46.

19 Marie-Louise Barron, 'De Simone de Beauvoir à Amour Digest. Les croisés de l'émancipation par le sexe', *Les Lettres françaises* (1949), 23 June. Ibid. p. 128.

20 Armand Hoog, 'Madame de Beauvoir et son sexe', *La Nef* (1949), August. Ibid. p. 161.

21 FC 192ff.

22 Cited in Brooke Horvath, *Understanding Nelson Algren*, Columbia, SC: University of South Carolina Press, 2005, p. 7.

23 FC 207.

24 SS 330.

25 SS 644.

26 Claire Laubier (ed.), *The Condition of Women in France, 1945–Present: A Documentary Anthology*, London: Routledge, 1990, p. 1.

27 SS 607.

28 SS 641, 644.

29 SS 645.

30 Cited in SdB to Sartre, 19 January 1940, LS 262.

31 SS 724–5.

32 SS 310, 311.

33 MDD 148.

34 SS 442.

35 Cited in PL 327.

36 SS 816.

37 SS 37. Beauvoir did not deny that women could authentically love men monogamously or children maternally. But the necessary condition for doing so wasn't monogamy or motherhood per se, but *the situation* in which particular women live those vocations. However, many of her first readers were so shocked by her claims that they were blinded to their nuances.

38 André Rousseaux, 'Le Deuxième Sexe', *Le Figaro littéraire* (1949), 12 November. Ibid. p. 210.

39 Emmanuel Mounier, *L'Esprit*, December 1949.

40 FC 200.

41 See Ingrid Galster, '"The limits of the abject": The Reception of *The Second Sex* in 1949', in *A Companion to Simone de Beauvoir*, ed. Laura Hengehold and Nancy Bauer, Oxford: Wiley, 2017, p. 40.

42 Cited in Galster, '"The limits of the abject", p. 39.

43 SS 127.

44 This section is indebted to Manon Garcia's excellent discussion of Beauvoir's method in *The Second Sex* in, *On ne naît pas femme, on le devient*, Paris: Flammarion, 2018, p. 93.

45 See Garcia, *On ne naît pas femme*, p. 109.

46 George Eliot, *Middlemarch*, Oxford: Oxford University Press, 1988, p. 159.

47 On Beauvoir's phenomenological method in *The Second Sex*, see Garcia, *On ne naît pas femme*, p. 124 ff.

48 'Simone de Beauvoir: Le Deuxième Sexe', actualité du livre, Institut National de l'Audiovisuel, France. https://www.ina.fr/audio/PH806055647/simone-de-beauvoir-le-deuxieme-sexe-audio.html

49 This letter, dated 29 January 1958, is cited in Marine Rouch, '"Vous êtes descendue d'un piédestal": une appropriation collective des Mémoires de Simone de Beauvoir par ses lectrices (1958–1964)' *Littérature* 191 (September 2018): 72.

50 Michèle Le Doeuff, *Hipparchia's Choice: An Essay Concerning Women and Philosophy*, trans. Trista Selous, New York: Columbia University Press, 2007, p. 34.

51 See, for example, Eva Lundgren-Gothlin, who argues that Beauvoir's reliance on Hegel made her work 'androcentric', to the extent that it 'sometimes verges on being misogynist'. *Sex and Existence: Simone de Beauvoir's* The Second Sex, trans. Linda Schenck, Hanover, NH: Wesleyan University Press, 1996.

52 C. B. Radford, 'Simone de Beauvoir: Feminism's Friend or Foe?' Part II, *Nottingham French Studies* 7 (May 1968): 44. On 'energetic anger' see Margaret Crosland, *Simone de Beauvoir: The Woman and Her Work*, London: Heinemann, 1992, p. 359.

53 Kathryn T. Gines, 'Comparative and Competing Frameworks of Oppression in Simone de Beauvoir's *The Second Sex*', *Graduate Faculty Philosophy Journal* 35 (1–2) (2014): 251–73.

54 Beauvoir, 'Introduction to *Women Insist*', trans. Marybeth Timmerman, in FW 250.

55 Moi, *Simone de Beauvoir*, p. 28.

Chapter 13

1 See 'Chronologie', MPI xcviii.

2 'It's About Time Women Put a New Face on Love', *Flair* 1(3), April 1950: 76–7. Included in FW.

3 'It's About Time', FW 76.

4 'It's About Time', FW 78.

5 'It's About Time', FW 79.

6 SdB to Sartre, early July 1950, *Lettres à Sartre*, p. 370.

7 SdB to Sartre, 2 September 1950.

8 SdB to Sartre, 20 August 1950, LS 474.

9 FC 245.

10 TALA 434.

11 SdB to NA, 30 October 1951 TALA 434, 435.

12 SdB to NA, 30 October 1951, TALA 436.

13 FC 267–8.

14 SdB to NA, 9 November 1951, TALA 440.

15 Sylvie Chaperon, 'The reception of The Second Sex in Europe', *Encyclopédie pour une histoire nouvelle de l'Europe*, 2016.

16 SdB to NA, 3 December 1951, TALA 446.

17 FC 170.

18 FC 291.

19 FC 268. On Sartre's adoption of some of Beauvoir's views by the time he published *Saint Genet* in 1952, see Webber, *Rethinking Existentialism*.

20 FC 269.

21 FC 296–7.

22 FC 291.

23 FC 291.

24 Sartre, in 'Sartre on Literature and Politics: A Conversation with Redmond O'Hanlon', *The Crane Bag* 7(1), *Socialism and Culture* (1983): 83.

25 Claude Lanzmann to SdB; Sylvie Le Bon de Beauvoir archives, cited in Rowley, *Tête-à-tête*, p. 214.

26 FC 294.

27 Gerassi interview with Sartre, 12 March 1971.

28 See Josée Dayan and Malka Ribowska *Simone de Beauvoir*, text published by Gallimard: Paris, 1979; based on a film made in 1978.

29 FC 297.

30 FC 297–8.

31 FC 298. See also Claude Lanzmann, *The Patagonian Hare: A Memoir*, trans. Frank Wynne, London: Atlantic Books, 2012, p. 244 on becoming part of 'the family'.

32 Lanzmann, *Patagonian*, p. 265.

33 Lanzmann, *Patagonian*, p. 259.

34 The sale to Yale included 112 letters, however in 2008 Lanzmann referred to having 300. See Claude Lanzmann, 'Le Sherpa du 11bis', in Julia Kristeva, Pascale Fautrier, Pierre-Louis Fort, Anne Strasser (eds) *(Re)Découvrir l'oeuvre de Simone de Beauvoir: Du Dexuième Sexe à La Cérémonie des Adieux*, Paris: Le Bord de L'eau, 2008, p. 20.

35 Cited in Franck Nouchi, 'L'exil américain des lettres d'amour de Simone de Beauvoir à Claude Lanzmann', *Le Monde*, 19 January 2018.

36 See Introduction to SS 12.

37 See Toril Moi, 'While We Wait: The English Translation of *The Second Sex*', *Signs* 27(4): 1005–35 (2002).

38 Blanche Knopf to Harold Parshley, 2 November 1951, cited in Rosie Germain, 'Reading *The Second Sex* in 1950s America', *The Historical Journal* 56(4) 2013: 1041–62.

39 Parshley, 'Introduction', SSP vi.

40 Parshley, 'Introduction', SSP x.

41 Beauvoir, in SdB, Simons and Todd, 'Two Interviews with Simone de Beauvoir', p. 20.

42 Clyde Kluckholm, 'The Female of our Species', *New York Times Book Review*, 22 February 1953, 3, 33.

43 Charles J. Rolo, 'Cherchez la femme', *The Atlantic*, April 1953, 86.

44 Margaret Mead, in 'A SR Panel Takes Aim at *The Second Sex*', *Saturday Review*, 21 February 1953.

45 In the United States Beauvoir's book appeared amidst a cluster of contemporary books about 'woman'. Alfred Kinsey's *Sex and the Human Male* was published in 1946 – and, just as Beauvoir had wished in her letters to Algren – books were beginning to appear about female sexuality. Ashley Montagu's *The Natural Superiority of Women* was published in 1952; Kinsey's *Sex and the Human Female* and Mirra Komaraovksy's *Women in the Modern World* appeared in 1953.

46 Carol Giardina, *Freedom for Women: Forging the Women's Liberation Movement, 1953–1979*, Gainesville: University Press of Florida, 2010, 79.

47 For more on the reception of *The Second Sex* in 1950s America, see Rosie Germain's excellent article 'Reading *The Second Sex* in 1950s America'.

48 SdB to NA, April 1953, TALA 479.

49 Lanzmann, *Patagonian*, p. 235.

50 SdB to Sartre, summer 1953 (n.d.), LS 493.

51 SdB to NA, 15 February 1954, p. 492.

52 FC 323.

53 FC 326.

54 FC 328.

55 'Les prix Goncourt et Renaudot', *Journal les actualités françaises*, 10 December 1954, Institut National de l'Audovisuel, France, https://www.ina.fr/video/AFE85007180/les-prix-goncourt-et-renaudot-video.html

56 SdB to NA, 9 January 1955, p. 512.

57 Colette Audry, 'Notes pour un portrait de Simone de Beauvoir', *Les Lettres françaises*, 17–24 December, 1954, p. 5.

58 Beauvoir, 'A Story I Used to Tell Myself' [1963], UM 159.

59 FC 328.

60 FC 282.

61 FC 283.

62 FC 328.

63 A. Blanchet, 'Les Prix littéraires', *Études* 284 (1955): 96–100, here p. 98.

64 G. Charensol, 'Quels enseignements peut-on tirer des chiffres de tirage de la production littéraire actuelle?', *Informations sociales* (1957): 36–45.

65 G. J. Joyaux, 'Les problèmes de la gauche intellectuelle et Les Mandarins de Simone de Beauvoir', *Kentucky Foreign Language Quarterly* 3 (1956): 121.

66 FC 328.

67 Doris Lessing, 'Introduction' to M 9.

68 M 48

69 M 107.

70 M 203.

71 TALA 511.

72 Lanzmann, *Patagonian*, p. 257.

73 FC 336.

74 SdB to S, late May 1954 [undated], LS 505.

75 FC 361.

76 FC 332.

77 PW 7.

78 'What is Existentialism?' PW 324.

79 'What is Exisentialism?' PW 324.

80 FC 358–9.

81 LM 32.

82 FC 487.

83 I am not at liberty to cite the Lanzmann letters directly, but the letters in question are from August and September 1956, available at the Beinecke Rare Book & Manuscript Library, Yale University. The quotation from C. Wright Mills is from *The Power Elite*, Oxford: Oxford University Press, 2000, p. 3.

84 See Sandrine Sanos, *Simone de Beauvoir*, p. 117. Margaret Simons, 'Beauvoir's Ironic Sacrifice; or Why Philosophy Is Missing from her Memoirs', forthcoming.

85 TLM 130.

86 This information is taken from 1956 (tome I) and 1958 (tome II) NRF editions of *Le Deuxième Sexe* (Paris: Gallimard).

87 TALA 526, 1 January 1957.

88 FC 398.

89 Unpublished journal, 25 May 1958, Sylvie Le Bon de Beauvoir archives, cited in the 'Introduction' to MPI ix.

90 FC 443.

91 See 'Notice' to *Mémoires d'une jeune fille rangée*, in MPI 1226, on the absence of what Philippe Lejeune called 'the autobiographical pact', by which the author commits to telling the reader the truth about herself (see *Le pacte autobiographique*, Paris: Seuil, 1975).

92 'Texte de Présentation de l'Édition Originale', Simone de Beauvoir, *Mémoires d'une Jeune Fille Rangée*', MPI 352.

93 'essai sur l'écrivain', cited in MPI, 'Introduction', xv.

94 FC 448.

95 Lanzmann, *Patagonian*, p. 329.

96 Lanzmann, *Patagonian*, p. 330.

97 FC 614.

98 Letter from a reader, dated 20 June 1959; cited in Marine Rouch, '"Vous êtes descendue d'un piédestal": une appropriation collective des Mémoires de Simone de Beauvoir par ses lectrices (1958–1964)' *Littérature* 191 (September 2018): 68.

99 See Marine Rouch, 'Vous êtes descendue d'un piédestal', p. 72.

100 Letter from a reader, dated 15 November 1959; cited in Rouch, 'Vous êtes descendue d'un piédestal', p. 71.

101 MDD 360.

102 FC 456.

Chapter 14

1 In her published collection of letters from Sartre, Beauvoir records that his letter from 25 July 1963 was the last he wrote to her because from that point on they used the telephone during their separations. QM 304.

2 SdB to NA, September 1959, TALA 530.

3 FC 466.

4 Lanzmann, *Patagonian*, p. 330.

5 *Brigitte Bardot and the Lolita Syndrome*, trans. Bernard Frechtman, London: Four Square, 1962. First published in *Esquire in* August 1959.

6 BB 36.

7 BB 30.

8 TALA 528, SdB to NA, 2 January 1959.

9 'Chronologie', MPII xiv; xvi. We know from Sylvie Le Bon de Beauvoir's 'Chronologie' that there are several surviving (unpublished) journals, extracts from which were published in MPI and II in 2018.

10 Simone de Beauvoir, *Extraits du journal*, May 1959, MPI 349.

11 Simone de Beauvoir, *Extraits du journal*, May 1959, MPI 349.

12 FC 479–80.

13 October 1959, QM 295.

14 Sartre to SdB, October 1959 [undated], QM 297.

15 FC 480.

16 FC 511.

17 FC 487.

18 'Preface to *The Great Fear of Loving*', FW 84.

19 SLBdB, 'Chronologie', MPII xvii.

20 FC 503.

21 Nelson Algren, 'People', *Time*, 2 July 1956, p. 33.

22 SLBdB, 'Chronologie', MPII xvii.

23 SdB to NA, 1 January 1957, p. 526.

24 FC 506.

25 See SdB to S, August 1958 (n.d.), LS 514.

26 Cohen-Solal, *Sartre*, p. 419 ff.

27 Cohen-Solal, *Sartre*, p. 428.

28 SLBdB, 'Chronologie', MPII xx.

29 SdB to NA, 16 November 1960, TALA 538.

30 Lamblin, *A Disgraceful Affair*, p. 148.

31 SdB, in interview with Madeleine Gobeil, 'The Art of Fiction No. 35', *Paris Review* 34 (Spring–Summer 1965).

32 See 'Introduction' to MPI xxxviii.

33 SdB to NA, 16 November 1960, TALA 538.

34 SdB to NA, December 1960, TALA 539.

35 PL 220.

36 The French text reads: 'il faudrait plutôt expliquer comment certains individus sont capables de mener à bein ce délire concerté qu'est un système et d'où leur vient l'entêtement qui donne à leurs aperçus la valeur des clés universelles. J'ai dit déjà que la condition féminine ne dispose pas à ce genre d'obstination'.

37 PL 221.

38 SLBdB, 'Chronologie', MPII xxii.

39 David Macey, *Frantz Fanon: A Biography*, London: Verso Books, 2012, pp. 455–6.

40 FC 606–7.

41 FC 611.

42 SLBdB, 'Chronologie', MPII xxiii. Some of the stolen material reappeared subsequently in private sales.

43 He wouldn't stay there for long – in December he moved to 222 boulevard Raspail.

44 ASD 306.

45 Cohen-Solal, *Sartre*, p. 406.

46 See Gary Gutting, *Thinking the Impossible: French Philosophy Since 1960*, Oxford: Oxford University Press, 2011, chapter 4.

47 Although Friedan only admitted this later: see Sandra Dijkstra, 'Simone de Beauvoir and Betty Friedan: The Politics of Omission', *Feminist Studies* 6(2) (Summer 1980): 293–4.

48 Cited in Gonzague de Saint-Bris and Vladimir Fedorovksi in *Les Egéries Russes*, Paris: Lattès, 1994, p. 282.

49 VED 29.

50 SdB to NA, December 1963, p. 555.

51 VED 31.

52 'Maladie de ma mère', ff. 254, 287, 311. Cited in 'Notice' MPII 1276.

53 VED 24.

54 VED 19–20.

55 VED 76.

56 ASD 135.

57 ASD 75.

58 SLBdB, 'Chronologie', dates the submission of the manuscript to 7 May 1963.

59 FC 199.

60 FC 202.

61 FC 202.

62 FC 203.

63 FC 202.

64 Simone de Beauvoir, 'Une interview de Simone de Beauvoir par Madeleine Chapsal', in *Les écrivains en personne* (Paris: Julliard, 1960, pp. 17–37), reprinted in *Les écrits de Simone de Beauvoir*, ed. Claude Francis and Fernand Gontier, Paris: Gallimard, 1979, p. 396.

65 FC 674.

66 Françoise d'Eaubonne, *Une femme nommée Castor*, Paris: Harmattan, 2008, p. 253. See also MPII 1017ff on 'j'ai été flouée'.

67 SLBdB, 'Chronologie', MPII xxvi.

68 Simone de Beauvoir, in interview with Madeleine Gobeil, 'The Art of Fiction No. 35', *Paris Review* 34 (Spring–Summer 1965). See also SLBdB 'Chronologie', MPII xxviii for information about dating.

69 Letter dated 29 October 1964, cited in Rouch, 'Vous êtes descendue d'un piédestal', p. 81.

70 FC 133.

71 FC 133–4.

72 Jacques Ehrmann, 'The French Review', *The French Review* 37(6) 1964: 698–9, 699.

73 G. Ménie, 'Le Prix d'une révolte', *Esprit* 326(3) 1964 (March): 488–96, 493.

74 Francine Dumas, 'Une response tragique', *Esprit* 326(3) 1964 (March): 496–502.

75 SdB to NA, December 1963, TALA 556.

76 Nelson Algren, 'I ain't Abelard', *Newsweek*, 28 December 1964, 58–9.

77 Nelson Algren, 'The Question of Simone de Beauvoir', *Harper's*, May 1965, 136.

78 See note in TALA 559.

79 http://www.lepoint.fr/actualites-litterature/2007-01-18/simone-de-beauvoir-ces-lettres-qui-ebranlent-un-mythe/1038/0/45316

80 Kurt Vonnegut, *Fates Worse than Death: An Autobiographical Collage of the 1980s*, New York: 2013, 60. Vonnegut's claim is based on Bair's biography of Beauvoir.

81 'Preface to *The Sexually Responsive Woman*', first published in English in 1964; no surviving French version; FW 97.

82 See Jean-Louis Jeannelle and Eliane Lecarme-Tabone, 'Introduction', MPI xliv.

83 Sara Ahmed, 'Feminist Killjoys (and Other Wilful Subjects)', *Scholar and Feminist Online* 8(3), Summer 2010: 4.

84 SLBdB 'Chronologie', MPII xxvi.

85 'What Love Is – And Isn't', *McCall's* 71, August 1965, 133. (In FW 100.)

86 'Sartre Talks of Beauvoir', *Vogue*, July 1965, p. 73.

87 'Notes' autour de *Tout compte fait*, MPII 973.

88 'Notes' autour de *Tout compte fait*, MPII 978.

89 'Notes' autour de *Tout compte fait*, MPII 997–8.

90 ASD 275.

91 'The Situation of Women Today', FW 145.

92 'The Situation of Women Today', FW 133, 134

93 'The Situation of Women Today', FW 139.

94 'Women and Creativity', FW 158.

95 'Les Belles Images (par Simone de Beauvoir, *Gallimard*)', *La Cité*, May 1967, p. 14.

96 SLBdB, 'Chronologie', MPII xxxi.

97 ASD 144.

98 BI 151.

99 SdB Interview with Jacqueline Piatier, *Le Monde*, 23 December 1966.

100 BI 183.

101 SLBdB, 'Chronologie', MPII xxxi.

102 ASD 414.

103 See ASD 369 for Beauvoir's discussion.

104 ASD 142.

105 'Preface to *Through Women's Eyes*', trans. Marybeth Timmermann, FW 253.

106 TWD 13.

107 TWD 70.

108 TWD 80.

109 TWD 107.

110 Henri Clouard, 'La Revue littéraire', *Revue des deux mondes*, March 1968: 115–24, p. 118.

111 Clouard 'La Revue littéraire', pp. 118–19.

112 Jacqueline Piatier, 'Le Démon du bien: "La Femme rompue" de Simone de Beauvoir', *Le Monde*, 1968.

113 ASD 144.

114 ASD 143.

115 ASD 147.

116 ASD 490.

117 Bruno Vercier, 'Les livres qui ont marqué la pensée de notre époque', *Réalités*, August 1971.

118 'Libération des femmes, année zéro', *Partisans* 54–55: 1970, Maspero.

119 Beauvoir claimed that they approached her in ASD; Anne Zelinsky claimed that Beauvoir approached them (in 'Castor for ever', in *Le cinquantenaire du 'Deuxième Sexe'*, 310–13).

120 According to Sylvie Le Bon de Beauvoir, Beauvoir never had an abortion. She believed that abortion should be freely available, but that the availability of contraception would mean that abortion would play 'only a marginal role' (Schwarzer, p. 30).

Chapter 15

1 ASD 131.

2 From Gide's old character, la Pérouse: quoted in OA 237.

3 Woolf, 29 December 1940, cited in OA 514.

4 OA 244.

5 OA 410.

6 OA 547.

7 Revue des livres, *Vie Sociale*, March 1970, pp. 157–160. http://gallica.bnf.fr/ark:/12148/bpt6k62832097/f34.item.r=beauvoir

8 Henry Walter Brann, review of '*La Vieillesse* by Simone de Beauvoir', *The French Review* 44(2), December 1970: 396–7.

9 Edward Grossman, 'Beauvoir's Last Revolt', *Commentary* 54(2), 1 August 1972: 56–9, here 56.

10 ASD 147.

11 OA 148.

12 Simone de Beauvoir, in *A Walk Through the Land of Old Age*, in PolW 363.

13 Schwarzer, Introduction, p. 13.

14 See A 10–11.

15 'Response to Some Women and a Man', FW 209.

16 'Response', FW 210.

17 'Response', FW 210.

18 'Beauvoir's Deposition at the Bobigny Trial', FW 220.

19 'Beauvoir's Deposition at the Bobigny Trial', FW 226.

20 'Beauvoir's Deposition at the Bobigny Trial', FW 226.

21 'Abortion and the Poor', FW 217.

22 ASD 134.

23 Jean-Marie Domenach, 'Simone de Beauvoir: Tout compte fait', *Esprit* 1972 (December): 979–80.

24 ASD 154.

25 See ASD 57ff, 163.

26 Carlo Jansiti, *Violette Leduc*, Paris: Grasset, 1999, 447–8.

27 ASD 193.

28 ASD 484.

29 ASD 489.

30 ASD 500.

31 November 1949 interview with Clodine Chonez, retransmitted by the radio programme 'Les jours du siècle', France Inter, 17 February 1999.

32 Francis Jeanson, *Simone de Beauvoir ou l'entreprise de vivre, suivi d'entretiens avec Simone de Beauvoir*, Paris: Seuil, 1966, p. 258.

33 FC 202.

34 Alice Schwarzer, 'I am a feminist', in *Simone de Beauvoir Today: Conversations 1972–1982*, London: Hogarth Press, 1984, p. 16. See also pp. 29ff. For an excellent discussion of the continuity of Beauvoir's feminism in 1949 and the 1970s see Sonia Kruks, 'Beauvoir and the Marxism Question', in Laura Hengehold and Nancy Bauer (eds), *A Companion to Simone de Beauvoir*, Oxford: Wiley-Blackwell, 2017.

35 Schwarzer, p. 34.

36 Schwarzer, pp. 37–8.

37 'Preface to *Stories from the French Women's Liberation Movement*', trans. Marybeth Timmermann, FW 260.

38 Alice Schwarzer, 'The Rebellious Woman – An Interview with Alice Schwarzer', trans. Marybeth Timmermann, FW 197.

39 Sylvie Chaperon, 'Introduction' to 'The MLF and the Bobigny Affair', FW 189.

40 Claire Etcherelli, 'Quelques photos-souvenirs', *Les Temps Modernes* 63(647–8), January–March 2008: 60. Lanzmann introduced Beauvoir to Etcherelli's book *Élise ou la vrai vie*: it was a story of forbidden love between an Algerian man and a female factory worker during the War of Independence. The book went on to win prizes, and in the 1970s Etcherelli joined Beauvoir and Lanzmann as editorial staff at *Les Temps Modernes*.

41 Etcherelli, 'Quelques photos-souvenirs', p. 61.

42 Bair, p. 676 n. 13.

43 A 54.

44 A 63.

45 Cohen-Solal, *Sartre*, p. 500.

46 Preface to 'Everyday Sexism', *Les Temps Modernes* 329 (December 1973), trans. Marybeth Timmerman, in FW 240.

47 Simone de Beauvoir, 'Preface to *Divorce in France*', trans. Marybeth Timmerman, FW 248. First published in Claire Cayron, *Divorce en France*, Paris: Denoël-Gonthier, 1974.

48 'Introduction to *Women Insist*', trans. Marybeth Timmerman, FW 250.

49 See ASD 499.

50 Gerassi, p. 30. December 1970 interview.

51 Gerassi, p. 32. December 1970 interview.

52 This interview appeared in weekly instalments in *Le Nouvel Observateur*, 23, 30 June and 7 July, 1975. Cited in Hazel Rowley, *Tête-à-tête*, p. 333.

53 'Simone de Beauvoir interroge Jean-Paul Sartre', in *Situations* X, 'Politique et autobiographie', Paris: Gallimard, 1976, pp. 116–17.

54 Schwarzer, p. 73.

55 'My Point of View: An Outrageous Affair', trans. Debbie Mann and Marybeth Timmermann, FW 258.

56 'When All the Women of the World …', trans Marybeth Timmermann, FW 256.

57 A 100.

58 A 110–11.

59 'D'abord, je ne donnais pas à lire mes manuscrits – à personne sauf à Simone de Beauvoir – avant qu'ils sont imprimés: par consequent, elle avait un rôle essentiel et unique.' (Michel Sicard, 'Interférences: entretien avec Simone de Beauvoir et Jean-Paul Sartre', *Obliques* 18–19 (1979): 326.)

60 Xavier Delacourt, 'Simone de Beauvoir adaptée: Une fidélité plate', *Le Monde*, 1978. http://www.lemonde.fr/archives/article/1978/01/30/simone-de-beauvoir-adaptee-une-fidelite-plate_3131878_1819218.html#YOXP2bX45I01dulu.99

61 WT, pp. 74–5.

62 Josée Dayan and Malka Ribowska, *Simone de Beauvoir*, text published by Gallimard: Paris, 1979; based on a film made in 1978. http://www.ina.fr/video/CAB7900140801

63 Video: 'Film "Simone de Beauvoir"' sur Samedi et demi, Institut National de l'Audiovisuel, France, https://www.ina.fr/video/CAB7900140801/film-simone-de-beauvoir-video.html

64 Julien Cheverny, 'Une bourgeoise modèle: Simone de Beauvoir', *Figaro Magazine*, 17 February 1979, p. 57.

65 Schwarzer, p. 103.

Chapter 16

1 Charles Hargrove, 'Thousands escort Sartre's coffin', *The Times* [London, England] 21 April 1980: 4. The Times Digital Archive. Online, 27 March 2018.

2 Bair, p. 587.

3 Bair, p. 588.

4 Sylvie Le Bon de Beauvoir, interview with Magda Guadalupe dos Santos, 'Interview avec Sylvie Le Bon de Beauvoir', *Sapere Aude*, Belo Horizonte, v. 3, n. 6, pp. 357–65, 2 semestre 2012, p. 364.

5 Bair, p. 512.

6 A 3.

7 Bair, p. 595.

8 'La fin d'un philosophe', *Le Point*, 23–29 November 1981.

9 A 254, 353.

10 Hazel E. Barnes, 'Beauvoir and Sartre: The Forms of Farewell', *Philosophy and Literature* 9(1): 28–9.

11 Cohen-Solal, *Sartre*, p. 518.

12 FC 328.

13 Beauvoir, cited in interview with Alice Schwarzer, p. 107.

14 http://www.lemonde.fr/archives/article/1980/05/12/la-mort-de-jean-paul-sartre_2822210_1819218.html?xtmc=jean_paul_sartre_deces&xtcr=11

15 https://www.lexpress.fr/culture/livre/sartre-face-a-son-epoque_486893.html

16 'Jean-Paul Sartre dies in Paris hospital,' *The Times* [London, England] 16 April 1980: 1. The Times Digital Archive. Online, 27 March 2018.

17 'Obituary', *The Times* [London, England] 16 April 1980: 16. The Times Digital Archive. Online, 27 March 2018.

18 Schwarz, W. (1980, 16 April). 'Sartre, sage of left, dies', *The Guardian* (1959–2003).

19 J-P Sartre: As influential as Rousseau (1980, 16 April), *The Guardian* (1959–2003).

20 https://archive.nytimes.com/www.nytimes.com/learning/general/onthisday/bday/0621.html

21 https://www.washingtonpost.com/archive/local/1980/04/16/jean-paul-sartre-existential-author-dramatist-dies/120a0b98-9774-4248-a123-1efab2d68520/?utm_term=.2cad98e8c74e

22 Simone de Beauvoir to Bianca Lamblin, autumn 1982, cited in Lamblin, *A Disgraceful Affair*.

23 Bair, p. 598.

24 See Lanzmann, *Patagonian*, p. 352.

25 Bair, p. 601.

26 Michèle le Doeuff, 'Sartre; l'unique sujet parlant', *Esprit – changer la culture et la politique*, 5: 181–91.

27 SdB in Beauvoir, Simons and Todd, 'Two Interviews with Simone de Beauvoir', p. 24.

28 SdB in Schwarzer, *Simone de Beauvoir Today*, p. 210.

29 'Foreword to Deception Chronicles', FW 272.

30 'Women, Ads, and Hate', FW

31 'The Urgency of an Anti-Sexist Law', trans. Marybeth Timmermann, FW 266. First published in *Le Monde* as 'De l'urgence d'une loi anti-sexiste', March 18–19, 1979.

32 'Women, Ads, and Hate', FW 275.

33 Lanzmann, *Patagonian*, p. 257.

34 Cited in Lanzmann, *Patagonian*, pp. 258–9.

35 Schwarzer, p. 110.

36 Bair, p. 604.

37 Etcherelli, 'Quelques photos-souvenirs', p. 61.

38 Beauvoir, in SdB, Simons and Todd, 'Two Interviews with Simone de Beauvoir', p. 20.

39 Beauvoir, ibid.

40 The opening of *The Ethics of Ambiguity*, the concluding pages of *All Said and Done*, and the pages of Beauvoir's student diaries all refer to Pascal, who described human life as ambiguous in a similar sense.

41 Even Sartre excised or downplayed the influence of these thinkers from his published works, in favour of more fashionable philosophical currents like phenomenology (and, later, psychoanalysis and Marxism). See Kate Kirkpatrick, *Sartre on Sin*, Oxford: Oxford University Press, 2017; *The Mystical Sources of Existentialist Thought*, Abingdon: Routledge, 2018.

42 HdB, *Souvenirs*, p. 8.

43 HdB, *Souvenirs*, p. 12; Lanzmann, *Patagonian*, p. 525.

44 Claude Jannoud, 'L'Œuvre: Une vulgarisation plus qu'une création', *Le Monde*, 15 April 1986.

Chapter 17

1 Voltaire, 'Première Lettre sur Oedipe' in *Oeuvres* (1785) vol. 1.

2 'Simone De Beauvoir', *The Times* [London, England] 15 April 1986: 18. The Times Digital Archive. Online 24 March 2018.

3 Appreciation, Michael Dobbs, 15 April 1986, *The Washington Post*. https://www. washingtonpost.com/archive/lifestyle/1986/04/15/appreciation/39084b0c-a652-4661-b226-3ad12385b4d3/?utm_term=.55d325922220

4 Liliane Lazar, 'Simone de Beauvoir (9 January 1908–14 April 1986)', *Dictionary of Literary Biography Yearbook: 1986*, edited by J. M. Brook, Gale, 1987, pp. 199–206, here pp. 200, 201.

5 P. de Boisdeffre, 'LA REVUE LITTERAIRE: Deux morts exemplaires, un même refus: Jean Genet et Simone de Beauvoir', *Revue des deux mondes* (1986): 414–28, here pp. 416, 419, 420.

6 Richard Heller, 'The Self-centered Love of Madame Yak-Yak', *Mail on Sunday*, 1 December 1991, p. 35.

7 Lanzmann, *Patagonian* p. 351. In 1990, Beauvoir's letters to Sartre were published by Sylvie Le Bon de Beauvoir. Claude Lanzmann wrote that: 'I know that Castor would never have published them nor allowed them to be published like that. I know this because she told me so, because she states as much in her introduction to the edition of Sartre's letters published in 1983, and because I shared her life'. For Sylvie's reasons for publishing see Ursula Tidd, 'Some Thoughts on an Interview with Sylvie le Bon de Beauvoir: Current issues in Beauvoir studies', *Simone de Beauvoir Studies* 12 (1995): 17–26.

8 Lamblin, p. 137.

9 'Simone de Beauvoir interroges Jean-Paul Sartre', in *Situations* X, 'Politique et autobiographie', Paris: Gallimard, 1976, pp. 116–17.

10 ASD 143.

11 See Cohen-Solal, *Sartre*, p. 261. See also Marine Rouch 2018 on the way Beauvoir's readers idolized her ('"Vous êtes descendue d'un piédestal": une appropriation collective des Mémoires de Simone de Beauvoir par ses lectrices (1958–1964)', *Littérature* 191 (September 2018)).

12 SdB in Alice Schwarzer, *Simone de Beauvoir Today*, p. 93.

13 ASD 144.

14 *Simone de Beauvoir*, film by Josée Dayan and Malka Ribowska, text published by Gallimard: Paris, 1979; film made in 1978.

15 Schwarzer, *Simone de Beauvoir Today*, p. 37.

16 Moi, 2008, p. 39.

17 Beauvoir in SdB, Simons and Todd, 'Two Interviews with Simone de Beauvoir', p. 24.

18 Sorokine found *The Blood of Others* boring (see SdB to Sartre, 27 January 1944, LS 384). Algren said it had 'too much philosophy' (SdB to NA, Friday, 20 August 1948, TALA 210, 212).

19 SdB to Schwarzer, *Simone de Beauvoir Today*, p. 110.

20 FC 283. Emphasis added.

21 PL 606. Recent decades have seen scholars reconsider the question of influence between Sartre and Beauvoir which gives greater attention to Beauvoir's 'I' than previous generations have shown. According to Sylvie le Bon de Beauvoir,

Beauvoir described her relationship with Sartre with the image of '*astres jumeux*', twin stars, claiming it was one of 'absolute fraternity' and mutual support. All the same, Le Bon de Beauvoir published Beauvoir's *Cahiers* in French in 2008 because she believed they would enable us to do greater justice to who Beauvoir was, 'intellectually and personally, to what she thought, wanted, and planned for herself, before meeting Sartre, before becoming the Simone de Beauvoir that we know'. Sylvie Le Bon de Beauvoir, in Magda Guadalupe dos Santos 'Interview avec Sylvie Le Bon de Beauvoir', *Sapere Aude*, Belo Horizonte, 3(6), 357–65, 2 semestre 2012, p. 359.

22 ASD 235.

23 ASD 619.

24 See DPS 58–61, 66 especially 16 August 1926.

25 Nietzsche, 'Schopenhauer as Educator', in *Untimely Meditations*, trans. R. J. Hollingdale, Cambridge: Cambridge University Press, 1997, 163.

26 See Plato's *Symposium*.

27 SS 166.

28 Elizabeth Fallaize, *The Novels of Simone de Beauvoir*, 'Introduction', p. 1.

29 PC 120.

Select Bibliography

Algren, Nelson, 'Last Rounds in Small Cafés: Remembrances of Jean-Paul Sartre and Simone de Beauvoir', *Chicago*, December 1980.

Algren, Nelson, 'People', *Time*, 2 July 1956.

Altman, Meryl, 'Beauvoir, Hegel, War', *Hypatia* 22(3) (2007): 66–91.

Anon. 'Views and Reviews', *New Age* 1914 (15/17).

Arp, Kristana, *The Bonds of Freedom: Simone de Beauvoir's Existentialist Ethics*, Chicago: Open Court, 2001.

Audry, Colette, 'Portrait de l'écrivain jeune femme', *Biblio* 30:9 (November 1962).

Audry, Colette, 'Notes pour un portrait de Simone de Beauvoir', *Les Lettres françaises* 17–24 December 1954.

Aury, Dominique, 'Qu'est-ce que l'existentialisme? Escarmouches et patrouilles', *Les Lettres françaises*, 1 December 1945.

Bair, Deirdre, *Simone de Beauvoir: A Biography*, London: Jonathan Cape, 1990.

Barrett, William, *Irrational Man: A Study in Existential Philosophy*, New York: Doubleday, 1958.

Barron, Marie-Louise, 'De Simone de Beauvoir à Amour Digest. Les croisés de l'émancipation par le sexe', *Les lettres françaises*, 23 June 1949.

Baruzi, Jean, *Leibniz: Avec de nombreux textes inédits*, Paris: Bloud et cie, 1909.

Battersby, Christine, 'Beauvoir's Early Passion for Schopenhauer: On Becoming a Self', forthcoming.

Bauer, Nancy, *Simone de Beauvoir, Philosophy, and Feminism*, New York: Columbia University Press, 2001.

Bauer, Nancy, 'Introduction' to 'Femininity: The Trap', in Simone de Beauvoir, *Feminist Writings*, ed. Margaret A. Simons and Marybeth Timmerman, Urbana: University of Illinois Press, 2015.

Beauvoir, Hélène de, *Souvenirs*, Paris: Séguier, 1987.

Beauvoir, Simone de – see *Abbreviations on pp. xii–xiv for all primary sources cited.*

Beauvoir, Simone de, in discussion with Claudine Chonez, 'Simone de Beauvoir: Le Deuxième Sexe' (actualité du livre), 30 November 1949, Institut National de l'Audovisuel, France. https://www.ina.fr/audio/PH806055647/simone-de-beauvoir-le-deuxieme-sexe-audio.html

Beauvoir, Simone de, in interview with Madeleine Gobeil, 'The Art of Fiction No. 35', *Paris Review* 34 (Spring–Summer 1965).

Beauvoir, Simone de, in Interview with Margaret A. Simons and Jane Marie Todd, 'Two Interviews with Simone de Beauvoir', *Hypatia* 3:3 (1989).

Bergson, Henri, *Time and Free Will: An Essay on the Immediate Data of Consciousness*, trans. F. L. Pogson, New York: Dover, 2001.

Bergson, Henri, *The Creative Mind: An Introduction to Metaphysics*, trans. Mabelle L. Anderson, New York: Citadel Press, 1992.

Blanchet, A., 'Les Prix littéraires', *Études* 284 (1955): 96–100.

Boisdeffre, P. de 'LA REVUE LITTERAIRE: Deux morts exemplaires, un même refus: Jean Genet et Simone de Beauvoir', *Revue des deux mondes* (1986): 414–28.

Boulé, Jean-Pierre, *Sartre, Self-formation, and Masculinities*, Oxford: Berghahn, 2005.

Carter, Angela, 'Colette', *London Review of Books*, 2:19, 2 October 1980.

Challaye, Félicien, letter to Amélie Gayraud, in *Les Jeunes filles d'aujourd hui*, Paris: G. Oudin, 1914.

Chaperon, Sylvie, 'The reception of The Second Sex in Europe', *Encyclopédie pour une histoire nouvelle de l'Europe*, 2016.

Charensol, G. 'Quels enseignements peut-on tirer des chiffres de tirage de la production littéraire actuelle?', *Informations sociales* (1957): 36–45.

Churchwell, Sarah, *The Many Lives of Marilyn Monroe*, New York: Picador, 2005.

Cleary, Skye, *Existentialism and Romantic Love*, Basingstoke: Palgrave Macmillan, 2015.

Cohen-Solal, Annie, *Sartre: A Life*, London: Heinemann, 1987.

Collingnon, A. 'Bouches inutiles aux Carrefours', *Opéra*, 31 October 1944.

Conant, James, 'Philosophy and Biography', lecture given at 'Philosophy and Biography' symposium, 18 May 1999, published online by the Wittgenstein Initiative: http://wittgenstein-initiative.com/philosophy-and-biography/

Cottrell, Robert D., *Simone de Beauvoir*, New York: Frederick Ungar, 1975.

Crosland, Margaret, *Simone de Beauvoir: The Woman and Her Work*, London: Heinemann, 1992.

Dayan, Josée and Malka Ribowska, *Simone de Beauvoir*, Gallimard: Paris, 1979.

Deguy, Jacques and Sylvie Le Bon de Beauvoir, *Simone de Beauvoir: Ecrire la liberté*, Paris: Gallimard, 2008.

Delacourt, Xavier, 'Simone de Beauvoir adaptée: Une fidélité plate', *Le Monde*, 1978.

Descartes, René, *Oeuvres de Descartes*, ed. Charles Adam and Paul Tannery, volume I, Paris: Cerf, 1897.

Dijkstra, Sandra, 'Simone de Beauvoir and Betty Friedan: The Politics of Omission', *Feminist Studies* 6:2 (Summer 1980).

d'Eaubonne, Françoise, *Une femme nommée Castor*, Paris: Harmattan, 2008.

Eliot, George, *Middlemarch*, Oxford: Oxford University Press, 1988.

Emerson, Ralph Waldo, 'Considerations by the Way', from *Complete Works*, vol. 6, 'The Conduct of Life', 1904.

Fallaize, Elizabeth, *The Novels of Simone de Beauvoir*, London: Routledge, 1990.

Fallaize, Elizabeth, (ed.) *Simone de Beauvoir: A Critical Reader*, London: Routledge, 1998.

Fouillée, Alfred, *La Liberté et le déterminisme*, 3rd edn, Paris: Alcan, 1890.

Francis, Claude and Fernande Gontier, *Les écrits de Simone de Beauvoir*, Paris: Gallimard, 1979.

Fullbrook, Edward and Kate Fullbrook, *Sex and Philosophy: Rethinking de Beauvoir and Sartre*, London: Continuum, 2008.

Galster, Ingrid, *Le Deuxième Sexe de Simone de Beauvoir*, Paris: Presse universitaire Paris-Sorbonne, 2004.

Galster, Ingrid, *Beauvoir dans tout ses états*, Paris: Tallandier, 2007.

Galster, Ingrid, 'Simone de Beauvoir et Radio-Vichy: A propos de quelques scenarios retrouvés', *Romanische Forschungen* 108. Bd. H. 1/2 (1996).

Galster, Ingrid, '"The limits of the abject": The Reception of *The Second Sex* in 1949', in Laura Hengehold and Nancy Bauer (eds), *A Companion to Simone de Beauvoir*, Oxford: Wiley-Blackwell, 2017.

Garcia, Manon, *On ne naît pas femme, on le devient*, Paris: Flammarion, 2018.

Gayraud, Amélie, *Les Jeunes filles d'aujourd hui*, Paris: G. Oudin, 1914.

Germain, Rosie, 'Reading *The Second Sex* in 1950s America', *The Historical Journal* 56(4) (2013): 1041–62.

Gerassi, John, *Jean Paul Sartre: Hated Conscience of His Century*, vol. 1, London: University of Chicago Press, 1989.

Gerassi, John, *Talking with Sartre: Conversations and Debates*, New Haven: Yale University Press, 2009.

Gheerbrant, Jacqueline and Ingrid Galster, 'Nous sentions un petit parfum de soufre ...' *Lendemains* 94 (1999).

Giardina, Carol, *Freedom for Women: Forging the Women's Liberation Movement, 1953–1979*, Gainesville: University Press of Florida, 2010.

Gide, André, *The Journals of André Gide*, trans. Justin O'Brien, New York: Knopf, 1948, vol. II: 1914–27.

Gines, Kathryn T., 'Comparative and Competing Frameworks of Oppression in Simone de Beauvoir's *The Second Sex*', *Graduate Faculty Philosophy Journal* 35 (1–2) (2014).

Grell, Isabelle, *Les Chemins de la liberté de Sartre: genèse et écriture (1938–1952)*, Bern: Peter Lang, 2005.

Guidette-Georis, Allison, 'Georges Sand et le troisième sexe', *Nineteenth Century French Studies* 25:1/2 (1996): 41–9.

Gutting, Gary, *Thinking the Impossible: French Philosophy Since 1960*, Oxford: Oxford University Press, 2011.

Heilbrun, Carolyn, *Writing a Woman's Life*, London: The Women's Press, 1988.

Heller, Richard, 'The Self-centred Love of Madame Yak-yak', *The Mail on Sunday*, 1 December 1991.

Hengehold, Laura and Nancy Bauer (eds), *A Companion to Simone de Beauvoir*, Oxford: Wiley-Blackwell, 2017.

Hirschman, Sarah, 'Simone de Beauvor: professeur de lycée', *Yale French Studies* 22 (1958–9).

Hoog, Armand, 'Madame de Beauvoir et son sexe', *La Nef*, August 1949.

hooks, bell, 'True Philosophers: Beauvoir and bell', in Shannon M. Mussett and William S. Wilkerson (eds), *Beauvoir and Western Thought from Plato to Butler*, Albany, NY: SUNY Press, 2012.

Horvath, Brooke, *Understanding Nelson Algren*, Columbia, SC: University of South Carolina Press, 2005.

Jannoud, Claude, 'L'Œuvre: Une vulgarisation plus qu'une création', *Le Monde*, 15 April 1986.

Jansiti, Carlo, *Violette Leduc*. Paris: Grasset, 1999.

Jeannelle, Jean-Louis and Eliane Lecarme-Tabone, 'Introduction', in Simone de Beauvoir, *Mémoires*, tome I, ed. Jean-Louis Jeannelle and Eliane Lecarme-Tabone, Bibliothèque de la Pléiade, Paris: Gallimard, 2018.

Jeanson, Francis, *Simone de Beauvoir ou l'entreprise de vivre*, Paris: Seuil, 1966.

Joyaux, G. J. 'Les problèmes de la gauche intellectuelle et Les Mandarins de Simone de Beauvoir', *Kentucky Foreign Language Quarterly* 3 (1956).

Kaplan, Gisela, *Contemporary Western European Feminism*, London: UCL Press, 1992.

Kluckholm, Clyde, 'The Female of our Species', *New York Times Book Review*, 22 February 1953.

Kristeva, Julia and Philippe Sollers, *Marriage as a Fine Art*, trans. Lorna Scott Fox, New York: Columbia University Press, 2016.

Kristeva, Julia, Pascale Fautrier, Pierre-Louis Fort and Anne Strasser (eds), *(Re)Découvrir l'oeuvre de Simone de Beauvoir: Du Dexuième Sexe à La Cérémonie des Adieux*, Paris: Le Bord de L'eau, 2008.

Kruks, Sonia, *Situation and Human Existence: Freedom, Subjectivity, and Society*, London: Unwin Hyman, 1990.

Kunda, Z. and R. Sanitioso, 'Motivated Changes in the Self-concept', *Journal of Experimental Social Psychology* 25 (1989): 272–85.

Lacoin, Elisabeth, *Zaza: Correspondence et carnets d'Elisabeth Lacoin (1914–29)*, Paris: Seuil, 1991.

Lacroix, Jean, *Maurice Blondel: Sa vie, son oeuvre, avec un exposé de sa philosophie*, Paris: Presses Universitaires de France, 1963.

Lacroix, Jean, 'Charité chrétienne et justice politique', *Esprit* 1945 (February).

Lagneau, Jules, *De l'existence de Dieu*, Paris: Alcan, 1925.

Lamblin, Bianca, *A Disgraceful Affair*, trans. Julie Plovnick, Boston: Northeastern University Press, 1996 [Fr. 1993].

Lanzmann, Claude, *The Patagonian Hare: A Memoir*, trans. Frank Wynne, London: Atlantic Books, 2012.

Lanzmann, Claude, 'Le Sherpa du 11bis', in Julia Kristeva, Pascale Fautrier, Pierre-Louis Fort, Anne Strasser (eds), *(Re)Découvrir l'oeuvre de Simone de Beauvoir: Du Dexuième Sexe à La Cérémonie des Adieux*, Paris: Le Bord de L'eau, 2008.

Laubier, Claire (ed.), *The Condition of Women in France, 1945–Present: A Documentary Anthology*, London: Routledge, 1990.

Le Bon de Beauvoir, Sylvie, 'Chronologie', in Simone de Beauvoir, *Mémoires*, tome I, ed. Jean-Louis Jeannelle and Eliane Lecarme-Tabone, Bibliothèque de la Pléiade, Paris: Gallimard, 2018.

Le Bon de Beauvoir, Sylvie, 'Avant-propos', Simone de Beauvoir et Jacques-Laurent Bost, *Correspondence croisée*, Paris: Gallimard, 2004.

Le Bon de Beauvoir, Sylvie, interview with Magda Guadalupe dos Santos, 'Interview avec Sylvie Le Bon de Beauvoir', *Sapere Aude*, Belo Horizonte, 3(6), 357–65, 2 semestre 2012.

Lecarme-Tabone, Eliane, 'Simone de Beauvoir's "Marguerite" as a Possible Source of Inspiration for Jean-Paul Sartre's "The Childhood of a Leader"', trans. Kevin W. Gray, in Christine Daigle and Jacob Golomb, *Beauvoir & Sartre: The Riddle of Influence*, Bloomington: Indiana University Press, 2009.

Le Doeuff, Michèle, *Hipparchia's Choice: An Essay Concerning Women and Philosophy*, trans. Trista Selous, New York: Columbia University Press, 2007.

Lee, Hermione, *Virginia Woolf*, London: Vintage, 1997.

Lejeune, Philippe, *Le pacte autobiographique*, Paris: Seuil, 1975.

Lennon, Kathleen, *Imagination and the Imaginary*, London: Routledge, 2015.

Lessing, Doris, 'Introduction' to *The Mandarins*, trans. Leonard Friedman, London: Harper Perennial, 2005.

Lundgren-Gothlin, Eva, *Sex and Existence: Simone de Beauvoir's The Second Sex*, trans. Linda Schenck, Hanover, NH: Wesleyan University Press, 1996.

Macey, David, *Frantz Fanon: A Biography*, London: Verso Books, 2012.

Martin, Andy, 'The Persistence of "The Lolita Syndrome"', *The New York Times*, 19 May 2013. https://opinionator.blogs.nytimes.com/2013/05/19/savile-beauvoir-and-the-charms-of-the-nymph/

Martin Golay, Annabelle, *Beauvoir intime et politique: La fabrique des Mémoires*, Villeneuve d'Ascq: Presses Universitaires du Septentrion, 2013.

Mauriac, François, 'Demande d'enquête', *Le Figaro*, 30 May 1949.

Maza, Sarah, *Violette Nozière: A Story of Murder in 1930s Paris*, Los Angeles: University of California Press, 2011.

Mead, Margaret, 'A SR Panel Takes Aim at *The Second Sex*', *Saturday Review*, 21 February 1953.

Merleau-Ponty, Maurice, 'Metaphysics and the Novel', trans. Hubert Dreyfus and Patricia Allen Dreyfus, *Sense and Nonsense*, Evanston, IL: Northwestern University Press, 1991.

Moi, Toril, *Simone de Beauvoir: The Making of an Intellectual Woman*, 2nd edn, Oxford: Oxford University Press, 2008.

Moi, Toril, 'While We Wait: The English Translation of *The Second Sex*', *Signs* 27:4 (2002): 1005–35.

Mussett, Shannon M. and William S. Wilkerson (eds), *Beauvoir and Western Thought from Plato to Butler*, Albany: State University of New York Press, 2012.

Myrdal, Gunnar, with Richard Sterner and Arnold Rose, *An American Dilemma: The Negro Problem and Modern Democracy*, New York: Harper, 1944.

Nouchi, Franck, 'L'exil américain des lettres d'amour de Simone de Beauvoir à Claude Lanzmann', *Le Monde*, 19 January 2018.

Parshley, Howard, 'Introduction' to *The Second Sex*, trans. H. M. Parshley, New York: Random House, Vintage, 1970.

Pattison, George and Kate Kirkpatrick, *The Mystical Sources of Existentialist Thought*, Abingdon: Routledge, 2018.

Radford, C. B., 'Simone de Beauvoir: Feminism's Friend or Foe?' Part II, *Nottingham French Studies* 7 (May 1968).

Rolo, Charles J., 'Cherchez la femme', *The Atlantic*, April 1953.

Rouch, Marine, '"Vous êtes descendue d'un piédestal": une appropriation collective des Mémoires de Simone de Beauvoir par ses lectrices (1958–1964)' *Littérature* 191 (September 2018).

Rousseaux, André, 'Le Deuxième Sexe', *Le Figaro littéraire*, 12 November 1949.

Rowbotham, Sheila, 'Foreword' to *The Second Sex*, trans. Constance Borde and Sheila Malovany-Chevallier, London: Vintage, 2009.

Rowley, Hazel, *Tête-à-tête: The Lives and Loves of Simone de Beauvoir and Jean-Paul Sartre*, London: Vintage, 2007.

Rubenstein, Diane, '"I hope I am not fated to live in Rochester": America in the Work of Beauvoir', *Theory & Event* 15:2 (2012).

Rudman, Laurie A., Corinne A. Moss-Racusin, Julie E. Phelan and Sanne Nauts, 'Status Incongruity and Backlash Effects: Defending the Gender Hierarchy Motivates Prejudice against Female Leaders', *Journal of Experimental and Social Psychology* 48 (2012): 165–79.

Saint-Bris, Gonzague de and Vladimir Fedorovksi, *Les Egéries Russes*, Paris: Lattès, 1994.

Sanitioso, R., Z. Kunda and G. T. Fong, 'Motivated Recruitment of Autobiographical Memories', *Journal of Personality and Social Psychology* 59 (1990): 229–41.

Sanitioso, R. and R. Wlordarski, 'In Search of Information that Confirms a Desired Self-perception: Motivated Processing of Social Feedback and Choice of Social Interactions', *Personality and Social Psychology Bulletin* 30 (2004): 412–22.

Sanos, Sandrine, *Simone de Beauvoir: Creating a Feminist Existence in the World*, Oxford: Oxford University Press, 2017.

Sartre, Jean-Paul, *Écrits de jeunesse*, Paris: Gallimard, 1990.

Sartre, Jean-Paul, *Carnets de la drôle de guerre*, Paris: Gallimard, 1995.

Sartre, Jean-Paul, *War Diaries*, trans. Quintin Hoare, London: Verso, 1984.

Sartre, Jean-Paul, *Being and Nothingness*, trans. Hazel Barnes, London: Routledge, 2003.

Sartre, Jean-Paul, with Michel Contat and Alexandre Astruc, *Sartre by Himself*, New York: Urizen Books, 1978.

Schwarzer, Alice, *After the Second Sex: Conversations with Simone de Beauvoir*, trans. Marianne Howarth, New York: Pantheon Books, 1984.

Schwarzer, Alice, *Simone de Beauvoir Today: Conversations 1972–1982*, London: Hogarth Press, 1984.

Sevel, Geneviève, 'Je considère comme une grande chance d'avoir pu recevoir son enseignement', *Lendemains* 94 (1999).

Simons, Margaret A., *Beauvoir and The Second Sex: Feminism, Race, and the Origins of Existentialism*, New York: Rowman & Littlefield, 2001.

Simons, Margaret A., 'Introduction', to Simone de Beauvoir, *Philosophical Writings*, ed. Margaret Simons with Marybeth Timmerman and Mary Beth Mader, Chicago: University of Illinois Press, 2004.

Simons, Margaret A., 'Introduction' to Simone de Beauvoir, *Feminist Writings*, ed. Margaret A. Simons and Marybeth Timmerman, Urbana: University of Illinois Press, 2015.

Simons, Margaret A., 'Introduction' to 'Literature and Metaphysics', Beauvoir, *Philosophical Writings*, ed. Margaret Simons with Marybeth Timmerman and Mary Beth Mader, Chicago: University of Illinois Press, 2004.

Simons, Margaret A., 'Beauvoir's Ironic Sacrifice; or Why Philosophy is Missing from her Memoirs', forthcoming.

Simons, Margaret A. (ed.) *The Philosophy of Simone de Beauvoir: Critical Essays*, Bloomington: Indiana University Press, 2006.

Simons, Margaret A. and Hélène N. Peters, 'Introduction' to 'Analysis of Bernard's Introduction', Beauvoir, *Philosophical Writings*, ed. Margaret Simons with Marybeth Timmerman and Mary Beth Mader, Chicago: University of Illinois Press, 2004.

Spiegelberg, Herbert, *The Phenomenological Movement: A Historical Introduction*, volume 2, The Hague: Springer, 2013.

Tidd, Ursula, *Simone de Beauvoir*, London: Reaktion, 2009.

Tidd, Ursula, 'Some Thoughts on an Interview with Sylvie le Bon de Beauvoir', *Simone de Beauvoir Studies* 12 (1995).

TIME, 'Existentialism', 28 January 1946, pp. 28–9.

Times, The [London], 'Simone de Beauvoir', 15 April 1986, p. 18.

Viellard-Baron, Jean-Louis, 'Présentation' to Jean Baruzi, *L'Intelligence Mystique*, Paris: Berg, 1985.

Vintges, Karen, 'Introduction' to 'Jean Paul Sartre', in *Philosophical Writings*, ed. Margaret Simons with Marybeth Timmerman and Mary Beth Mader, Chicago: University of Illinois Press, 2004.

Vintges, Karen, 'Simone de Beauvoir: A Feminist Thinker for the Twenty-First Century', in Margaret Simons (ed.), *The Philosophy of Simone de Beauvoir*, Bloomington, IN: Indiana University Press, 2006.

Voltaire, 'Première Lettre sur Oedipe', in *Œuvres complètes*, tome I, Kehl: Imprimerie de la Société littéraire typographique, 1785.

Waelhens, A. de, compte-rendu de Francis Jeanson, *Le problème moral et la pensée de Sartre*, *Revue Philosophique de Louvain* 10 (1948).

Wahl, Jean, *Petite histoire de 'l'existentialisme'*, Paris: Éditions Club Maintenant, 1947.

Webber, Jonathan, *Rethinking Existentialism*, Oxford: Oxford University Press, 2018.

Woolf, Virginia, *A Room of One's Own/Three Guineas*, London: Penguin Classics, 2000.

Wright Mills, C., *The Power Elite*, Oxford: Oxford University Press, 2000.

Acknowledgements

It's very hard to know when this book's life started – and when to stop thanking people for the ways they have inspired and supported it. For igniting and stoking my loves of philosophy and French literature I'd like to thank Françoise Bayliss, Randall Morris, Meg Werner, Pamela Sue Anderson, Jeanne Treuttel, Michèle Le Doeuff, George Pattison and Marcelle Delvaux-Abbott – and my family.

This book offers my portrait of Beauvoir, but it rests on the foundation of many scholars' pioneering work in Beauvoir studies. In particular I would like to thank Margaret Simons and all of the translators, editors and introduction-writers of the Beauvoir Research Series published by the University of Illinois Press, as well as Michèle Le Doeuff, Elizabeth Fallaize, Sonia Kruks, bell hooks, Nancy Bauer, Stella Sandford, Meryl Altman, Toril Moi, Tove Pettersen and Barbara Klaw. I am grateful to the welcoming and generous discussions of members of the International Simone de Beauvoir Society, who gave me glimpses into their Beauvoirs and enriched my own.

I offer my thanks to Aaron Gabriel Hughes for their excellent research assistance in tracking down obscure French reviews; to Emily Herring, for bringing Bergsonmania to life; to Marine Rouch for generously sharing her research on Beauvoir's letters from readers; to the Beinecke Rare Book and Manuscript Library at Yale University; to Eric Legendre at the Gallimard archives; to Jean-Louis Jeannelle for newspaper articles and a conversation about sources; and especially to Sylvie Le Bon de Beauvoir, for taking the time to be interviewed for this book and for generously replying to my questions afterwards, too.

Becoming Beauvoir wouldn't exist at all were it not for the initial enthusiasm of Liza Thompson at Bloomsbury, and it wouldn't have become what it is without her insightful criticisms: I'm very grateful for both the enthusiasm and the criticism. My thanks also go to Daisy Edwards, Lucy Russell and Kealey Rigden at Bloomsbury for their work on the project. For reading the manuscript during its development I am grateful to Bloomsbury's anonymous reviewers, and also to Clare Carlisle and Suzannah Lipscomb.

For their interest and encouragement at various stages of this project's development I would like to thank my students and colleagues at the University of Oxford, UH Philosophy and King's College London.

Every writer knows that a book takes a village, and I'm grateful to have such a wonderful village of friends and family – thanks especially to Sophie Davies-Jones, Melanie Goodwin, Phyllis Goodwin, Suzie and Tom, Naomi and Joseph, Mary and Ard, and Angela and Simon.

Finally, thank you to my creative and inspiring children – whose teasing question, 'Simone de Beauvoir: Who's she?' became a motto of sorts – and to my husband: *vous et nul autri*.

Picture credits

The author gratefully acknowledges permission for the images included in this book:

1 Collection Sylvie Le Bon de Beauvoir, © Diffusion Gallimard.

2 Collection Sylvie Le Bon de Beauvoir, © Diffusion Gallimard.

3 Collection Sylvie Le Bon de Beauvoir, © Diffusion Gallimard.

4 Photo: Frédéric Hanoteau/Collection Sylvie Le Bon de Beauvoir, © Diffusion Gallimard.

5 Photo: Frédéric Hanoteau/Collection Sylvie Le Bon de Beauvoir, © Diffusion Gallimard.

6 Collection Sylvie Le Bon de Beauvoir, © Diffusion Gallimard.

7 Robert Doisneau/Gamma-Legends Collection/Getty Images.

8 Robert Doisneau/Gamma-Legends Collection/Getty Images.

9 Collection Sylvie Le Bon de Beauvoir, © Diffusion Gallimard.

10 Collection Sylvie Le Bon de Beauvoir, © Diffusion Gallimard.

11 Bettmann/Bettmann Collection/Getty Images.

12 Collection Sylvie Le Bon de Beauvoir, © Diffusion Gallimard.

13 Jacques Pavlovsky/Sygma Collection/Getty Images.

14 Eric Bouvet/Gamma-Rapho Collection/Getty Images.

Index